Student Workbook

for use with

Managerial Economics

Eighth Edition

Christopher R. Thomas
University of South Florida at Tampa

S. Charles Maurice
Texas A&M University
late Professor Emeritus

Prepared by
Christopher R. Thomas
University of South Florida at Tampa

McGraw-Hill
Irwin

Boston   Burr Ridge, IL   Dubuque, IA   Madison, WI   New York   San Francisco   St. Louis
Bangkok   Bogotá   Caracas   Kuala Lumpur   Lisbon   London   Madrid   Mexico City
Milan   Montreal   New Delhi   Santiago   Seoul   Singapore   Sydney   Taipei   Toronto

McGraw-Hill
Irwin

Student Workbook for use with
MANAGERIAL ECONOMICS
Christopher R. Thomas, S. Charles Maurice

Published by McGraw-Hill/Irwin, an imprint of The McGraw-Hill Companies, Inc., 1221 Avenue of the Americas, New York, NY 10020. Copyright © 2005 by The McGraw-Hill Companies, Inc. All rights reserved.

1 2 3 4 5 6 7 8 9 0 2QPD/2QPD 0 9 8 7 6 5 4

ISBN 0-07-294103-0

www.mhhe.com

Acknowledgments

I would like to thank Victoria Perk at University of South Florida's Center for Urban Transportation Research for her extensive review of the problems in this Student Workbook. I also wish to thank Chris Colaco, a student at the St. Petersburg campus of University of South Florida, for his numerous helpful comments on the previous edition of this Workbook, all of which have been adopted in this edition.

In this edition of the Student Workbook, I received substantial assistance from several people at McGraw-Hill. Teri Baldini undertook a remarkably thorough editorial review of the manuscript that greatly improved the readability and look of the final version of this Workbook. Matthew Perry, the Supplement Producer at McGraw-Hill, provided me with valuable advice on how to improve the printed quality of the more than 200 graphs in this Workbook. Finally, I would like especially to thank Katie Crouch, my Development Editor, for putting up with me through the many deadlines involved in getting the textbook and all its supplements to press on time.

Although this edition of the Workbook has been more carefully edited and reviewed than any previous edition, there nonetheless remains a small chance that some errors may have slipped by me. As always, I encourage instructors and students to contact me with any corrections or comments you might have. Your input is greatly appreciated.

C.R.T.
cthomas@coba.usf.edu
Tampa, Florida
January 19, 2004

To the Student

This Workbook is intended to do one thing—help you learn managerial economics. The most effective way for you to learn and understand managerial economics is to work as many problems as possible. For this reason, I believe it is beneficial for you to solve an additional set of problems for which you have answers. For each chapter of the textbook, I have compiled a group of problems covering every important concept in the chapter. If you work and understand all of the problems in each chapter of this Workbook, you will be well-prepared for exams.

Each chapter of this Workbook consists of the following six parts:

Learning Objectives. Students frequently get bogged down by the details of a chapter and lose sight of what they are supposed to have learned. Each chapter of this Workbook begins with a list of the main things you should learn from the chapter.

Essential Concepts. This part of the Workbook briefly summarizes the major principles set forth in the text. You should review these concepts before attempting to work the problems. If any of these points are unclear, you should review the material in the text. The *Essential Concepts* section provides a handy summary of the chapter that you can refer to as you work the problems.

Matching Definitions. Here you will find a review of the margin definitions in the chapter. Students tell me they like to do matching exercises, and so, never one to ignore market demand, I have provided such a section.

Study Problems. This part of the Workbook contains a battery of problems designed to cover every topic in the chapter. These problems are quite similar to the Technical Problems in your textbook. You will also find some *Computer Problems* in those chapters that use statistical analysis. Answers to *Study Problems* are provided at the end of each Workbook chapter. You should work these problems *without* looking at the answers. Use the answers to *check* your work, not to *guide* your work!

Multiple Choice/True-False. Since instructors sometimes use the multiple choice/true-false format for testing, each chapter of the Workbook contains some of these types of questions. The answers, along with brief explanations, are given at the end of chapters.

Homework Exercises. A final section of this Workbook contains one or two representative problems from each chapter. The chapters that cover statistical analysis also have *Computer Exercises*. Your instructor has the solutions to these problems, and he or she may ask you to hand them in for grading. If not, you should work the *Homework Exercises* anyway and check your answers with classmates or with your instructor.

Because managerial economics applies microeconomic theory to business decision making, you need to be comfortable using a number of fundamental mathematical skills from high school algebra. To help refresh you, this Workbook provides a *Review of Fundamental Mathematics*. For many students, the mathematical review is a particularly valuable part of this Workbook.

C. R. T.

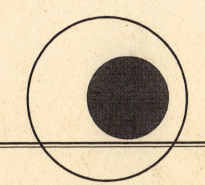

STUDENT WORKBOOK
Table of Contents

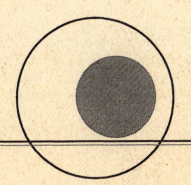

Review of Fundamental Mathematics

As explained in the Preface and in Chapter 1 of your textbook, managerial economics applies microeconomic theory to business decision making. The decision-making tools that you will learn can provide numerical answers to questions such as:

➤ What price should Harley-Davidson charge for its 2005 model Sportster?
➤ At Doctors Walk-In Clinic, what combination of doctors and nurses provides the expected level of medical services at the lowest possible total cost?
➤ What is the forecasted price of West Texas crude oil six months from now?
➤ How many PCs should Hewlett-Packard manufacture and sell each month in order to maximize profit?

In order to apply the decision-making rules developed in managerial economics, you need to understand some fundamental mathematics, most of which you learned in high school algebra. No calculus is used in the body of the textbook, and none is required to work the *Technical Problems* and *Applied Problems* at the end of each chapter in the textbook. Exercises are provided throughout this Review. Answers to the exercises can be found at the end of this Review.

Mathematical Functions

CONCEPT OF A FUNCTION

The relation between decision-making variables such as output, labor and capital employment, price, cost, and profit can be expressed using mathematical *functions*. A function shows mathematically the relation between a *dependent* variable and one or more *independent* variables. The dependent variable is often denoted by y, and the independent variable is denoted by x. The idea that "y is related to x" or that "y is a function of x" is expressed symbolically as

$$y = f(x)$$

This mathematical notation expresses the relation between y and x in the most *general* functional form. In contrast to this general form of expression, a *specific* functional form uses an equation to show the exact mathematical relation between y and x using an equation. For example,

$$y = 100 - 2x$$

gives a specific function relating y to values of x.

The equation showing the specific functional relation between y and x provides a "formula" for calculating the value of y for any specific value of x. In the specific function given above, when x equals 20, y equals 60 ($=100-2\times20$). In economic analysis, it is frequently convenient to denote the dependent and independent variable(s) using notation that reminds us of the economic variables involved in the relation. Suppose, for example, that the quantity of golfing lessons (q) that a professional golf instructor gives each week depends on the price charged by the golf pro (p). The specific functional relation — which is called the golf pro's "demand" for lessons — can be expressed as

$$q = f(p) = 100 - 2p$$

Instead of using the "generic" mathematical names y and x, the dependent variable is denoted by q to suggest "quantity," and the independent variable is denoted by p to suggest "price." If the golf pro charges $40 per lesson, then she will give 20 ($=100-2\times40$) lessons per week.

INVERSE FUNCTIONS

Sometimes it is useful to "reverse" a functional relation so that x becomes the dependent variable and y becomes the independent variable:[1]

$$x = f^{-1}(y)$$

This function, known as an *inverse function*, gives the value of x for given values of y. The inverse of $y = f(x)$ can be derived algebraically by expressing x as a function of y.[2] Consider again the demand for golfing lessons. The inverse function gives the price that a golf pro can charge for a given quantity of lessons each week:

$$p = f(q) = 50 - 0.5q$$

If the golf pro wishes to sell 20 lessons per week, she charges a price of $40 ($=50-0.5\times20$) per lesson. Notice that all of the values of q and p satisfying the function $q = 100 - 2p$ also satisfy the inverse function $p = 50 - 0.5q$.

FUNCTIONS OF TWO OR MORE INDEPENDENT VARIABLES

In many economic relations, the dependent variable is a function of, or depends on, the values of more than one independent variable. If y depends on both w and z, for example, the general functional relation is expressed as

$$y = f(w,z)$$

Suppose a firm employs two inputs, labor and capital, to produce its product. The price of labor is $30 per hour, and the price of using capital is $60 per hour. The total cost of production (C) can be expressed as a function of the amount of labor employed per hour (L) and the amount of capital used per hour (K):

$$C = f(L,K) = 30L + 60K$$

---

[1] For the function $y = f(x)$, mathematicians denote its inverse function as $x = f^{-1}(y)$. The "-1" is not an exponent here, but rather it denotes this function to be the inverse function of $y = f(x)$.

[2] Inverse functions do not exist for all functions. In this review, we will not investigate the conditions that ensure the existence of an inverse. In cases where inverse functions are required for managerial decision making, the required inverse functions generally do exist and can be rather easily derived.

From this cost function, the manager calculates the cost of employing 10 workers and 5 units of capital to be $600 ($= 30 \times 10 + 60 \times 5$).

Exercises (Answers to Exercises follow this Review on pages 17-18.)

1. In the following functions, find the value of the dependent variable when $x = 10$.
   a. $y = 300 - 20x$ $300 - 20(10) = 300 - 200 = \underline{100}$
   b. $y = 10 + 3x + x^2$ $10 + 30 + 100 = \underline{140}$
   c. $w = -20 + 3x$ $-20 + 3(10) = \underline{10}$
   d. $s = 40x + 2$ $400 + 2 = \underline{402}$

2. Find the inverse functions.
   a. $y = 450 + 15x$
   b. $q = 1,000 - 25p$

3. In the functions below, find the value of the dependent variable for the values of the independent variables given.
   a. $y = f(x, w) = x^2 + w^2$, for $x = 25$ and $w = 5$
   b. $z = f(w, r) = 50w + 150r$, for $w = 200$ and $r = 32$

Linear Functions

Functions can be either *linear* or *nonlinear* in form. This section of the Review discusses the properties of linear functions, and then the next section examines nonlinear functions. The primary distinction between linear and nonlinear functions is the nature of their slopes: linear functions have constant slopes while curvilinear (i.e., nonlinear) functions have varying slopes.

DEFINITION OF LINEAR FUNCTIONS

A function, $y = f(x)$, is a linear function if a graph of all the combinations of x and y that satisfy the equation $y = f(x)$ lie on a straight line. Any linear relation between y and x can be expressed in the algebraic form

$$y = a + bx$$

where y is the dependent variable, x is an independent variable, a is the *intercept parameter*, and b is the *slope parameter*. The terms a and b are called *parameters*, rather than *variables*, because their values do not change along the graph of a specific linear function. The intercept parameter, a, gives the value of y when $x = 0$. For the line representing $y = f(x)$, when $x = 0$ the line crosses the y-axis. Hence the name "intercept" parameter.[3] Every line is characterized by a unique pair of values for a and b.

---

[3]Sometimes a is called the *y-intercept*. When the dependent variable is not named y, the term *y-intercept* can be confusing. It is best to think of the intercept parameter a as giving the point where the line for this function crosses the axis of the variable "on the other side of the equal sign." If, for example, $c = 30 - 5q$, the line passes through the c axis at the value $c = 30$ ($= 30 - 5 \times 0$). Also note that c need not be graphed on the vertical axis; 30 is where the line crosses the c-axis whether c is plotted on the vertical or on the horizontal axis.

Figure A.1 shows a graph of the golf pro's demand function which relates the number of lessons given each week (q) to the price charged for a lesson (p). The values of the parameters of this linear function are $a = 100$ and $b = -2$. Notice that the line passes through the q axis at 100 lessons per week. The slope of the line is -2. The slope of lines and curves are so important that we will now discuss in detail the meaning of the slope of a line and the slope of a curve.

FIGURE A.1: Demand function for golfing lessons

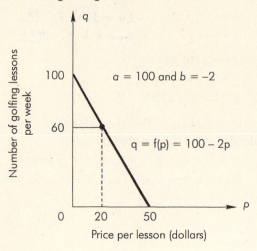

SLOPE OF A LINE

The slope of a line representing the function $y = f(x)$ is defined as the change in the dependent variable y divided by the change in the independent variable x:

$$slope\ of\ a\ line = b = \frac{\Delta y}{\Delta x}$$

where the Δ symbol indicates the *change* in a variable.[4] When y is plotted on the vertical axis and x is plotted on the horizontal axis, the change is y can be called *rise*, the change in x can be called *run*, so the slope of the line is frequently referred to as *rise over run*. In Figure A.1, moving from the top of the line where it intersects the q axis down to the bottom of the line where it intersects the p axis, the rise is $-100 (= \Delta q)$. The run is $+50$ (Δp), and so the slope is -2.

The slope of a line can be either positive, negative, or zero. If x and y move in the same direction, Δx and Δy have the same algebraic sign. When an increase (decrease) in x causes an increase (decrease) in y, x and y are said to be *directly* or *positively* related. When x and y are directly or positively related, the slope of $y = f(x)$ is positive (i.e., $b > 0$). The graph of a line is upward sloping when x and y are directly or positively related. See Panel A in Figure A.2 for an example of a direct or positive relation.

Alternatively, x and y may move in opposite directions: an increase (decrease) in x causes a decrease (increase) in y. In this situation, x and y are said to be *inversely* or *negatively* related, and the slope of $y = f(x)$ is negative (i.e., $b < 0$). The graph of a line is downward sloping when variables are inversely or negatively related. See Panel B in Fig-

---

[4]The change in a variable is calculated by taking the final value of the variable (x_1) and subtracting the initial value (x_0): $\Delta x = x_1 - x_0$. When a variable increases (decreases) in value, the final value is greater (less) than the initial value of the variable, and the change in the variable is positive (negative).

ure $A.2$ for an example of an inverse or negative relation.

In some situations, changes in x do not cause y to increase or to decrease. If changes in x have no effect on y, x and y are unrelated or independent. Suppose, for example, $y = 50$ for all values of x. The parameter values for this situation are $a = 50$ and $b = 0$. The graph of this linear function is a horizontal line at $y = 50$ (see Panel C of Figure $A.2$). In general, when x and y are independent, the slope of the line is zero.

FIGURE A.2: The slope of a line

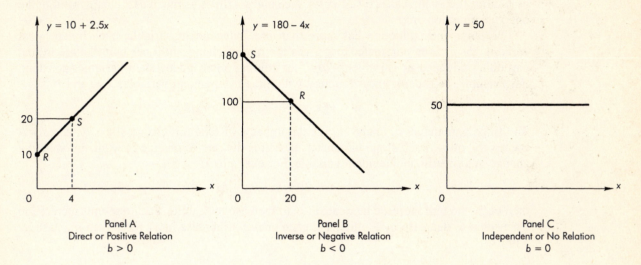

Panel A	Panel B	Panel C
Direct or Positive Relation	Inverse or Negative Relation	Independent or No Relation
$b > 0$	$b < 0$	$b = 0$

CALCULATING THE SLOPE OF A LINE

Calculating the slope of a line is straightforward. First, locate any two points on the line. Then calculate Δy and Δx between the two points. Finally, divide Δy by Δx. Consider, for example, points R and S in Panel A of Figure $A.2$. Moving from R to S, $\Delta y = 20 - 10 = +10$ and $\Delta x = 4 - 0 = +4$. Now divide: $\Delta y / \Delta x = +10 / +4 = +2.5$. Since the slope is positive, the line is upward sloping and the variables y and x are directly (or positively) related.

As discussed above, when variables are inversely (negatively) related, the slope of the line is negative. In Panel B of Figure $A.2$, consider moving from R to S. Note that $\Delta y = 180 - 100 = +80$ because the movement from R to S is *upward* (by 80 units). Since moving from R to S is a leftward movement, the change in x is negative: $\Delta x = 0 - 20 = -20$. Now divide the changes in y and x: $\Delta y / \Delta x = +80 / -20 = -4$.

Moving along the line in Panel C, Δy is always zero for any change in x. Thus, the slope of the horizontal line is zero.

INTERPRETING THE SLOPE OF A LINE AS A RATE OF CHANGE

Students usually learn to calculate the slope of lines rather quickly. It is surprising, however, that many students who can correctly calculate the slope of a line cannot explain the meaning of slope or interpret the numerical value of slope. To understand the meaning and usefulness of slope in decision making, you must learn to think of slope as the rate of change in the dependent variable as the independent variable changes. Since the slope parameter is a ratio of two changes, Δy and Δx, slope can be interpreted as the *rate of change in y per unit change in x*.

In Panel *A* of Figure *A*.2, the slope of the line is 2.5 ($b = \Delta y/\Delta x = +2.5$). This means that *y* changes 2.5 units for every one-unit change in *x*, and *y* and *x* move in the same direction (since $b > 0$). Thus, if *x* increases by 2 units, *y* increases by 5 units. If *x* decreases by 6 units, then *y* decreases by 15 units. *Y* changes 2.5 times as much as *x* changes and in the same direction as *x* changes.

In Panel *B* of Figure *A*.2, the slope of the line is −4 ($b = \Delta y/\Delta x = -4$). This means that *y* changes 4 units for every one unit *x* changes, and *y* and *x* move in opposite directions (since $b < 0$). Thus, if *x* increases by 2 units, *y* decreases by 8 units. If *x* decreases by 6 units, then *y* increases by 24 units. *Y* changes 4 times as much as *x* changes but in the opposite direction of *x*.

When a linear function has more than one independent variable, each independent variable has a slope parameter that gives the rate of change in *y* per unit change in that particular independent variable *by itself*, or holding other independent variables constant. For example, consider a linear function with three independent variables *x*, *y*, and *z*:

$$w = f(x, y, z) = a + bx + cy + dz$$

The slope parameters *b*, *c*, and *d* give the impacts of one-unit changes in *x*, *y*, and *z*, respectively, on *w*. Each slope parameter measures the rate of change in *w* attributable to a change in a specific independent variable. For example, if

$$w = 30 + 2x - 3y + 4z$$

then each one unit increase in *x* causes *w* to increase by 2 units, each one-unit increase in *y* causes *w* to decrease by 3 units, and each one-unit increase in *z* causes *w* to increase by 4 units.

Exercises

4. Consider again the golf pro's demand for lessons, which is graphed in Figure *A*.1. Let the golf pro increases the price of her lessons from $20 to $25.
    a. The quantity of lessons given at a price of $25 is _____ lessons per week.
    b. The change in *p* is Δp = ____.
    c. The change in *q* is Δq = ____.
    d. The slope of the demand line is _____.
    e. Since a $1 increase in price causes the quantity of lessons each week to _____ by ____ lessons per week, a $5 increase in price causes the quantity of lessons per week to _____ by ____ lessons per week.

5. In Panel *A* of Figure *A*.2, change the coordinates of point *S* to *x* = 30 and *y* = 100. Let point *R* continue to be at *x* = 0 and *y* = 10.
    a. Moving from point *R* to the new point *S*, Δy = ____ − ____ = ____.
    b. Moving from point *R* to the new point *S*, Δx = ____ − ____ = ____.
    c. The slope of the line = _____.
    d. The equation of the new line is _____.
    e. Along the new line, *y* changes _____ times as much as *x* changes and in the _____ direction.
    f. If *x* increases by 4 units, *y* _____ by _____ units.
    g. The parameter values for the new line are *a* = _____ and *b* = _____.

6. In Panel B of Figure $A.2$, change the coordinates of point R to $x = 40$ and $y = 40$. Let point S continue to be at $x = 0$ and $y = 180$.
    a. Moving from the new point R to point S, $\Delta y =$ ____ – ____ = ____.
    b. Moving from the new point R to point S, $\Delta x =$ ____ – ____ = ____.
    c. The slope of the line = _____.
    d. The equation of the new line is _____.
    e. Along the new line, y changes _____ times as much as x changes and in the _____ direction.
    f. If x increases by 5 units, y _____ by _____ units.
    g. The parameter values for the new line are $a =$ _____ and $b =$ _____.

7. Let $w = 30 + 2x - 3y + 4z$.
    a. Evaluate w at $x = 10$, $y = 20$, and $z = 30$.
    b. If x decreases by 1 unit, w _____ by _____ units.
    c. If y increases by 1 unit, w _____ by _____ units.
    d. If z increases by 3 units, w _____ by _____ units.
    e. Evaluate w at $x = 9$, $y = 21$, and $z = 33$. Compare this value of w to the value of w in part a: the change in w equals _____.
    f. Add the individual impacts on w in parts b, c, and d. Does the sum of the individual impacts equal the total change in w found in part e?

Curvilinear Functions

Linear functions are easy to use because the rate of change in the dependent variable as the independent variable changes is constant. For many relations, however, the rate of change in y as x changes is not constant. Functions for which the rate of change, or slope, varies are called *curvilinear* functions. As the name suggests, the graph of a curvilinear function is a curve rather than a straight line. While some curvilinear functions can be difficult to use, the curvilinear functions used in managerial economics are generally quite easy to use and interpret.

Any relation between y and x that cannot be expressed algebraically in the form $y = a + bx$ is a curvilinear function. Examples of curvilinear functions include: $y = a + bx + cx^2$, $y = \sin x$, $y = \ln x$, and $y = e^x$. We begin this section with a discussion of how to measure and interpret the slope of a curvilinear function. Then we examine the properties of polynomial functions and logarithmic functions.

MEASURING SLOPE AT A POINT ON A CURVE

The slope of a curve varies continuously with movements along the curve. It is useful in studying decision making to be able to measure the slope of a curve at any one point of interest along the curve. You may recall from high school algebra or a pre-calculus class in college that the slope at a point on a curve can be measured by constructing the tangent line to the curve at the point.[5] The slope of a curve at the point of tangency is equal to the slope of the tangent line itself.

To illustrate how to measure the slope of a curve at a point, consider the curvilinear function $y = f(x) = 800x - 0.5x^2$, which is graphed in Figure $A.3$. As x increases, the value of y increases (the curve is positively sloped), reaches its peak value at $x = 800$ (point M), and then decreases until $y = 0$ at $x = 1,600$. Let's find the slope of this curve at

---

[5]When a line is tangent to a curve, it touches the curve at only one point. For smooth, continuous curves, there is one and only one line that is tangent to a curve at any point on the curve. Consequently, the slope of a curve at a point is unique and equal to the slope of the tangent line.

point A, which is the point $x = 1,000$ and $y = 300,000$. First, a tangent line labeled TT' in the figure, is constructed at point A.[6] Then, the slope of TT' is calculated to be -200 $(= -500,000/2,500)$. The slope of the curve at point A indicates that y changes 200 times as much as x changes, and in the opposite direction because the slope is negative.

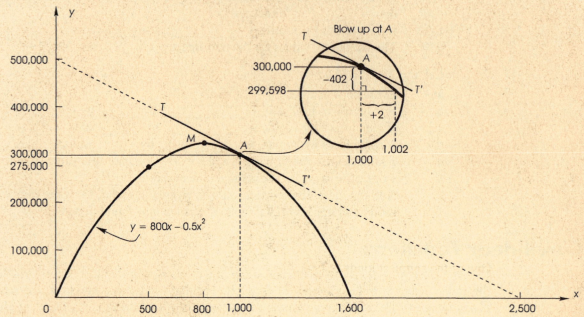

It is important to remember that the slope of a curve at a point measures the rate of change in y at precisely that point. If x changes by more than an infinitesimal amount, which it usually does in practical applications, the slope of the tangent measures only approximately the rate of change in y relative to the change in x. However, the smaller the change in x, the more precisely the change in y can be approximated by the slope of the tangent line.

To illustrate this rather subtle point, let x increase by 2 units from 1,000 (at point A) to 1,002. Since the slope of the curve at point A is -200, the increase in x of 2 units causes y to decrease by approximately 400 units. We say y decreases by "approximately" 400 units, because a 2-unit change in x, which is a rather small change when x is equal to 1,000, is still large enough to create a tiny amount of error. Since the change in x is quite small relative to the point of measure, the actual change in y will be quite close to -400 though not exactly -400. The blow up at point A in Figure A.3 confirms that the change in y is not exactly -400 but rather is -402. When the change in x is "small," we must emphasize that the tiny error can be ignored for practical purposes.

---

[6]A tangent line that you draw will only approximate an exact tangent line because your eyesight is probably not so sharp that you can draw precisely a line tangent to a curve. Fortunately, for the purposes of managerial economics, you only need to be able to sketch a line that is approximately tangent to a curve. If you have taken a course in calculus, you know that taking the derivative of a function and evaluating this derivative at a point is equivalent to constructing a tangent line and measuring its slope.

Exercises

8. Calculate the slope at point A on the following curves:

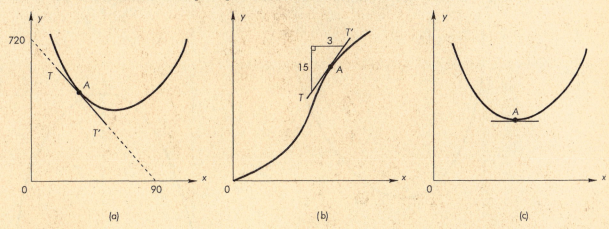

(a)   (b)   (c)

9. In Figure A.3, find the slope of the curve at $x = 500$. [Hint: Use a ruler and a sharp pencil to draw the appropriate tangent line.]

POLYNOMIAL FUNCTIONS

One of the simplest kinds of curvilinear functions is a *polynomial function*. A polynomial function takes the form

$$y = f(x) = a_0 + a_1 x + a_1 x^2 + \dots + a_n x^n$$

where n is an integer and $a_0, a_1, a_2, \dots , a_n$ are parameters. The highest power to which the independent variable x is raised is called the *degree* of the polynomial. Many of the curvilinear relations in managerial economics involve polynomial functions of degree 2 or degree 3. A polynomial of degree 1 is a linear function, which we have discussed.

When the relation between y and x is a polynomial of degree 2, the function is known as a *quadratic* function, which can be expressed as follows:

$$y = a + bx + cx^2$$

The graph of a quadratic function can be either ∪-shaped or ∩-shaped, depending on the algebraic signs of the parameters. Two of the most common quadratic functions in managerial economics have the properties shown in Panels A and B of Figure $A.4$.

We now discuss the restrictions on the algebraic signs of the parameters associated with the ∪-shaped or ∩-shaped curves shown in Figure $A.4$. As shown in Figure $A.4$, when b is negative (positive) and c is positive (negative), the quadratic function is ∪-shaped (∩-shaped).[7] Point M, which denotes either the minimum point for a ∪-shaped curve in Panel A or the maximum point for a ∩-shaped curve in Panel B, occurs at $x = -b/2c$ in either case. As just mentioned, b and c are of opposite algebraic signs, thus x is positive when these curves reach either a minimum or a maximum.[8]

---

[7]In Panel b, the constant term is zero ($a = 0$) because the curve passes through the origin.

[8]Since economic variables generally take only positive values, an additional mathematical property, $b^2 < 4ac$, ensures that point M occurs at a positive, rather than negative, value of y. We do not emphasize this property here or in the textbook because, as it turns out, the condition is always met in practice when the parameters of the quadratic equation are estimated using economic data for which x and y take only positive values.

FIGURE A.4: Two common quadratic functions

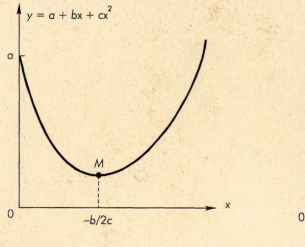

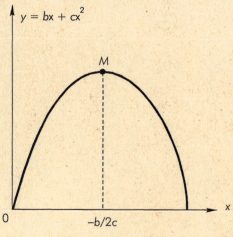

Panel A
$$y = a + bx + cx^2$$
$$a > 0$$
$$b < 0$$
$$c > 0$$

Panel B
$$y = bx + cx^2$$
$$b > 0$$
$$c < 0$$

A polynomial function of degree 3 is often referred to as a *cubic* function. The specific form of a cubic function used in managerial economics takes the form:

$$y = ax + bx^2 + cx^3$$

Figure *A*.5 summarizes the shapes of two cubic functions that you will see later in this course. The graph of a cubic function is either *S*-shaped or reverse *S*-shaped, depending on the values of the parameters. In Panel *A*, the reverse *S*-shaped cubic function is characterized by parameters with algebraic signs $a > 0$, $b < 0$, and $c > 0$. In Panel *B*, the *S*-shaped cubic function has parameter restrictions $b > 0$ and $c < 0$. (Note that $a = 0$ in Panel *B*.)[9]

---

[9]For cubic equations, the condition $b^2 < 4ac$ ensures that the slope of the curve at the point of inflexion (*I*) is upward (positive). As explained in footnote 8, this condition is not usually of much concern in practice.

FIGURE A.5: Two common cubic functions

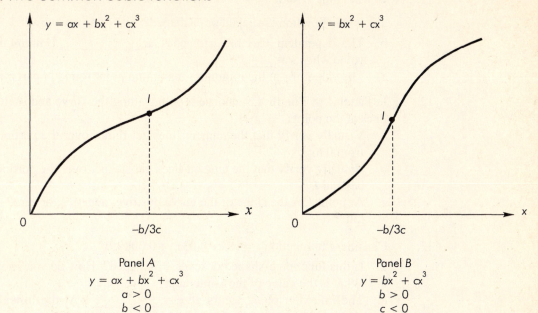

Panel A
$$y = ax + bx^2 + cx^3$$
$$a > 0$$
$$b < 0$$
$$c > 0$$

Panel B
$$y = bx^2 + cx^3$$
$$b > 0$$
$$c < 0$$

The *inflexion point* on an *S*-shaped or a reverse *S*-shaped curve is the point at which the *slope* of the curve reaches either its minimum value (Panel *A*) or its maximum value (Panel *B*). Consider Panel *A*. Beginning at zero and moving toward the point of inflexion (labeled "*I*" in both panels), the slope of the curve is decreasing. Then, beyond the inflexion point, the slope of the curve begins increasing.[10] Note that y is always *increasing* as x increases, but at first (over the range 0 to I) y increases at a decreasing rate, then beyond I, y increases at an increasing rate. It follows that the slope is smallest at point I in Panel *A*. In Panel *B*, y first increases at an increasing rate, and then beyond the inflexion point, y increases at a decreasing rate. Thus, the rate of change in y is greatest at inflexion point I in Panel *B*. The point of inflexion I occurs at $x = -b/3c$ for both *S*-shaped and reverse *S*-shaped curves.

Exercises

10. Consider the function $y = 10 - 0.03x + 0.00005x^2$.

   a. Is this function ∪-shaped or ∩-shaped? How do you know?
   b. The dependent variable y reaches a _____(minimum, maximum) value when $x =$ _____.
   c. The value of y at the minimum/maximum point found in part b is _____.

_____

[10]To "see" that slope is decreasing over the segment of the curve from 0 to I, visualize a series of lines tangent to the curve at points along the curve between 0 and I. Since these "visualized" tangent lines are getting flatter between 0 and I, the slope of the curve is getting smaller. Moving beyond I, the "visualized" tangent lines are getting steeper, so the slope of the curve is rising.

11. Consider the function $y = -0.025x^2 + 1.45x$.

    a. Is this function ∪-shaped or ∩-shaped? How do you know?

    b. The dependent variable y reaches a _____(minimum, maximum) value when $x =$ _____.

    c. The value of y at the minimum/maximum point found in part b is _____.

12. In Panel A of Figure $A.5$, choose 5 points along the curve and sketch the tangent lines at the points.

    a. Visually verify that the tangent lines get flatter over the portion of the curve from 0 to I.

    b. Visually verify that the tangent lines get steeper over the portion of the curve beyond I.

    c. At point I, is the slope of the curve positive, negative, or zero? How can you tell?

13. Consider the function $y = 10x - 0.03x^2 + 0.00005x^3$.

    a. Is this function S-shaped or reverse S-shaped? How do you know?

    b. What is the value of the y-intercept?

    c. The inflexion point occurs at $x =$ _____. At the inflexion point, the slope of the curve reaches its _____ (maximum, minimum) value.

    d. What is the value of y when $x = 1,000$?

EXPONENTIAL AND NATURAL LOGARITHMIC FUNCTIONS

We now discuss two more curvilinear functions, exponential functions and natural logarithmic functions, which have mathematical properties that can be quite useful in many applications arising in managerial economics and finance.

Exponential Functions

An *exponential function* takes the form

$$y = f(x) = a^x$$

where a is any positive constant (called the "base" of the exponent), and the independent variable x is the power to which the base is raised. Exponential functions differ from polynomial functions, such as $y = ax + bx^2 + cx^3$, because x is an *exponent* in exponential functions but is a *base* in polynomial functions.

Exponential functions have numerous algebraic properties that are quite helpful in applications you will see later in this course.

1. $a^n = a \times a \times ... \times a$ (*n times*)

2. $a^0 = 1$

3. $a^{-n} = \dfrac{1}{a^n}$

4. $a^i a^j = a^{i+j}$

5. $(a^i)^j = a^{ij}$

6. $\dfrac{a^i}{a^j} = a^{i-j}$

A commonly used base in economics and finance applications is the constant e, which is the limiting value of the expression $(1 + \frac{1}{n})^n$, as n gets very large (i.e., approaches infinity):

$$e = \lim_{n \to \infty} \left(1 + \frac{1}{n}\right)^n \cong 2.718$$

Nearly all hand calculators have a key labeled "e" or "e^x" that enters the value 2.718... into the calculator's display for exponential computations. Verify that you can use this key on your calculator by making the calculation $e^4 = 54.5981$.

Natural Logarithms

Natural logarithms are logarithms for which e is the base

$$y = e^x$$

where x is the power to which e must be raised to get y. For example, e must be raised to the power of 4 to obtain the number 54.5981. Thus, the natural logarithm of 54.5981 is 4. In general, the natural logarithm of any *positive* number y can be expressed as

$$x = \ln y$$

The symbol "ln" is used to distinguish this base e logarithm from the base 10 logarithm that is used in some scientific applications.[11] Notice that the natural logarithmic function $x = \ln y$ is the inverse of the exponential function $y = e^x$. Figure A.6 illustrates the inverse nature of the two functions.

Natural logarithms have the following convenient algebraic properties that can be quite useful:

1. $\ln rs = \ln r + \ln s$

2. $\ln r^s = s \ln r$

3. $\ln\left(\dfrac{r}{s}\right) = \ln r - \ln s$

FIGURE A.6: The inverse relation between exponential and natural logarithmic functions

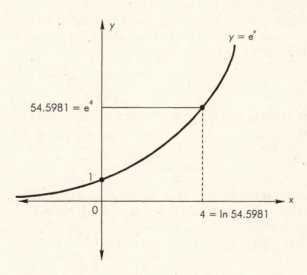

[11]The natural logarithm function key on your hand calculator is labeled "ln" or "ln x," whereas the key for base 10 logarithms is usually labeled "log" or "log10." You will always use the "ln" or "ln x" key in this Workbook (and Textbook).

Exercises

14. Evaluate the following:

a. 5^0

b. $2^3 \cdot 2^2$

c. $(K^a)^b$

d. L^{a+b}/L^b

e. $e = \lim\limits_{n \to \infty} \left(1 + \dfrac{1}{n}\right)^n$

f. e^{-4}

g. e^3

h. $\ln 8$

i. $\ln 1,000$

j. $\ln(ax^b)$

k. $\ln(K/L)$

l. e^0

Finding Points of Intersection

You may recall from your algebra courses that the point at which two lines intersect can be found mathematically by solving two equations containing the two variables. Similarly, the two points where a straight line crosses a quadratic function can be found using the quadratic formula. While you no doubt hoped to avoid seeing these techniques again, you will see that finding points of intersection plays a crucial role in solving many business decision-making problems. We now review this important algebraic skill.

FINDING THE INTERSECTION OF TWO LINES

Consider two lines represented by the two linear equations

$$y = a + bx$$
$$y = c + dx$$

The point at which these two lines intersect—assuming they are not parallel ($b = d$)—can be found algebraically by recalling that the values of y and x at the point of intersection solve both equations. Setting the two equations equal to each other and solving for x provides the value of x at the point of intersection ($\bar{x}$)

$$\bar{x} = \frac{a - c}{d - b}$$

To find the value of y at the point of intersection, $\bar{x}$ is substituted into either linear equation to find $\bar{y}$

$$\bar{y} = \frac{ad - bc}{d - b}$$

Figure $A.8$ illustrates how to find the point of intersection of the two linear equations: $y = 10 - x$ and $y = 2 + x$. In this example, $a = 10$, $b = -1$, $c = 2$, and $d = 1$. Substituting these parameter values into the above formulas, the solution is found to be $\bar{x} = 4$ and $\bar{y} = 6$. Verify that the point $\bar{x} = 4$, $\bar{y} = 6$ solves both equations.

FIGURE A.8: Finding the intersection of two lines

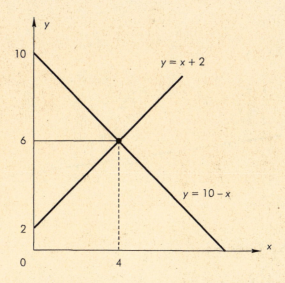

FINDING THE INTERSECTION OF A LINE AND A QUADRATIC CURVE

A line crosses a quadratic curve—either a ∪-shaped or a ∩-shaped curve—at two points. Figure $A.9$ shows the linear function $y = 56 - 0.02x,$ as well as the quadratic function $y = 20 - 0.14x + 0.003x^2.$ As in the case of intersecting lines, the values of y and x at the points of intersection between a line and a quadratic curve solve both equations. In general, to find the points of intersection, the equations for the line and the quadratic curve are set equal to each other and then solved for the two values of x at which the line and the curve cross.

To illustrate this technique, set the equation for the line, $y = 56 - 0.02x$, equal to the equation for the curve, $y = 20 - 0.14x + 0.003x^2$

$$56 - 0.02x = 20 - 0.14x + 0.0003x^2$$

Now there is one variable in one equation, and the equation is a quadratic equation. To solve a quadratic equation, the quadratic equation must be expressed in the form

$$0 = A + Bx + Cx^2$$

where A is the constant term, B is the coefficient on the linear term, and C is the coefficient on the quadratic term. After setting expressions equal, terms are rearranged to get zero on one side of the equality:

$$0 = -36 - 0.12x + 0.0003x^2$$

It is important to note that A and B are *not* equal to the parameter values a and b of the quadratic curve. In this problem, for example, $a = 20$ and $b = -0.14$, but $A = -36$ and $B = -0.12$. The solution to the quadratic equation $0 = A + Bx + Cx^2$ is the familiar *quadratic formula*:

$$x_1, x_2 = \frac{-B \pm \sqrt{B^2 - 4AC}}{2C}$$

Substituting the values of A, B, and C into the quadratic formula yields the two solutions for x: $x_1 = -200$ and $x_2 = 600$.

FIGURE A.9: Finding the intersection of a line and a quadratic curve

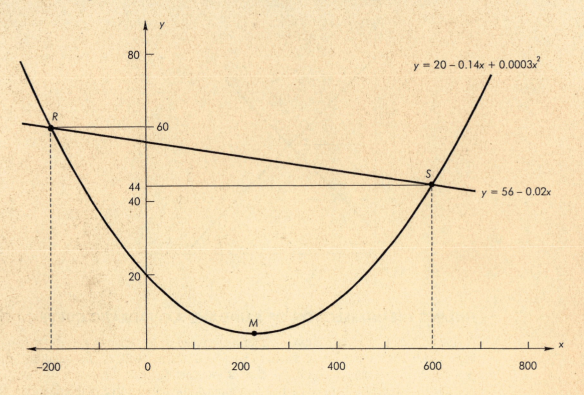

Exercises

15. Find the point of intersection of the following two lines:
$$y = 1,000 - 20x \quad \text{and} \quad y = 25 + 5x$$

16. Consider the following linear function and quadratic function:
$$y = 32 - 0.02x$$
$$y = 50 - 0.2x + 0.00025x^2$$
The line intersects the quadratic curve at two points: $x_1 =$ _____ , $y_1 =$ _____ and $x_2 =$ _____ , $y_2 =$ _____ .

ANSWERS TO EXERCISES

1. a. $y = 100\ (= 300 - 200)$
   b. $y = 140\ (= 10 + 30 + 100)$
   c. $w = 10\ (= -20 + 30)$
   d. $s = 402\ (= 400 + 2)$

2. a. $x = f(y) = -30 + 0.067y$
   b. $p = f(q) = 40 - 0.04q$

3. a. $y = 650\ (= 625 + 25)$
   b. $z = 14,800\ (= 10,000 + 4,800)$

4. a. $50\ (= 100 - 2 \times 25)$
   b. $+5\ (= 25 - 20)$
   c. $-10\ (= 50 - 60)$
   d. $-2\ (= \Delta q / \Delta p = -10/+5)$
   e. decrease; 2; decrease; 10

5. a. $\Delta y = 100 - 10 = +90$
   b. $\Delta x = 30 - 0 = +30$
   c. $+3\ (= \Delta y / \Delta x = +90/+30)$
   d. $y = 10 + 3x$
   e. 3; same
   f. increases; 12
   g. $a = 10; b = 3$

6. a. $\Delta y = 180 - 40 = +140$
   b. $\Delta x = 0 - 40 = -40$
   c. $-3.5\ (= \Delta y / \Delta x = +140/-40)$
   d. $y = 180 - 3.5x$
   e. 3.5; opposite
   f. decreases; 17.5
   g. $a = 180; b = -3.5$

7. a. $110\ (= 30 + 2 \times 10 - 3 \times 20 + 4 \times 30)$
   b. decreases; 2
   c. decreases; 3
   d. increases; 12
   e. $+7$; because $30+(2\times9)+(-3\times21)+(4\times33)=117$, which is 7 units greater than the value of w in part a.
   f. $(\Delta x \times 2)+(\Delta y \times -3)+(\Delta z \times 4) = -2 + -3 + 12 = +7$; yes, $\Delta w = +7$

8. a. slope at point A = slope of $TT' = -720/90 = -8$
   b. slope at point A = slope of $TT' = 15/3 = +5$
   c. slope at point A = slope of tangent = 0 a the minimum point

9. When $x = 500$, $y = 275,000$ (confirm this with the equation). Construct a tangent line at the dot on the curve at $x = 500$ and $y = 275,000$, and extend the tangent line to cross the y-axis. If precisely drawn, the tangent line crosses the y-axis at 125,000. If your tangent line is precisely constructed, the slope of the tangent line is $+300\,[= (275,000 - 125,000)/500]$. Be satisfied if you came close to $+300$; calculus is required to get a precisely accurate measure of slope.

10. a. U-shaped; The polynomial is a quadratic and the parameters have the sign pattern associated with a U-shaped curve: $a > 0$, $b < 0$, $c > 0$.
    b. minimum; 300 $(= -b/2c = 0.03/0.0001)$
    c. $5.5\ [= 10 - 0.03(300) + 0.00005(300)^2]$

11. a. ∩-shaped; The polynomial is a quadratic and the parameters have the sign pattern associated with a ∩-shaped curve:, $b > 0$, $c < 0$.
     b. maximum; 29 $(= -b/2c = -1.45 / -0.05)$
     c. 21.025 $[= -0.025(29)^2 + 1.45(29)]$

12. The figure shows the "sketched" tangent lines at five additional points along the curve in Panel A of Figure $A.5$.
     a. You can verify visually that the three tangent lines between 0 and I get flatter as x increases.
     b. You can verify visually that the two tangent lines to the right of point I get flatter as x increases. *Steeper*

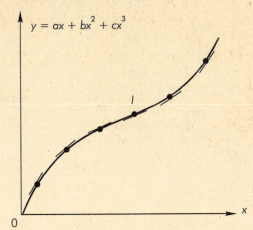

$$y = ax + bx^2 + cx^3$$

     c. At point I, the slope is positive because the sketched tangent line at point I slopes upward.

13. a. Reverse S-shaped, as in Panel A of Figure $A.5$. The parameters have the signs $a > 0$, $b < 0$, and $c > 0$.
     b. 0
     c. 200; minimum
     d. 30,000 $[= 10(1,000) - 0.03(1,000)^2 + 0.00005(1,000)^3]$

14. a. 1
     b. $32 = 2^5 = 2^{3+2}$
     c. K^{ab}
     d. $L^a = L^{a+b-b}$
     e. $2.718... = e$
     f. 0.01832
     g. 20.0855
     h. 2.0794
     i. 6.9077
     j. $\ln a + b \ln x$
     k. $\ln K - \ln L$
     l. 1, because $a^0 = 1$

15. $\bar{x} = (1,000 - 25) / (5 - (-20)) = 39$ and $\bar{y} = 1,000 - (20 \times 39) = 220 = 25 + (5 \times 39)$

16. Solve the quadratic equation, $0 = 18 - 0.18x + 0.00025x^2$, to get two solutions for x:
     $x_1 = 600$, $y_1 = 20$
     $x_2 = 120$, $y_2 = 29.6$

Managers, Profits, and Markets

Learning Objectives

After reading Chapter 1 and working the problems for Chapter 1 in the textbook and in this Workbook, you should be able to:

➢ Explain the role of economic theory in managerial economics.

➢ Measure the explicit opportunity cost of using market-supplied resources to produce goods or services.

➢ Measure the implicit opportunity cost of using owner-supplied resources to produce goods or services.

➢ Compute total economic cost of using resources by summing explicit and implicit opportunity costs of resource use. Calculate economic profit and accounting profit.

➢ Define the value of a firm and explain the relation between maximizing profit and maximizing the firm's value.

➢ Discuss the problems arising from separation of ownership and control in businesses and suggest some corporate control mechanisms to address these problems.

➢ Explain the difference between price-taking firms to price-setting firms.

➢ Provide an answer to the question "what is a market?"

➢ List and explain the characteristics of four market structures.

➢ Discuss implications for managerial decision making of globalization of markets.

Essential Concepts

1. Managerial economics applies microeconomic theory—the study of the behavior of individual economic agents—to business problems in order to teach business decision makers how to use economic analysis to make decisions that will achieve the firm's goal—maximization of profit.

2. Economic theory helps managers understand real-world business problems by using simplifying assumptions to abstract away from irrelevant ideas and information and turn complexity into relative simplicity.

3. The economic cost of using resources to produce a good or service is the opportunity cost to the owners of the firm using those resources. The opportunity

cost of using any kind of resource is what the owners of the firm must give up to use the resource.

4. Total economic cost is the sum of the opportunity costs of market-supplied resources plus the opportunity costs of owner-supplied resources. The opportunity costs of using market-supplied resources are the out-of-pocket monetary payments made to the owners of resources, which are called *explicit costs*. The opportunity cost of using an owner-supplied resource is the best return the owners of the firm could have received had they taken their own resource to market instead of using it themselves. Such nonmonetary opportunity costs are called *implicit costs*.

5. Businesses may incur numerous kinds of implicit costs, but the three most important types of implicit costs are (1) the opportunity cost of cash provided by owners, known as equity capital, (2) the opportunity cost of using land or capital owned by the firm, and (3) the opportunity cost of the owner's time spent managing the firm or working for the firm in some other capacity.

6. Economic profit is the difference between total revenue and total economic cost:

    Economic profit = Total revenue − Total economic cost

    = Total revenue − Explicit costs − Implicit costs

    Economic profit belongs to the owners and will increase the wealth of the owners. When revenues fall short of total economic cost, economic profit is negative, and the loss must be paid for out of the wealth of the owners.

7. When accountants calculate business profitability for financial reports, they follow a set of rules known as "generally accepted accounting principles" or GAAP. These rules, which are constructed by the Securities and Exchange Commission (SEC) and the Financial Accounting Standards Board (FASB) do not allow accountants to deduct most types of implicit costs for the purposes of calculating taxable accounting profit. Thus, accounting profit differs from economic profit because accounting profit does not subtract from total revenue the implicit costs of using resources.

    Accounting profit = Total revenue − Explicit costs

8. Since the owners of firms must cover the costs of all resources used by the firm, maximizing economic profit, rather than accounting profit, is the objective of the firm's owners.

9. The value of a firm is the price for which it can be sold, and that price is equal to the present value of the expected future profit of the firm.

10. The risk associated with not knowing future profits of a firm is accounted for by adding a risk premium to the discount rate used for calculating the present value of the firm's future profits. The larger (smaller) the risk associated with future profits, the higher (lower) the risk premium used to compute the value of the firm, and the lower (higher) the value of the firm will be.

11. If cost and revenue conditions in any period are independent of decisions made in other time periods, a manager will maximize the value of a firm by making decisions that maximize profit in every single time period.

12. In firms for which the manager is not also the owner, the managers are agents of the owners, or principles. A principal-agent problem exists when agents have

objectives different from those of the principal, and the principal either has difficulty enforcing agreements with the agent or finds it too difficult and costly to monitor the agent to verify that the agent is furthering the principal's objectives.

13. Agency problems arise because of moral hazard. Moral hazard exists when either party to an agreement has an incentive not to abide by all provisions of the agreement, and one party cannot cost-effectively find out if the other party is abiding by the agreement, or cannot enforce an agreement even when information is available.

14. In order to address agency problems, shareholders can employ a variety of corporate control mechanisms. Shareholders can reduce agency problems by:

    (1) requiring managers to hold a stipulated amount of the firm's equity,
    (2) increasing the percentage of outsiders serving on the company's board of directors, and
    (3) financing corporate investments with debt instead of equity. Corporate takeovers also create an incentive for managers to make decisions that maximize the value of a firm.

15. A price-taking firm cannot set the price of the product it sells because price is determined strictly by the market forces of demand and supply.

16. A price-setting firm sets the price of its product because it possesses some degree of market power, which is the ability to raise price without losing all sales.

17. A market is any arrangement that enables buyers and sellers to exchange goods and services, usually for money payments. Markets exist to reduce transaction costs, the costs of making a transaction.

18. Market structure is a set of characteristics that determines the economic environment in which a firm operates:

    (1) the number and size of firms operating in the market,
    (2) the degree of product differentiation, and
    (3) the likelihood of new firms' entering.

19. Markets may be structured as one of four types:

    (1) A perfectly competitive market has a large number of relatively small firms selling an undifferentiated product in a market with no barriers to entry.
    (2) A monopoly market is one in which a single firm, protected by a barrier to entry, produces a product that has no close substitutes.
    (3) In monopolistically competitive markets, a large number of relatively small firms produce differentiated products without any barriers to entry.
    (4) In oligopoly markets, there are only a few firms whose profits are interdependent—each firm's decisions about pricing, output, advertising, and so forth affects all other firms' profits—with varying degrees of product differentiation.

20. Globalization of markets is the economic integration of markets located in nations around the world. Globalization provides managers with both an opportunity to sell more goods and services to foreign buyers as well as the threat of increased competition from foreign producers.

Matching Definitions

- accounting profit
- economic profit
- equity capital
- explicit costs
- globalization of markets
- implicit costs
- market
- market power
- market structure
- market-supplied resources
- moral hazard
- opportunity cost
- owner-supplied resources
- price-setting firm
- price-taking firm
- principal-agent problem
- risk premium
- total economic cost
- transaction costs
- value of a firm

1. OPPURTUNITY COST — What a firm's owners give up to use resources to produce goods or services.

2. MKT SUPPLIED RES'S — Resources owned by others and hired, rented, or leased in resource markets.

3. OWNER SUP'D RES'S — Resources owned and used by a firm.

4. TTL ECON COSTS — Sum of opportunity costs of market-supplied resources plus opportunity costs of owner-supplied resources.

5. EXPLICIT — Monetary opportunity costs of using market-supplied resources.

6. IMPLICIT — Nonmonetary opportunity costs of using owner-supplied resources.

7. EQ CAPITAL — Money provided to businesses by the owners.

8. ECON PROFIT — Amount that total revenue exceeds total economic cost.

9. ACCT'G PROFIT — Difference between total revenue and explicit costs.

10. VALUE OF A FIRM — Price for which a firm can be sold, or equivalently, the present value of the expected future profits of the firm.

11. RISK PREM — Amount added to the riskless discount rate to account for uncertainty associated with the expected future profits.

12. P-A PROBLEM — Conflict arising when the objectives of the agent differ from those of the principal, and the principal has difficulty enforcing and monitoring the agent.

13. MORAL HAZ — Exists when either party to an agreement has an incentive not to abide to the agreement and one party cannot cost-effectively monitor the agreement or cannot effectively enforce the agreement.

14. P-T FIRM — A firm that cannot set the price of the product it sells, since market forces determine the price.

15. P-S FIRM — A firm that has the ability to raise the price of its product without losing all of its sales.

16. MARKET POWER — Ability to raise price without losing all sales.

17. MARKET — Any arrangement through which buyers and sellers interact to exchange products, services, resources for production, or in general, anything of value.

18. TRANS COSTS   Additional costs over and above the price paid that arise in the process of making transactions.

19. MARKET STRUCT   Set of characteristics that determines the economic environment in which a firm does business.

20. GLOB OF MARKETS   Economic integration of markets located in nations around the world.

Study Problems

1. In 2004 Terry Brady, the legendary athlete from Indiana, decided to leave his job as head football coach at Mattoon High School to open Brady Advantage, his own sporting goods store, in Terre Haute. By locating Brady Advantage halfway between St. Louis and Indianapolis, Brady hoped to attract customers from both large metropolitan markets. A partial income statement for Brady Advantage follows:

	2004
Revenues	
Revenue from sales of goods and services	$210,000
Operating costs and expenses	
Costs of products and services sold	$82,000
Selling expenses	$6,000
Administrative expenses	$12,000
Total Operating Costs & Expenses	$100,000
Income from operations	$110,000
Interest expense (bank loan)	$14,000
Non-recurring expenses to start business	$8,000
Income taxes	$16,000
Net income	$72,000

Terry Brady's coaching job at Mattoon High paid $45,000 of annual salary and benefits. To get the sporting goods store opened, Brady used $50,000 of his personal savings, which was earning a guaranteed 12 percent annual rate of return. Brady opened his store in a building that he owned in Terre Haute. Prior to opening his store, the building was rented for $24,000 per year.

a. In 2004, Brady Advantage incurs $_____ of total explicit costs for using market-supplied resources.

b. In 2004, the opportunity cost of Brady's equity capital is $_____.

c. The total implicit cost of using owner-supplied resources in 2004 is $_____.

d. The total opportunity cost of resources used by Brady Advantage in 2004 is $_____. The total economic cost in 2004 is $_____.

e. The accounting profit for Brady Advantage in 2004 is $_____.

f. Based on his profit in 2004, did Terry Brady increase his wealth by quitting his job at Mattoon High and opening Brady Advantage? Explain your answer carefully. [Hint: Compute economic profit in 2004].

2. During a year of operation, a firm collects $5,000,000 in revenue and spends $3,500,000 on labor expense, raw materials, rent, and utilities. The firm's owner has provided $1,000,000 of her own money instead of investing the money and earning a 12 percent annual rate of return.

    a. The explicit costs of the firm are $_____. The implicit costs are $_____. Total economic cost is $_____.

    b. The firm earns accounting profit of $_____.

    c. The firm's economic profit is $_____.

    d. If the owner could earn 15 percent annually on the money she has invested in the firm, the economic profit of the firm would be _____ (when revenue is $5,000,000).

3. Over the next three years, a firm is expected to earn economic profit of $700,000 in the first year, $800,000 in the second year, and $500,000 in the third year. After the end of the third year, the firm goes out of business.

    a. If the risk-adjusted discount rate is 16 percent for each of the next three years, the value of the firm is $_____. The firm can be sold today for a price of $_____.

    b. If the risk-adjusted discount rate is 10 percent for each of the next three years, the value of the firm is $_____. The firm can be sold today for a price of $_____.

4. For each of the following managers, decide whether the manager is likely to be a price-setter (possesses market power) or a price-taker (does not possess market power).

    a. The loan officer at a bank decides what interest rate to charge on car loans made to Chicago-area buyers of new cars.

    b. The manager of FastCo Inc., a manufacturer of standardized fasteners, such as screws and machine bolts.

    c. The CEO of Bombardier, a manufacturer of a popular brand of jet skis.

    d. The owner-manager of a McDonald's hamburger restaurant, which is the first hamburger restaurant to open in a new suburban neighborhood.

5. For each of the firms below, identify the market structure that best matches the competitive characteristics found in that firm's market.

    a. Microsoft Corporation, in the market for business-application software, such as word processing, spreadsheet, and database.

    b. Becker Farms, a 1,000-acre wheat farm near Beaver City, Nebraska.

    c. Robo Wash, the only coin-operated car wash in Monroe, Louisiana.

    d. The Jumping Bean, a family-owned Mexican food restaurant in San Antonio, Texas.

    e. Après Ski, one of only two restaurants licensed to operate at the base of the main ski lift in Park City, Utah.

6. The *Wall Street Journal* (Special Report on Executive Pay April 6, 2000) reported that some stockholders of Ben & Jerry's Homemade, Inc. were upset that the firm's new senior director of business development was given a guaranteed bonus of at least $75,000 in his two-year contract.

   a. What is the problem with a guaranteed bonus for managers?

   b. In light of the problem discussed in part *a*, why might Ben & Jerry's nonetheless wish to offer new managers guaranteed bonuses?

Multiple Choice / True-False

1. Economic theory is a valuable tool for business decision making because it
   a. assumes away the problem.
   b. identifies for managers the essential information for making a decision.
   c. creates a realistic, complex model of the business firm.
   d. provides an easy solution to complex business problems.

2. The total opportunity cost of using owner-supplied resources
   a. does not involve monetary payments and so can be ignored when computing economic profit.
   b. is part of the business firm's total economic cost.
   c. equals the sum of all opportunity costs of using resources obtained by the firm in various resource markets.
   d. must be covered by revenues or economic profit will be negative and owner's wealth will be reduced.
   e. both *b* and *d*.

3. Economic profit equals
   a. total revenue minus implicit costs.
   b. total revenue minus explicit costs.
   c. accounting profit minus explicit costs.
   d. accounting profit minus the total cost of using owner-supplied resources.
   e. accounting profit plus the total costs of using market-supplied resources.

4. When economic profit is positive,
   a. total revenue exceeds total economic cost, and the business owners' wealth increases.
   b. the firm may not earn enough to cover the costs of using owner-supplied resources.
   c. the firm earns more than enough revenue to cover the opportunity costs of all of the resources it uses.
   d. both *a* and *c*.

5. The value of a firm is
   a. smaller the higher is the risk premium used to compute the firm's value.
   b. larger the higher is the risk premium used to compute the firm's value.
   c. the price for which the firm can be sold minus the present value of expected future profits.
   d. equal to the dollar value of a firm's ownership stake in the capital equipment holdings of the firm.

6. Suppose Maverick, the owner-manager of Western Wear Depot, earned $240,000 in revenue last year. Maverick's explicit costs of operation totalled $300,000. Maverick has a bachelor's degree in education and could be earning $40,000 annually as a high school teacher.
   a. Maverick's total economic cost is $300,000.
   b. Maverick's accounting profit is −$100,000.
   c. Maverick incurs $40,000 of implicit costs.
   d. Maverick's economic profit is −$60,000.
   e. both *c* and *d*.

7. A risk premium
   a. is subtracted from the discount rate when calculating the present value of a future stream of risky profits.
   b. accounts for the riskiness of future profits.
   c. is lower the more risky the future stream of profits.
   d. is an additional compensation paid to the workers of a business enterprise.

8. Owners of a firm want the managers to make business decisions that will
   a. maximize the value of the firm.
   b. maximize expected profit in each period of operation.
   c. maximize the market share of the firm.
   d. both *a* and *b* when revenue and cost conditions in one time period are independent of revenues and costs in future time periods.

9. The principal-agent problem arises when the principal
   a. and the agent have different objectives.
   b. cannot enforce the contract agent or finds it too costly to monitor the agent.
   c. cannot decide whether the firm should seek to maximize the expected future profits of the firm or maximize the price for which the firm can be sold.
   d. both *a* and *b*.
   e. both *a* and *c*.

10. Moral hazard
    a. occurs when managers pursue maximization of profit without regard to the interests of society in general.
    b. exists when either party to a contract has an incentive to cancel the contract.
    c. occurs only rarely in modern corporations.
    d. is the cause of principal-agent problems.
    e. both *a* and *c*.

11. A price-taking firm can exert no control over price because
    a. price is determined by market forces.
    b. price is determined by the intersection of demand and supply.
    c. the firm's individual production is insignificant relative to production in the industry.
    d. many other firms produce a product that is nearly identical to its product.
    e. all of the above.

12. A price-setting firm
    a. can lower the price of its product and sell more units.
    b. can raise the price of its product and sell fewer units but will not lose all of its sales.
    c. possesses market power.
    d. sells a product that is somehow differentiated from the product sold by its rivals or sells in a limited geographic market area with only one or a few sellers.
    e. all of the above.

13. Which of the following is NOT one of the features characterizing market structures?
    a. The number and size of firms.
    b. The likelihood of new firms entering a market.
    c. The level of capital investment in research and development.
    d. The degree of product differentiation.

14. In markets characterized by monopolistic competition,
    a. a large number of relatively small firms sell a differentiated product.
    b. a small number of relatively large firms sell a standardized product.
    c. entry into the market is relatively easy so that profit in the long run is zero.
    d. entry into the market is restricted to that profit may be positive in the long run.
    e. both *a* and *c*.

15. Which of the following is NOT a characteristic of monopoly market structures?
    a. A single firm produces the entire market output.
    b. The greater the ability of consumers to find imperfect substitutes for the firm's product the lower will be the firm's market power.
    c. There are no barriers to entry.
    d. No close substitutes for the product are available.

16. T F The effectiveness of a board of directors in monitoring managers will be enhanced by appointing members from the firm who are well-informed about the management problems facing the firm.

17. T F If accounting profit is positive, economic profit must also be positive.

18. T F The value of a firm is smaller the higher is the risk premium used to compute the firm's value.

19. T F In markets characterized by oligopoly, interdependence of firms means that actions of any one firm in the market will have an effect on the sales and profits of all other firms in the market.

20. T F Economic profit is the best measure of a firm's performance because the opportunity cost of using *all* resources is subtracted from total revenue.

Answers

1. opportunity cost
2. market-supplied resources
3. owner-supplied resources
4. total economic cost
5. explicit costs
6. implicit costs
7. equity capital
8. economic profit
9. accounting profit
10. value of the firm
11. risk premium
12. principal-agent problem
13. moral hazard
14. price-taking firm
15. price-setting firm
16. market power
17. market
18. transaction costs
19. market structure
20. globalization of markets

STUDY PROBLEMS

1. a. $138,000 = $82,000 + $6,000 + $12,000 + $14,000 + $8,000 + $16,000

   b. $6,000 = $50,000 × 0.12 (Note that the *amount* of equity capital is $50,000 while the *opportunity cost* of using the $50,000 of equity capital is the forgone return caused by removing the $50,000 from its present investment earning 12 percent annually–i.e., $6,000 per year.)

   c. There are three owner-supplied resources in this problem: Brady's time away from his high school coaching job, his equity capital, and his building that he could have rented. The total implicit cost = $75,000 (= $45,000 + $6,000 + $24,000).

   d. $213,000 (= $138,000 + $75,000); $213,000. (Note: Total economic cost is defined as the opportunity cost of *all* resources used by the firm.)

   e. $72,000 = Total revenue – explicit costs = $213,000 – $138,000. Note that accounting profit is frequently called "net income" in financial statements (as in this problem.)

   f. Terry Brady's wealth decreased in 2004 because economic profit is –$3,000 (= $210,000 – $138,000 – $75,000). Only when the owners of businesses earn positive economic profits do they experience an increase in their wealth. Remember, the value of their firm, which is part (or perhaps all) of their wealth, depends on the future stream of economic profit earned by the firm. A year in which profit is zero adds nothing to owner wealth. A year in which profit is negative reduces owner wealth. The value of economic profit, –$3,000, indicates Brady would have been $3,000 better off had he NOT owned and operated Brady Advantage in 2004 but instead collected salary as high school coach of $45,000, interest of $6,000, and rent of $24,000 (which totals $75,000). As you can see, accounting profit in this example must exceed $75,000 in order for Brady to break even.

2. a. $3,500,000; $120,000; $3,620,000
   b. $1,500,000
   c. $1,380,000

d. $1,350,000

3. a. Value of the firm:

$$\frac{\$700,000}{(1.16)^1} + \frac{\$800,000}{(1.16)^2} + \frac{\$500,000}{(1.16)^3}$$

$$= \$603,448 + \$594,530 + \$320,329$$

$$= \$1,518,307 = \text{price of the firm}$$

b. Value of the firm:

$$\frac{\$700,000}{(1.10)^1} + \frac{\$800,000}{(1.10)^2} + \frac{\$500,000}{(1.10)^3}$$

$$= \$636,364 + \$661,157 + \$375,657$$

$$= \$1,673,178 = \text{price of the firm}$$

4. a. *Price-taker*. Many banks provide car loans in Chicago. The price of a car loan, which is the interest rate, is determined by market forces of demand and supply.

b. *Price-taker*. FastCo Inc. will lose most, if not all, of its sales if it tries to raise its price above the price charged by its rivals—all of which produce a standardized product. FastCo has no market power and is a price-taking firm.

c. *Price-setter*. Bombardier enjoys a substantial amount of brand loyalty that gives its manager the ability to raise the price of its jet skis without losing all sales.

d. *Price-setter*. At this time, McDonald's is the only hamburger restaurant in the area and consequently enjoys some degree of market power. Over time, however, new restaurants will enter the market if a profit can be earned.

5. a. *Oligopoly*. In office applications, Microsoft is one of just a few firms providing such software and the firms recognize their mutual interdependence in matters of pricing, software features, and service.

b. *Perfect Competition*. Becker Farms is one of thousands of relatively small producers of a standardized product. Furthermore, there are no barriers to entry in wheat farming.

c. *Monopoly*. For now, Robo Wash is the only coin-op car wash in Monroe. Robo Wash probably has sufficient market power to be able to raise price without losing all its sales. However, as price goes up, people will turn to substitutes—drive to a nearby town with a car wash, wash the car less frequently, or wash the car at home. In time, high prices will attract entry of new coin-op car washes.

d. *Monopolistic competition.* The market for Mexican food in San Antonio is characterized by a large number of restaurants producing somewhat differentiated dining experiences without any protection from entry of new rival restaurants.

e. *Oligopoly*. The two restaurants face interdependent profits and, in this case, also enjoy an entry barrier (the license).

6. a. Principal-agent problems can be mitigated to some extent by linking manager compensation to the performance of the firm. Guaranteed bonuses are paid no matter how well the firm performs, and so undermine the incentive of a manager to make decisions that maximize the value of a firm.

b. Maximizing the value of a firm also requires hiring successful managers (or taking greater risk by hiring inexperienced managers). If labor markets for managerial talent are tight, then firms may be required to increase compensation to attract talented managers. By guaranteeing a bonus, Ben & Jerry's not only increases a manager's compensation by $75,000, but also reduces the risk associated with that compensation (it is guaranteed).

MULTIPLE CHOICE / TRUE-FALSE

1. b   Theory provides important clues to managers about the kinds and amounts of information that will be needed to make decisions.

2. e   The cost of owner-supplied resources may not involve an out-of-pocket payment, but these implicit costs are nonetheless costs to owners and must be covered to retain the use of the owner-supplied resources.

3. d   Economic profit = Accounting profit—Implicit costs. Implicit costs are the opportunity costs of using owner-supplied resources.

4. d   Both *a* and *c* are true by the definition of economic profit, and the wealth of owners increases only when economic profit is positive.

5. a   The higher is the risk premium, the larger is the risk-adjusted discount rate used to calculate the present value of future profits.

6. c   The implicit cost of Maverick's time is $40,000, so economic profit is $-\$100,000$ ($= 240,000 - 300,000 - 40,000$).

7. b   This is the definition of risk premium.

8. d   Making business decisions that maximize profit in each separate time period will result in maximization of the value of the firm, as long as revenue and cost conditions in any single period are unrelated to revenues and costs in other time periods.

9. d   Both *a* and *b* follow from the discussion of principal-agent problems in the textbook.

10. d   Principal-agent problems arise when there is a moral hazard.

11. e   Price-taking firms cannot control the price of their product because there are too many producers selling an identical product. The price, under these circumstances, is determined not by one firm, but by the market forces of demand and supply.

12. e   Price-setting firms can control the price of their products by increasing or decreasing production along their downward sloping demand curves. They possess this market power because consumers do not have many substitutes from which to choose.

13. c   Research and development expenditure is not a characteristic of market structure, although such expenditures may be part of a strategic plan by management to create barriers to entry or to differentiate a product in the future.

14. e   Both *a* and *c* are characteristics of monopolistic competition.

15. c   A monopoly requires an entry barrier, otherwise, raising price above cost results in new firms entering, which eliminates the monopoly.

16. F   The opposite is true; outsiders on the board of directors tend to enhance the monitoring function of a board.

17. F   Accounting profit can be positive, but when the opportunity cost of using resources owned by the firm is subtracted from positive accounting profit, the resulting economic profit may be zero or negative.

18. T   Risk is an undesirable attribute of business profits. For a given level of expected profit, the smaller the associated risk, the more investors are willing to pay for a claim on this profit.

19. T   Interdependence of sales and profits is the hallmark of oligopoly.

20. T   As emphasized in the text, owners of businesses recognize that costs of using all resources, whether the resources are purchased in resource markets or owned by the firm. Only economic profit subtracts from total revenue all costs of using resources.

Homework Exercises

1. A partial income statement from CenTer Realty, Inc. is shown below:

	2005
Revenues	
Revenue from sales of goods and services	$53,750,000
Operating costs and expenses:	
Cost of products and services sold *E*	$26,000,000
Selling expenses *E*	$5,235,000
Administrative expenses *E*	$4,237,000
Total operating costs and expenses	$35,472,000
Income from operations	$18,278,000
Interest expense (corporate bonds & loans) *E*	$875,000
Non-recurring legal expenses *E*	$585,000
Income taxes *E*	$10,245,000
Net income	$6,573,000

In 2005, CenTer Realty owned and occupied an office building in downtown Kansas City. The building could have been leased to other businesses for $3,000,000 in lease income for 2005. CenTer Realty also owned undeveloped land valued at $32,000,000. Owners of CenTer Realty can earn a 9 percent rate of return on funds invested elsewhere.

a. In 2005, CenTer Realty's total explicit costs of using market-supplied resources are $ _47 177,000_ .

b. CenTer's total implicit costs of using owner-supplied resources equals $_____ in 2005.

c. Total economic cost is $_____.

d. CenTer's accounting profit is $_____.

e. Economic profit in 2005 is $_____.

f. The Board of Directors believes CenTer's owners can earn 14 percent, rather than 12 percent on funds invested elsewhere. At a 14 percent rate of return, economic profit in 2005 is $_____.

2. At the beginning of 2005, market analysts expect Atlantis Company, holder of a valuable patent, to earn the following stream of economic profits over the next five years. At the end of five years, Atlantis will lose its patent protection, and analysts expect economic profit to be zero after five years.

Year	Expected Economic Profit
2005	$2,000,000
2006	$3,000,000
2007	$4,000,000
2008	$5,000,000
2009	$2,000,000

   a. If investors apply an annual risk-adjusted discount rate of 8 percent, the value of Atlantis Company in 2005 is $_____, which is also the maximum price they would be willing to pay for Atlantis.

   b. If investors apply an annual risk-adjusted discount rate of 12 percent, the value of Atlantis Company in 2005 is $_____, which is also the maximum price they would be willing to pay for Atlantis.

3. For each of the firms below, identify the market structure that best matches the competitive characteristics found in that firm's market:
   a. _____   *BusinessWeek* magazine
   b. _____   Exxon Corporation
   c. _____   Dow Chemical, wholesale chemicals
   d. _____   Pfizer, Inc., supplier of Viagra

4. Explain why SunKist, a well-known citrus producer, is a price-taker.

5. Explain why the Lexus dealer in your city is a price-setting firm. Be sure to discuss the concept of market power.

Demand, Supply, and Market Equilibrium

Learning Objectives

After reading Chapter 2 and working the problems for Chapter 2 in the textbook and in this Workbook, you should be able to:

➢   List six principal variables that determine the quantity demanded of a good.

➢   Derive a demand function from a generalized demand function.

➢   Give two interpretations of a point on a demand curve.

➢   Find inverse demand functions.

➢   Distinguish between changes in "quantity demanded" and changes in "demand."

➢   Determine when to move along a demand curve and when to shift a demand curve.

➢   List six principal variables that determine the quantity supplied of a good.

➢   Distinguish between changes in "quantity supplied" and changes in "supply."

➢   Give two interpretations of a point on a supply curve.

➢   Find inverse supply functions.

➢   Explain why market equilibrium occurs at the price for which quantity demanded equals quantity supplied.

➢   Analyze the impact on equilibrium price and quantity of a shift in either the demand curve or the supply curve, while the other curve remains constant.

➢   Analyze simultaneous shifts in both demand and supply curves.

➢   Explain the impact of government imposed price ceilings and price floors.

Essential Concepts

1.   The amount of a good or service that consumers are willing and able to purchase during a given period of time is called *quantity demanded* (Q_d). Six principal variables influence quantity demanded: (1) the price of the good or service (P), (2) the incomes of consumers (M), (3) the prices of related goods and services (P_R), (4) the taste patterns of consumers ($\Im$), (5) the expected price of the product in some future period (P_e), and (6) the number of consumers in the market (N). The relation between quantity demanded and the six factors that influence the quantity demanded of a good is called the *generalized demand function* and is expressed as follows:

$$Q_d = f(P, M, P_R, \Im, P_e, N)$$

The generalized demand function shows how all six variables *jointly* determine the quantity demanded.

2. The impact on Q_d of changing one of the six factors *while the other five remain constant* is summarized below.

    (1) The quantity demanded of a good is inversely related to its own price by the *law of demand*. Thus $\Delta Q_d / \Delta P$ is negative.

    (2) A good is said to be *normal* (*inferior*) when the amount consumers demand of a good varies directly (inversely) with income. Thus $\Delta Q_d / \Delta M$ is positive (negative) for normal (inferior) goods.

    (3) Commodities that are related in consumption are said to be *substitutes* if the demand for one good varies directly with the price of another good so that $\Delta Q_d / \Delta P_R$ is positive. Alternatively, two goods are said to be *complements* if the demand for one good varies inversely with the price of another good so that $\Delta Q_d / \Delta P_R$ is negative.

    (4) When buyers expect the price of a good or service to rise (fall), demand in the current period of time increases (decreases). Thus, $\Delta Q_d / \Delta P_e$ is positive.

    (5) A movement in consumer tastes toward (away from) a good, as reflected by an increase (decrease) in the consumer taste index $\Im$, will increase (decrease) demand for a good. Thus $\Delta Q_d / \Delta \Im$ is positive.

    (6) An increase (decrease) in the number of consumers in a market will increase (decrease) the demand for a good. Thus $\Delta Q_d / \Delta N$ is positive.

3. The generalized demand function can be expressed in linear functional form as

$$Q_d = a + bP + cM + dP_R + e\Im + fP_e + gN$$

where the slope parameters *b, c, d, e, f,* and *g* measure the effect on Q_d of changing one of the six variables (P, M, P_R, $\Im$, P_e, or N) while holding the other five variables constant. For example, b ($= \Delta Q_d / \Delta P$) measures the change in Q_d per unit change in P holding M, P_R, $\Im$, P_e, and N constant. When the slope parameter of a particular variable is positive (negative), Q_d is directly (inversely) related to that variable. The following table summarizes the interpretation of the parameters in the general linear demand function.

Variable	Relation to Quantity Demanded	Sign of Slope Parameter
P	Inverse	$b = \Delta Q_d / \Delta P$ is negative
M	Direct for normal goods Inverse for inferior goods	$c = \Delta Q_d / \Delta M$ is positive $c = \Delta Q_d / \Delta M$ is negative
P_R	Direct for substitute goods Inverse for complement goods	$d = \Delta Q_d / \Delta P_R$ is positive $d = \Delta Q_d / \Delta P_R$ is negative
$\Im$	Direct	$e = \Delta Q_d / \Delta \Im$ is positive
P_e	Direct	$f = \Delta Q_d / \Delta P_e$ is positive
N	Direct	$g = \Delta Q_d / \Delta N$ is positive

4.   A *demand function*, or simply *demand*, shows the relation between price and quantity demanded when all other factors that affect consumer demand are held constant. The "other things" held constant are the five variables other than price that can affect demand $(M, P_R, \Im, P_e, N)$. The demand equation expresses quantity demanded as a function of product price only:

$$Q_d = f(P)$$

The variables M, P_R, $\Im$, P_e, and N are assumed to be constant and therefore do *not* appear as variables in the demand function.

5.   When graphing demand curves, economists traditionally plot the independent variable price (P) on the vertical axis and Q_d, the dependent variable, on the horizontal axis. The equation so plotted is actually the *inverse* of the demand function $P = f^{-1}(Q_d)$.

6.   A point on a demand curve shows either: (1) the maximum amount of a good that will be purchased if a given price is charged; or (2) the maximum price consumers will pay for a specific amount of the good. This maximum price is sometimes referred to as the *demand* price for that amount of the good.

7.   The *law of demand* states that quantity demanded increases when price falls and quantity demanded decreases when price rises, other things held constant. The law of demand implies $\Delta Q_d / \Delta P$ must be negative; Q_d and P are inversely related.

8.   When the price of a good changes, the "quantity demanded" changes. A change in a good or service's own price causes a change in quantity demanded, and this change in quantity demanded is represented by a movement along the demand curve.

9.   The five variables held constant in deriving demand $(M, P_R, \Im, P_e, N)$ are called the *determinants of demand* because they determine where the demand curve is located. When there is a change in any of the five determinants of demand, a "change in demand" is said to occur, and the demand curve shifts either rightward or left-

ward. An increase (decrease) in demand occurs when demand shifts rightward (leftward). The determinants of demand are also called the "demand-shifting variables."

10. The quantity supplied (Q_s) of a good depends most importantly upon six factors: (1) the price of the good itself (P), (2) the price of inputs used in production (P_I), (3) the prices of goods related in production (P_r), (4) the level of available technology (T), (5) the expectations of producers concerning the future price of the good (P_e), and (6) the number of firms producing the good or the amount of productive capacity in the industry (F). The *generalized supply function* shows how all six of these variables *jointly* determine the quantity supplied

$$Q_s = g(P, P_I, P_r, T, P_e, F)$$

11. The impact on Q_s of changing one of the six factors *while the other five remain constant* is summarized below.

   (1)   The quantity supplied of a good is directly related to the price of the good. Thus $\Delta Q_s / \Delta P$ is positive.

   (2)   As input prices increase (decrease), production costs rise (fall), and producers will want to supply a smaller (larger) quantity at each price. Thus $\Delta Q_s / \Delta P_I$ is negative.

   (3)   Goods that are related in production are said to be *substitutes in production* if an increase in the price of good X relative to good Y causes producers to increase production of good X and decrease production of good Y. Thus $\Delta Q_s / \Delta P_r$ is negative for substitutes in production. Goods X and Y are said to be *complements in production* if an increase in the price of good X relative to good Y causes producers to increase production of both goods. Thus $\Delta Q_s / \Delta P_r$ is positive for complements in production.

   (4)   Advances in technology (reflected by increases in T) reduce production costs and increase the supply of the good. Thus $\Delta Q_s / \Delta T$ is positive.

   (5)   If firms expect the price of a good they produce to rise in the future, they may withhold some of the good, thereby reducing supply of the good in the current period. Thus, $\Delta Q_s / \Delta P_e$ is negative.

   (6)   If the number of firms producing the product increases (decreases) or the amount of productive capacity in the industry increases (decreases), then more (less) of the good will be supplied at each price. Thus $\Delta Q_s / \Delta F$ is positive.

12. The generalized supply function can be expressed in linear functional form as

$$Q_s = h + kP + lP_I + mP_r + nT + rP_e + sF$$

where the slope parameters are interpreted as summarized in the following table:

Variable	Relation to Quantity Supplied	Sign of Slope Parameter
P	Direct	$k = \Delta Q_s / \Delta P$ is positive
P_I	Inverse	$l = \Delta Q_s / \Delta P_I$ is negative
P_r	Inverse for substitutes in production (wheat and corn)	$m = \Delta Q_s / \Delta P_r$ is negative
	Direct for complements in production (oil and gas)	$m = \Delta Q_s / \Delta P_r$ is positive
T	Direct	$n = \Delta Q_s / \Delta T$ is positive
P_e	Inverse	$r = \Delta Q_s / \Delta P_e$ is negative
F	Direct	$s = \Delta Q_s / \Delta F$ is positive

13. A *supply function* gives the quantity supplied at various prices and may be expressed mathematically as

$$Q_s = g(P)$$

where $P_I, P_r, T, P_e,$ and F are assumed to be constant and therefore do not appear as variables in the supply function. An increase (decrease) in price causes an increase in quantity supplied, which is represented by an upward (downward) movement along a given supply curve.

14. A point on the supply curve indicates either (1) the maximum amount of a good or service that will be offered for sale at a given price, or (2) the minimum price necessary to induce producers voluntarily to offer a particular quantity for sale. This minimum price is sometimes referred to as the *supply price* for that level of output.

15. When any of the five determinants of supply (P_I, P_r, T, P_e, F) change, "supply" (not "quantity supplied") changes. A change in supply results in a shift of the supply curve. Only when the price of a good changes does the quantity supplied change.

16. The equilibrium price and quantity in a market are determined by the intersection of demand and supply curves. At the point of intersection, quantity demanded equals quantity supplied, and the market clears. Buyers can purchase all they want and sellers can sell all they want at the "market-clearing" (equilibrium) price.

17. Since the location of the demand and supply curves is determined by the five determinants of demand and the five determinants of supply, a change in any one of these ten variables will result in a new equilibrium point. The following figure summarizes the results when either demand or supply shifts while the other curve remains constant.

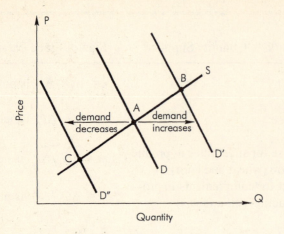

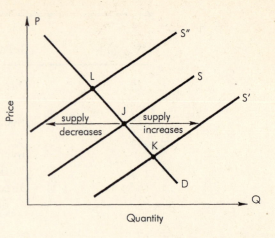

Panel A: Shifts in demand (supply constant)   **Panel B**: Shifts in supply (demand constant)

When demand increases and supply remains constant, price and quantity sold both rise, as shown by the movement from point *A* to *B* in Panel *A* above. A decrease in demand, supply constant, causes both price and quantity sold to fall, as shown by the movement from point *A* to *C*. When supply increases and demand remains constant, price falls and quantity sold rises, as shown by the movement from point *J* to *K* in Panel *B* above. A decrease in supply, demand constant causes price to rise and quantity to fall, as shown by the movement from *J* to *L*.

18. When both supply and demand shift simultaneously, it is possible to predict either the direction in which price changes or the direction in which quantity changes, but not both. The change in equilibrium quantity or price is said to be indeterminate when the direction of change depends upon the relative magnitudes by which demand and supply shift. The four possible cases for simultaneous shifts in demand and supply are summarized in Figure 2.9 of your textbook.

19. When government sets a ceiling price below the equilibrium price, a shortage results because consumers wish to buy more of the good than producers are willing to sell at the ceiling price. If government sets a floor price above the equilibrium price, a surplus results because producers offer for sale more of the good than buyers wish to consume at the floor price.

Matching Definitions

ceiling price
change in demand
change in quantity demanded
change in quantity supplied
complements
complements in production
decrease in demand
decrease in supply
demand
demand price
determinants of demand
determinants of supply
equilibrium price

equilibrium quantity
excess demand (shortage)
excess supply (surplus)
floor price
generalized demand function
generalized supply function
increase in demand
increase in supply
indeterminate
inferior good
inverse demand function
inverse supply function
law of demand

market clearing price
market equilibrium
normal good
qualitative forecasts
quantitative forecasts
quantity demanded
quantity supplied
slope parameters
substitutes
substitutes in production
supply
supply price
technology

1. _____ Amount of a good or service that consumers are willing and able to purchase during a given period of time.

2. _____ Relation between quantity demanded and the six principal variables affecting quantity demanded.

3. _____ A good for which demand decreases with decreases in income.

4. _____ A good for which demand increases with decreases in income.

5. _____ Two goods for which an increase in the price of one causes an increase in consumption of the other, all other things constant.

6. _____ Two goods for which a decrease in the price of one causes an increase in consumption of the other, all other things constant.

7. _____ Parameters in a linear function that measure the effect on the dependent variable of a one-unit change in the value of an independent variable, holding all others variables constant.

8. _____ The relation that shows how quantity demanded varies with price, holding all other factors constant.

9. _____ Price is expressed as a function of quantity demanded.

10. _____ The maximum price consumers will pay for a specific amount of a good.

11. _____ Quantity demanded increases when price falls and decreases when price rises, other things held constant.

12. _____ A movement along a given demand curve caused by a change in the good's own price.

13. _____ Quantity demanded increases at every price.

14. _____ Quantity demanded decreases at every price.

15. _____ The five principal variables that determine the location of the demand curve $(M, P_R, \Im, P_e, N)$. These are the demand shifting variables.

16. _____ A shift in demand that occurs when one of the demand shifting variables changes.

17. _____ The amount of a good or service offered for sale per time period.

18. _____ The relation between quantity supplied and the six principal factors affecting the quantity supplied.

19. _____ Two goods for which an increase in the price of one good causes a decrease in the production of the other good.

20. _____ Two goods for which an increase in the price of one good causes an increase in the production of the other good.

21. _____ The state of knowledge about how to combine resources to produce goods and services.

22. _____ The functional relation between price and quantity supplied, holding all other factors constant.

23. _____ The five principal variables that determine the location of the supply curve (P_I, P_r, T, P_e, F). These are the supply shifting variables.

24. _____ A movement along the supply curve caused by a change in the price of the good.

25. _____ Price is expressed as a function of quantity supplied.

26. _____ The minimum price necessary to induce producers voluntarily to offer a given quantity for sale.

27. _____ Rightward shift of a supply curve when quantity supplied increases at every price.

28. _____ Leftward shift of a supply curve when quantity supplied decreases at every price.

29. _____ Buyers can purchase all of a good they wish and producers can sell all they wish at the prevailing price.

30. _____ The price at which quantity demanded equals quantity supplied.

31. _____ The amount of a good or service that is demanded and sold in market equilibrium.

32. _____ When quantity supplied is greater than quantity demanded.

33. _____ When quantity demanded is greater than quantity supplied.

34. _____ Another name for equilibrium price.

35. _____ Forecasts that predict only the direction in which economic variables will move.

36. _____ Forecasts that predict both the direction in which economic variables will move and the magnitudes of the changes.

37. _____ Term referring to the condition in which it is impossible to predict the direction of the change in either equilibrium quantity or equilibrium price.

38. _____ The maximum price government permits seller to charge for a good.

39. _____ The minimum price government permits seller to charge for a good.

Study Problems

1. What happens to the demand for Sony color television sets when each of the following changes occurs?

   _____ a. The price of Zenith color television sets rises.

   _____ b. The price of a Sony rises.

   _____ c. Personal income falls (color televisions are normal goods).

   _____ d. Technological advances result in dramatic price reductions for video tape recorders.

   _____ e. Congress is persuaded to impose tariffs on Japanese television sets starting next year.

2. What happens to the supply of random access memory (RAM) chips, a component in the manufacture of personal computers, when each of the following changes occurs?

   _____ a. Two huge new manufacturing plants begin operation in South Korea.

   _____ b. Scientists discover a new production technology that will lower the cost of making RAM chips.

   _____ c. The price of silicon, a key ingredient in RAM chip production, rises sharply.

   _____ d. The price of RAM chips increases.

   _____ e. The market for personal computers turns sour and RAM chip makers now expect RAM chip prices to fall by 25 percent next quarter.

3. "The salaries of chief executive officers (CEOs) are unreasonably high." Critically evaluate this statement.

4. Suppose the quantity demanded of good (Q_d) depends only on the price of the good (P), monthly income (M), and the price of a related good R (P_R):

$$Q_d = 180 - 10P - 0.2M + 10P_R$$

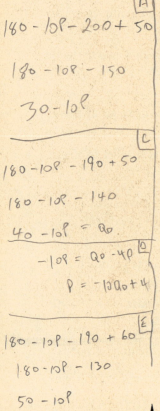

(handwritten, box A)
$180 - 10P - 200 + 50$
$180 - 10P - 150$
$30 - 10P$

(handwritten, box C)
$180 - 10P - 190 + 50$
$180 - 10P - 140$
$40 - 10P = Q_0$
$-10P = Q_0 - 40$
$P = -\frac{1}{10}Q_0 + 4$

(handwritten, box E)
$180 - 10P - 190 + 60$
$180 - 10P - 130$
$50 - 10P$

a. On the axes below, construct the demand curve for the good when $M =$ $1,000 and $P_R =$ $5. The equation for demand is

$Q_d =$ __30 - 10P__ .

b. Interpret the intercept and slope parameters for the demand equation in part *a*.

c. Let income decrease to $950. Construct the new demand curve. This good is __NORMAL__ (normal, inferior). Explain using your graph.

d. For the demand curve in part *c*, find the inverse demand function:

$P =$ _____ .

e. Let the price of good R increase to $6 (income remaining at $950). Construct the new demand curve. Good R is a __SUBSTITUTE__ (substitute, complement) good. Explain using your graph.

f. For the demand curve in part *e*, the demand price for 20 units is $ __3.00__ . At a price of $4, the maximum amount consumers are willing and able to purchase is __10__ units.

g. For the demand curve in part *e*, find the equilibrium price and quantity when supply is $Q_s = -10 + 10P$.

$P_E =$ __3.00__ and $Q_E =$ __20.__

Construct the supply curve and verify your answer.

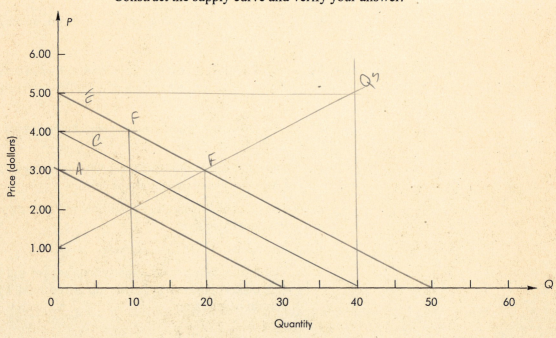

5. Consider the following demand and supply functions for tomatoes:

$$Q_d = 6,000 - 4,000P$$
$$Q_s = -1,000 + 10,000P$$

a. Plot the demand and supply functions on the axes below.

b. At a price of $1.00 per tomato, ___2000___ tomatoes is the maximum amount that can be sold. A price of $ _0.30_ per tomato is the maximum price that consumers will pay for 2,000 tomatoes, which is the demand price for 2,000 tomatoes.

c. The maximum amount of tomatoes that producers will offer for sale if the price of tomatoes is $0.30 is ___2000___. The minimum price necessary to induce producers to offer voluntarily 2,000 tomatoes for sale is $_0.30_, which is called the supply price for 2,000 tomatoes.

d. In equilibrium, the price of tomatoes is $ _0.50_ and ___4000___ tomatoes will be sold.

e. In equilibrium, the quantity of tomatoes produced is _4,000_ tomatoes.

f. In equilibrium, the quantity of tomatoes consumed is _4,000_ tomatoes.

g. Are your answers to parts e and f the same? Why or why not?

h. Congress imposes a $0.30 per tomato ceiling price on tomatoes. This results in a ___SHORTAGE___ (surplus, shortage) of ___2000___ tomatoes.

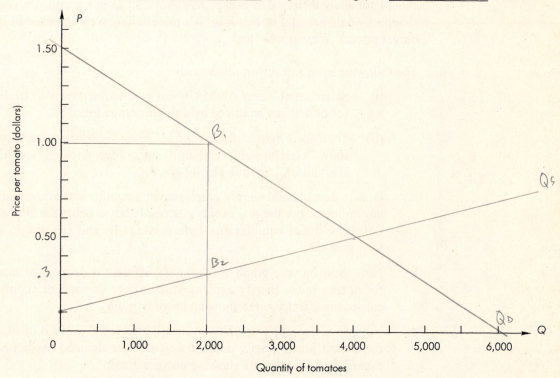

6. "A decrease in the supply of crude oil will cause a shortage of crude oil." Evaluate this statement with a concise narrative and graphical analysis.

7. "An increase in the demand for electricity will cause a shortage of electricity." Evaluate this statement with a concise narrative and graphical analysis.

8. Determine the effect on equilibrium price and quantity if the following changes occur in a particular market:

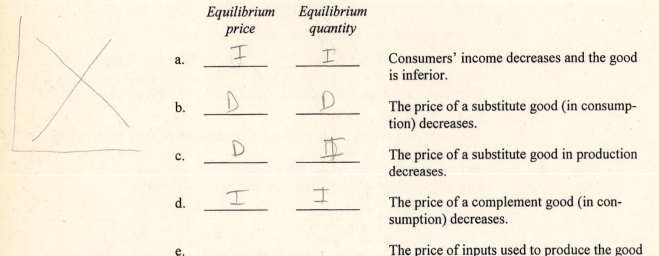

	Equilibrium price	*Equilibrium quantity*	
a.	I	I	Consumers' income decreases and the good is inferior.
b.	D	D	The price of a substitute good (in consumption) decreases.
c.	D	I	The price of a substitute good in production decreases.
d.	I	I	The price of a complement good (in consumption) decreases.
e.			The price of inputs used to produce the good decrease.

9. At the meat counter of a local supermarket, two shoppers were overheard complaining about the high price of hamburger. They concluded that government should not allow the price of beef to rise above $2.25 per pound. Do you think the shoppers would actually be better off if a price ceiling were imposed to lower hamburger prices? Why or why not?

10. The following events occur simultaneously:

    (i) Scientists at Texas A&M University discover a way to triple the number of oranges produced by a single orange tree.

    (ii) The *New England Journal of Medicine* publishes research results that show "conclusively" that drinking orange juice reduces the risk of heart attack and stroke by 40 percent.

    a. Draw a demand-and-supply graph showing equilibrium in the market for orange juice before the two events described above. Label the axes and curves. Label the initial equilibrium—before events (i) and (ii)—as P_0 and Q_0 on your graph.

    b. Now show on your graph how event (i) affects the demand or supply curves for orange juice. Briefly explain which of the demand or supply variables caused the effect you are showing on your graph.

    c. Now show on your graph how event (ii) affects the demand or supply curves for orange juice. Briefly explain which of the demand or supply variables caused the effect you are showing on your graph.

    d. Based on your graphic analysis, what do you predict will happen to the equilibrium price of orange juice? The equilibrium quantity of orange juice?

Multiple Choice / True-False

1. Which one of the following will NOT cause an increase in the demand for Whirlpool dishwashers?
    a. A decline in home mortgage interest rates.
    b. An increase in real disposable income.
    c. General Electric raises the price of its dishwashers.
    d. Introduction of new semiconductors reduces the per unit cost of producing dishwashers.

2. The quantity supplied of coffee beans decreases when
    a. average annual rainfall decreases due to a drought in Central and South America.
    b. the price of coffee beans falls.
    c. the price of tea rises.
    d. a labor union for coffee bean pickers forms and wages rise.

3. Which of the following statements correctly describes market equilibrium?
    a. Consumers can buy all of the good they wish at the market price.
    b. Producers can sell all of the good they wish at the market price.
    c. Neither a surplus nor a shortage exists.
    d. All of the above.

Use the figure below to answer questions 4 and 5.

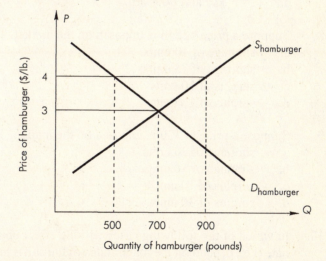

4. Suppose government sets a floor of $4 on the price of beef. This results in
    a. a surplus of 400 tons of hamburger.
    b. a surplus of 200 tons of hamburger.
    c. a shortage of hamburger.
    d. consumers purchasing 900 tons of hamburger at a price of $4.

5.	Suppose government imposes a ceiling price of $4 on hamburger. This results in
	a.	a surplus of 400 tons of hamburger.
	b.	a surplus of 200 tons of hamburger.
	c.	a shortage of hamburger.
	d.	consumers purchasing 700 tons of hamburger at a price of $3.

6.	When the Super Bowl was played in Tampa, some fans complained that there were not enough hotel rooms. We can conclude that
	a.	the game should have been played in a bigger city.
	b.	the market for hotel rooms was in equilibrium.
	c.	the city council should have done a study so that the hotel industry would have constructed more hotel rooms.
	d.	the price of hotel rooms was below the market-clearing price.

Use the following supply and demand functions to answer Questions 7 - 9:

$$Q_d = 100 - 2P$$

$$Q_s = -20 + P$$

7.	What are equilibrium price and quantity?
	a.	$P_E = \$20$ and $Q_E = 100$
	b.	$P_E = \$40$ and $Q_E = 20$
	c.	$P_E = \$60$ and $Q_E = 40$
	d.	$P_E = \$30$ and $Q_E = 40$

8.	Suppose a price of $46 is imposed on the market. This results in a
	a.	shortage of 10 units.
	b.	shortage of 26 units.
	c.	surplus of 10 units.
	d.	surplus of 18 units.

9.	Suppose a price of $30 is imposed on the market. This results in a
	a.	shortage of 30 units.
	b.	shortage of 10 units.
	c.	surplus of 10 units.
	d.	surplus of 30 units.

10.	In which of the following cases will the effect on equilibrium output be indeterminate (i.e., depend on the magnitudes of the shifts in supply and demand)?
	a.	Demand increases and supply increases.
	b.	Demand decreases and supply decreases.
	c.	Demand decreases and supply increases.
	d.	Demand remains constant and supply increases.

46

The generalized linear demand function below is used to answer the next three questions:

$$Q_d = a + bP + cM + dP_R$$

where Q_d = quantity demanded, P = the price of the good, M = household income, P_R = the price of a good related in consumption.

11. The law of demand requires that
    a. $a < 0$.
    b. $b < 0$.
    c. $P < 0$.
    d. $a < 0$ and $b < 0$.
    e. $b < 0$ and $P < 0$.

12. If $c = 0.01$ and $d = -32$, the good is
    a. a normal good.
    b. an inferior good.
    c. a substitute for good R.
    d. a complement with good R.
    e. both a and d.

13. For the generalized linear demand function given above
    a. $\Delta Q_d / \Delta M = c$.
    b. d is the effect on the quantity demanded of the good of a one-dollar change in the price of the related good, all other things constant.
    c. b is the effect on the quantity demanded of the good of a one-dollar change in the price of the good, all other things constant.
    d. all of the above.

14. In which of the following case(s) must equilibrium quantity always fall?
    a. Demand increases and supply increases.
    b. Demand decreases and supply decreases.
    c. Supply decreases and demand remains constant.
    d. Demand decreases and supply increases.
    e. Both b and c.

15. T F A decrease in supply causes a shortage.

16. T F When demand decreases, supply constant, equilibrium output rises.

17. T F Predicting that price will rise by 10 percent as a result of an increase in the price of labor is a *qualitative* forecast.

18. T F A market is in equilibrium when supply equals demand.

19. T F A rise in the price of aluminum will cause an increase in the demand for steel and plastic.

20. T F Only a change in a good's own price will cause a change in the quantity demanded of the good.

Answers

MATCHING DEFINITIONS

1.	quantity demanded		21.	technology
2.	generalized demand function		22.	supply
3.	normal good		23.	determinants of supply
4.	inferior good		24.	change in quantity supplied
5.	substitutes		25.	inverse supply function
6.	complements		26.	supply price
7.	slope parameters		27.	increase in supply
8.	demand		28.	decrease in supply
9.	inverse demand function		29.	market equilibrium
10.	demand price		30.	equilibrium price
11.	law of demand		31.	equilibrium quantity
12.	change in quantity demanded		32.	excess supply (surplus)
13.	increase in demand		33.	excess demand (shortage)
14.	decrease in demand		34.	market clearing price
15.	determinants of demand		35.	qualitative forecasts
16.	change in demand		36.	quantitative forecasts
17.	quantity supplied		37.	indeterminate
18.	generalized supply function		38.	price ceiling
19.	substitutes in production		39.	price floor
20.	complements in production			

STUDY PROBLEMS

1.
   a. Demand increases (shifts rightward)
   b. Nothing happens to Sony demand; demand does not shift. Quantity demanded, however, decreases.
   c. Demand decreases (shifts leftward)
   d. Demand increases (shifts rightward)
   e. Demand in the current time period increases (shifts rightward) since consumers expect price to be higher next year.

2.
   a. Supply increases (shifts rightward)
   b. Supply increases (shifts rightward)
   c. Supply decreases (shifts leftward)
   d. Nothing happens to RAM chip supply; supply does not shift. Quantity supplied, however, increases.
   e. Supply in the current time period increases (shifts rightward) as producers increase production in the current time period to sell more chips at a price that is higher relative to the price they expect to receive in the next quarter.

3. The salaries of CEOs are determined by supply and demand. If supply were greater or demand smaller, then the salaries of CEOs would be lower.

4.   The three demand curves for parts *a*, *c*, and *e*, and the supply curve in part *g* are plotted below:

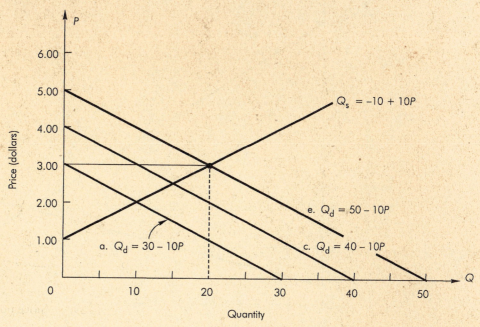

a. $Q_d = 30 - 10P$. The demand curve is shown in the figure above.

b.   Intercept parameter $a = 30$:   If price is zero, consumers will take only 30 units.

Slope parameter $b = -10$:   For each $1 increase in price, consumers buy 10 fewer units.

c.   The demand curve is shown in the figure above as $Q_d = 40 - 10P$. Inferior, since *decreasing* income from $1,000 to $950 results in an increase in demand, which can only happen for inferior goods.

d. $P = 4 - 1/10 Q_d$

e.   The demand curve is shown in the figure above as $Q_d = 50 - 10P$. Substitutes, since increasing the price of R from $5 to $6 results in an increase in demand.

f. $3 ($= 5 - (1/10) \times 20$, which is the inverse demand in part *e*); 10 ($= 50 - 10 \times 4$)

g.   Set $Q_d = Q_s$: $50 - 10P = -10 + 10P$. Solve to get $P_E = 3. Substituting $3 into either the demand equation or the supply equation:

$$50 - 10 \times 3 = -10 + 10 \times 3 = 20 = Q_E$$

$$50 - 30 \div 3 = 20$$

5.   a.   Your demand and supply curves should look like this:

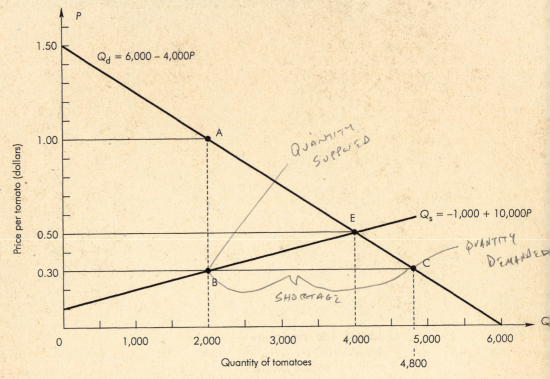

b. $2,000 \; (=6,000-4,000\times1.00)$ see point A; $1

c. $2,000 \; (=-1,000+10,000\times0.30)$ see point B; $0.30

d. $0.50; 4,000 (see point E)

e.   4,000

f.   4,000

g.   Yes, in equilibrium quantity consumed equals quantity produced ($Q_d = Q_s$).

h.   Shortage; 2,800. Notice that at $0.30, quantity demanded is 4,800 $(=6,000-4,000\times0.30)$, and quantity supplied is 2,000 $(=-1,000+10,000\times0.30)$. Thus, the shortage is 2,800 ($=4,800-2,000$).

6.   A decrease in the supply of crude oil will not cause a shortage as long as the price of crude oil is allowed to rise to the market clearing level. After a decrease in supply, the crude oil market will continue to clear but at a higher price. At the higher equilibrium price of crude oil, consumers can buy all they want and producers can sell all they want. Only if government places a ceiling price below the market clearing price can there be a shortage of crude oil when supply decreases. Shortages are not caused by decreases in supply. The following graph shows a decrease in crude oil supply as a leftward shift in supply from S_A to S_B, which causes equilibrium in the crude oil market to move from point A to point B and the market clearing price of crude oil rises from P_A to P_B.

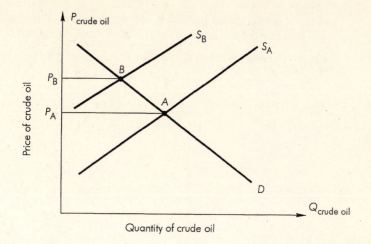

Quantity of crude oil

7. An increase in the demand for electricity will not cause a shortage as long as the price of electricity is allowed to rise to the market clearing level. After an increase in demand, the electricity market will continue to clear but at a higher price. At the higher equilibrium price of electricity, consumers can buy all they want and producers can sell all they want. Only if government places a ceiling price below the market clearing price can there be a shortage of electricity when demand increases. Shortages are not caused by increases in demand. The graph below shows an increase in electricity demand as a rightward shift in demand from D_A to D_B, which causes equilibrium in the electricity market to move from point A to point B and the market clearing price of electricity rises from P_A to P_B.

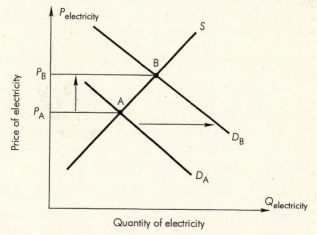

Quantity of electricity

8. a. The increase in demand results in an increase in both P_E and Q_E.
    b. The decrease in demand results in a decrease in both P_E and Q_E.
    c. The increase in supply results in a decrease in P_E and increase in Q_E.
    d. The increase in demand results in an increase in both P_E and Q_E.
    e. The increase in supply results in a decrease in P_E and increase in Q_E.

9. If the government imposed price ceiling is lower than the market clearing price, then a shortage will result; that is, quantity demanded of hamburger will exceed the quantity supplied. Consumers will not be able to purchase all the hamburger they desire at the artificially low price. Some form of hamburger rationing must be devised. Frequently used rationing devices include waiting lines, lotteries, black markets, and bureaucratic schedules based upon "need." Experience with price ceilings has consistently

demonstrated that most consumers prefer paying the market-clearing price rather than face the inefficiencies involved in rationing schemes.

10.   Your graph should look like, for the most part, the following figure:

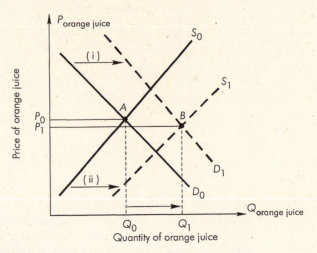

a.   See the preceding graph.

b.   You could explain event (i) as either an increase in productive capacity, F, (capacity has tripled for the same number of trees) or as an improvement in technology, T. Either way you explain it, event (i) causes an increase in supply of orange juice as shown by the rightward shift from S_0 to S_1.

c.   You could explain event (ii) as either an increase in the number of buyers of orange juice, N, or as an increase in consumer tastes toward consuming more orange juice, $\Im$. Either way you explain it, event (ii) causes an increase in demand for orange juice as shown by the rightward shift from D_0 to D_1.

d.   The simultaneous increase in demand and supply cause equilibrium quantity to increase, but equilibrium price of orange juice could rise, fall, or stay the same depending on the magnitudes of the shifts in demand and supply. Thus, the predicted change in the price of orange juice is indeterminate.

MULTIPLE CHOICE/TRUE-FALSE

1.   d   New semiconductors that reduce production costs causes *supply* to increase.

2.   b   Only a change in the price of coffee beans causes a change in the quantity supplied of coffee beans. Since P and Q_s are directly related, a decrease in the price of coffee beans causes a decrease in the quantity supplied of coffee beans.

3.   d   All of these are true in equilibrium. (See the definition of market equilibrium.)

4.   a   At a price of $4, $Q_s > Q_d$ (900 > 500), so there is a surplus of 400 tons of hamburger.

5.   d   Since the ceiling price is set *higher* than the equilibrium price, it has no effect on the market. Equilibrium is reached at $3 and 700 tons of hamburger.

6.   d   Since $Q_d > Q_s$, the price of hotel rooms must have been below equilibrium.

7.   b $100 - 2P = -20 + P \Rightarrow 120 = 3P \Rightarrow P_E = \$40.$ $Q_E = 100 - 2(40) = 20$.

8.   d $Q_d = 100 - 2(46) = 8;$ $Q_s = -20 + 46 = 26 \Rightarrow$ surplus of $26 - 8 = 18$ units.

9.   a $Q_d = 100 - 2(30) = 40;$ $Q_s = -20 + 30 = 10 \Rightarrow$ shortage of $40 - 10 = 30$ units.

10. c   Practice drawing the situation depicted in Panels B and C in Figure 2.9 of your textbook. You should try not to rely on memorization, but rather you should be able to derive these graphs on your own.

11. b   Law of demand states that Q_d and P are inversely related, so b is negative.

12. e   Since $c > 0$, the good is normal. Since $d < 0$, the related good R is a complement.

13. d   All of the choices are true.

14. e   See the movement from point A to C in Panel B of Figure 2.12 of your text and Panel D of Figure 2.9 of your text.

15. F   Decreasing supply (demand constant) causes Q_E to decrease, but there is no shortage.

16. F   Equilibrium output falls.

17. F   This is a quantitative forecast since the magnitudes of change are forecast.

18. F   Equilibrium occurs when quantity demanded equals quantity supplied.

19. T   Steel and plastic are substitutes for aluminum.

20. T Q_d is inversely related to P. Changes in the variables held constant along a demand curve causes demand to shift.

Homework Exercises

Consider the market for new, single-family homes in New Orleans. The generalized demand function for new housing in New Orleans is estimated to be

$$Q_d = 15 - 2P + 0.05M + 0.10R$$

where Q_d is the monthly quantity demanded, P is the price per square foot, M is average monthly income in New Orleans, and R is the average monthly rent for a three-bedroom apartment in New Orleans. Q_d is measured in units of 1,000 square feet per month.

1. New housing in New Orleans is a(n) _____ (normal, inferior) good. How can you tell from the generalized demand function?

2. New housing and three-bedroom apartments are _____ (substitutes, complements) in New Orleans. How can you tell from the generalized demand function?

3. If average monthly income is $1,500 and the monthly rental rate for three-bedroom apartments is $700, then the demand function for new housing in New Orleans is

    $Q_d =$ _____.

4. Graph the demand curve for new housing in New Orleans on the axes provided below. Label the demand curve D_0.

The generalized supply function for new housing in New Orleans is estimated to be

$$Q_s = 96 + 2P - 10P_L - 4P_K$$

where P is the price per square foot of new housing in New Orleans, P_L is the average hourly wage rate for construction workers, and P_K is the price of capital (as measured by the average rate of interest paid on loans to home builders). Q_s is measured in units of 1,000 square feet per month.

5. Does it make sense for P_L and P_K to have negative coefficients in the generalized supply function? Explain why or why not.

6. If the average hourly wage rate for construction workers is $10 per hour and the average rate of interest on loans to builders is 9 percent (i.e., $P_K = 9$), then the supply function for new housing is

$Q_s =$ _____.

7. Graph the supply curve for new housing in the graph below. Label supply S_0.

8. Solve mathematically for equilibrium price and quantity. Show your work:

$P_E = \$$_____ per square foot.

$Q_E =$ _____ square feet per month (in 1,000s).

9. Do your supply and demand curves intersect at P_E and Q_E found in question 8 above? Should they?

10. Suppose New Orleans suffers a serious recession that causes average monthly income to fall from $1,500 to $1,100 per month. If other things remain the same, the demand for new housing in New Orleans is now:

$Q_d =$ _____.

Plot this new demand curve in the figure below. Label it D'.

11. Suppose that because of the recession in New Orleans, the wage rate for construction workers falls to $8 per hour. If other things remain the same, the supply of new housing in New Orleans is now:

$Q_s =$ _____.

Plot this new supply curve in the figure. Label the new supply curve S'.

12. After income falls to $1,100 and wages fall to $8, new equilibrium price and quantity are

$P_E = \$$_____ per square foot

$Q_E =$ _____ square feet per month (in 1,000s)

Housing Market in New Orleans

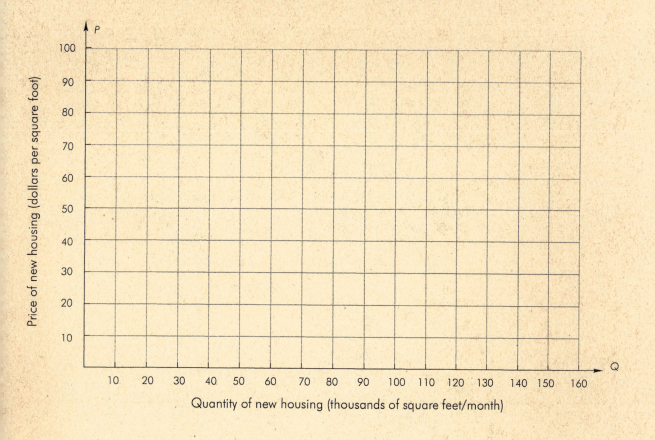

Marginal Analysis for Optimal Decision Making

Learning Objectives

After reading Chapter 3 and working the problems for Chapter 3 in the textbook and in this Workbook, you should be able to:

➤ Employ marginal analysis to find the optimal levels of activities in unconstrained maximization problems.

➤ Explain why sunk costs, fixed costs, and average costs are irrelevant for determining the optimal levels of activities.

➤ Employ marginal analysis to find the optimal levels of two or more activities in constrained maximization and minimization problems.

Essential Concepts

1. Formulating an optimization problem involves specifying three things: (1) the objective function to be either maximized or minimized, (2) the activities or choice variables that determine the value of the objective function, and (3) any constraints that may restrict the range of values that the choice variables may take.

2. *Marginal analysis* involves changing the value of a choice variable by a small amount to see if the objective function can be further increased (in the case of maximization problems) or further decreased (in the case of minimization problems).

3. *Net benefit* from an activity (NB) is the difference between total benefit (TB) and total cost (TC) for the activity: $NB = TB - TC$. The net benefit function is the objective function to be maximized in unconstrained maximization problems. The optimal level of the activity (A^*) is the level of activity that maximizes net benefit.

4. The *choice variables* determine the value of the objective function. Choice variables can be either *continuous* or *discrete*. A choice variable is continuous if the decision maker can choose from an uninterrupted span (or continuum) of values. A discrete choice variable is one for which the decision maker chooses from a span of values that is interrupted by gaps.

5. *Marginal benefit* (MB) is the change in total benefit caused by an incremental change in the level of activity. *Marginal cost* (MC) is the change in total cost caused by an incremental change in the level of activity. An "incremental change" in activity is a small positive or negative change in activity, usually a one-unit

increase or decrease in activity. Marginal benefit and marginal cost can be expressed mathematically as

$$MB = \frac{\text{change in total benefit}}{\text{change in activity}} = \frac{\Delta TB}{\Delta A}$$

$$MC = \frac{\text{change in total cost}}{\text{change in activity}} = \frac{\Delta TC}{\Delta A}$$

where the symbol Δ means *the change in* and A denotes the level of activity.

6. Because "marginal" variables measure rates of change in corresponding "total" variables, marginal benefit and marginal cost are also slopes of total benefit and total cost curves, respectively. Marginal benefit (cost) of a particular unit of activity is measured by the slope of the line tangent to the total benefit (total cost) curve at that point of activity.

7. If, at a given level of activity, a small increase or decrease in activity causes net benefit to increase, then this level of activity is not optimal. The activity must then be increased (if marginal benefit exceeds marginal cost) or decreased (if marginal cost exceeds marginal benefit) to reach the highest net benefit. The optimal level of the activity is attained when no further increases in net benefit are possible for any changes in the activity. This point occurs at the activity level for which marginal benefit equals marginal cost: $MB = MC$.

8. When a manager faces an unconstrained maximization problem and must choose among discrete levels of an activity, the manager should increase the activity if $MB > MC$ and decrease the activity if $MB < MC$. The optimal level of activity is the last level for which MB exceeds MC.

9. *Sunk costs* are costs that have previously been paid and cannot be recovered. *Fixed costs* are costs that are constant and must be paid no matter what level of activity is chosen. *Average (or unit) cost* is the cost per unit of activity, which is computed by dividing total cost by the number of units of activity. Decision makers wishing to maximize net benefit should ignore any sunk costs, any fixed costs, and the average costs associated with the activity because none of these costs affect the marginal cost of the activity, and so are irrelevant for making optimal decisions.

10. The ratio of marginal benefit divided by the price of an activity (MB/P) tells the decision maker the additional benefit of that activity per additional dollar spent on that activity. In constrained optimization problems, the ratios of marginal benefits to prices of the various activities are used by managers to determine how to allocate a fixed number of dollars among activities.

11. To maximize or minimize an objective function subject to a constraint, the ratios of the marginal benefit to price must be equal for all activities,

$$\frac{MB_A}{P_A} = \frac{MB_B}{P_B} = \cdots = \frac{MB_Z}{P_Z}$$

and the values of the choice variables must meet the constraint.

Matching Definitions

activities or choice variables
average (or unit) cost
constrained optimization
continuous variable
discrete variable
fixed costs
marginal analysis
marginal benefit

marginal cost
maximization problem
minimization problem
objective function
optimal level of activity
sunk costs
unconstrained optimization

1. _____ Function to be either maximized or minimized.

2. _____ Optimization problem in which the decision maker is trying to maximize some activity.

3. _____ Optimization problem in which the decision maker is trying to minimize some activity

4. _____ The determinants of the values of objective functions.

5. _____ A variable that cannot take a continuum of values.

6. _____ A variable that can take any value between two end points.

7. _____ A situation in which a manager may choose the optimal levels of activities from an unrestricted set of values.

8. _____ A situation in which a manager may choose the optimal levels of activities from a restricted set of values.

9. _____ The analytical process of making incremental changes to the level of the choice variables to arrive at the point where no further improvements in the objective function are possible.

10. _____ The level of activity that maximizes net benefit.

11. _____ The additional benefits derived per unit increase in activity.

12. _____ The additional cost realized per unit increase in activity.

13. _____ Costs that have already been paid and cannot be recovered.

14. _____ Costs that are constant and must be paid no matter what level of activity is chosen.

15. _____ Total cost divided by the number of units of activity.

Study Problems

1. a. Fill in the missing numbers below.

A	Total Benefit	Total Cost	Marginal Benefit	Marginal Cost	Net Benefit
0	0	0	XX	XX	0
1	10	2	10	2	8
2	19	5	9	3	14
3	25	9	6	4	16
4	30	15	5	6	15
5	34	22	4	7	12

b. Define "optimal level of activity." In part a, what is the optimal level of activity? Why?

c. In part a, marginal benefit does not equal marginal cost for any quantity. Does this mean there is no optimal level of activity? Why or why not? *No, pick*

d. At the optimal level of activity, could you increase the level of activity and get an increase in total benefit? If so, why should the manager *not* increase the activity further?

2. The manager of a firm estimates that the sales of her firm are related to radio and newspaper advertising in the following way:

$$S = 12,000 + 1,800AR, \text{ where}$$

S = the number of units sold,
A = the number of quarter-page newspaper advertisements, and
R = the number of minutes of radio spots.

a. Derive the marginal benefit of newspaper and radio advertising. [Hint: The marginal benefit of advertising can be found by determining how much S changes for each one-unit change in A, holding R constant.]

$$\frac{\Delta S}{\Delta A} = \underline{\hspace{2cm}} \quad \text{and} \quad \frac{\Delta S}{\Delta R} = \underline{\hspace{2cm}}$$

b. If the newspaper ads cost \$600 per quarter-page ad ($P_A = \$600$) and the radio ads cost \$200 per minute ($P_R = \$200$), find the combination of radio and television ads that maximizes sales when the advertising budget is \$7,200. Also compute the optimal level of sales.

[Hint: Set $MB_A/P_A = MB_R/P_R$, then solve for either A or R and substitute this expression into the budget constraint $600A + 200R = \$7,200$ to solve for A^* and R^*.]

$$A^* = \underline{\hspace{2cm}}$$
$$R^* = \underline{\hspace{2cm}}$$
$$S^* = \underline{\hspace{2cm}}$$

c. Suppose the advertising budget is cut so that only \$4,800 can be spent on advertising. Now what are the sales-maximizing values of A, R, and S?

$$A^* = \underline{\hspace{2cm}}$$
$$R^* = \underline{\hspace{2cm}}$$
$$S^* = \underline{\hspace{2cm}}$$

d. Based on parts b and c, what is the effect of changing the advertising budget constraint on the optimal level of sales?

$$\frac{\Delta S^*}{\Delta B} = \underline{\hspace{2cm}},$$

where ΔB is the change in the advertising budget. Do you expect this number to be positive or negative?

3. A life-insurance salesman spends 9 hours a week on the telephone soliciting new clients. From past experience, the salesman estimates that each hour spent calling students, blue-collar workers, and professionals will produce the following number of additional sales:

	Number of Additional Sales		
Hours Calling	Students	Blue-Collar Workers	Professionals
1	10	8	14
2	8	6	11
3	6	4	8
4	4	3	6
5	1	1	4
6	0	0	1

a. How should the life-insurance salesman allocate his phone-calling time to maximize the number of sales?

Hours spent calling students = _____

Hours spent calling blue-collar workers = _____

Hours spent calling professionals = _____

b. Now suppose the salesman decides to spend 16 hours a week soliciting new clients. How should he allocate his time?

Hours spent calling students = _____

Hours spent calling blue-collar workers = _____

Hours spent calling professionals = _____

4. Use the figure below to answer the following questions

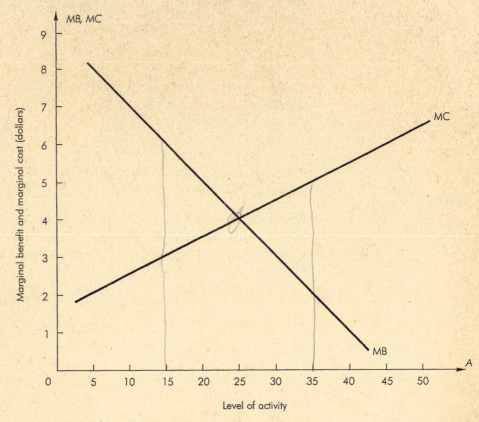

a. At 15 units of the activity, marginal benefit is $__6__ and marginal cost is $__3__.

b. Adding the 15th unit of activity causes net benefit to __I__ (increase, decrease) by $__3__.

c. At 35 units of the activity, marginal benefit is $__2__ and marginal cost is $__5__.

d. Subtracting the 35th unit of activity causes net benefit to __I__ (increase, decrease) by $__3__.

e. The optimal level of activity is __25__ units, MB = $__4__ and MC = $_____.

f. Can you compute total benefit, total cost, and net benefit for the optimal level of activity? If so, how? If not, why not?

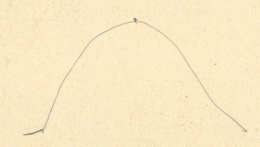

5. Activity A has the following marginal benefit (MB) and marginal cost (MC) functions:

$$MB = 10 - 0.05A \quad \text{and} \quad MC = 2 + 0.05A$$

where MB and MC are measured in dollars.

a. The 70th unit of activity increases total benefit by $_____$ and increases total cost by $_____$. Since marginal benefit is $_____$ (greater, less) than marginal cost, adding the 70th unit of the activity $_____$ (increases, decreases) net benefit by $_____$.

b. The 110th unit of activity increases total benefit by $_____$ and increases total cost by $_____$. Since marginal benefit is $_____$ (greater, less) than marginal cost, adding the 110th unit of the activity $_____$ (increases, decreases) net benefit by $_____$.

c. The optimal level of activity is $_____$ units. At the optimal level of activity, marginal benefit is $_____$ and marginal cost is $_____$.

The total benefit (TB) and total cost (TC) functions for the activity are

$$TB = 10A - 0.025A^2 \quad \text{and} \quad TC = 2A + 0.025A^2$$

where TB and TC are measured in dollars.

d. For the optimal level of activity in part c, the total benefit is $_____$, the total cost is $_____$, and the net benefit is $_____$.

e. Compute the net benefit for one unit more and one unit less than the level of activity found to be optimal in part c (i.e., compute NB for $A^* + 1$ and $A^* - 1$). Are your results consistent with the definition of "optimal"? Explain.

6. Evaluate the following statements:

a. "The optimal level of an activity is that level for which marginal benefit exceeds marginal cost by the greatest possible amount."

b. "The ratio of marginal benefit to marginal cost of an activity measures the additional benefit attributable to increasing the activity by one unit."

c. "At the optimal level of activity, further increases in the activity necessarily decrease total benefit."

d. "This is a lousy vacation resort, and it's been raining the whole time. I'd leave but I've already paid for the hotel for the week, so I guess I will stay."

e. "I hate golf, but I paid so much for the clubs that I can't give it up."

f. "The cost of my yearly business license is doubling next year, so I must plan to increase output next year in order to cover the additional cost of doing business."

g. "Now is the perfect time to buy more television ads because the TV networks are offering us lower prices on any extra ads we purchase."

7. Suppose a manager wishes to find the optimal level of two activities X and Y, which yield the total benefits presented in the table below. The price of X is $40 per unit, and the price of Y is $100 per unit.

Level of Activity	Total Benefit of Activity X (TB_X)	Total Benefit of Activity Y (TB_Y)
0	0	0
1	800	1,000
2	1,440	1,900
3	2,000	2,700
4	2,360	3,400
5	2,680	4,000
6	2,960	4,500
7	3,200	4,900
8	3,400	5,200

a. The manager faces a budget constraint of $500 for expenditures on activities X and Y. The optimal levels of activities of X and Y when the manager can spend only $500 are $X^* =$ _____ and $Y^* =$ _____.

b. In part a, the total benefit associated with the optimal level of X and Y is $ _____.

c. Now let the budget constraint increase to $780. The optimal levels of activities of X and Y when the manager can spend $780 are $X^* =$ _____ and $Y^* =$ _____.

d. In part c, the total benefit associated with the optimal level of X and Y is $ _____.

Multiple Choice / True-False

1. For an unconstrained optimization problem with a continuous choice variable, the optimal level of an activity is that level of activity for which
   a. total benefit exceeds total cost by the greatest amount possible.
   b. marginal benefit minus marginal cost equals zero.
   c. total benefit equals total cost.
   d. marginal benefit is zero.
   e. both *a* and *b*.

In Questions 2 – 6, consider an activity A that has the following marginal benefit (MB) and marginal cost (MC) functions:

$$MB = 50 - 0.025A \quad \text{and} \quad MC = 40 + 0.025A$$

and the following total benefit (TB) and total cost (TC) functions:

$$TB = 50A - 0.0125A^2 \quad \text{and} \quad TC = 40A + 0.0125A^2 .$$

2. Undertaking the 100th unit of the activity
   a. reduces total benefit by $2.50 and increases total cost by $2.50.
   b. increases total benefit by $2.50 and reduces total cost by $2.50.
   c. causes net benefit to fall.
   d. maximizes net benefit because $MB = MC$ at 100 units.
   e. none of the above.

3. Undertaking the 400th unit of the activity
   a. reduces total benefit by $10 and increases total cost by $10.
   b. increases total benefit by $40 and increases total cost by $50.
   c. causes net benefit to fall.
   d. both *a* and *c*.
   e. both *b* and *c*.

4. What is the optimal level of activity?
   a. 100
   b. 200
   c. 300
   d. 400
   e. 500

5. For the optimal activity level in question 4, total benefit, total cost, and net benefit are respectively
   a. $9,500, $8,500, and $1,000
   b. $21,875, $23,125, and –$1,250
   c. $23,125, $21,875, and –$1,250
   d. $13,875, $13,125, and $750
   e. none of the above.

6. What level of activity maximizes TOTAL benefit?
    a. 500
    b. 1,500
    c. 1,750
    d. 1,850
    e. 2,000

In questions 7 – 9, a firm can spend $1,150 monthly on advertising in either the newspaper or on the radio. Marketing experts estimate that monthly sales can be increased by the following amounts:

Number of Ads Monthly	Additional Units Sold Monthly	
	Newspaper	Radio
1	1,000	1,800
2	750	1,500
3	500	1,200
4	400	1,000
5	250	600

The prices of newspaper and radio ads are $250 and $300 respectively.

7. In order to maximize monthly sales, the advertising budget should be allocated so that
    a. 1 newspaper ad and 1 radio ad are purchased monthly.
    b. 1 newspaper ad and 2 radio ads are purchased monthly.
    c. 2 newspaper ads and 2 radio ads are purchased monthly.
    d. 3 newspaper ads and 1 radio ad are purchased monthly.
    e. none of the above.

8. If the advertising budget is increased to $2,250 per month, how should the budget be allocated to maximize sales?
    a. 2 newspaper ads and 2 radio ads are purchased monthly.
    b. 3 newspaper ads and 3 radio ads are purchased monthly.
    c. 3 newspaper ads and 4 radio ads are purchased monthly.
    d. 3 newspaper ads and 5 radio ads are purchased monthly.
    e. none of the above.

9. In question 8 above, the values of MB_N / P_N and MB_R / P_R are both equal to
    a. 1
    b. 2
    c. 3
    d. 4
    e. none of the above

10. If the marginal benefit of the last unit of activity X is 100 and the price of X is $25,
    a. the last unit of X causes total benefit to rise by 4.
    b. the last unit of X causes total benefit to rise by 100.
    c. spending one more dollar on X causes total benefit to rise by 100.
    d. spending one more dollar on X causes total benefit to rise by 4.
    e. both b and d.

Use the following graph showing the marginal benefit and marginal cost curves for activity A to answer questions 11 – 14.

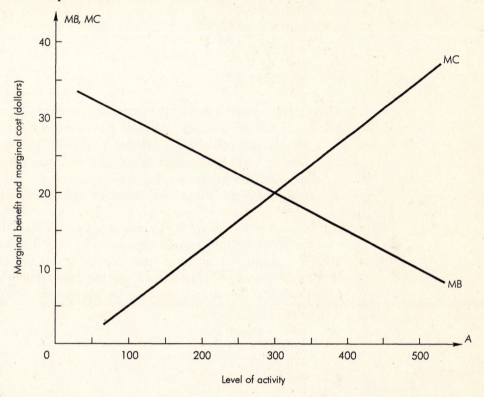

11. If the firm is using 100 units of the activity, marginal benefit is $_____ and marginal cost is $_____.
    a. $20; $20
    b. $30; $5
    c. $5; $30
    d. $25; $25
    e. $30; 25

12. If the firm is using 100 units of the activity, the firm can _____ (increase, decrease) the activity by one unit and increase net benefit by $_____.
    a. decrease; $25
    b. decrease; $35
    c. increase; $30
    d. increase; $25

13. If the firm is using 500 units of the activity, it can _____ (increase, decrease) the activity by one unit and increase net benefits by $_____.
   a. decrease; $25
   b. decrease; $35
   c. increase; $25
   d. increase; $30

14. To maximize net benefits the firm should use _____ units of the activity, at which point _____.
   a. 300; $MB > MC$
   b. 200; $MB = MC = \$25$
   c. 400; $MB < MC$
   d. 300; $MB = MC = \$20$
   e. 400; $MB = MC$

15. When marginal cost is greater than marginal benefit at the current activity level, the decision maker can increase net benefit by decreasing the activity because
   a. total benefit will rise by more than total cost will rise.
   b. total cost will fall by more than total benefit will fall.
   c. net benefit is upward sloping at this point.
   d. marginal cost is rising faster than marginal benefit is falling.

16. A firm is currently buying 30 TV ads at $200 each and 20 newspaper ads at $100 each for a total advertising expenditure of $8,000. The additional sales from the last TV ad were 300 units and from the last newspaper ad were 200 units. If the firm buys 2 more newspaper ads it can increase sales by _____ units and keep advertising cost the same by reducing TV ads by _____ units.
   a. 300; 1
   b. 100; 2
   c. 100; 1
   d. 400; 2
   e. 500; 3

17. T   F   At the optimal level of an activity, total cost is minimized and total benefit is maximized.

18. T   F   The solution to an unconstrained minimization problem is the same as the solution to the unconstrained maximization problem for which the net benefit function is the negative of the net cost function.

19. T   F   As a rule, the optimal number of product defects is zero.

20. T   F   When a manager faces an objective function with more than one choice variable, the firm attains a maximum of its objective function when the marginal benefit from each activity equals its marginal cost.

Answers

MATCHING DEFINITIONS

1. objective function
2. maximization problem
3. minimization problem
4. activities or choice variables
5. discrete variable
6. continuous variable
7. unconstrained optimization
8. constrained optimization

9. marginal analysis
10. optimal level of activity
11. marginal benefit
12. marginal cost
13. sunk costs
14. fixed costs
15. average (or unit) costs

STUDY PROBLEMS

1. a.

A	Total Benefit	Total Cost	Marginal Benefit	Marginal Cost	Net Benefit
0	0	0	xx	xx	0
1	10	2	10	2	8
2	19	5	9	3	14
3	25	9	6	4	16
4	30	15	5	6	15
5	34	22	4	7	12

b. The level of activity that maximizes the objective function (net benefit) is called the *optimal level of activity*. $A^* = 3$ because at this value, net benefit is maximized.

c. When the choice variable (in this case A) is not continuous, the objective function may reach its maximum value at a level of activity where marginal benefit does *not* equal marginal cost. Marginal analysis still leads to the optimal value, however. At a quantity of 3, marginal benefit (= $6) exceeds marginal cost (= $4). Clearly, producing the third unit increases profit. For the fourth unit of activity, marginal cost (= $6) exceeds marginal benefit (= $5), and net benefit would decrease if it were produced. Thus, 3 units is the optimal level.

d. Because MB is positive at the optimal level, TB could be further increased by increasing the level of activity. This is not desirable because the increase in TB would be accompanied by a decrease in NB (since $MB < MC$).

2. a. $\Delta S/\Delta A = 1800R$; $\Delta S/\Delta R = 1800A$

b. The optimal levels of R and A must satisfy two conditions:

  (i) $MB_A/P_A = MB_R/P_R$
   $(1800R/600) = (1800A/200) \Rightarrow R = 3A$

  (ii) $P_R R + P_A A = 7{,}200$
   $200R + 600A = 7{,}200$
   These two conditions are simultaneously satisfied if
   $200(3A) + 600A = 7{,}200 \Rightarrow A^* = 6, R^* = 18$, and $S^* = 206{,}400$

c. $R^* = 12$; $A^* = 4$; $S^* = 98{,}400$

d. $\Delta S^*/\Delta B = 108{,}000/2{,}400 = 45$. Positive because an increase (decrease) in the advertising budget will increase (decrease) sales.

3. a. 3; 2; 4 (*MB* per hour = $MB/1$ = 6 for all 3 and total number of hours = 9)
   b. 5; 5; 6 ($MB/1$ = 1 for all 3 and total number of hours = 16)

4. a. MB_{15} = $6; MC_{15} = $3 [Note: These numbers are read from the figure.]
   b. increase; $3
   c. MB_{35} = $2; MC_{35} = $5
   d. increase; $3
   e. 25; $4; $4
   f. No, because you are only given marginal benefit and marginal cost. You cannot compute total benefit, total cost, and net benefit using the information given.

5. a. $6.50 [= 10 − 0.05(70)]; $5.50 [= 2 + 0.05(70)]; greater; increases; $1 (= 6.50 − 5.50)
   b. $4.50 [= 10 − 0.05(110)]; $7.50 [= 2 + 0.05(110)]; less; decreases; $3 (= 7.50 − 4.50)
   c. A^* = 80 units (set $MB = MC$ and solve for A^*);
      $6; $6 [Note: $MB_{80} = MC_{80}$ = 10 − 0.05(80) = 2 + 0.05(80) = 6.]
   d. TB = $640; TC = $320; NB = $320
   e. A^* + 1 = 81 and NB_{81} = $319.95;
      A^* − 1 = 79 and NB_{79} = $319.95;
      Since NB_{80} (= $320) exceeds both NB_{79} and NB_{81}, these computations are consistent with NB being maximized at 80 units.

6. a. The optimal level of an activity is that level for which *total* benefit exceeds *total* cost by the greatest possible amount.
   b. *MB/MC* gives the additional benefit for *spending one more dollar* on the activity, not for increasing the activity by one more unit. Only if MC = $1 would spending one more dollar on the activity also result in one more unit of the activity being undertaken.
   c. This statement is generally incorrect. At the optimal level of activity, further increases in the activity cause total benefit to decrease *only* if MB is negative. MB equals MC at the optimal level activity level. Because MC cannot be negative, MB cannot be negative at the optimal activity level. Since MB cannot be negative, total benefit cannot fall as activity increases beyond X^*. It is true (by definition) that net benefit *falls* as X increases beyond the optimal level of activity.
   d. Bad reasoning. What has already been paid for the room is a sunk cost and is irrelevant. This person should weigh the expected marginal benefits and costs, then make the decision about whether to stay.
   e. What was paid for the golf clubs is a sunk cost and should be ignored.
   f. After paying for the more expensive business license, presumably a once-a-year fee paid at the beginning of the year, the cost is sunk and has no effect on marginal cost (or marginal revenue, for that matter). Thus, ignore the sunk cost and plan to produce the same level of output, unless something else causes a change in either MB or MC.
   g. Extra ads are only worth purchasing if, at the lower price, the marginal cost of buying more ads is less than the marginal benefit of running more ads. It is indeed possible that by lowering the price of additional advertising spots, ad buyers will find it optimal to buy more ads. Of course, it is also possible that even at "low" prices, extra ads are not worth the added cost.

7. a. X^* = 5; Y^* = 3
   b. $5,380 since $TB_{X=5}$ = $2,680 and $TB_{Y=3}$ = $2,700
   c. X^* = 7; Y^* = 5
   d. $7,200 since $TB_{X=7}$ = $3,200 and $TB_{Y=5}$ = $4,000

1. e   Since $NB = TB - TC$, maximizing NB implies TB exceeds TC by the greatest amount possible. For a continuous choice variable, $MB = MC$ at the optimal level of an activity. Thus $MB - MC = 0$ at the optimal level of activity.

2. e   Undertaking the 100th unit of activity increases total benefit by $47.50 (= 50 - 0.025 \times 100)$ and increases total cost by $42.50 (= 40 + 0.025 \times 100)$. This would cause net benefit to rise by $5. Thus, none of the choices are correct.

3. e   Undertaking the 400th unit of activity increases total benefit by $40 (= 50 - 0.025 \times 400)$ and increases total cost by $50 (= 40 + 0.025 \times 400)$. This would cause net benefit to fall (by $10). Thus, both b and c are correct.

4. b   At 200 units, MB equals $45 (= 50 - 0.025 \times 200)$ and MC equals $45 (= 40 + 0.025 \times 200)$.

5. a $TB = \$9,500 (= 50 \times 200 - 0.025 \times 200^2)$; $TC = \$8,500 (= 40 \times 200 + 0.025 \times 200^2)$; $NB = \$1,000 (= \$9,500 - \$8,500)$.

6. e   Total benefit is maximized at the activity level for which $MB = 0$. Thus, solve $0 = 50 - 0.025A$ to get the activity level where MB reaches its peak: $A = 2,000$.

7. e   The optimal number of newspaper and radio ads are $N^* = 1$ and $R^* = 3$.

8. d   At $N^* = 3$ and $R^* = 5$, $MR/P = 2$ for both newspaper and radio ads, and $2,250 is spent.

9. b   See the answer to question 8 above.

10. e   Since $MB = 100$, the last unit of X increases total benefit by 100. Since $MB/P = 100/25 = 4$, spending one more dollar of activity X increases total benefit by 4.

11. b   From the graph at $A = 100$, $MB = 30$, $MC = 5$.

12. d   Total benefit rises by $30 and total cost rises by $5, so net benefit rises by $25.

13. a   Total benefit falls by $30 and total cost falls by $5, so net benefit falls by $25.

14. d $\Delta MB = MC = \$20$ at $A = 300$.

15. b   Decreasing A causes TC and TB to fall. In this case, $MC > MB$, so TC falls by more than TB falls, and NB rises.

16. c   If 2 more newspaper adds are purchased sales will rise by 400 units (200 more units at the margin for each extra newspaper ad), and if 1 less TV ad is purchased sales will fall by 300 units. Thus, if 2 more newspaper ads are purchased while 1 less TV ad is purchased, then sales will rise by 100 units $(= 400 - 300)$, and total cost remains $8,000 because the increased expenditure on newspaper ads is exactly equal to the reduced expenditure on TV ads.

17. F   Neither TB nor TC is maximized or minimized at the optimal level of activity. It is NB that is being maximized.

18. T   Unconstrained minimization involves multiplying net cost (NC) by -1 to get net benefit (NB), which is then maximized by finding the level of activity for which $MB = MC$.

19. F MB generally does not equal MC at zero defects because the marginal cost of eliminating the last defective product is generally expensive.

20. T $MB_X = MC_X$; $MB_Y = MC_Y$; and so on.

Homework Exercises

1.   Use the figure below to fill in the blanks in the following questions.

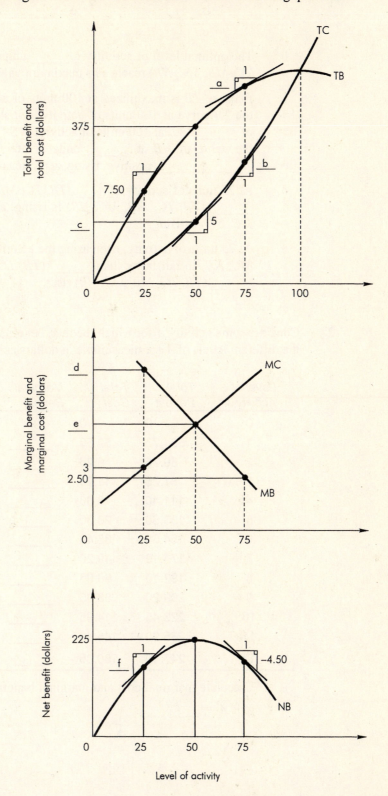

a. The values that belong in the blanks $a - f$ in the figure on the previous page are:

a. _____   d. _____

b. _____   e. _____

c. _____   f. _____

b. The optimal level of activity is _____ units of activity where _____ (TB, TC, MB, MC, NB) reaches its maximum value of $_____.

c. Because TB is maximized at 100 units of activity, a line drawn tangent to the TB curve at 100 units of activity (*not* shown in the figure) has a slope of _____. NB at 100 units of activity is $_____, which is identical to the value of NB at _____ units of activity. Beyond 100 units, NB is _____ (positive, rising, zero, negative).

d. At 25 units of activity, _____ (TB, TC, MB, MC, NB) is rising faster than _____ (TB, TC, MB, MC, NB) is rising, and thus _____ (TB, TC, MB, MC, NB) is rising.

e. At 75 units of activity, decreasing the activity causes _____ (TB, TC, MB, MC, NB) to fall faster than _____ (TB, TC, MB, MC, NB) falls, and thus _____ (TB, TC, MB, MC, NB) rises.

2. Consider some activity A for which the total benefits and total costs associated with the different levels of A are measurable in dollars as tabulated below.

Level of Activity A	Total Benefit	Total Cost	Marginal Benefit	Marginal Cost	Net Benefit
0	0	0	xx	xx	_____
1	$31.75	$2.50	_____	_____	_____
2	60.75	6.25	_____	_____	_____
3	87.25	11.25	_____	_____	_____
4	111.40	18.00	_____	_____	_____
5	133.60	26.30	_____	_____	_____
6	154.60	35.40	_____	_____	_____
7	174.10	49.20	_____	_____	_____
8	192.10	66.95	_____	_____	_____
9	209.20	88.95	_____	_____	_____
10	223.45	114.95	_____	_____	_____
11	235.90	145.45	_____	_____	_____
12	247.10	180.05	_____	_____	_____

a. Calculate marginal cost and marginal benefit. The optimal level of activity A is $A^* = $ _____.

b. Explain carefully, using the logic of marginal analysis, why $A = 4$ is *not* the optimal level of activity A.

c. Explain carefully, using the logic of marginal analysis, why $A = 12$ is *not* the optimal level of activity A.

d. Now calculate the net benefit for each level of A and tabulate the values in the last column of the table. Inspect net benefit and determine the level of A that maximizes net benefit.
    $A^* =$ _____.
    Is this the same value as in part a?

3. A manager can spend $7,000 on two activities (X and Y) that generate benefits for the firm. The price of X is $1,000 per unit and the price of Y is $2,000 per unit. The table below gives the total benefits for various levels of activities X and Y.

Level of Activity X	Total Benefit of Activity X	Total Benefit of Activity Y
0	0	0
1	$ 30,000	$ 70,000
2	55,000	110,000
3	75,000	140,000
4	90,000	164,000
5	100,000	186,000
6	105,000	206,000

a. The optimal levels of activities X and Y when the manager faces a budget constraint of $7,000 are $X^* =$ _____ and $Y^* =$ _____. The total benefit to the firm of engaging in the optimal levels of activities X and Y is $_____.

b. Now let the budget increase to $17,000. The optimal levels of activities X and Y when the manager faces a budget constraint of $17,000 are $X^* =$ _____ and $Y^* =$ _____. The total benefit to the firm of engaging in the optimal levels of activities X and Y is $_____.

4. Circle the correct words to go in the blanks below.

    a. If marginal benefit exceeds marginal cost, then _____ (increasing, decreasing) the level of activity by one unit increases _____(total, marginal, net) benefit by more than it _____(increases, decreases) _____ (total, marginal) cost. Therefore _____ (increasing, decreasing) the level of activity by one unit must increase net benefit. The decision maker should continue to _____ (increase, decrease) the level of activity until marginal benefit and marginal cost are both _____ (zero, equal).

    b. If marginal cost exceeds marginal benefit, then _____ (increasing, decreasing) the level of activity by one unit decreases _____(total, marginal, net) benefit by less than it _____(increases, decreases) _____ (total, marginal) cost. Therefore, _____ (increasing, decreasing) the level of activity by one unit must increase net benefit. The decision maker should continue to _____ (increase, decrease) the activity until marginal benefit and marginal cost are both _____ (zero, equal).

5. Several years ago, Nabisco spent $330 million building a facility in Brazil to produce Oreo cookies and Ritz crackers for sale in their South American markets. At a recent board meeting, managers at Nabisco were discussing closing the Brazilian plant because profits from South American sales declined sharply last year. One senior vice president opposed shutting down the Brazilian plant saying, "We spent so much money getting our Brazilian facility going, we just can't quit now." Evaluate the vice president's advice. Explain why you agree or disagree.

6. Consider this statement: "Conservationists want to save too many spotted owls." Use graphical analysis accompanied by a concise narrative discussion to explain circumstances under which this statement would be true. Make sure your graphs have clearly labeled axes and curves. [Note: Good answers are dispassionate and logical.]

7. A publisher of a new novel has spent $250,000 setting the type. The publisher must spend $1 million advertising the new book. It is now ready to print the book. For practical purposes, as many books as they like can be printed. In deciding how many copies to run,

    a. does the cost of typesetting have any influence on the publisher's decision? Explain.

    b. does the cost of advertising have any influence on the publisher's decision? Explain.

8.	The southeast sales manager for Manufacturer's Aluminum Supply makes most of her outside sales by playing either golf or tennis with potential clients. From much past experience, she estimates that various levels of playing golf and tennis generate the following amounts of additional sales (MB):

Number of rounds of golf (G)	Additional sales generated (MB_G)	Number of tennis matches (T)	Additional sales generated (MB_T)
1	$2,500	1	$2,400
2	2,000	2	2,250
3	1,750	3	2,100
4	1,375	4	1,800
5	1,250	5	1,500
6	1,200	6	1,050
7	1,125	7	750
8	1,100	8	600

One round of golf (18 holes) takes 5 hours to play (including a half-hour stop at the clubhouse), and one tennis match (best two out of three sets) takes 3 hours to complete. The sales manager can get away from the office to play golf and tennis only 20 hours each week.

a.	What is the optimal number of rounds of golf to play and the optimal number of tennis matches to play?

b.	Suppose the sales manager gets sick one week and can only play 12 hours of golf and tennis. What level of golf and tennis play is optimal?

Basic Estimation Techniques

Learning Objectives

After reading Chapter 4 and working the problems for Chapter 4 in the textbook and in this Workbook, you should be able to:

➤ Set up a regression equation that can be estimated using a computerized regression routine.

➤ Interpret and understand how to use the computer output to investigate problems that are of interest to managers of a firm.

In order to accomplish these two goals, you must know how to:

➤ Specify a relation or model between a dependent variable and the appropriate independent variable(s) that can be estimated using regression techniques.

➤ Interpret the estimated parameters of regression equations.

➤ Determine whether estimated parameters are statistically significant using either a t-test or a p-value associated with the parameter estimate.

➤ Evaluate how well the regression equation "fits" the data by examining the R^2 statistic (also known as the coefficient of determination).

➤ Test for statistical significance of the whole regression equation using an F-test.

➤ Use linear regression techniques to estimate the parameters of two common nonlinear models: (1) quadratic regression models and (2) log-linear regression models.

Essential Concepts

1. A simple linear regression model relates a dependent variable Y to a single independent (or explanatory) variable X in a linear fashion

$$Y = a + bX$$

The *intercept parameter* (a) gives the value of Y at the point where the regression line crosses the Y-axis, which is the value of Y when X is zero. The *slope parameter* (b) gives the change in Y associated with a one-unit change in X ($b = \Delta Y / \Delta X$).

2. Because the variation in Y is affected not only by variation in X but also by various random effects as well, the actual value of Y cannot be predicted exactly. The regression equation is correctly interpreted as providing the average value, or the expected value, of Y for a given value of X.

3. Parameter estimates are obtained by choosing values of a and b that minimize the sum of the squared residuals. The residual is the difference between the actual value of Y and the fitted value of Y, $Y_i - \hat{Y}_i$. This method of estimating a and b is called the *method of least-squares*, and the estimated regression line, $Y = \hat{a} + \hat{b}X$, is called the *sample regression line*. The sample regression line is an estimate of the true regression line.

4. The estimates $\hat{a}$ and $\hat{b}$ do not, in general, equal the true values of a and b. Since $\hat{a}$ and $\hat{b}$ are computed using data from a random sample, the estimates themselves are random variables—the estimates would vary in value from one random sample to another random sample. Statisticians have shown that the distribution of values that the estimates might take is centered around the true value of the parameter. An estimator is *unbiased* if the average value, or the expected value, of the estimator is equal to the true value of the parameter. The method of least-squares can produce unbiased estimates of a and b.

5. It is the randomness of the parameter estimates that necessitates testing for statistical significance. Just because the estimate $\hat{b}$ is not zero does not mean the true value of b is not zero. Even when b does equal zero, it is still possible that the sample will produce a least-squares estimate $\hat{b}$ that is different from zero. Thus, it is necessary to determine if there is sufficient statistical evidence in the sample to indicate that Y is truly related to X (i.e., $b \neq 0$).

6. There are two ways to determine whether an estimated parameter is statistically significant. Either a t-test can be performed or the p-value for the parameter estimate can be examined.

7. To perform a t-test for significance, a researcher must first determine the level of significance for the test. The *significance level* of a test is the probability of finding a parameter estimate to be significantly different from zero when, in fact, b is zero. This mistake is called a *Type I error*. Lower levels of significance, other things equal, are more desirable. One minus the level of significance is called the *level of confidence*.

    Once the level of significance is chosen, the t-ratio is computed as

    $$t = \frac{\hat{b}}{S_{\hat{b}}}$$

    where $S_{\hat{b}}$ is the standard error of the estimate $\hat{b}$. Next, the critical value of t is found in the t-table at the end of your textbook. Choose the critical t-value with $n - k$ degrees of freedom for the desired level of significance, where n is the number of observations and k is the number of parameters being estimated. If the absolute value of the t-ratio is greater (less) than the critical t-value, then $\hat{b}$ is (is not) statistically significant.

8. An alternative method of assessing the statistical significance of parameter estimates is to treat as statistically significant only those parameter estimates whose p-values are smaller than the maximum acceptable significance level. The p-value gives the exact level of significance for a parameter estimate, which is the probability of finding significance when none exists.

9. The coefficient of determination R^2 measures the percentage of the total variation in the dependent variable that is explained by the regression equation. The value of R^2 ranges from 0 to 1. A high R^2 indicates Y and X are highly correlated and the scatter diagram tightly fits the sample regression line.

10. The F-test is used to test for significance of the overall regression equation. The F-statistic from the computer printout is compared to the critical F-value obtained from the F-table at the end of your textbook. The critical F-value is identified by two separate degrees of freedom and the significance level. The first of the degrees of freedom is $k-1$ and the second is $n-k$. If the value for the calculated F-statistic (calculated by the computer) exceeds the critical F-value, the regression equation overall is statistically significant at the specified significance level. Alternatively, if the p-value for the F-statistic is smaller than the acceptable level of significance, the equation as a whole is statistically significant.

12. Multiple regression uses more than one explanatory variable to explain the variation in the dependent variable. The coefficient for each of the explanatory variables measures the change in Y associated with a one-unit change in that explanatory variable ($b = \Delta Y / \Delta X$).

13. Two types of nonlinear models can be easily transformed into linear models that can be estimated using linear regression analysis. These are quadratic regression models and log-linear regression models.

   (a) *Quadratic regression models* are appropriate when the curve fitting the scatter plot is either ∪-shaped or ∩-shaped. A quadratic equation, $Y = a + bX + cX^2$, can be transformed into a linear form by computing a new variable $Z = X^2$, which is then substituted for X^2 in the regression. Then, the regression equation to be estimated is $Y = a + bX + cZ$.

   (b) *Log-linear regression models* are appropriate when the relation takes the multiplicative exponential form: $Y = aX^bZ^c$. The equation is transformed by taking natural logarithms:

   $$\ln Y = \ln a + b \ln X + c \ln Z$$

   The coefficients b and c are elasticities. For example, b measures the percent change in Y that results when X changes by 1 percent.

Matching Definitions

coefficient of determination (R^2)
critical value of t
cross-sectional data set
degrees of freedom
dependent variable
estimates
estimators
explanatory variables
fitted or predicted value
F-statistic
hypothesis testing
intercept parameter
level of confidence

level of significance
log-linear regression model
method of least-squares
multiple regression model
parameter estimation
parameters
population regression line
p-value
quadratic regression model
random error term
regression analysis
relative frequency distribution on b
residual

sample regression line
scatter diagram
slope parameter
statistically significant
time series data set
t-ratio
true (or actual) relation
t-statistic
t-test
Type I error
unbiased estimator

1. _____ The coefficients in an equation that determine the exact mathematical relationship between the variables.

2. _____ The process of finding estimates of the numerical values of the parameters in an equation.

3. _____ The technique that uses data on variables to determine a mathematical equation that describes the relationship between the variables.

4. _____ The variable whose variation is to be explained.

5. _____ Variables thought to affect the value of the dependent variable.

6. _____ The parameter that gives the value of the dependent variable (Y) when the explanatory variable (X) is zero.

7. _____ A parameter that gives the change in the dependent variable per one-unit change in one of the explanatory variables.

8. _____ The unknown relationship that exists between Y and X and is to be discovered through regression analysis.

9. _____ Captures the effects of all the minor, unpredictable factors that cannot reasonably be accounted for in the hypothesized model.

10. _____ Data on explanatory and dependent variables that is collected over time.

11. _____ Data that is collected from many different firms or industries at one point in time.

12. _____ A graph that plots the value of the dependent variable against the value of the explanatory variable.

13. _____ The equation or line that represents the exact relationship between the independent variable and explanatory variables.

14. _____ The line that best fits the sample data.

15. _____ Method of fitting a line through a scatter of data that minimizes the sum of squared distance from each sample point and the fitted point.

16. _____ Values of Y obtained by entering a value for X into the least-squares regression line.

17. _____ The observed difference between the value estimated by the regression line and the actual value.

18. _____ The formulas by which the estimates of the intercept parameter and the slope parameters are calculated.

19. _____ The values of the intercept and slope parameters that are calculated using the formulas (i.e., the estimators) for the least-squares lines.

20. _____ Sample data contain sufficient evidence that the true value of a coefficient or parameter is not zero.

21. _____ A statistical technique for making probabilistic statements about the true value of a parameter.

22. _____ Graph showing the distribution of values that $\hat{b}$ might take given the random sample of observations on Y and X.

23. _____ An estimator which, on average, gives the true value of the parameter it seeks to estimate.

24. _____ Statistical test for testing the hypothesis that the true value of a parameter is equal to zero.

25. _____ The ratio of an estimated regression parameter divided by its standard error.

26. _____ The numerical value of the t-ratio.

27. _____ The value the t-statistic must exceed in order to reject the hypothesis that the true value of the parameter is equal to zero.

28. _____ Parameter estimate is found to be statistically significant when the true parameter value is equal to zero.

29. _____ The probability of making a Type I error.

30. _____ When the true value of a parameter is zero, this gives the probability of (correctly) failing to find statistical significance.

31. _____ The number of observations in a sample minus the number of parameters being estimated.

32. _____ The exact level of significance associated with a particular test statistic, such as a t-statistic or an F-statistic.

33. _____ The fraction of the total variation that is explained by the relationship with the independent variables.

34. _____ A statistic used to test whether the overall regression equation is statistically significant.

35. _____ A regression having more than one explanatory variable to explain the variation in the dependent variable.

36. _____ A regression that fits a ∪- or ∩-shaped pattern of data.

37. _____ A multiplicative nonlinear regression model in which the slope parameters are elasticities.

Study Problems

1. A simple linear regression equation relates G and H as follows:

$$G = a + bH$$

a. The explanatory variable is _____, and the dependent variable is _____.

b. The slope parameter is _____, and the intercept parameter is _____.

c. When H is zero, G equals _____.

d. For each one unit increase in H, the change in G is _____ units.

2. Using the statistical tables in your textbook, find the values of the appropriate test statistic in the following two situations:

a. Testing for statistical significance (at the 10 percent level of significance) of the individual regression coefficients in the model

$$Y = a + bX + cZ + dR$$

which is estimated using a time-series sample containing monthly observations over a two-year period.

b. Testing the statistical significance (at the 95 percent level of confidence) of the overall regression equation

$$Z = a + bY + cX$$

which is estimated using cross-section data on 21 firms.

3. The linear regression equation in question 1 above is estimated using 22 observations on G and H. The least-squares estimate of b is –210.4, and the standard error of the estimate is 80.92. Perform a t-test for statistical significance at the 2 percent level of significance.

a. There are _____ degrees of freedom for this t-test.

b. The value of the t-statistic is _____. The critical t-value for the test is _____.

c. Is $\hat{b}$ statistically significant? Explain.

d. The p-value for the t-statistic is 0.017. The p-value gives the probability of rejecting the hypothesis that _____ ($b = 0, b \neq 0$) when b is truly equal to _____. The exact level of significance for $\hat{b}$ is _____ percent.

4. Thirty data points on Y and X are employed to estimate the parameters in the linear relation

$$Y = a + bX$$

The computer output from the regression analysis is shown at the top of the next page:

DEPENDENT VARIABLE:	Y	R-SQUARE	F-RATIO	P-VALUE ON F	
OBSERVATIONS:	30	0.5223	8.747	0.0187	
VARIABLE		PARAMETER ESTIMATE	STANDARD ERROR	T-RATIO	P-VALUE
INTERCEPT		800.0	189.125	4.23	0.0029
X		–2.50	0.850	–2.94	0.0187

a. The equation of the sample regression line is _____.

b. Test the intercept and slope estimates for statistical significance at the 5 percent significance level. The critical t-value is _____. The parameter estimate for a is _____, which _____ (is, is not) statistically significant. The parameter estimate for b is _____, which _____ (is, is not) statistically significant.

c. Interpret the p-values for the parameter estimates.

d. Test the overall equation for statistical significance at the 5 percent significance level. Explain how you performed this test and present your results. Interpret the p-value for the F-statistic.

e. If X equals 500, the fitted (or predicted) value of Y is _____.

f. The fraction of the total variation in Y explained by the regression is _____ percent.

5. A manager wishes to determine the relation between a firm's sales and its level of advertising in the newspaper. The manager believes sales (S) and advertising expenditures (A) are related in a nonlinear way:

$$S = a + bA + cA^2 + dA^3$$

Explain how to transform this nonlinear model into a linear regression model.

6. Suppose Y is related to X, W, and Z in the following nonlinear way:

$$Y = aX^b W^c Z^d$$

a. This nonlinear relation can be transformed into the linear regression model

_____ .

The computer output from the regression analysis is shown below.

DEPENDENT VARIABLE: LNY	R-SQUARE	F-RATIO	P-VALUE ON F		
OBSERVATIONS: 25	0.7360	19.52	0.0001		
VARIABLE	PARAMETER ESTIMATE	STANDARD ERROR	T-RATIO	P-VALUE	
INTERCEPT	3.1781	1.1010	2.89	0.0088	
LNX	-2.173	0.6555	-3.32	0.0033	
LNW	1.250	1.780	0.70	0.4902	
LNZ	-0.8415	0.1525	-5.52	0.0001	

b. At the 99 percent level of confidence, perform t-tests for statistical significance of $\hat{b}$, $\hat{c}$, and $\hat{d}$.

c. This regression leaves _____ percent of the variation in the dependent variable unexplained.

d. The estimated value of a is _____ .

e. If $X = 10$, $W = 5$, and $Z = 2$, the expected value of Y is _____ .

f. If Z decreases by 10 percent (all other things constant), Y will _____ (increase, decrease) by _____ percent.

g. If W decreases by 12 percent (all other things constant), Y will _____ (increase, decrease) by _____ percent.

7. A multiple regression model, $Y = a + bX + cX^2$, is estimated by creating a new variable named "X2" that equals X^2. A computer package produces the following output:

DEPENDENT VARIABLE: Y	R-SQUARE	F-RATIO	P-VALUE ON F		
OBSERVATIONS: 27	0.8766	85.25	0.0001		
VARIABLE	PARAMETER ESTIMATE	STANDARD ERROR	T-RATIO	P-VALUE	
INTERCEPT	8000.00	3524.0	2.27	0.0325	
X	-12.00	4.50	-2.67	0.0135	
X2	0.005	0.002	2.50	0.0197	

a. The regression has _____ degrees of freedom.

b. Test to see if the estimates of a, b, and c are statistically significant at the 5 percent significance level.

c. The exact levels of significance of $\hat{a}, \hat{b},$ and $\hat{c}$ are _____, _____, and _____, respectively.

d. _____ percent of the total variation in Y is explained by the regression. _____ percent of the variation in Y is unexplained by the regression.

e. The critical value of the F-statistic at the 5 percent level of significance is _____. Is the overall regression equation statistically significant at the 5 percent level? The exact level of significance of the equation as a whole is _____ percent.

f. If X is equal to 1,200, then $Y =$ _____.

Computer Problem

1. Use the following 12 observations on Y and X and a computer regression package, such as the Student Edition of Statistix 8, to work this computer problem.

Observation	X	Y
1	15	75
2	20	150
3	30	125
4	35	250
5	40	200
6	50	225
7	55	300
8	60	200
9	70	250
10	75	175
11	80	225
12	90	175

Run the appropriate regression to estimate the parameters of the linear model: $Y = a + bX$.

a. At the 5 percent level of significance, does X play a significant role in explaining the variation in Y? Explain.

b. What percentage of the variation in Y is explained by variation in the explanatory variable X? What percentage of the variation in Y is unexplained by this model?

c. Using the computer software package, plot a scatter diagram of the data. (Plot Y on the vertical axis and X on the horizontal axis.) By looking at the scatter diagram, can you see why the R^2 for the linear model is low or high? Explain.

Now run the appropriate regression to estimate the parameters of the curvilinear model: $Y = a + bX + cX^2$.

d. Does the curvilinear model seem more appropriate for this data? Explain carefully using the regression results for the curvilinear model.

Multiple Choice / True-False

1. Using regression analysis for a linear equation $Y = a + bX$, the objective is to
    a. estimate the parameters a and b.
    b. fit a straight line through the data scatter in such a way that the sum of the squared errors is minimized.
    c. estimate the variables Y and X.
    d. both a and b.
    e. all of the above.

2. In a linear regression equation of the form $Y = a + bX$, the slope parameter b shows
    a. $\Delta X / \Delta Y$.
    b. $\Delta X / \Delta b$.
    c. $\Delta Y / \Delta b$.
    d. $\Delta Y / \Delta X$.
    e. none of the above

3. In a linear regression equation of the form $Y = a + bX$, the intercept parameter a shows
    a. the value of Y when X is zero.
    b. the value of X when Y is zero.
    c. the amount that Y changes when X changes by one unit.
    d. the amount that X changes when Y changes by one unit.

In questions 4 – 10, use the following estimation results for $Y = a + bX$:

DEPENDENT VARIABLE: Y	R-SQUARE	F-RATIO	P-VALUE ON F		
OBSERVATIONS: 22	0.4815	18.57	0.0003		
VARIABLE	PARAMETER ESTIMATE	STANDARD ERROR	T-RATIO	P-VALUE
INTERCEPT	276.320	105.060	2.63	0.0160
X	−24.291	5.636	−4.31	0.0003

4. What is the critical value of the t-statistic at the 1 percent level of significance?
    a. 1.725
    b. 1.717
    d. 2.819
    e. 2.845

5. Which of the following statements is true?
   a. Since $5.1885 > 2.819$, $\hat{b}$ is statistically significant.
   b. Since $4.31 > 2.819$, $\hat{b}$ is statistically significant.
   c. Since $5.1885 > 2.845$, $\hat{b}$ is statistically significant.
   d. Since $4.31 > 2.845$, $\hat{b}$ is statistically significant.

6. Given the t-ratio calculated for $\hat{b}$, what would be the lowest level of significance that would allow the hypothesis $b = 0$ to be rejected in favor of the alternative hypothesis $b \neq 0$?
   a. 0.03 percent
   b. 1.0 percent
   c. 1.6 percent
   d. 48.57 percent
   e. 51.43 percent

7. What is the critical value for F at the 1 percent level of significance?
   a. 4.35
   b. 5.93
   c. 7.94
   d. 8.10

8. Which of the following is true?
   a. Since $4.35 < 21.177$, the regression equation is statistically significant.
   b. Since $4.35 < 21.177$, the regression equation is statistically significant.
   c. Since $21.177 > 8.10$, the regression equation is statistically significant.
   d. Since $21.177 > 7.94$, the regression equation is statistically significant.

9. R^2 tells us
   a. the amount of variation in Y that is unexplained.
   b. the percent of the variation in X that is explained.
   c. that 51.43 percent of the total variation in Y is explained by the regression.
   d. that 48.57 percent of the total variation in Y is explained by the regression.

10. If $X = 40$, then $Y =$ _____.
    a. -840.32
    b. -695.32
    c. 1,478.32
    d. 1,845.32
    e. 1,945.32

Questions 11 – 13 cover topics presented in the Appendix to Chapter 4 in the textbook.

11. Multicollinearity will most likely be a problem when
    a. time-series data are used.
    b. cross-section data are used.
    c. the explanatory variables are not independent.
    d. endogenous variables are not independent.

12. Autocorrelation will most likely be a problem when
    a. time-series data are used.
    b. cross-section data are used.
    c. the explanatory variables are not independent.
    d. endogenous variables are not independent.

13. Heteroscedasticity will most likely be a problem when
    a. time-series data are used.
    b. cross-section data are used.
    c. the explanatory variables are not independent.
    d. endogenous variables are not independent.

14. T F   Generally, each and every data point in the sample lies on the sample regression line.

15. T F   In the model $Y = a + bX$, a high R^2 tells us that the variation in Y is caused by the variation in X.

16. T F   The amount of energy consumed each month at a specific factory is an example of a time-series data set.

17. T F   If the regression equation is statistically significant, then all of the individual parameters are statistically significant.

18. T F   If $\hat{b}$ is statistically significant at a 10 percent significance level, then $\hat{b}$ is far enough from zero that there is only a 10 percent probability that the true value of b equals zero.

19. T F   The method of least-squares produces unbiased estimates of parameters; therefore, $\hat{b} = b$ when the least-squares technique is employed to estimate the parameters of a regression model.

20. T F   The p-value gives the probability of making a Type I error, which is the probability of finding significance when none exists.

Answers

MATCHING DEFINITIONS

1. parameters
2. parameter estimation
3. regression analysis
4. dependent variable
5. explanatory variables
6. intercept parameter
7. slope parameter
8. true (or actual) relation
9. random error term
10. time series data set
11. cross-sectional data set
12. scatter diagram
13. population regression line
14. sample regression line
15. method of least-squares
16. fitted or predicted value
17. residual
18. estimators
19. estimates
20. statistically significant
21. hypothesis testing
22. relative frequency distribution on $\hat{b}$
23. unbiased estimator
24. t-test
25. t-ratio
26. t-statistic
27. critical value of t
28. Type I error
29. level of significance
30. level of confidence
31. degrees of freedom
32. p-value
33. coefficient of determination (R^2)
34. F-statistic
35. multiple regression model
36. quadratic regression model
37. log-linear regression model

STUDY PROBLEMS

1.
   a. H; G
   b. b; a
   c. a
   d. b

2.
   a. $t_{20} = 1.725$ (at the 10 percent significance level with $24 - 4 = 20$ degrees of freedom)
   b. $F_{k-1, n-k} = F_{2, 18} = 3.55$

3.
   a. 20
   b. $-2.60 = -210.4/80.92$; $t_{critical} = 2.528$
   c. The estimated value of b is (just) statistically significant because the calculated value

of the t-ratio, in absolute value, is greater than the critical value from the t-table: 2.60 > 2.528. There is no more than a 2% chance that the true value of b is zero when the t-ratio is -2.60.

    d. $b = 0$; zero; 1.7 (There is exactly a 1.8% chance that the true value of b is zero when the t-ratio is -2.60.)

4.   a. $\hat{Y} = 800.0 - 2.50X$

    b. $t_{critical} = 2.048$; 800.0; is; -2.50; is

    c.   The p-value gives the probability of committing a Type I error; that is rejecting the hypothesis that a parameter's true value is zero when the parameter value really is zero. For the intercept parameter estimate, there is only a 0.29% chance that $a = 0$, given the t-ratio of 4.23. For the slope parameter estimate, there is only a 1.87% chance that $b = 0$, given the t-ratio of -2.94.

    d.   The critical value of the F-statistic is $F_{k-1,n-k} = F_{1,28} = 4.20$. Since the calculated F-statistic, 8.747, exceeds the critical value of F, the equation is statistically significant. The p-value for the F-ratio indicates there is only a 1.82% chance the equation is *not* truly significant when the F-ratio is as large as 8.747.

    e. $-450 = 800.0 + (-2.50)(500) = 800.0 - 1,250$

    f.   52.23%

5.   Two new variables must be computed and substituted for A^2 and A^3. Let $X = A^2$ and $Z = A^3$ so that the nonlinear relation can be written in linear form as: $S = a + bA + cX + dZ$.

6.   a. $\ln Y = \ln a + b \ln X + c \ln W + d \ln Z$

    b.   The critical value of the t-statistic for $n - k = 25 - 4 = 21$ degrees of freedom and a 1 percent significance level is 2.831. When t-ratios are negative, their absolute values are used in their t-tests. Since $\left|t_{\hat{b}}\right|$ and $\left|t_{\hat{d}}\right|$ both exceed 2.831, the estimates of b and d are statistically significant. Since $t_{\hat{c}}$ is less than 2.831, the estimate of c is *not* statistically significant.

    c.   26.4% of the variation in $\ln Y$ is unexplained.

    d.   The intercept estimate provides an estimate for log a, (i.e., 3.1781 is an estimate of the *natural log* of a.) Therefore, $\hat{a}$ is found by taking the antilog: $\hat{a} = e^{3.1781} = 24.00$. If the intercept estimate (of $\ln a$) is statistically significant, then the estimate of a (24.00) is also statistically significant. Since the t-statistic for the intercept is 2.89 ($= 3.1781/1.1010$) exceeds 2.831 (barely), the estimate of a ($\hat{a} = 24$) is statistically significant.

    e.   When $X = 10$, $W = 5$, and $Z = 2$, $Y = 0.6724$ $[= 24(10)^{-2.1730}(5)^{1.2500}(2)^{-0.8415}]$

    f.   increase; 8.415 ($= 10 \times 0.8415$)

    g.   decrease; 15 ($= 12 \times 1.2500$)

7.   a. $24 = 27 - 3$

    b.   The critical value of the t-statistic is 2.064 at the 5% level of significance with 24 degrees of freedom. Since all three calculated t-ratios (2.27, -2.67, and 2.50) exceed the critical t-value, all three parameter estimates are statistically significant at the 5% level of significance.

    c.   3.25%; 1.35%; 1.97%

    d.   87.66%; 12.34%

    e.   3.40; The equation is statistically significant at the 5% level. The p-value for the F-statistic indicates the exact level of significance is much better than 5%: there is less than a 0.01% chance the equation as a whole is not statistically significant.

    f.   800 ($= 8,000 - 12 \times 1,200 + 0.005 \times 1,200^2$)

COMPUTER PROBLEM

Your regression printout for the linear model $Y = a + bX$ should look like this:

DEP. VARIABLE:	Y	R-SQUARE	F-RATIO	P-VALUE ON F	
OBS:	12	0.2026	2.54	0.1420	
		PARAMETER	STD.		
VARIABLE		ESTIMATE	ERROR	T-RATIO	P-VALUE
INTERCEPT		137.242	40.2942	3.41	0.0067
X		1.13402	0.71138	1.59	0.1420

1. a. No. The t-ratio for $\hat{b}$, 1.59, is less than the critical t ($= 2.228$) for a 5 percent level of significance and 10 ($= n - k = 12 - 10$) degrees of freedom. The p-value for $\hat{b}$ reveals that the exact level of significance is 14.20 percent.

   b. 20.26% of the variation in Y is explained by X, which is the only explanatory variable in the model. This leaves 79.74% of the variation in Y unexplained.

   c. Your scatter diagram should look like the following:

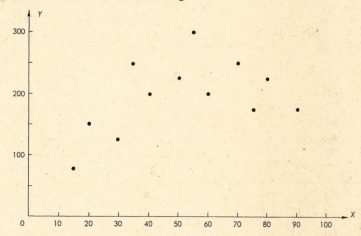

As you can see, a straight line fits the scatter of data points rather poorly, and this explains the low R^2 and F-statistic in the linear model.

Your regression printout for the curvilinear model $Y = a + bX + cX^2$ should look like:

DEP. VARIABLE:	Y	R-SQUARE	F-RATIO	P-VALUE ON F	
OBS:	12	0.6379	7.93	0.0103	
		PARAMETER	STD.		
VARIABLE		ESTIMATE	ERROR	T-RATIO	P-VALUE
INTERCEPT		−31.774	58.8211	−0.54	0.6021
X		9.31115	2.53695	3.67	0.0052
X2		−0.07900	0.02402	−3.29	0.0094

Note that a new variable, $X2$, was created by squaring X ($X2 = X^2$).

   d. Yes. For the curvilinear regression, the F-ratio and R^2 are higher than the linear model, which indicates a better fit. Looking at the scatter diagram, you can also see a curvature to the data pattern. More important, however, X and X2 are both significant explanatory variables as $\hat{b}$ and $\hat{c}$ are significant at better than the 1 percent level, as indicated by their p-values. The lack of significance for the intercept estimate, $\hat{a}$, indicates the true curvilinear relation may pass through the origin (i.e., the true value of a is zero.)

1.   d   Least-squares estimation is equivalent to fitting a line through a scatter of data points.

2.   d   The slope parameter b gives the rate of change in the dependent variable as the independent variable changes.

3.   a   The intercept parameter a gives the value of the dependent variable when the line crosses the axis on which the dependent variable is plotted.

4.   d   From the t-table at the end of your textbook, the critical value of t with $n - k = 22 - 2 = 20$ degrees of freedom and a 99% confidence level is 2.845.

5.   d   Since $|t_{\hat{b}}| > t_{critical}$, $\hat{b}$ is statistically significant.

6.   a   The p-value for $\hat{b}$ is 0.0003, which gives the lowest level of significance for which the hypothesis $b = 0$ can be rejected.

7.   d   For the 99 percent level of confidence, $F_{n-k, k-1} = F_{20, 1} = 8.10$.

8.   c   Since $F_{calculated} > F_{critical}$, the regression equation is statistically significant.

9.   c   51.43% of variation in Y is explained by the equation, while 48.57% is unexplained.

10.   b $-695.32 \ (= 276.32 - 24.291 \times 40)$

11.   c   Multicollinearity arises when explanatory variables are correlated with one another.

12.   a   Autocorrelation is most common in time series data because random effects tend to "carry-over" from one time period to the next.

13.   b   Heteroscedasticity is most common in cross-section data.

14.   F   The sample regression line is the best-fitting line, but it cannot pass through every data point in a scatter diagram (unless all points lie perfectly on a straight line, which is an extremely unlikely occurrence).

15.   F   A high degree of correlation does not imply *causality*. Two variables may be highly correlated even though changes in one variable do not cause changes in the other.

16.   T   This is indeed a time-series data set. A cross-section data set would contain energy consumption for all factories in a given month.

17.   F   It is possible for the equation as a whole to be significant without all of the individual parameters being significant.

18.   T   The level of significance is the probability that b is actually zero when $\hat{b}$ is found to be statistically significant.

19.   F   Unbiasedness only means that if you collected many random samples and calculated $\hat{b}$ the estimates *on average* would be equal to the true value.

20.   T   This is the definition of p-values.

Homework Exercises

1. Thirty data points on Y and X are employed to estimate the parameters in the linear relation $Y = a + bX$. The computer output from the regression analysis is

DEPENDENT VARIABLE: Y	R-SQUARE	F-RATIO	P-VALUE ON F		
OBSERVATIONS: 30	0.3301	13.79	0.0009		
VARIABLE	PARAMETER ESTIMATE	STANDARD ERROR	T-RATIO	P-VALUE	
INTERCEPT	93.54	46.210	2.02	0.0526	
X	−3.25	0.875	−3.71	0.0009	

a. The equation of the sample regression line is $\hat{Y} = $ _____.

b. There are _____ degrees of freedom for the t-test. At the 1% level of significance, the critical t-value for the test is _____ .

c. At the 1% level of significance, $\hat{a}$ _____ (is, is not) significant, and $\hat{b}$ _____ (is, is not) significant.

d. At the 2% level of significance, the critical t-value for a t-test is _____ . At the 2% level of significance, $\hat{a}$ _____ (is, is not) significant, and $\hat{b}$ _____ (is, is not) significant.

e. The p-value for $\hat{b}$ indicates that the exact level of significance is _____ percent, which is the probability of _____
_____ .

f. At the 1% level of significance, the critical value of the F-statistic is _____ . The model as a whole _____(is, is not) significant at the 1% level.

g. If X equals 500, the fitted (or predicted) value of Y is _____ .

h. The percentage of the total variation in Y *not* explained by the regression is _____ percent.

i. Explain why it is necessary to assess the statistical significance of the parameter estimates.

2. Suppose Y is related to R and S in the following nonlinear way:

$$Y = aR^b S^c$$

a. In order to estimate the parameters a, b, and c, the equation must be transformed into the form: _____ .

Twenty-six observations are used to obtain the following regression results:

DEPENDENT VARIABLE:	LNY	R-SQUARE	F-RATIO	P-VALUE ON F	
OBSERVATIONS:	26	0.3647	4.21	0.0170	
VARIABLE		PARAMETER ESTIMATE	STANDARD ERROR	T-RATIO	P-VALUE
INTERCEPT		2.9957	0.3545	8.45	0.0001
LNR		2.34	0.87	2.69	0.0134
LNS		-0.687	0.334	-2.06	0.0517

b. There are _____ degrees of freedom for the t-test. At the 1% level of significance, the critical t-value for the test is _____ .

c. At the 1% level of significance, $\hat{a}$ _____ (is, is not) significant, $\hat{b}$ _____ (is, is not) significant, and $\hat{c}$ _____ (is, is not) significant.

d. The estimated value of a is _____ .

e. The p-value for $\hat{b}$ indicates that the exact level of significance is _____ percent, which is the probability of _____

_____ .

f. At the 1% level of significance, the critical value of the F-statistic is _____ . The model as a whole _____ (is, is not) significant at the 1% level.

g. If $R = 12$ and $S = 30$, the fitted (or predicted) value of Y is _____ .

h. The percentage of the total variation in the dependent variable *not* explained by the regression is _____ percent.

i. If R increases by 14%, Y will increase by _____ percent.

j. A 6.87% increase in Y will occur if S _____ (increases, decreases) by _____ percent.

3. **_COMPUTER EXERCISE_**

Use a computer regression package, such as the Student Edition of Statistix 8, to work this computer exercise.

In Illustration 4.3 on page 144 of the textbook, a linear regression model was employed to determine whether the auto insurance premiums (P) can be adequately explained differences in costs across counties in California. Two variables were used to measure costs: (1) the number of claims per thousand insured vehicles (N), and the average dollar amount of each bodily injury claim (C).

a. Estimate the following log-linear regression model using the data provided in Illustration 4.3.

$$P = aN^b C^c$$

Note: The bodily injury claim data in Illustration 4.3 are stored in a Statistix 8 data file, which is included on the Statistix 8 disk that came with your textbook.

b. In order to estimate the parameters a, b, and c, the equation must be transformed into the form: _____.

c. The estimated log-linear model of bodily injury claims is

$$\hat{P} = \underline{\hspace{1cm}} N \underline{\hspace{1cm}} C \underline{\hspace{1cm}}$$

d. There are _____ degrees of freedom for the t-test. At the 2% level of significance, the critical t-value for the test is _____.

e. At the 2% level of significance, $\hat{a}$ _____ (is, is not) significant, $\hat{b}$ _____ (is, is not) significant, and $\hat{c}$ _____ (is, is not) significant.

f. If N increases by 6%, auto premiums (P) are predicted to increase by _____ percent. Show your work here:

g. According to the estimated equation, auto premiums would be expected to rise by 10% if the average amount of each claim (C) _____ (increases, decreases) by _____ percent. Show your work here:

h. Compare the F-ratios and R^2s of the linear and log-linear models. Which model does a better job overall of explaining the variation in auto premiums (P)? Briefly explain.

Theory of Consumer Behavior

Learning Objectives

After reading Chapter 5 and working the problems in this chapter of your Workbook, you should be able to:

➤ Explain the concept of utility and the assumptions underlying consumer preferences.

➤ Explain the equilibrium condition for an individual consumer to be maximizing utility subject to a budget constraint.

➤ Use indifference curves to derive a demand curve for an individual consumer.

➤ Identify the substitution, income, and total effects of a change in the price of a good.

➤ Explain why demand curves are downward sloping.

➤ Derive a market demand curve from the individual demand curves.

Essential Concepts

1. The benefits consumers obtain from the goods and services they consume is called *utility*. A *utility function* shows an individual's perception of the level of utility that would be attained from consuming each conceivable bundle of goods.

2. The theory of consumer behavior assumes that consumers have complete information about the availability and prices of all goods and services and the capacity of these goods and services to satisfy or provide utility. Consumers can also rank all conceivable bundles of goods on the basis of the ability of each bundle to provide utility. For any pair of bundles *A* and *B*, the consumer can make one of three possible responses: (*i*) I prefer bundle *A* to bundle *B*, (*ii*) I prefer bundle *B* to bundle *A*, or (*iii*) I am indifferent between the two bundles.

3. Indifference curves provide a means of depicting graphically the preferences of a consumer. An *indifference curve* is a locus of points, representing different bundles of goods and services, each of which yields the same level of total utility or satisfaction.

4. Indifference curves are negatively sloped and convex. Therefore, if the consumption of one good is increased, consumption of the other must be reduced to maintain a constant level of utility. The *marginal rate of substitution (MRS)*—the absolute value of the slope of the indifference curve—diminishes as the consumer moves downward along an indifference curve, increasing X and decreasing Y.

5. An *indifference map* consists of several indifference curves. The higher (or further to the right) an indifference curve is on the map, the greater the level of utility associated with the curve.

6. *Marginal utility* is the addition to total utility that is attributable to the addition of one unit of a good to the current rate of consumption, holding constant the amounts of all other goods consumed ($MU = \Delta U / \Delta X$).

7. The marginal rate of substitution shows the rate at which one good can be substituted for another while keeping utility constant. It can be interpreted as the ratio of the marginal utility of X divided by the marginal utility of Y:

$$MRS \equiv -\frac{\Delta Y}{\Delta X} = \frac{MU_x}{MU_y}$$

where $-\Delta Y / \Delta X$ is the negative of the slope of the indifference curve.

8. The consumer's budget line shows all possible commodity bundles that can be purchased at given prices with a fixed amount of money income. The relation between money income (M) and the amount of goods X and Y purchased can be expressed as

$$M = P_x X + P_y Y$$

Alternatively, the equation for the budget line can be rewritten in the form of a straight line

$$Y = \frac{M}{P_y} - \frac{P_x}{P_y} X$$

The first term, M/P_y, gives the amount of Y the consumer can buy if no X is purchased. The term P_x/P_y is the absolute value of the slope of the budget line.

9. An increase (decrease) in money income causes a parallel outward (backward) shift in the budget line. An increase (decrease) in the price of X causes the budget line to pivot inward (outward) around the original vertical intercept.

10. A consumer maximizes utility subject to a limited money income at the combination of goods for which the indifference curve is just tangent to the budget line. At this combination, the marginal rate of substitution (the absolute value of the slope of the indifference curve) is equal to the price ratio (the absolute value of the slope of the budget line)

$$MRS = -\frac{\Delta Y}{\Delta X} = \frac{MU_x}{MU_y} = \frac{P_x}{P_y}$$

Thus a consumer allocates money income so that the marginal utility per dollar spent on each good is the same for all commodities purchased

$$\frac{MU_x}{P_x} = \frac{MU_y}{P_y}$$

and all income is spent.

11. The demand curve of an individual for a specific commodity relates utility-maximizing quantities purchased to market prices, holding constant money income and the prices of all other goods. The slope of the demand curve illustrates the law of demand: quantity demanded varies inversely with price.

12. When the price of a good changes, the total change in quantity demanded can be decomposed into two parts: (*i*) the substitution effect, and (*ii*) the income effect. The *substitution effect* is the change in consumption of a good after a change in its price, when the consumer is forced by a change in money income to consume at some point on the original indifference curve. Considering the substitution effect only, the amount of the good consumed must vary inversely with its price. The *income effect* of a price change is the change in the consumption of a good resulting strictly from the change in purchasing power. The total effect of a price change is equal to the sum of the substitution and income effects:

Total effect of price change = Substitution effect + Income effect

13. Considering the substitution effect alone, an increase (decrease) in the price of a good causes less (more) of the good to be demanded. For a normal good, the income effect adds to (or reinforces) the substitution effect. The income effect in the case of an inferior good offsets (or takes away from) the substitution effect.

14. *Market demand* is a list of prices and the quantities consumers are willing and able to purchase at each price in the list, other things being held constant. Market demand is derived by horizontally summing the demand curves for all the individuals in the market.

Matching Definitions

budget line
Giffen good
income effect
indifference curves
marginal rate of substitution
marginal utility

market demand
substitution effect
total effect
utility
utility function

1. _____ The benefits consumers receive from consuming goods or services.

2. _____ Equation showing a consumer's perception of the total utility forthcoming from consuming each bundle of goods and services.

3. _____ A set of consumption bundles each and every one of which provides a consumer with exactly the same level of total utility.

4. _____ The number of units of Y that must be given up for total utility to remain the same when one more unit of X is consumed.

5. _____ The addition to total utility attributable to consuming one more unit of a good, holding the consumption of all other goods constant.

6. _____ Line showing all bundles of goods that can be purchased at given prices if the entire income is spent.

7. _____ The change in the consumption of a good that would result if the consumer remained on the original indifference curve after the price of the good changes.

8. _____ The change in consumption of a good resulting strictly from the change in purchasing power after the price of a good changes.

9. _____ The sum of the substitution and income effects.

10. _____ A good for which quantity demanded varies directly with price, causing an upward sloping demand curve.

11. _____ A list of prices and the corresponding quantity consumers are willing and able to purchase at each price.

Study Problems

1. The following figure shows a portion of a consumer's indifference map. The consumer faces the budget line ZL, and the price of Y is $20.

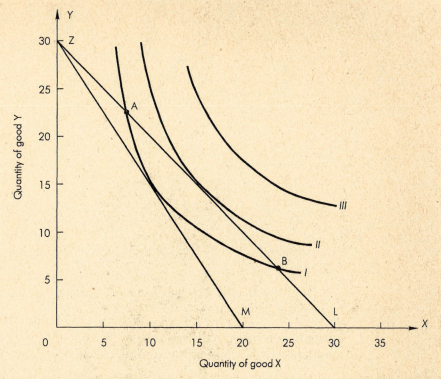

a. The consumer's income = $_____. The price of X is $_____.

b. The equation for the budget line ZL is Y = _____.

c. What combination of X and Y would the consumer choose? Why?

d. The marginal rate of substitution at the combination in part c is _____.

e. Explain in terms of the MRS why the consumer would not choose either combination A or B.

f. If the budget line pivots to ZM, the consumer chooses _____ units of good X and _____ units of good Y.

g. Along budget line ZM, the price of X is $_____ and the price of Y is $_____.

h. The new MRS is equal to _____.

2. The figure below shows a portion of a consumer's indifference map, and a budget line. The consumer's income is $1,200 and the price of Y is $6.

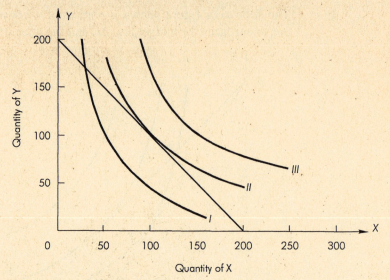

a. Using the given budget line, what is one point on the consumer's demand for X?

b. Pivot the budget line and derive two other points on the consumer's demand for X.

3. Using the consumer's indifference map shown in the figure below, derive the total, substitution, and income effects caused by a decrease in the price of X.

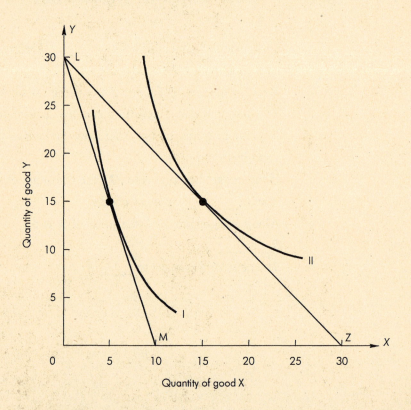

4. Suppose the marginal utility of the last unit of X consumed is 40, and the marginal utility of the last unit consumed of Y is 30. The prices of X and Y are $4 and $2, respectively. Should the consumer increase or decrease consumption of X? Explain carefully.

5. Suppose there are four consumers in the market for good X. The quantities demanded by each of the four consumers at each price between $1 and $5 are shown in the table below:

	Quantity Demanded				
Price of X	Consumer 1	Consumer 2	Consumer 3	Consumer 4	Market Demand
$1	5	12	8	3	_____
$2	4	10	7	2	_____
$3	3	8	6	1	_____
$4	2	6	3	0	_____
$5	1	4	1	0	_____

a. Fill in the blanks in the table for the market quantity demanded at each price.
b. Using the following graph, draw the demand curves for each of the four consumers. Label them D_1, D_2, D_3, and D_4.
c. Construct the market demand curve in the graph and label it $D_{market\ demand}$.

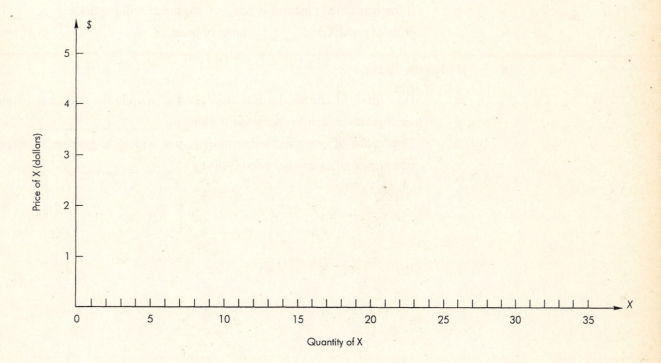

6. A consumer is indifferent between 6X and 4Y and 4X and 8Y.

    a. The marginal rate of substitution between these points is equal to _____.

    b. Over this range, the consumer is just willing to give up _____ units of Y to obtain another X.

    c. Over this range, the consumer is just willing to give up _____ units of X to obtain another Y.

7. The following table shows the marginal utility for each of six units of X and Y. The price of X is $4 and the price of Y is $2.

Quantity	MU_X	MU_Y
1	20	14
2	16	12
3	12	8
4	10	6
5	8	5
6	6	4

    a. If the consumer's income is $20, the consumer will purchase _____ units of good X and _____ units of good Y.

    b. If the consumer's income is $26, the consumer will purchase _____ units of good X and _____ units of good Y.

8. Fill in the blanks.

    a. How much of one good a consumer must give up in the market to obtain another unit of some other good is given by _____.

    b. How much of one good a consumer is just willing to give up to obtain one more unit of another good is given by _____.

Multiple Choice / True-False

For questions 1 and 2 use the figure below that shows a consumer's indifference map.

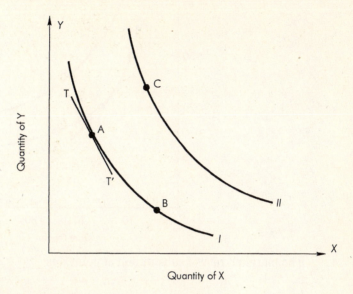

Quantity of X

1. Which of the following statements is (are) true?
   a. The consumer is indifferent between bundles A and B.
   b. The consumer prefers bundle B to C.
   c. Bundle B is less expensive than bundle A.
   d. both a and c.
   e. both a and b.

2. The marginal rate of substitution at point A
   a. is equal to the absolute value of the slope of the tangent line TT'.
   b. is smaller than the MRS at point B.
   c. measures the increase in total satisfaction from consuming one more unit of X and one less unit of Y.
   d. is equal to the MRS at point B.

3. Which of the following is NOT one of the assumptions for the theory of consumer behavior?
   a. Consumers have complete knowledge regarding their money income, the prices of all goods and services, and the capacity of each good to satisfy the consumer.
   b. More of a good is preferred to less of a good.
   c. Consumers can rank order all bundles of goods.
   d. Indifference curves are concave.

Use the following figure to answer Questions 4 – 7. This figure shows two indifference curves for a consumer.

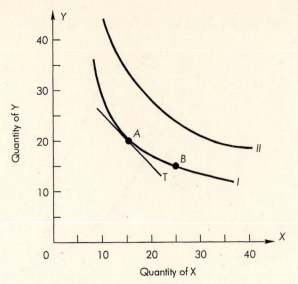

4. The marginal rate of substitution at point A is _____.
    a. 1
    b. 2
    c. 3
    d. 4
    e. 5

5. The marginal rate of substitution between points A and B is _____.
    a. 1
    b. 2
    c. 1/2
    d. 2/3
    e. 3/2

6. If the consumer moves from B to A, that consumer is willing to give up X for Y at the rate _____ X for _____ Y.
    a. 1; 1
    b. 1/2; 1
    c. 3; 2
    d. 2; 1
    e. 1; 2

7. If utility-maximizing equilibrium is at point A, what could make the consumer move to a point on curve II?
    a. The price of Y falls.
    b. The price of X falls.
    c. Income rises.
    d. All of the above.
    e. None of the above.

Use the following figure to answer questions 8 – 13. The consumer's income is $500.

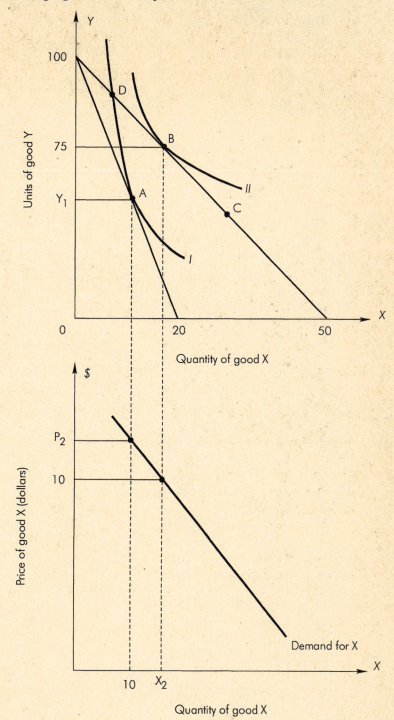

8. The price of Y is _____.
   a. $1
   b. $2
   c. $4
   d. $5
   e. $10

9. The value of P_2 is _____.
   a. $1
   b. $5
   c. $10
   d. $20
   e. $25

10. The value of X_2 is _____.
    a. 5
    b. 10
    c. 12.5
    d. 15
    e. 20

11. The value of Y_1 is _____.
    a. 5
    b. 10
    c. 15
    d. 20
    e. 50

12. Commodity bundle C costs _____.
    a. $100.
    b. $250.
    c. $500.
    d. $750.
    e. none of the above

13. At point D, _____.
    a. $MRS < 2$
    b. $MRS > 5$
    c. $MU_x < MU_y$
    d. $P_x < P_y$
    e. $MU_x/MU_y < P_x/P_y$

Use the following figure to answer questions 14 – 17. In the figure, assume the price of *X* increases.

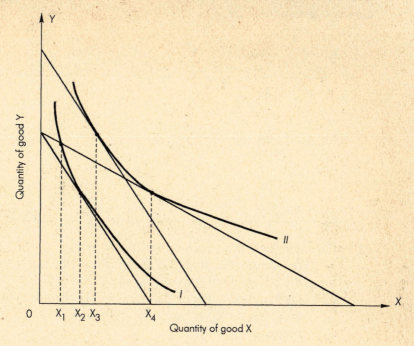

14. The substitution effect is the movement from
    a. X_3 to X_2.
    b. X_2 to X_1.
    c. X_1 to X_2.
    d. X_3 to X_1.
    e. X_4 to X_3.

15. The income effect is the movement from
    a. X_3 to X_2.
    b. X_2 to X_1.
    c. X_1 to X_2.
    d. X_3 to X_1.
    e. X_4 to X_3.

16. Good *X* is
    a. normal.
    b. inferior.
    c. a Giffen good.
    d. both *b* and *c*.

17. The total effect is the movement from
    a. X_3 to X_2.
    b. X_4 to X_1.
    c. X_3 to X_1.
    d. X_4 to X_2.
    e. X_2 to X_4.

Assume that an individual consumes two goods, X and Y. The total utility (assumed measurable) of each good is independent of the rate of consumption of other goods. The prices of X and Y are respectively $2 and $3. Use the following table of total utilities to answer questions 18 – 20.

Units of Good	Total Utility of X	Total Utility of Y
1..............	20	45
2..............	38	78
3..............	54	108
4..............	68	135
5..............	80	159
6..............	90	180

18. If the consumer buys the fourth unit of X,
    a. the marginal utility of the fourth unit is 14 units of satisfaction.
    b. the marginal utility per dollar spent on X is 7.
    c. the marginal utility of the fourth unit is 10 units of satisfaction.
    d. the marginal utility per dollar spent on X is 14.
    e. both a and b.

19. If the consumer has $26 to spend on X and Y, the utility maximizing bundle (given the budget constraint) is
    a. $7X$ and $7Y$.
    b. $4X$ and $6Y$.
    c. $6X$ and $4.67Y$.
    d. $6X$ and 4Y.
    e. $2X$ and $4Y$.

20. If the consumer has $16 to spend on X and Y, which combination will the consumer choose?
    a. $5X$ and $2Y$
    b. $2X$ and $1Y$
    c. $2X$ and $3Y$
    d. $2X$ and $4Y$
    e. The consumer is indifferent between a and d.

Use the following information to answer questions 21 – 23. A consumer with an income of $240 is spending it all on 12 units of good X and 18 units of good Y. The price of X is $5 and the price of Y is $10. The marginal utility of the last X is 20 and the marginal utility of the last Y is 30.

21. What should the consumer do?
    a. Nothing, this is the utility maximizing choice.
    b. Buy more Y and less X because MU_y is higher than MU_x.
    c. Buy more Y and less X because the marginal utility per dollar of Y is higher.
    d. Buy more X and less Y because the price of X is lower.
    e. Buy more X and less Y because the marginal utility per dollar of X is higher.

22. If the consumer buys one less Y this person can, spending the same income,
    a. increase total utility by 40 with two more units of X.
    b. buy two more X but lose 10 units of utility.
    c. buy two more X and increase utility by 10.
    d. buy one more X and reduce utility by 10.
    e. none of the above.

23. When the consumer attains equilibrium,
    a. MU_x will be lower than 20.
    b. MU_y will be higher than 30.
    c. MU_y will be double MU_x.
    d. All of the above.
    e. None of the above.

24. T   F   Demand curves are downward sloping because the income effect always reinforces the substitution effect.

25. T   F   In utility-maximizing equilibrium it must be the case that the marginal rate of substitution equals the ratio of the prices of the two goods and the marginal utilities per dollar of each of the goods are equal.

26. T   F   A consumer maximizes utility from a given income by choosing the combination of goods so the marginal utilities are equal.

27. T   F   Market demand is the horizontal sum of the demands of all consumers in the market.

28. T   F   An indifference curve shows all combinations of two goods that can be purchased from a given income.

29. T   F   A consumer in equilibrium can reach a higher indifference curve if and only if income increases.

30. T   F   A budget line gives the amount of one good that can be purchased at each amount of the other good with a given income and prices.

Answers

1. utility
2. utility function
3. indifference curves
4. marginal rate of substitution
5. marginal utility
6. budget line
7. substitution effect
8. income effect
9. total effect
10. Giffen good
11. market demand

STUDY PROBLEMS

1.
   a. $600; $20
   b. $30 - 1.0X$
   c. The consumer chooses $15X$ and $15Y$. This combination lies on the highest indifference curve that can be attained with budget line ZL.
   d. $MRS = 1(P_x/P_y = \$20/\$20)$
   e. At A, $MRS > P_x/P_y$ and at B, $MRS < P_x/P_y$. Therefore, at $A(B)$ the consumer is willing to give up more $Y(X)$ in order to get more $X(Y)$ than the amount that must be given up in the market.
   f. $10X$ and $15Y$
   g. $P_x = \$30$, $P_y = \$20$
   h. $MRS = 30/20 = 1.5$

2.
   a. $P_x = \$1,200/200 = \$6$ and $X = 100$
   b. The graph below shows the derivation of the other two combinations.

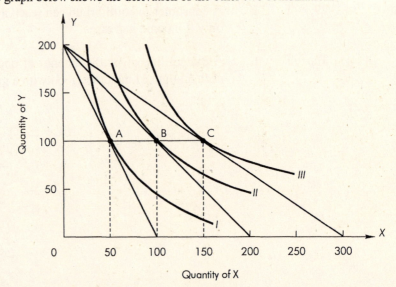

   At A, $P_x = \$1,200/100 = \$12$ and $X = 50$. At B, $P_x = \$1,200/200 = \$6$ and $X = 100$ as above. At C, $P_x = \$1,200/300 = \$4$ and $X = 150$.

3. The figure below illustrates how to isolate the substitution and income effects for a decrease in the price of X, shown by the outward rotation from LM to LZ. First isolate the substitution effect by laying a ruler (or any straight-edge) along the new budget line LZ. Now move your ruler carefully backwards and parallel to LZ until it is just tangent to the original indifference curve I at Point C. The change in X caused by moving along the original indifference curve (point A to point C) is +5 units because $X = 5$ at point A and $X = 10$ at point C. [Note: You get the values of X by "eye-balling" their locations on the graph. No formulas are used in this problem.] The income effect is the change in X when the hypothetically removed income is restored, and the budget line shifts rightward to LZ. The movement from bundle C to bundle B causes consumption of X to change by +5 units (from 10 to 15 units). Again the values of X are found by visual inspection, not mathematical formulas. The total effect is +10 because consumption of X increases from 5 to 15 units as a result of the decrease in the price of X.

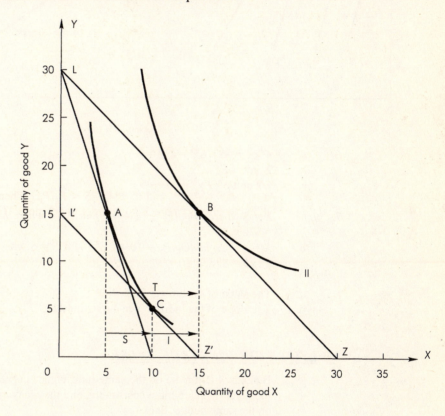

4. Since $MU_x/P_x = 40/4 = 10 < 15 = 30/2 = MU_y/P_y$, the consumer should spend more on Y and less on X. The reduction in utility from spending one less dollar on X (10 units of utility) is less than the increase in utility from spending one more dollar on Y (15 units of utility).

5. The following figure shows the individual demand curves for the four consumers and the market demand curve (the horizontal sum of the four individual curves).

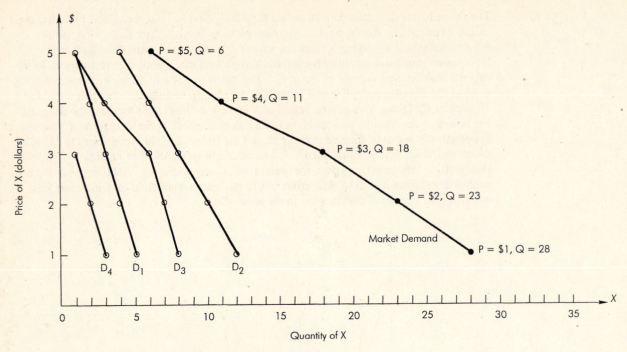

6. a. $MRS = -\Delta Y/\Delta X = 4/2 = 2$
    b. 2 units of Y
    c. 1/2 unit of X

7. a. $X = 3$ where $MU_x/P_x = 12/4 = 3$ and $Y = 4$ where $MU_y/P_y = 6/2 = 3$. $\$4 \times 3 + \$2 \times 4 = \$20$
    b. $X = 4$ where $MU_x/P_x = 10/4 = 2.5$ and $Y = 5$ where $MU_y/P_y = 5/2 = 2.5$. $\$4 \times 4 + \$2 \times 5 = \$26$

8. a. The slope of the budget line: P_x/P_y
    b. The slope of the indifference curve: the MRS

MULTIPLE CHOICE / TRUE-FALSE

1. a   Bundles A and B lie on the same indifference curve. Note that you cannot tell from the graph which bundle costs more, and they may even cost the same if they both lie on the same budget line.

2. a $MRS =$ slope of indifference curve = slope of tangent line

3. d   Indifference curves are assumed to be convex.

4. a   Extend tangent T to both axes. The slope is $35/35 = 1$

5. c $MRS = -\Delta Y/\Delta X = 5/10 = 1/2$

6. d   Since $-\Delta Y/\Delta X = 1/2$, $-\Delta X/\Delta Y = 2$

7. d   Each change would move the budget line outward.

8. d   Since the Y–intercept is 100, 100 units of Y (and zero units of X) can be purchased with an income of \$500. Thus, the price of Y must be \$5.

9. e   Since the slope at point A is 5(= $\Delta Y/\Delta X$ = 100/20) and since the slope of the budget line equals P_x/P_y, it follows that $P_x/5 = 5$. Therefore, P_2 must equal $25.

10. c   At point B, $375 is being spent on Y ($5×75). Since income is equal to $500, $125 (= $500 – $375) is being spent on X. The price of X along the budget line passing through point B is $10. If the consumer spends $125 on X at a price of $10/unit of X, then 12.5 units of X are purchased.

11. e   At point A, $250 (= $25×10) is being spent on X leaving $250 to spend on Y. Since P_y = $5, Y_1 must be 50.

12. c   Bundle C costs the same as bundle B because they are on the same budget line.

13. b   Since MRS = 5 at point A, and since MRS diminishes along an indifference curve, $MRS > 5$ at point D.

14. e   The increase in P_x causes consumption of X to decrease from X_4 to X_3 along the original indifference curve.

15. a   Taking away the hypothetical income that was given to the consumer to isolate the substitution effect causes the budget line to shift parallel backwards. Consumption of X decreases from X_3 to X_2.

16. a   Good X is normal because the income and substitution effects move in the same direction.

17. d   From indifference curve II to I.

18. e TU_3 = 54 and TU_4 = 68 ⇒ MU_4 = 14 units of satisfaction. The marginal utility per dollar spent on X is 7(= MU_x/P_x = 14/2).

19. b   At $4X$ and $6Y$, $MU_x/P_x = MU_y/P_y = 7$ and all $26 dollars are spent.

20. d   At $2X$ and $4Y$, $MU_x/P_x = MU_y/P_y = 9$ and all $16 dollars are spent.

21. e $MU_x/P_x = 4 > MU_y/P_y = 3$

22. c   Utility falls by 30 with one less Y but rises by 40 with two more X at $5 each.

23. d   In equilibrium, $MU_x/5 = MU_y/10$.

24. F   Income effect can work in the opposite direction of substitution effect.

25. T   One condition implies the other.

26. F   The marginal utilities per dollar are equal.

27. T   This is the definition of market demand.

28. F   This is the definition of a budget line.

29. F   A consumer can also reach higher indifference curve if the price of one or both goods falls.

30. T   A budget line is $Y = M/P_y - (P_x/P_y)X$.

Homework Exercises

1. Use the information given in the figure below to answer the following questions.

   a. The consumer's income is $_____.

   b. The price of Y is $_____.

   c. When the price of X is $2, the marginal rate of substitution is _____.

   d. The equation of the budget line passing through point A is $Y =$ _____.

   e. At point D on the demand curve for X, the price of X is $_____.

   f. At point D on the demand curve for X, the quantity demanded is _____.

   g. At point B on the indifference curve II, the MRS is _____.

   h. At point B, the consumer's budget is $_____.

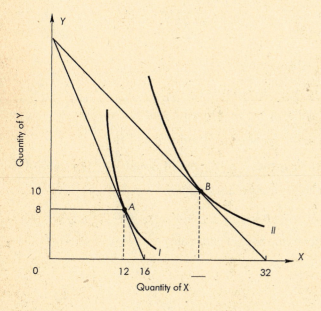

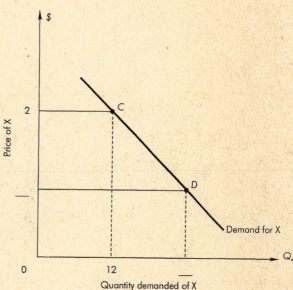

2. Assume that an individual consumes two goods, X and Y. The total utility (assumed measurable) of each good is independent of the rate of consumption of other good. The price of X and Y are respectively $40 and $60. Use the following table of total utilities to answer the following questions.

Units of Good	Total Utility of X	Total Utility of Y
1.....	20	45
2.....	38	78
3.....	54	108
4.....	68	135
5.....	80	159
6.....	90	180

a. The marginal utility of the fifth unit of Y is _____.

b. The marginal utility of the sixth unit of X is _____.

c. The marginal utility per dollar spent on the fourth unit of X is _____.

d. The marginal utility per dollar spent on the third unit of Y is _____.

e. If the consumer has $420 to spend, _____ unit of X and _____ units of Y maximize utility subject to the budget constraint.

f. If the consumer has $220 to spend, _____ units of X and _____ units of Y maximize utility subject to the budget constraint.

Elasticity and Demand

Learning Objectives

After reading Chapter 6 and working the problems for Chapter 6 in the textbook and in this Workbook, you should be able to:

➢ Explain how price elasticity of demand (E) is used to measure the responsiveness or sensitivity of consumers to a change in the price of a good.

➢ Explain the role that price elasticity plays in determining how a change in the price of a commodity affects the total revenue ($TR = P \times Q$) received.

➢ List and explain several factors that affect the elasticity of demand.

➢ Calculate the elasticity of demand (a) over an interval using the interval (or arc) formula, and (b) at a point on a demand curve.

➢ Define and compute the income elasticity of demand (E_M) and the cross-price elasticity of demand (E_{XY}).

➢ Relate marginal revenue to total revenue and demand elasticity.

➢ Write the marginal revenue equation for linear inverse demand functions.

Essential Concepts

1. The price elasticity of demand (E) measures the responsiveness or sensitivity of consumers to changes in the price of a good by taking the ratio of the percentage change in quantity demanded to the percentage change in the price of the good:

$$E = \frac{\%\Delta Q}{\%\Delta P}$$

Since P and Q are inversely related by the law of demand, the numerator and denominator of E always have opposite algebraic signs, and E is always negative. The larger the absolute value of E, the more sensitive buyers will be to a change in price.

2. Demand is elastic when $|E| > 1$, demand is inelastic when $|E| < 1$, and demand is unitary elastic when $|E| = 1$. [Note: The symbol "$|\ |$" denotes the absolute value.]

3. Using price elasticity, the percentage change in quantity demanded ($\%\Delta Q_d$) can be predicted for a given percentage change in price ($\%\Delta P$) as

$$\%\Delta Q_d = \%\Delta P \times E$$

Alternatively, the percentage change in price required for a given change in quantity demanded can be predicted as

$$\%\Delta P = \%\Delta Q_d \div E$$

4. The effect of a change in price on total revenue ($TR = P \times Q$) is determined by the price elasticity of demand. When demand is elastic (inelastic), the quantity (price) effect dominates. Total revenue always moves in the same direction as the variable (P or Q) having the dominant effect. When demand is unitary elastic, neither effect dominates, and changes in price leave total revenue unchanged. These results are summarized in the following table:

Relations Between Price Elasticity (E) and Total Revenue (TR)

	Elastic	Unitary elastic	Inelastic
	$\|\%\Delta Q\| > \|\%\Delta P\|$	$\|\%\Delta Q\| = \|\%\Delta P\|$	$\|\%\Delta Q\| < \|\%\Delta P\|$
	Q-effect dominates	No dominant effect	P-effect dominates
Price rises	TR falls	No change in TR	TR rises
Price falls	TR rises	No change in TR	TR falls

5. Several factors affect the elasticity of demand for a good: (1) the better and more numerous the substitutes for a good, the more elastic is the demand for the good, (2) the greater the percentage of the consumers' budgets spent on the good, the more elastic is demand, and (3) the longer the time period consumers have to adjust to price changes, the more responsive they will be and the more elastic is demand.

6. When calculating the value of E, computing percentage changes can be avoided by using a simpler formula for computing elasticity which can be obtained through the following algebraic operations:

$$E = \frac{\%\Delta Q}{\%\Delta P} = \frac{\dfrac{\Delta Q}{Q} \times 100}{\dfrac{\Delta P}{P} \times 100} = \frac{\Delta Q}{\Delta P} \cdot \frac{P}{Q}$$

Thus, price elasticity can be calculated by multiplying the slope of demand ($\Delta Q/\Delta P$) times the ratio of price to quantity (P/Q), which avoids making tedious percentage change computations.

7. Price elasticity can be measured either (1) over an interval (or arc) along demand, or (2) at a specific point on the demand curve. In either case, E still measures the sensitivity of consumers to changes in the price of the commodity. The choice of whether to measure demand elasticity at a point or over an interval of demand depends on the length of demand over which E is measured. If the change in price is relatively small, a point measure is generally suitable. Alternatively, when the price change spans a sizable arc along the demand curve, the interval measurement of elasticity provides a better measure of consumer responsiveness than the point measure.

8. When calculating the price elasticity of demand over an interval of demand, use the arc or interval elasticity formula:

$$E = \frac{\Delta Q}{\Delta P} \cdot \frac{\text{Average } P}{\text{Average } Q}$$

9. When calculating the price elasticity of demand at a point on demand, multiply the slope of demand ($\Delta Q/\Delta P$), computed at the point of measure, times the ratio P/Q, computed using the values of P and Q at the point of measure. The method of measuring the point elasticity depends on whether demand is linear or curvilinear.

Point Elasticity when Demand is Linear

For a generalized linear demand function of the form $Q = a + bP + cM + dP_R$, let income and the price of the related good take specific values of $\hat{M}$ and $\hat{P}_R$, respectively. The demand equation can then be expressed as $Q = a' + bP$, where $a' = a + c\hat{M} + d\hat{P}_R$ and the slope parameter b measures the rate of change in quantity demanded per unit change in price ($b = \Delta Q/\Delta P$). The price elasticity of a linear demand can be computed using either of two formulas that give the same value for E:

$$E = b\frac{P}{Q} \quad \text{or} \quad E = \frac{P}{P - A}$$

where P and Q are the values of price and quantity demanded at the point of measure along demand, and $A\ (=-a'/b)$ is the price-intercept of demand.

Point Elasticity when Demand is Curvilinear

For curvilinear demand functions, the price elasticity at a point can be computed using either of two equivalent formulas:

$$E = \frac{\Delta Q}{\Delta P}\frac{P}{Q} = \frac{P}{P - A}$$

where $\Delta Q/\Delta P$ is the slope of the curved demand at the point of measure (which is the inverse of the slope of the tangent line at the point of measure), P and Q are the values of price and quantity demanded at the point of measure, and A is the price-intercept of the tangent line extended to cross the price-axis.

10. In general, the price elasticity of demand varies along a demand curve. For linear demand curves, price and $|E|$ vary directly: the higher (lower) the price, the more (less) elastic is demand. For a curvilinear demand, there is no general rule about the relation between price and elasticity, except for the special case of $Q = aP^b$, which has a constant demand (equal to b) for all prices.

11. Marginal revenue (MR) is the change in total revenue per unit change in output:

$$MR = \frac{\Delta TR}{\Delta Q}$$

Since MR measures the rate of change in total revenue as quantity changes, MR is the slope of the total revenue (TR) curve. When MR is positive (negative), TR is rising (falling). When MR is zero, TR is neither rising nor falling; TR is at its maximum value.

12. When inverse demand is linear, $P = A + BQ$, marginal revenue is also linear, intersects the vertical (price) axis at the same point demand does, and is twice as steep as demand. The equation of the linear marginal revenue cure is $MR = A + 2BQ$.

13. For any demand curve (linear or curvilinear), when demand is elastic ($|E| > 1$), MR is positive. When demand is inelastic ($|E| < 1$), MR is negative. When demand is unitary elastic ($|E| = 1$), MR is zero.

Marginal Revenue, Total Revenue, and Price Elasticity of Demand

Marginal Revenue	Total Revenue	Price Elasticity
$MR > 0$	Increases as Q increases	Elastic ($|E| > 1$)
$MR = 0$	Is maximized	Unit Elastic ($|E| = 1$)
$MR < 0$	Decreases as Q increases	Inelastic ($|E| < 1$)

14. For all demand and marginal revenue curves, the relation between marginal revenue, price, and elasticity can be expressed as

$$MR = P\left(1 + \frac{1}{E}\right)$$

15. Income elasticity (E_M) measures the responsiveness of quantity demanded to changes in income, holding the price of the good and all other demand determinants constant.

$$E_M = \frac{\%\Delta Q_d}{\%\Delta M} = \frac{\Delta Q_d}{\Delta M} \cdot \frac{M}{Q_d}$$

Income elasticity is positive (negative) if the good is normal (inferior).

16. Cross-price elasticity (E_{XY}) measures the responsiveness of quantity demanded of good X to changes in the price of related good Y, holding the price of good X and all other demand determinants for good X constant.

$$E_{XY} = \frac{\%\Delta Q_X}{\%\Delta P_Y} = \frac{\Delta Q_X}{\Delta P_Y} \cdot \frac{P_Y}{Q_X}$$

Cross-price elasticity is positive (negative) when the two goods are substitutes (complements).

17. To calculate interval measures of income and cross-price elasticities, the following formulas can be employed:

$$E_M = \frac{\Delta Q}{\Delta M} \cdot \frac{\text{Average } M}{\text{Average } Q} \quad \text{and} \quad E_{XR} = \frac{\Delta Q}{\Delta P_R} \cdot \frac{\text{Average } P_R}{\text{Average } Q}$$

For the linear demand function $Q_X = a + bP_X + cM + dP_Y$, point measures of income and cross-price elasticities can be calculated as

$$E_M = c\frac{M}{Q} \quad \text{and} \quad E_{XR} = d\frac{P_R}{Q}$$

Matching Definitions

interval (or arc) elasticity
cross-price elasticity
price elasticity of demand
elastic demand
income elasticity
inelastic demand
inframarginal units

marginal revenue
point elasticity
price effect
quantity effect
total revenue
unitary elastic demand

1. _____ A measure of consumers' sensitivity or responsiveness to changes in the price of a good or service.

2. _____ When the percentage change in price (in absolute value) is *more* than the percentage change in quantity demanded (in absolute value).

3. _____ When the percentage change in quantity demanded (in absolute value) is *more* than the percentage change in price (in absolute value).

4. _____ When the percentage change in quantity demanded (in absolute value) is *just equal* to the percentage change in price (in absolute value).

5. _____ Total amount paid to a producer for a good or service: $P \times Q$.

6. _____ The effect on total revenue of a change in price, holding quantity constant.

7. _____ The effect on total revenue of a change in quantity, holding price constant.

8. _____ An elasticity calculated over an interval of a demand curve or demand schedule.

9. _____ An elasticity calculated at a specific price or point on a demand curve.

10. _____ A measure of how responsive quantity demanded is to a change in income, all other things constant.

11. _____ A measure showing how responsive the quantity demanded of one good is to changes in the price of another good, other factors constant.

12. _____ The additional revenue received by producing and selling one more unit of output.

13. _____ Units of output that could have been sold at a higher price had the firm not lowered its price to sell additional (marginal) units.

Study Problems

1. Moving along a demand curve, quantity demanded decreases 21 percent when price increases 7 percent.

    a. The price elasticity of demand elasticity is calculated to be _____ .
    b. Given the price elasticity calculated in part *a*, demand is _____ (elastic, inelastic, unitary elastic) along this portion of the demand curve.
    c. For this interval of demand, the percentage change in quantity is _____ (greater than, less than, equal to) the percentage change in price.

2. Fill in the blanks:

    a. The price elasticity of demand for a firm's product is equal to −0.5 over the range of prices being considered by the firm's manager. If the manager decreases the price of the product by 12 percent, the manager predicts the quantity demanded will _____ (increase, decrease) by _____ percent.
    b. The price elasticity of demand for an industry's demand curve is equal to −0.5 for the range of prices over which supply increases. If total industry output is expected to increase by 6 percent as a result of the supply increase, managers in this industry should expect the market price of the good to _____ (increase, decrease) by _____ percent.

3. Fill in the blanks:

    a. When the price effect dominates the quantity effect, demand is _____ .
    b. When the quantity effect dominates the price effect, demand is _____ .
    c. When the quantity effect and price effect exactly offset one another, demand is _____ .
    d. When a change in price causes a change in quantity demanded, total revenue always moves in the _____ direction as the variable (*P* or *Q*) having the _____ effect.

4. Fill in the blanks:

    a. When demand is elastic, a decrease in price causes quantity demanded to _____ and total revenue to _____ .
    b. When demand is inelastic, an increase in price causes quantity demanded to _____ and total revenue to _____ .
    c. When demand is unitary elastic, a decrease in price causes quantity demanded to _____ and total revenue to _____ .
    d. If quantity decreases and total revenue falls, demand must be _____ .
    e. If quantity decreases and total revenue stays the same, demand must be _____ .
    f. If quantity increases and total revenue rises, demand must be _____ .

5. Use the graph below of a linear demand curve to answer questions 5 and 6:

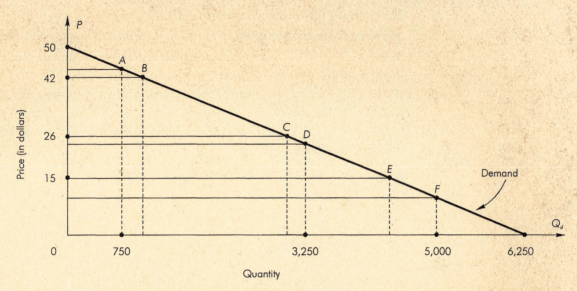

a. The equation for the linear demand in the figure above is $Q_d =$ _____ .

b. The equation for the *inverse* linear demand is $P =$ _____ .

c. Using the equations in parts a and b, find the missing prices and quantities at points $A - F$:

A: $P = \$$_____   C: $Q =$ _____   E: $Q =$ _____
B: $Q =$ _____   D: $P = \$$_____   F: $P = \$$_____

d. Compute the following interval (or arc) elasticities:

Interval A to B: $E_{AB} =$ _____

Interval C to D: $E_{CD} =$ _____

Interval E to F: $E_{EF} =$ _____

e. Compute the following point elasticities using the two formulas $E = (\Delta Q / \Delta P) \times (P / Q)$ and $E = P /(P - A)$:

Point	$E = \dfrac{\Delta Q}{\Delta P} \cdot \dfrac{P}{Q}$	$E = \dfrac{P}{P - A}$
A	$E_A =$_____	$E_A =$_____
C	$E_C =$_____	$E_C =$_____
E	$E_F =$_____	$E_F =$_____

f. Demand is unitary elastic at a price of \$ _____ and quantity of _____ .

g. As quantity increases along the demand curve, demand becomes _____ (more, less) elastic. As price falls along the demand curve, demand becomes _____ (more, less) elastic.

6. Use the figure in question 5 to answer the following:

   a. The equation for marginal revenue is $MR =$ _____.

   b. MR crosses the price-axis at $P = \$$_____. MR is zero at $Q =$ _____.

   c. If MR is _____ (rising, falling, zero, positive, negative), then demand is elastic.

   d. If MR is _____ (rising, falling, zero, positive, negative), then demand is unitary elastic.

   e. If MR is _____ (rising, falling, zero, positive, negative), then demand is inelastic.

7. Use the figure below to answer the following questions:

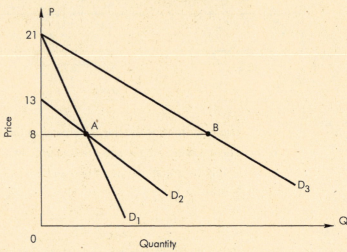

   a. Compute the point elasticity of demand at a price of $8 for D_1, D_2, and D_3.

$$D_1: \quad E = \underline{\hspace{2cm}}$$

$$D_2: \quad E = \underline{\hspace{2cm}}$$

$$D_3: \quad E = \underline{\hspace{2cm}}$$

   b. At what price is demand unitary elastic for each of these three demand curves?

$$D_1: \quad P = \underline{\hspace{2cm}}$$

$$D_2: \quad P = \underline{\hspace{2cm}}$$

$$D_3: \quad P = \underline{\hspace{2cm}}$$

   c. At a price of $8, the point price elasticity of demand for D_1 and D_3 are _____. Explain this result.

8. If a firm sells an additional unit of output and total revenue rises, then marginal revenue must be _____ (negative, positive) and demand must be _____ (elastic, inelastic, unitary elastic). Alternatively, if a firm sells an additional unit and total revenue falls, then marginal revenue must be _____ (negative, positive) and demand must be _____ (elastic, inelastic, unitary elastic).

9. Suppose the demand for good X is $Q_d = 100P^{-1}$.

    a. What is total revenue when $P = \$2$? When $P = \$4$? When $P = \$10$?

    b. This demand curve has a _____ (rising, constant, falling) elasticity of demand equal to _____.

10. Use the figure below to answer the following questions:

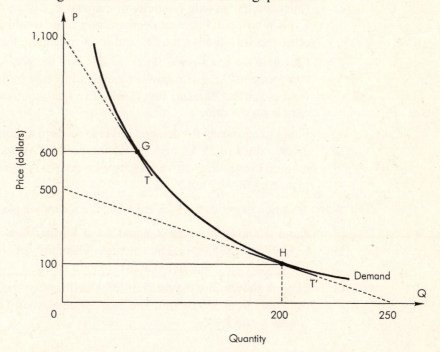

    a. Using the formula $E = (\Delta Q / \Delta P)(P / Q)$, the computed value of the price elasticity at point H is $E = $ _____.

    b. Using the formula $E = P /(P - A)$, the computed value of the price elasticity at point H is $E = $ _____.

    c. Compare the elasticities in parts a and b. Are they equal? Should they be equal?

    d. Calculate price elasticity at point G.

    e. Which formula did you use to compute elasticity at point G in part d? Why?

11. The generalized linear demand for good X is estimated to be

$$Q = 125,000 - 400P - 0.76M + 360P_R$$

where P is the price of good X, M is average income of consumers who buy good X, and P_R is the price of related good R. The values of P, M, and P_R are expected to be $200, $45,000, and $120, respectively. Use these values at this point on demand to make the following computations.

a. Compute the quantity of good X demanded for the given values of P, M, and P_R.

b. For the quantity in part a, calculate the point price elasticity of demand. At this point on the demand, is demand elastic, inelastic, or unitary elastic? How would decreasing the price of X affect total revenue? Explain.

c. Calculate the income elasticity of demand E_M. Is good X normal or inferior? Explain how a 3.5 percent decrease in income would affect demand for X, all other factors affecting the demand for X remaining the same.

d. Calculate the cross-price elasticity E_{XR}. Are the goods X and R substitutes or complements? Explain how a 6 percent increase in the price of related good R would affect demand for X, all other factors affecting the demand for X remaining the same?

e. Find the equations for demand, inverse demand and marginal revenue for the given values of P, M, and P_R. At the point on demand in parts a and b, is marginal revenue positive, negative or zero? Is this as you expected? Explain why or why not.

12. When the price of good X is $75, calculate the following elasticities:

a. Panel A shows how the demand for X shifts when income increases from $33,000 to $35,000. The income elasticity of demand for X equals _____. Good X is a(an) _____ good.

b. Panel B shows how the demand for X shifts when the price of related good Y decreases from $80 to $60. The cross-price elasticity equals _____. Goods X and Y are _____.

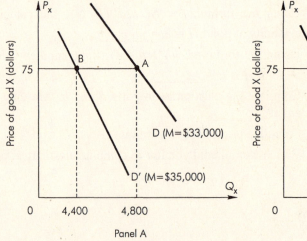

Panel A

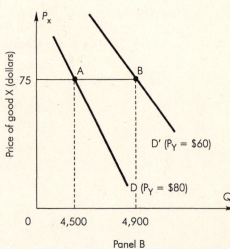

Panel B

13. The following figure shows a linear demand curve. Fill in the blanks *a* through *l* as indicated in the following figure:

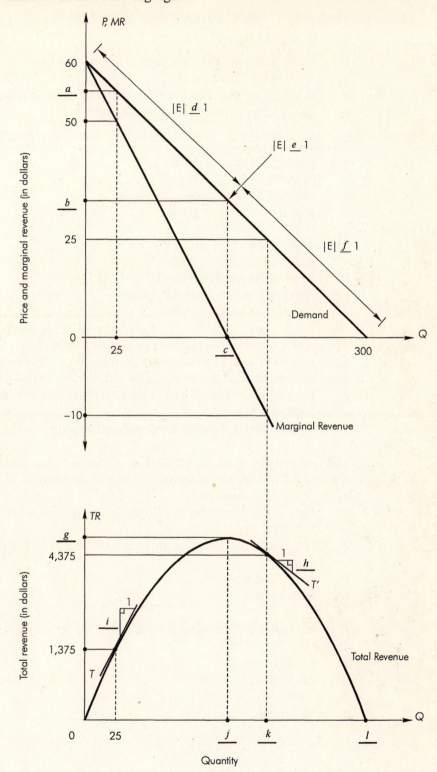

Multiple Choice / True-False

1. The absolute value of price elasticity of demand $|E|$
   a. is $|\%\Delta P| \div |\%\Delta Q_d|$
   b. is less than one when marginal revenue is positive.
   c. is always greater than one.
   d. is always greater than one when marginal revenue is negative.
   e. gets smaller as price falls along demand.

2. The cross-price elasticity is
   a. positive for normal goods.
   b. negative for substitute goods.
   c. negative for complementary goods.
   d. positive for inferior goods.

3. The income elasticity of demand is
   a. positive for normal goods.
   b. negative for substitute goods.
   c. negative for complementary goods.
   d. positive for inferior goods.

4. The interval method is used to compute price elasticity
   a. when a price change causes a relatively large movement along demand.
   b. so elasticity can be computed for rather small changes in price.
   c. for nonlinear demand curves because point elasticity cannot be computed for curves.
   d. because demand curves are downward sloping.

5. The demand for most agricultural products is rather inelastic. Thus, when bad weather reduces the size of crops (i.e., supply decreases),
   a. farmers' incomes rise.
   b. the marginal revenue of selling one more unit of an agricultural product is negative.
   c. the percentage decrease in crop sales exceeds the percentage increase in price.
   d. both a and b.
   e. both b and c.

6. If price elasticity of demand is −1.8 and price falls by 20 percent, then sales increase by
   a. 11.1 percent.
   b. 36 percent.
   c. 9 percent.
   d. 90 percent.

7. If price falls along a segment of demand that is price inelastic,
    a. arrows representing the price and quantity effects both point down.
    b. an arrow representing the price effect points down and is longer than an arrow for the quantity effect.
    c. an arrow representing the price effect points down and is shorter than an arrow for the quantity effect.
    d. arrows representing the price and quantity effects both point up.

8. If price rises along a segment of demand that is price elastic,
    a. an arrow representing the quantity effect points down and is longer than an arrow for the price effect.
    b. an arrow representing the quantity effect points up and is longer than an arrow for the price effect.
    c. total revenue moves in the direction of the arrow for the price effect.
    d. the arrows for the price and quantity effects point in opposite directions and are of equal length.

9. Which of the following would *NOT* tend to make demand for a good X more elastic?
    a. A major competitor of good X goes out of business.
    b. Product X is improved so that it becomes more durable.
    c. Incomes fall, which increases the share of families' budgets spent on X.
    d. both a and c.

Use the figure below to answer questions 10–12:

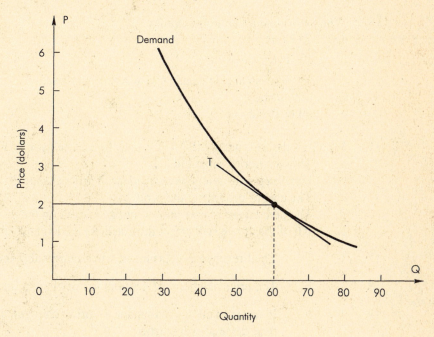

10. The point elasticity of demand when price is $2 is
    a. −6/90.
    b. −15.
    c. −1/2.
    d. −2.

11. If price falls from $2 to $1.99, then
    a. total revenue rises because $E = -15$.
    b. total revenue falls because $E = -1/2$.
    c. marginal revenue must be positive because total revenue rises.
    d. total revenue equals $1.99.

12. When price is $2, marginal revenue is
    a. negative.
    b. zero.
    c. positive.
    d. equal to price.

13. If the income elasticity of demand is –0.80 and quantity demanded increases by 10 percent as a result of a change in income, the income must have
    a. increased by 8 percent.
    b. increased by 80 percent.
    c. decreased by 8 percent.
    d. decreased by 12.5 percent.

14. When demand is unitary elastic
    a. marginal revenue is zero.
    b. the percentage change in quantity equals the percentage change in price.
    c. an increase in price has no effect on the quantity demanded.
    d. both a and b
    e. all of the above

15. When marginal revenue is negative
    a. $MR < P$.
    b. $|E|$ is less than one.
    c. an increase in price causes total revenue to rise.
    d. both a and c
    e. all of the above

16. Which of the following will NOT affect the price elasticity for a product?
    a. The number of substitutes.
    b. How long consumers have to adapt to price changes.
    c. The cost of producing the product.
    d. The percentage of consumers' budgets spent on the product.
    e. All of the above will affect the elasticity of demand for a product.

17. T F Total revenue is maximized when marginal revenue is zero.

18. T F The price elasticity of demand varies along a linear demand curve.

19. T F If total revenue is constant as price changes along a demand curve, then demand is inelastic.

20. T F The shorter the period of time that consumers have to adjust to a change in the price of a good, the less elastic will be demand.

ANSWERS

MATCHING DEFINITIONS

1.	demand elasticity	8.	arc elasticity
2.	inelastic demand	9.	point elasticity
3.	elastic demand	10.	income elasticity
4.	unitary elastic demand	11.	cross-price elasticity
5.	total revenue	12.	marginal revenue
6.	price effect	13.	inframarginal units
7.	quantity effect		

STUDY PROBLEMS

1.   a. -3.00 $(= -21\% \div 7\%)$

    b.   elastic; $|E| > 1$

    c.   greater than (When $|E| > 1$, the numerator of E must be larger, in absolute value, than the denominator of E.)

2.   a.   decrease; 4.8% [Note that $E = -0.40 = \%\Delta Q \div +12\%$. Solve for $\%\Delta Q = -4.8\%$.]

    b.   decreased; 50% [Note that $E = -0.40 = 20\% \div \%\Delta P$. Solve for $\%\Delta P = -50\%$.]

3.   a.   inelastic

    b.   elastic

    c.   unit elastic

    d.   same; dominant

4.   a.   increase; increase

    b.   decrease; increase

    c.   increase; remain the same

    d.   elastic [If Q decreases, P must have increased. When price increases and revenue decreases, demand is elastic.]

    e.   unit elastic [No change in total revenue indicates demand is unitary elastic.]

    f.   elastic [If Q increases, P must have decreased. When price decreases and revenue increases, demand is elastic.]

5.   a. $Q_d = 6,250 - 125P$. Begin with the general linear form $Q_d = a + bP$. The intercept parameter, a, is the Q-intercept ($= 6,250$), and the slope parameter, b, measures $\Delta Q_d/\Delta P$ ($= -6,250/50 = -125$). If this is confusing, see *Linear Functions* on page 3 of this Workbook.

    b. $P = 50 - 0.008Q_d$. To find the inverse function, solve algebraically for P in the equation from part a. If this is confusing, see *Inverse Functions* on page 2 of this Workbook.

    c.   A: $P = \$44$ C: $Q = 3,000$ E: $Q = 4,375$

        B: $Q = 1,000$ D: $P = \$24$ F: $P = \$10$

    d. $E_{AB} = \dfrac{\Delta Q}{\Delta P} \cdot \dfrac{\text{Average } P}{\text{Average } Q} = \dfrac{+250}{-2} \cdot \dfrac{43}{875} = -6.14$

$$E_{CD} = \frac{\Delta Q}{\Delta P} \cdot \frac{\text{Average } P}{\text{Average } Q} = \frac{+250}{-2} \cdot \frac{25}{3,125} = -1.0$$

$$E_{EF} = \frac{\Delta Q}{\Delta P} \cdot \frac{\text{Average } P}{\text{Average } Q} = \frac{+250}{-2} \cdot \frac{12.50}{4,687.5} = -0.33$$

e. $$E_A = \frac{\Delta Q}{\Delta P} \cdot \frac{P}{Q} = -125 \cdot \frac{44}{750} = -7.33 = \frac{44}{44 - 50}$$

$$E_C = \frac{\Delta Q}{\Delta P} \cdot \frac{P}{Q} = -125 \cdot \frac{26}{3,000} = -1.08 = \frac{26}{26 - 50}$$

$$E_E = \frac{\Delta Q}{\Delta P} \cdot \frac{P}{Q} = -125 \cdot \frac{15}{4,375} = -0.43 = \frac{15}{15 - 50}$$

f. $25; 3,125. For a linear demand, the unit elastic point occurs at the midpoint of the demand line.

g. less; less. Moving down linear demand, Q increases, P decreases, and $|E|$ decreases.

6. a. $MR = 50 - 0.016Q$. Inverse demand and marginal revenue have the same intercept parameters and the slope parameter of MR is twice the slope parameter of inverse demand. Since inverse demand is $P = 50 - 0.008Q_d$, MR has an intercept of 50 and a slope of -0.016 ($= 2 \times -0.008$).

   b. 50; 3,125. Inverse demand and marginal revenue have the same vertical intercepts. If MR is twice as steep as inverse demand, then MR must cross the Q axis midway between 0 and 6,250.

   c. positive. See Figure 6.5 and Table 6.4 on page 229 of the textbook.

   d. zero. See Figure 6.5 and Table 6.4 on page 229 of the textbook.

   e. negative. See Figure 6.5 and Table 6.4 on page 229 of the textbook.

7. a. $E_{D1} = 8/(8 - 21) = 8/-13 = -0.615$

   $E_{D2} = 8/(8 - 13) = 8/-5 = -1.6$

   $E_{D3} = 8/(8 - 21) = 8/-13 = -0.615$

   b. $D_1 : P = \$10.50; \quad D_2 : P = \$6.50; \quad D_3 : P = \$10.50$

   c. equal; The two demand curves have equal point elasticities because they both have the same price-intercept ($a = \$21$). Measured at the same price (in this case, $P = \$8$), their point elasticities must be equal.

8. positive; elastic; negative; inelastic

9. a. $TR_{P=2} = P \times Q = 2 \times 50 = \$100$

   $TR_{P=4} = P \times Q = 4 \times 25 = \$100$

   $TR_{P=10} = P \times Q = 10 \times 10 = \$100$

   b. constant; -1

10. a. $$E_H = \frac{\Delta Q}{\Delta P} \cdot \frac{P}{Q} = \frac{+250}{-500} \cdot \frac{100}{200} = -0.25$$

b. $E_H = \dfrac{P}{P-A} = \dfrac{100}{100-500} = -0.25$

c. They *are* equal, as they should be, since the two formulas are equivalent methods of computing point elasticity.

d. $E_G = \dfrac{P}{P-A} = \dfrac{600}{600-1,100} = -1.2$

e. At point G, the formula $E = P/(P-A)$ must be used because the slope of T ($\Delta Q/\Delta P$) cannot be determined from the information given in the figure.

11. a. $54,000 \; [= 125,000 + (-400 \times 200) + (-0.76 \times 45,000) + (360 \times 120)$

   b. $E = b\dfrac{P}{Q} = -400\dfrac{200}{54,000} = -1.481$; elastic; decrease TR because demand is elastic.

   c. $E_M = c\dfrac{M}{Q} = -0.76\dfrac{45,000}{54,000} = -0.633$; inferior ($c < 0$); $\%\Delta Q = +2.21 (= -3.5 \times -0.633)$

   d. $E_{XR} = d\dfrac{P_R}{Q} = 360\dfrac{120}{54,000} = 0.80$; substitutes ($d > 0$); $\%\Delta Q = +4.8\% (= 6 \times 0.80)$

   e. Demand:

   $Q = (125,000 - 0.76 \times 45,000 + 360 \times 120) - 400P$

   $\quad = 134,000 - 400P$

   Inverse Demand:

   $P = -134,000/-400 + (1/-400)Q$

   $\quad = 335 - 0.0025Q$

   Marginal Revenue:

   $MR = 335 + 2 \times (-0.0025)Q$

   $\quad = 335 - 0.005Q$

   At $Q = 54,000$, $MR = 65$. MR is expected to be positive because demand is elastic at this quantity (Recall that $E = -1.481$ in part b).

12. a. $E_M = \dfrac{\Delta Q}{\Delta M} \cdot \dfrac{\text{Average } M}{\text{Average } Q} = \dfrac{-400}{+2,000} \cdot \dfrac{34,000}{4,600} = -1.48$; inferior

   b. $E_{XY} = \dfrac{\Delta Q_X}{\Delta P_Y} \cdot \dfrac{\text{Average } P_Y}{\text{Average } Q_X} = \dfrac{+400}{-20} \cdot \dfrac{70}{4,700} = -0.30$; complements

13. a. $50 TR is $1,375 at $Q = 25$, so P must be $55 (=1,375/25).

   b. $30   This is the unit elastic point on demand, so price is the midpoint between 0 and 60 on the vertical axis.

   c. 150   This is the unit elastic point on demand, so quantity is the midpoint between 0 and 300 on the horizontal axis.

   d. >   Since MR is positive over this range of demand, demand is elastic.

   e. =   Since MR is zero at this point on demand, demand is unitary elastic.

   f. <   Since MR is negative over this range of demand, demand is inelastic.

   g. $4,500 $TR = P \times Q = \$30 \times 150$.

h.   −10   The slope of *TR* is *MR*, which is shown to be −10 on the *MR* curve.

i.   50   The slope of *TR* is *MR*, which is shown to be 50 on the *MR* curve.

j.   150   Total revenue reaches its peak at the quantity where demand is unit elastic, which is 150 (see blank *c*).

l.   300   Total revenue equals zero at a positive output when *P* is zero, which occurs where the demand curve touches the horizontal axis.

MULTIPLE CHOICE/TRUE-FALSE

1.   e   The absolute value of price elasticity is directly related to price. Thus, as price falls along demand, so does $|E|$.

2.   c $E_{XY} < 0$ for complementary goods.

3.   a $E_M > 0$ for normal goods.

4.   a   An interval measure instead of a point measure of elasticity is used when price changes over a relatively wide arc of demand.

5.   d   When demand is inelastic, an increase in price (in this case due to bad weather) increases total revenue (income to farmers). It is also true that $MR < 0$ when $E < 1$.

6.   b $-1.8 = \dfrac{\%\Delta Q}{-20\%} \Rightarrow \%\Delta Q = +36$ percent

7.   b   When demand is inelastic, the price effect dominates. In this case, price falls and the arrow representing the price effect points down and is longer than the arrow for the output effect (which points up). Total revenue moves in the direction of the dominant effect, and so in this case total revenue falls.

8.   a   When demand is elastic, the quantity effect dominates. In this case, price rises and the arrow representing the quantity effect points down and is longer than the arrow for the price effect (which points up). Total revenue moves in the direction of the dominant effect, and so in this case total revenue falls.

9.   a   The exit of a major competitor would decrease the number of substitutes, thereby making demand *less* elastic.

10. c   Extend tangent line *T* to cross the *P*-axis to find the value of *A*, which equals 6. Then, substituting $A = 6$, $E = -1/2 = P/(P - A) = 2/(2 - 6)$. Since tangent line *T* crosses the Q-axis at 90, the same answer can be obtained using the equivalent formula: $-1/2 = (\Delta Q / \Delta P)(P / Q) = (90 / -6)(2 / 60)$.

11. b   Since demand is inelastic at $2, TR must fall when price decreases to $1.99.

12. a   Since total revenue is falling at $P = \$2$, marginal revenue must be negative (which must, of course, be less than the *positive* value of price).

13. d $-0.80 = \dfrac{+10\%}{\%\Delta M} \Rightarrow \%\Delta M = -12.5$ percent

14. d   When $E = -1$, $|\%\Delta Q| = |\%\Delta P|$. Since $MR = P(1 + 1/E)$, $MR = 0$ when $E = -1$.

15. e   All are true when $MR < 0$.

16. c   Cost of producing the product is a factor affecting supply not demand.

17. T   *MR* measures the rate of change in *TR* as *Q* changes ($MR = \Delta TR/\Delta Q$), which is the slope of *TR*. When *TR* reaches its peak, its slope is zero.

18. T   Along a linear demand curve, demand is elastic above the midpoint, inelastic below the midpoint, and unitary elastic at the midpoint.

19. F   If *TR* is constant as *P* changes, then demand is *unitary* elastic.

20. T   With little time to adjust to a price change, consumers will be less able to substitute.

HOMEWORK EXERCISES

1. Use the figure below to answer the following questions.

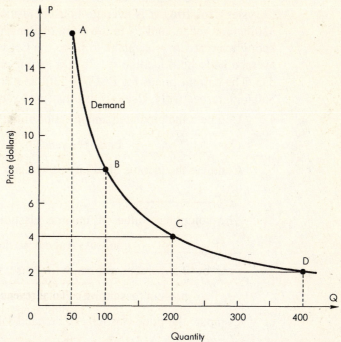

a. Calculate total revenue at points *A*, *B*, *C*, and *D*. If price falls from $16 to $8, total revenue _____ (increases, decreases, stays the same). If price falls from $8 to $4, total revenue _____ (increases, decreases, stays the same). If price falls from $4 to $2, total revenue _____ (increases, decreases, stays the same).

b. Given your answer in part *b*, is there any reason to believe this demand curve has a constant price elasticity of demand? Explain.

c. Write the equation of this demand curve in the form $Q = aP^b$: $Q =$ _____. Since $|b|$ is _____ (greater than, less than, equal to) one, demand is _____(elastic, inelastic, unitary elastic) at every price.

d. Compute point price elasticities for prices of $8, $4, and $2. [Hint: Use a straight-edge to carefully construct the appropriate tangent lines. Your tangent lines will be approximations since you are constructing them by sight.]
    $E_B =$ _____ $E_C =$ _____ $E_D =$ _____

e. Do the point elasticities in part *e* support your answer in part *d*? Explain why or why not.

2. Market researchers at Chrysler have estimated the demand for their new Chrysler Crossfire sports cars as follows:

$$Q_C = 1,050,000 - 95P_C + 14.25M + 60P_{BMW} + 25P_P$$

where Q_C is the quantity of Chrysler Crossfires sold annually, P_C is the price of a Chrysler Crossfire, M is average household income, P_{BMW} is the price of BMW's 330i sports sedan, and P_P is the price of Porsche's Boxster S sports car. The marketing team at Chrysler plans to price the Crossfire at $32,000. They predict that average household income is $75,000 for buyers in the market for their sports sedan. The current prices for BMW's 330i and Porsche's Boxster S are $34,000 and $50,000, respectively. Use this information to answer the following questions.

a. Compute the predicted annual sales of the Chrysler Crossfire:

$Q_C =$ _____ units per year.

b. Compute the income elasticity of demand for the Chrysler Crossfire:

$E_M =$ _____ .

The computed value of income elasticity indicates the Crossfire is a(n) _____ good. Average household income is predicted to fall next year by 2.5 percent, which will cause sales to _____ (rise, fall) by _____ percent (assuming other factors remain the same).

c. Compute the price elasticity of demand for the Chrysler Crossfire:

$E =$ _____ .

At the current price of $32,000, Chrysler is choosing to price in the _____ (elastic, inelastic) region of demand. At this point, a 5 percent increase in the price of Crossfires would be expected to cause sales to fall by _____ percent (assuming other factors remain the same).

d. Compute the cross-price elasticity of demand for Chrysler Crossfires with respect to changes in the price of the BMW 330i:
$E_{C-BMW} =$ _____ .

Compute the cross-price elasticity of demand for Chrysler Crossfires with respect to changes in the price of the Porsche Boxster S:
$E_{C-P} =$ _____ .

Both cross-price elasticities are _____ (positive, negative, greater than 1, less than 1) because these two cars are viewed by car-buyers as _____ (substitute, complement, inferior, normal) goods.

e. In part d, which of the two cross-price elasticities is larger in absolute value? Why do you suppose one is larger than the other?

3. Cactus Enterprises faces the following linear demand:

$$Q_d = 80 - 8P$$

a. Plot Cactus' demand curve in Panel A of the figure below. Label Cactus' demand curve "D."

b. The equation for Cactus Enterprises' marginal revenue curve can be expressed as $MR =$ _____. Plot Cactus' marginal revenue curve in Panel A of the figure below.

c. Over the range _____ to _____ units, total revenue is rising. Over the range _____ to _____ units, total revenue is falling. Total revenue is maximized at _____ units.

d. Compute the total revenue received by Cactus Enterprises for the levels of output $Q = 10, 20, 30, ..., 80$. Plot the total revenue curve in Panel B below.

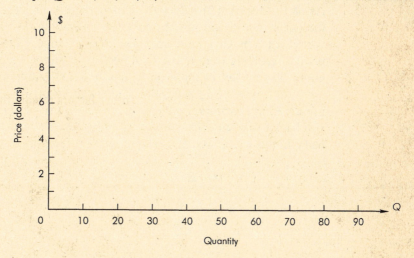

Panel A: Demand and Marginal Revenue

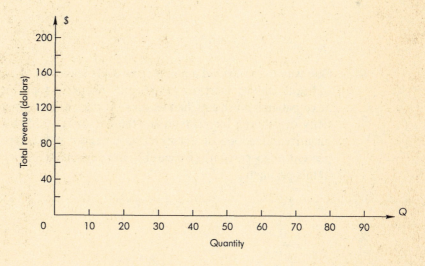

Panel B: Total Revenue

4. Over the past 30 years, cigarette makers did not worry too much about rising excise taxes on their product because they could simply raise prices to generate the extra revenue needed to pay the higher taxes. Apparently, according to recent stories in the *Wall Street Journal*, this pricing tactic no longer works. Explain carefully, using graphical analysis, why continued increases in the price of cigarettes eventually becomes an ineffective means of raising revenues.

5. As part of his plan to reduce the budget deficit, President Clinton proposed raising the excise tax on gasoline by 50 cents per gallon. While passage of this proposal was blocked by Congress, what would have happened to the sales of gasoline if the price of gasoline were to rise by 45 cents per gallon (i.e., producers cannot pass the entire 50-cent tax increase on to consumers)? Assume that the average price of gasoline is now $1.30 per gallon and use the short-run price elasticity for gasoline presented in Illustration 6.2 (page 235 of the text) to answer this question. Would you have expected consumers' total expenditure on gasoline to have risen or fallen had Clinton's proposed 50-cent-per-gallon excise tax been enacted? Explain.

6. One way to reduce the amount consumers spend on health care is to raise the price of health care by increasing the health insurance copayment (i.e., the portion of the price patients must pay themselves). At current copayment levels, if the price elasticity of demand for visits to see the doctor is –0.25, by what percentage will the quantity demanded of doctor visits decrease if the copayment is raised from 20 percent to 25 percent? (Be careful, the percentage change in price is *not* 5 percent in this problem.)

Demand Estimation and Forecasting

Learning Objectives

After reading Chapter 7 and working the problems for Chapter 7 in the textbook and in this Workbook, you should be able to:

➤ Specify an empirical demand function—both linear and nonlinear functional forms.

➤ Distinguish between "market-determined" and "manager-determined" prices and know whether to use the ordinary least-squares (OLS) or the two-stage least-squares (2SLS) method to estimate demand.

➤ For price-taking firms that face market-determined prices, you will learn to:

  ▪ determine whether the industry demand and supply function are identified.
  ▪ estimate industry demand (and supply) using two-stage least-squares (2SLS)

➤ For price-setting firms that face manager-determined prices, you will learn to:

  ▪ use the ordinary least-squares (OLS) method to estimate individual firms' demand functions.

➤ Forecast demand using time-series regression analysis.

➤ Employ dummy variables to account for cyclical or seasonal variation in sales.

➤ Forecast future sales and prices using econometric models that employ simultaneous equations for demand and supply.

➤ Discuss and explain several important problems that arise when using statistical methods to forecast demand.

Essential Concepts

1. *Empirical demand functions* are demand equations derived from actual market data. Empirical demand functions are extremely useful in making pricing and production decisions.

2. In *linear* form, an empirical demand function can be specified as

$$Q = a + bP + cM + dP_R$$

where Q is the quantity demanded, P is the price of the good or service, M is consumer income, and P_R is the price of some related good R.

In the linear form, $b = \Delta Q/\Delta P$, $c = \Delta Q/\Delta M$, and $d = \Delta Q/\Delta P_R$. The expected signs of the coefficients are: (1) b is expected to be negative, (2) if good X is normal (inferior), c is expected to be positive (negative), (3) if related good R is a substitute (complement), d is expected to be positive (negative).

The estimated elasticities of demand are computed as

$$\hat{E} = \hat{b}\,\frac{P}{Q} \qquad \hat{E}_M = \hat{c}\,\frac{M}{Q} \qquad \hat{E}_{XR} = \hat{d}\,\frac{P_R}{Q}$$

3. When demand is specified in *log-linear* form, the demand function can be written as

$$Q = aP^b M^c P_R^d$$

To estimate a log-linear demand function, the above equation must be converted to logarithms:

$$\ln Q = \ln a + b \ln P + c \ln M + d \ln P_R$$

In this log-linear form, the elasticities of demand are constant: $\hat{E} = \hat{b}$, $\hat{E}_M = \hat{c}$, and $\hat{E}_{XR} = \hat{d}$

4. The method of estimating the parameters of an empirical demand function depends on whether the price of the product is *market-determined* or *manager-determined*. Managers of price-taking firms do not set the price of the product they sell; rather, prices are endogenous or "market-determined" by the intersection of demand and supply. Managers of price-setting firms set the price of the product they sell by producing the quantity associated with the chosen price on the downward sloping demand curve facing the firm. Since price is manager-determined rather than market-determined, price is exogenous for price-setting firms.

5. When estimating industry demand for price-taking firms, the *problem of simultaneity* must be addressed. The simultaneity problem arises because the observed variation in equilibrium output and price is the result of changes in the determinants of both demand and supply. Because output and price are determined jointly by the forces of supply and demand, two econometric problems arise when a researcher tries to estimate the coefficients of demand: (i) the *identification problem* and (ii) the *simultaneous equations bias* problem.

    (i)   An industry demand equation is identified when it is possible to estimate the true demand function from a sample of observations of equilibrium output and price. Industry demand is identified when supply includes at least one exogenous variable that is not also in the demand equation.

    (ii) When market price is an endogenous variable, price will be correlated with the random error term in the demand equation, causing a simultaneous equations bias if the ordinary least-squares (OLS) method of estimation is applied. To avoid simultaneous equations bias, the two-stage least-squares method of estimation (2SLS) can be employed if the industry demand equation is identified.

6. The following steps, which are discussed in detail in the textbook (pp. 260–62), can be followed to estimate an industry demand function for a price-taking firm:

    Step 1: Specify the industry demand and supply equations.

Step 2: Check for identification of industry demand.

Step 3: Collect data for the variables in demand and supply.

Step 4: Estimate industry demand using 2SLS.

7. When a firm is a price-setting firm, the problem of simultaneity vanishes, and the demand curve for the firm can be estimated using the ordinary least-squares method of estimation. The following steps, which are discussed in detail in the textbook (pp. 264–69), can be followed to estimate the demand function for a price-setting firm:

    Step 1: Specify the price-setting firm's demand function.

    Step 2: Collect data for the variables in demand function.

    Step 3: Estimate the firm's demand using OLS.

8. A time-series model shows how a time-ordered sequence of observations on a variable, such as price or output, is generated. The simplest form of time-series forecasting is linear trend forecasting. In a linear trend model, sales in each time period (Q_t) are assumed to be linearly related to time (t):

    $$Q_t = a + bt$$

    and regression analysis is used to estimate the values of a and b. If $b > 0$, sales are increasing over time, and if $b < 0$, sales are decreasing. If $b = 0$, then sales are constant over time. The statistical significance of a trend is determined testing $\hat{b}$ for statistical significance or by examining the p-value for $\hat{b}$.

9. *Seasonal or cyclical variation* can bias the estimation of a and b in linear trend models. In order to account for seasonal variation in trend analysis, *dummy variables* are added to the trend equation. Dummy variables serve to shift the trend line up or down according to the particular seasonal pattern encountered. The significance of seasonal behavior is determined by using a t-test or p-value for the estimated coefficient on the dummy variable.

10. When using dummy variables to account for N seasonal time periods, $N-1$ dummy variables are added to the linear trend. Each dummy variable accounts for one of the seasonal time periods. The dummy variable takes a value of 1 for those observations that occur during the season assigned to that dummy variable, and a value of 0 otherwise.

11. Econometric models are statistical models that use an explicit model of the economic structure of a marketplace to explain and forecast the values of economic variables that are endogenous to the model. The technique of forecasting with simultaneous equations employs an estimated demand function and an estimated supply function to produce a forecasted value for sales (and price). The procedure can be summarized as follows:

    Step 1: The current (or prevailing) demand and supply functions are estimated using currently available data. Both equations must be identified, and both are estimated using two-stage least-squares (2SLS).

    Step 2: Future (forecasted) values of the exogenous variables are obtained either by estimation (e.g., linear trend forecasting) or from one of the forecasting models used by government agencies or private firms. The forecasted values of the exogenous variables are substituted into the demand and supply equations to obtain equations in the forecast period.

Step 3: The intersection of the future demand and supply equations is found. The values of P and Q at the intersection are the forecast values of sales and price for that period in the future.

12. The following problems and limitations are inherent in forecasting:

i. The further into the future the forecast is made, the wider is the confidence interval or region of uncertainty.

ii. If the model is misspecified by either excluding an important variable or by using an inappropriate functional form, then the reliability of the forecast will be reduced.

iii. Forecasts are incapable of predicting sharp changes that occur because of structural changes in the market itself.

Matching Definitions

dummy variable
econometric models
empirical demand functions
endogenous variable
exogenous variable
identification of demand
ordinary least-squares (OLS)
reduced-form equation

representative sample
response bias
seasonal or cyclical variation
simultaneity problem
simultaneous equations bias
time-series model
two-stage least-squares (2SLS)

1. _____ Demand equations derived from actual market data.

2. _____ A sample that has the same characteristics as the population as a whole.

3. _____ The difference between the response given by an individual to a hypothetical question and the action the individual takes when the situation actually occurs.

4. _____ A variable that is determined by a system of equations.

5. _____ A variable in a system of equations whose value is determined outside the system.

6. _____ Another name for standard regression analysis.

7. _____ A problem in estimating market demand that arises because variation in observed values of market quantity and price are simultaneously determined by changes in both supply and demand.

8. _____ An equation that expresses an endogenous variable as a function of the exogenous variables and random error terms.

9. _____ Determining whether the sample data will trace out the true demand curve.

10. _____ A method of estimating parameters of demand when price is endogenous or market-determined.

11. _____ A bias in estimating regression parameters that occurs when ordinary least squares (OLS) is used to estimate parameters of an equation for which one or more of the explanatory variables is an endogenous variable.

12. _____ A statistical model that uses only a time-series of observations on a variable to make forecasts of future values of the variable.

13. _____ The regular variation that time-series data frequently exhibits.

14. _____ A variable that can take only the value of 0 or 1.

15. _____ Statistical models that use an explicit structural model to explain the underlying economic relations.

Study Problems

1. Under what circumstances is it appropriate to estimate demand using the method of two-stage least-squares (2SLS)?

2. Suppose both the quantity demanded and the quantity supplied are specified to be functions of price only:

   $$Demand:\ Q = a + bP$$

   $$Supply:\ \ \ Q = e + fP$$

   a. Can you estimate this demand function using regression analysis? Why or why not?

   b. Suppose you added income (M) to the demand specification:

   $$Demand:\ Q = a + bP + cM$$

   Is demand identified now? Why or why not?

   c. Suppose that the price of labor (P_w) is added to the supply specification:

   $$Supply:\ \ \ Q = e + fP + gP_w$$

   Is demand identified now? Why or why not?

3. Under what circumstances is it appropriate to estimate demand using the method of ordinary least-squares (OLS)?

4. The following industry demand function for good X was estimated using 2SLS:

   $$Q = a + bP + cM + dP_R$$

   The demand function was first identified by specifying the supply function. The estimation results are:

Two-Stage Least-Squares Estimation				
DEPENDENT VARIABLE: QX				
OBSERVATIONS: 275				
VARIABLE	PARAMETER ESTIMATE	STANDARD ERROR	T-RATIO	P-VALUE
INTERCEPT	9500.4	3350.6	2.84	0.0049
P	−12.75	4.30	−2.87	0.0044
M	−0.0163	0.0066	−2.49	0.0135
PR	5.05	1.10	4.59	0.0001

   a. Is the sign of $\hat{b}$ as we would have predicted? Why or why not?

   b. Is this good normal or inferior good? Explain.

   c. Are goods X and R substitutes or complements? Explain.

   d. Which coefficients are significant at the 5 percent level of significance? Explain.

e. Using the values $P = \$20$, $M = \$50,000$, and $P_R = \$100$, calculate estimates of the following:

(i) The price elasticity of demand is _____.

(ii) The cross-price elasticity of demand is _____.

(iii) The income elasticity of demand is _____.

5. Consider the following nonlinear demand function, which is estimated for a price-setting firm. The method of least-squares is used to estimate the parameters.

$$Q = aP^b M^c P_R^d$$

The results of the estimation are:

DEPENDENT VARIABLE:	LNQ	R-SQUARE	F-RATIO	P-VALUE ON F	
OBSERVATIONS:	26	0.9248	90.18	0.0001	
VARIABLE		PARAMETER ESTIMATE	STANDARD ERROR	T-RATIO	P-VALUE
INTERCEPT		3.04	1.01	3.01	0.0064
LNP		−1.90	0.48	−3.96	0.0007
LNM		2.16	0.675	3.20	0.0041
LNPR		0.78	0.169	4.62	0.0001

a. Before the nonlinear demand equation can be estimated using regression analysis, the demand equation must be transformed into the following linear form:

$\ln Q =$ _____.

b. Are the parameter estimates statistically significant at the 5 percent level of significance?

c. The estimated value of a is equal to _____.

d. Is this good a normal or inferior good?

e. Is this good a substitute or complement with respect to related good R?

f. Compute estimates of the following elasticities:

(i) The price elasticity of demand is _____.

(ii) The income elasticity of demand is _____.

(iii) The cross-price elasticity of demand is _____.

g. A 23.15 percent decrease in household income, holding all other things constant, will cause quantity demanded to _____ (increase, decrease) by _____ percent.

h. All else constant, a 4 percent increase in price causes quantity demanded to _____ (increase, decrease) by _____ percent.

i. A 12.82 percent decrease in the price of R, holding all other things constant, will cause quantity demanded to _____ (increase, decrease) by _____ percent.

6. For the past 12 months you have been the night manager of Dixie Fried Chicken. In order to evaluate your performance as a manager, your boss estimates the following linear trend equation for nighttime sales (Q_t) over the last 12 months ($t = 1,..,12$):

$$Q_t = a + bt$$

where Q_t is the number of pieces of chicken sold nightly. The results of the regression are as follows:

DEPENDENT VARIABLE: QT	R-SQUARE	F-RATIO	P-VALUE ON F	
OBSERVATIONS: 12	0.8991	89.108	0.0001	
VARIABLE	PARAMETER ESTIMATE	STANDARD ERROR	T-RATIO	P-VALUE
INTERCEPT	175.0	38.88	4.50	0.0011
T	16.0	6.4	2.50	0.0314

a. Evaluate the statistical significance of the estimated coefficients. Does this estimation indicate a significant trend, either upward or downward, in sales during your tenure as night manager?

b. Perform an F-test for significance of the trend equation at the 5 percent level of significance.

c. If your boss uses the estimated linear trend to forecast your sales for months 14 and 16, how many units does he expect you to sell in these months?

$\hat{Q}_{t=14} = $ _____ and $\hat{Q}_{t=16} = $ _____

d. Comment on the precision of these two forecasts.

7. Suppose you manage the pro shop at a golf club in Miami and would like to be able to forecast the number of golf cart rentals on a quarterly basis. A simple linear trend model must account for the fact that demand for golf carts is always higher in the winter quarters (quarters 1 and 4) as tourists from northern states vacation in Florida. You decide to estimate the following equation:

$$Q_t = a + bt + cD$$

where D is a dummy variable equal to 1 for quarters 1 and 4, and zero otherwise. Using quarterly data from 2001–2004 ($t = 1,...,16$), you obtain the following estimation results:

DEPENDENT VARIABLE: QT	R-SQUARE	F-RATIO	P-VALUE ON F	
OBSERVATIONS: 16	0.9510	126.153	0.0001	
VARIABLE	PARAMETER ESTIMATE	STANDARD ERROR	T-RATIO	P-VALUE
INTERCEPT	3471.23	901.61	3.85	0.0020
T	−6.10	1.80	−3.39	0.0048
D	870.18	133.87	6.50	0.0001

a. Perform t- and F- tests to check for statistical significance (at the 99 percent confidence level) of the individual parameter estimates and the equation.

b. Is the downward trend in golf cart rentals statistically significant?

c. Calculate the intercept for winter quarters and summer quarters. What do the values imply?

d. Use the estimated equation to forecast golf cart rentals in the four quarters of 2005.

8. The following demand and supply functions are specified for the U.S. housing market:

Demand: $\quad\quad Q_H = a + bP_H + cM + dP_A + eR$

Supply: $\quad\quad Q_H = f + gP_H + hP_M$

The variables are measured in the following way:

Q_H = thousands of new homes sold
P_H = the median price of a new home in thousands of dollars
M = the median household income
P_A = the median monthly rental rate on apartments
R = the mortgage interest rate
P_M = an index of building materials prices

Using quarterly data for the period 1995I through 2004I, these equations are estimated using 2SLS:

Demand: $\quad\quad Q_H = 504,500 - 10.0P_H + 5M + 500P_A - 11,750R$

Supply: $\quad\quad Q_H = 326,000 + 15.0P_H - 1,800P_M.$

The predicted values for the exogenous variables for the first quarter of 2005 are obtained from a private econometrics firm. The predicted values are:

$M = \$52,000 \quad\quad P_A = \$400 \quad\quad R = 14\% \quad\quad P_M = 320$

a. Are the signs of the estimated coefficients as would be expected? Explain why for each one.

b. Forecast the price of housing in 2005I.

c. Forecast the sales of housing in 2005I.

Computer Problem

Use a computer regression package, such as the Student Edition of Statistix 8, and the following annual data for rutabagas in the United States to work this computer problem.

Year	Q	P	A	W
1980	4,459,637	4.5	49,500	115.6
1981	4,612,484	6.3	50,250	113.0
1982	4,941,674	7.9	49,000	110.5
1983	4,660,353	2.6	49,750	121.8
1984	5,272,535	7.4	54,000	118.2
1985	4,973,639	13.6	60,250	105.9
1986	5,439,800	8.2	48,250	112.9
1987	5,447,964	9.9	60,100	118.2
1988	5,428,675	12.7	62,750	113.4
1989	5,789,963	15.2	65,400	112.1
1990	5,238,036	11.5	58,500	111.6
1991	5,567,663	14.9	66,300	111.8
1992	5,150,214	15.3	67,800	109.0
1993	6,109,218	12.1	66,000	122.3
1994	5,746,473	19.1	72,250	107.8
1995	4,707,301	10.5	55,000	107.2
1996	5,365,661	7.1	53,400	119.1
1997	5,938,797	23.0	80,164	106.0
1998	6,125,474	19.1	84,000	119.7
1999	5,936,636	9.6	56,500	119.6
2000	5,131,297	12.3	62,000	111.6

Q is the number of pounds of rutabagas produced and sold annually in the United States, P is the inflation-adjusted price of rutabagas (in cents per pound), A is the inflation-adjusted annual expenditure on advertising (in dollars per year) by the American Rutabaga Growers Association (ARGA), and W is a weather index based on temperature and rainfall in the primary rutabaga-growing regions (W varies directly with conduciveness of weather for growing rutabagas).

a. Given the data provided in the table above, specify a linear empirical demand function for rutabagas in the United States:

   $Q =$ _____.

b. Should you use the ordinary least-squares (OLS) method or the two-stage least-squares (2SLS) method for estimating the market demand for rutabagas? Explain.

c. Given the data provided in the table above, specify a linear empirical supply function for rutabagas that will ensure the demand function specified in part *a* is identified:

$$Q = \underline{\hspace{6cm}}.$$

d. Using your statistical software, estimate the parameters of the empirical demand function specified in part *a*. Write your estimated demand for rutabagas:

$$\hat{Q}_d = \underline{\hspace{6cm}}.$$

Are the estimated slope parameters statistically significant at the 10 percent level?

e. What is the price elasticity of demand for rutabagas measured at the sample mean values of price and advertising? Is the demand for rutabagas elastic, inelastic, or unitary elastic when measured at the sample mean values of P and A? By approximately what percentage amount would the price of rutabagas have to fall in order for quantity demanded to increase by 5 percent?

f. What is the advertising elasticity of demand for rutabagas measured at the sample mean values of price and advertising? Approximately what percentage change in advertising would cause demand for rutabagas to increase by 5 percent?

g. Should you use the ordinary least-squares (OLS) method or the two-stage least-squares method (2SLS) method for estimating the market supply for rutabagas? Explain.

h. Using your statistical software, estimate the linear supply function that you suggested in part *c*. Your estimated supply equation for rutabagas is:

$$\hat{Q}_s = \underline{\hspace{6cm}}.$$

Are the estimated parameters statistically significant at the 10 percent level? At the 5 percent level?

i. You expect ARGA (the American Rutabaga Growers Association) to spend $75,000 (inflation adjusted) on advertising in 2006. Meteorological forecasts indicate the weather index for 2006 is likely to be 118.5. Forecast the market price and market output of rutabagas for 2006.

Multiple Choice / True-False

1. Which of the following is NOT a major problem inherent in forecasting?
    a. The further an exogenous variable is from its sample mean value, the less precise the forecast.
    b. Predicted values of exogenous variables are very difficult to find.
    c. Misspecifying the empirical demand equation can seriously reduce forecast accuracy.
    d. Structural changes in the economy can cause forecasts to completely miss abrupt changes in the value of the predicted variable.

2. If the demand curve is stable and the supply curve is shifting, estimation of $Q = a + bP$ will result in estimation of
    a. demand.
    b. supply.
    c. neither demand nor supply.
    d. both demand and supply.

3. In the following demand-supply system

    $$Demand: \qquad Q = a + bP + cM$$
    $$Supply: \qquad Q = d + eP + fP_L$$

    a. neither of the equations are identified.
    b. the demand function is identified but the supply function is not.
    c. the supply function is identified but the demand function is not.
    d. both equations are identified.

4. An identification problem will arise when
    a. the demand function is specified to be linear.
    b. the demand function includes too many exogenous variables.
    c. sample observations are the result of simultaneous interaction of supply and demand.
    d. the firm is a price-setting firm.

5. Two-stage least-squares estimation
    a. can only be used to estimate the parameters of an identified equation.
    b. eliminates the need to identify demand.
    c. produces parameter estimates that can be tested for statistical significance using the usual t-test or p-values.
    d. both a and c.
    e. both b and c.

In questions 6–12, suppose the following nonlinear demand function is estimated using 2SLS:

$$Q = aP^b M^c P_y^d$$

The estimation results are:

Two-Stage Least-Squares Estimation				
DEPENDENT VARIABLE: LNQ				
OBSERVATIONS: 44				
VARIABLE	PARAMETER ESTIMATE	STANDARD ERROR	T-RATIO	P-VALUE
INTERCEPT	-2.00	0.40	-5.00	0.0001
LNP	-1.10	0.44	-2.50	0.0166
LNM	2.40	0.60	4.00	0.0003
LNPR	-0.20	0.05	-4.00	0.0003

6. Which of the following supply equations result in the demand equation being identified?
   a. $Q = eP + fM + gP_y$
   b. $Q = eP + fM + gP_y + hZ$
   c. $\ln Q = \ln e + f \ln P + g \ln W$
   d. both b and c

7. These estimates indicate that the demand for the good is
   a. price inelastic since $\hat{E} = -1.10$.
   b. price elastic since $\hat{E} = -1.10$.
   c. price inelastic since $\hat{E} = -2.5$.
   d. price elastic since $\hat{E} = -2.5$.

8. The estimated own price elasticity of demand is
   a. statistically significant at the 5 percent significance level since $|-2.5| > 2.021$.
   b. *not* statistically significant at the 5 percent significance level since $0.004 < 2.021$.
   c. statistically significant at the 5 percent significance level since $|-2.5| > 2.000$.
   d. *not* statistically significant at the 5 percent significance level since $2.6 < 2.721$.

9. The estimates indicate that the income elasticity of demand is
   a. -0.20.
   b. -2.0.
   c. 2.4.
   d. 4.0.

10. The estimate of the cross-price elasticity indicates that the two goods are
    a. normal goods.
    b. substitute goods.
    c. inferior goods.
    d. complementary goods.
    e. none of the above.

11. According to the estimated demand equation, if the price of Y rises by 25 percent, then quantity demanded will
    a. increase by 5 percent.
    b. decrease by 5 percent.
    c. increase by 6 percent.
    d. decrease by 6 percent.

12. From the above estimates, we would expect quantity demanded to rise by 30 percent if income
    a. rises by 12.5 percent.
    b. rises by 8 percent.
    c. falls by 0.08 percent.
    d. falls by 125 percent.

13. Demand equations derived from actual market data are
    a. empirical demand functions.
    b. never estimated using consumer interviews.
    c. frequently estimated using regression analysis.
    d. both a and c.
    e. all of the above.

14. If demand is estimated using the empirical specification
    $$\ln Q = \ln a + b \ln P + c \ln M + d \ln P_R$$
    then an equivalent expression for demand is
    a. $\ln Q = a + bP + cM + dP_R$.
    b. $Q = a + bP + cM + dP_R$.
    c. $Q = e^a + bP + cM + dP_R$.
    d. $Q = abPcMdP_R$.
    e. none of the above.

15. For a linear demand function, $Q = a + bP + cM + dP_R$, the income elasticity is
    a. c.
    b. $c(M/Q)$.
    c. $c(Q/M)$.
    d. $-c$.
    e. $-c(Q/P_R)$.

16. A representative sample
    a. eliminates the problem of response bias.
    b. reflects the characteristics of the population.
    c. is frequently a random sample.
    d. both b and c.
    e. all of the above.

17. Why can we estimate the demand for a price-setting firm using ordinary least-squares whereas estimating market demand requires the two-stage least-squares method?
    a. For a firm, there are always exogenous variables in supply but not demand.
    b. For a firm, there are always exogenous variables in demand but not supply.
    c. The manager of the firm sets the price, so there is no simultaneity problem.
    d. both *a* and *c*.
    e. both *b* and *c*.

18. A market-determined price
    a. is determined by the manager of a firm.
    b. is determined by the intersection of demand and supply curves.
    c. is an endogenous variable.
    d. both *a* and *b*.
    e. both *b* and *c*.

19. Manager-determined prices are
    a. not determined by the forces of demand and supply.
    b. exogenous variables in a demand equations.
    c. associated with price-taking firms.
    d. both *a* and *b*.
    e. both *b* and *c*.

20. When price is endogenously determined
    a. two-stage least-squares (2SLS) estimation of parameters is appropriate.
    b. ordinary least-squares (OLS) estimation of parameters is appropriate.
    c. the problem of simultaneity arises.
    d. both *a* and *c*.
    e. both *b* and *c*.

The next 11 questions refer to the following:

The manufacturer of Cabbage Patch dolls used quarterly price data for the period $1997I - 2005IV$ ($t = 1, ..., 36$) and the regression equation
$$P_t = a + bt + c_1 D_1 + c_2 D_2 + c_3 D_3$$
to forecast doll prices in the year 2006. P_t is quarterly prices of dolls, and D_1, D_2, and D_3 are dummy variables for quarters *I*, *II*, and *III*, respectively.

DEPENDENT VARIABLE:	PT	R-SQUARE	F-RATIO	P-VALUE ON F	
OBSERVATIONS:	36	0.9078	76.34	0.0001	
VARIABLE		PARAMETER ESTIMATE	STANDARD ERROR	T-RATIO	P-VALUE
INTERCEPT		24.0	6.20	3.87	0.0005
T		0.800	0.240	3.33	0.0022
D1		–8.00	2.60	–3.08	0.0043
D2		–6.00	1.80	–3.33	0.0022
D3		–4.00	0.60	–6.67	0.0001

21. At the 2 percent level of significance, is there a statistically significant trend in price of dolls?
    a. Yes, because $0.0022 < 0.02$.
    b. No, because $0.0022 > 0.02$.
    c. Yes, because $0.800 > 0.02$.
    d. Yes, because $0.240 > 0.02$.
    e. Yes, because $3.33 > 0.02$.

22. The estimated *quarterly* increase in price is _____, and the estimated *annual* increase in price is _____ .
    a. $1.50; $6.00
    b. $1.40; $4.00
    c. $0.60; $2.40
    d. $0.80; $3.20
    e. none of the above

23. What is the estimated intercept of the trend line in the first quarter?
    a. 24
    b. −8
    c. 32
    d. 16
    e. none of the above

24. What is the estimated intercept of the trend line in the fourth quarter?
    a. 22.8
    b. 16
    c. 18
    d. 20
    e. none of the above

25. At the 2 percent level of significance, the estimation results indicate that price in the _____ quarter is significantly higher than in any other quarter.
    a. first
    b. second
    c. third
    d. fourth

26. At the 2 percent level of significance, the results indicate that price in the _____ quarter is significantly lower than in any other quarter.
    a. first
    b. second
    c. third
    d. fourth

27. In any given year price tends to vary as follows:
    a. $P_I > P_{II} > P_{III} > P_{IV}$
    b. $P_I > P_{IV} > P_{III} > P_{II}$
    c. $P_{II} > P_{III} > P_{IV} > P_I$
    d. $P_{III} > P_I > P_{II} > P_{IV}$
    e. $P_{IV} > P_{III} > P_{II} > P_I$

28. Using the estimated time-series regression, predicted price in the first quarter of 2006 is
    a. $53.60.
    b. $45.60.
    c. $56.00.
    d. $37.60.
    e. none of the above

29. Using the estimated time-series regression, predicted price in the second quarter of 2006 is
    a. $48.40
    b. $54.40
    c. $40.40
    d. $51.40
    e. none of the above

30. Using the estimated time-series regression, predicted price in the third quarter of 2006 is
    a. $55.20.
    b. $47.20.
    c. $58.00.
    d. $56.00.
    e. none of the above

31. Using the estimated time-series regression, predicted price in the fourth quarter of 2006 is
    a. $48.
    b. $50.
    c. $52.
    d. $56.
    e. none of the above

In questions 32–34, use the following estimates of the market supply and demand functions:

Demand: $Q_d = 16,000 - 20,000P + 4M$

Supply: $Q_s = 80,000 + 15,000P - 7,000P_1$

From a macroeconomic forecast, the predicted values for M and P_1 in 2006 are:

$\hat{M}_{2006} = 16,000$ and $\hat{P}_{I,2006} = 10$.

32. What is your price forecast for 2006?
    a. $1
    b. $2
    c. $3
    d. $4
    e. $5

33. What is your sales forecast for 2006?
    a. 10,000 units
    b. 20,000 units
    c. 30,000 units
    d. 40,000 units
    e. 50,000 units

34. If the 2006 forecast for P_1 had been 5, what would be your sales forecast for 2006?
    a. 60,000 units
    b. 70,000 units
    c. 80,000 units
    d. 90,000 units
    e. 100,000 units

35. T F In a simultaneous equations model containing a supply and a demand equation, both equations are identified if each one contains at least one exogenous variable that is not in the other equation.

36. T F Two-stage least-squares estimation cannot be used to estimate demand unless both supply and demand are identified.

37. T F Time-series models use the past behavior of sales to predict the future value of sales.

38. T F Dummy variables can only be used for adjusting time-series models for cyclical variations.

39. T F In the linear trend model of sales $Q_t = a + bt$, a negative value of b is, by itself, evidence of a downward trend in sales.

40. T F Time-series forecasting is too simple to be useful in real-world forecasting.

Answers

MATCHING DEFINITIONS

1.	empirical demand functions	11.	simultaneous equations bias
2.	representative sample	12.	time-series model
3.	response bias	13.	seasonal or cyclical variation
4.	endogenous variable	14.	dummy variable
5.	exogenous variable	15.	econometric models
6.	ordinary least-squares (OLS)		
7.	simultaneity problem		
8.	reduced-form equation		
9.	identification of demand		
10.	two-stage least-squares (2SLS)		

STUDY PROBLEMS

1. 2SLS is required when the firm is a price-taking firm because price is determined by the intersection of demand and supply curves. Since P is an endogenous variable, the problem of simultaneity arises. 2SLS eliminates the bias that would occur if OLS were used in this situation.

2. a. No. The demand equation is not identified.

   b. No. Identification of demand requires the supply equation to contain at least one exogenous variable not included in the demand equation. In this case, the demand equation contains an exogenous variable not included in the supply equation.

   c. Yes. Now supply contains an exogenous variable not included in the demand equation.

3. OLS is appropriate when the firm is a price-setting firm. In this case, movement along demand is caused not by shifts in an industry supply curve, but rather by the decisions made by the firm. Consequently, P is not an endogenous variable in a system of demand and supply equations.

4. a. Yes, Q should be inversely related to P along a demand curve.

   b. Inferior. Since $\hat{c}$ is negative, X is an inferior good.

   c. Substitutes. Since $\hat{d}$ $(= \Delta Q/\Delta P)$ is positive, goods X and R must be substitutes.

   d. The critical value of t for $n - k = 275 - 4 = 271$ degrees of freedom and the 5 percent level of significance is (approximately) 1.96. Since $|t| > 1.96$ for all four t-ratios, all four parameters are statistically significant. Also, the p-values are all smaller than 0.05, which indicates exact levels of significance smaller than 5%.

   e. $\hat{Q} = 8,942$ at $P = 20$, $M = 50,000$, $P_R = 100$

      (i) $\hat{E} = -0.028$ $[= -12.35 \times (20/8,942)]$

      (ii) $\hat{E}_{XR} = 0.056$ $[= 5.05 \times (100/8,942)]$

      (iii) $\hat{E}_M = -0.091$ $[= -0.0163 \times (50,000/8,942)]$

5. a. $\ln Q = \ln a + b\ln P + c\ln M + d\ln P_R$

   b. Yes, the absolute values of all t-ratios are greater than 2.074.

   c. $\hat{a} = e^{3.04} = 20.905$

d. The estimated value of c is positive, and significant, indicating this good is a normal good.

e. The estimated value of d is positive, and significant, indicating the two goods are substitutes.

    (i) $\hat{E} = \hat{b} = -1.90$

    (ii) $\hat{E}_M = \hat{c} = 2.16$

    (iii) $\hat{E}_{XR} = \hat{d} = 0.78$

f. decrease; 50%

g. decrease; 7.60%

h. decrease; 10%

6. a. $\hat{a}$: p-value is 0.0011, so $\hat{a}$ is statistically significant at better than the 1% level of significance (or 99% level of confidence). The probability that $a = 0$ (i.e., a Type I error) is quite small, about one-tenth of 1 percent.
$\hat{b}$: p-value is 0.0314, so $\hat{b}$ is statistically significant at the 5% level of significance (or 95% level of confidence). The probability that $b = 0$ is small, about a 3 percent chance.
Conclusion: Sales exhibit a statistically significant positive trend over time (i.e., $\hat{b} > 0$ and its p-value is acceptably small). The model as a whole is also explaining a statistically significant amount of the total variation in sales, as indicated by the very small p-value for the F-ratio.

b. From the F-table, $F_{1,10} = 4.96$. Since the calculated F-ratio is 89.108, the equation is significant at the 95 percent confidence level or 5 percent significance level.

c. $\hat{Q}_{14} = 175 + 16 \times 14 = 399$

   $\hat{Q}_{16} = 175 + 16 \times 16 = 431$

d. We would expect the confidence interval to be smaller for the forecast of sales in the 14th month because 14 is closer to the sample mean value of t ($\bar{t} = 6.5$) than is 16.

7. a. $t_{\hat{a}} = 3.85 > 3.012 \Rightarrow \hat{a}$ is statistically significant.
$\left| t_{\hat{b}} \right| = \left| -3.39 \right| > 3.012 \Rightarrow \hat{b}$ is statistically significant.
$t_{\hat{c}} = 6.5 > 3.012 \Rightarrow \hat{c}$ is statistically significant.
The calculated value of F of $126.153 > F_{2,13} = 6.70 \Rightarrow$ the equation as a whole is statistically significant.

b. Yes; the exact level of significance is 0.48% $\Rightarrow$ virtually no chance of committing a Type I error (finding significance when there is none).

c. The winter intercept $= \hat{a} + \hat{c} = 4341.41$.

The summer (i.e., "other" months) intercept $= \hat{a} = 3471.23$.

Since $\hat{c}$ is positive and statistically significant, the regression indicates that golf cart rentals increase in winter months (despite the overall downward trend in rentals).

d. First quarter 2005: $Q_{17} = 3{,}471.23 - 6.10(17) + 870.18(1) = 4{,}237.71$

Second quarter 2005: $Q_{18} = 3{,}471.23 - 6.10(18) + 870.18(0) = 3{,}361.43$

Third quarter 2005: $Q_{19} = 3{,}471.23 - 6.10(19) + 870.18(0) = 3{,}355.33$

Fourth quarter 2005: $Q_{20} = 3{,}471.23 - 6.10(20) + 870.18(1) = 4{,}219.41$

8.   a.   Yes. We would expect quantity demanded to be inversely related to the price of housing and mortgage interest rates, and directly related to income and the price of apartments. We would expect the quantity supplied to be directly related to the price of housing and inversely related to the price of building materials.

b and *c*.

Step 1:   Estimates of supply and demand are already done for you.

Step 2:   Demand:

$$\hat{Q}_H = 504,500 - 10.0P_H + 5(52,000) + 500(400) - 11,750(14)$$
$$= 800,000 - 10.0P_H$$

Supply:

$$\hat{Q}_H = 326,000 + 15P_H - 1,800(320)$$
$$= -250,000 + 15P_H$$

Step 3:   Find the intersection of supply and demand.

$$800,000 - 10P_H = -250,000 + 15P_H$$
$$1,050,000 = 25P_H$$
$$42,000 = P_H$$

and
$$Q_H = 800,000 - 10(42,000) = 380,000$$

So, P_{2005I} = \$42,000 and Q_{2005I} = 380,000 new homes per quarter

COMPUTER PROBLEM

a.   For the variables provided in the dataset, the most appropriate linear specification of demand is $Q_d = a + bP + cA$.

b.   Since rutabaga prices are determined by market forces of demand and supply, the demand for rutabagas should be estimated using 2SLS.

c. $Q_s = d + eP + fW$

d. $\hat{Q}_d = 1,378,514 - 105,420P + 85.5049A$

The two-stage least-squares computer printout looks like this:

	Two-Stage Least-Squares Estimation				
DEP. VARIABLE:	Q				
OBS:	21				
VARIABLE		PARAMETER ESTIMATE	STD. ERROR	T-RATIO	P-VALUE
INTERCEPT		1378514	1179956	1.17	0.2579
P		−105420	59748.1	−1.76	0.0946
A		85.5049	29.9106	2.86	0.0104

Both slope parameter estimates, $\hat{b}$ and $\hat{c}$, are statistically significant at the 10 percent level (see the *p*-values in the printout above).

e.   Use your software program to compute sample means for Q, P, and A. (You will need the sample mean of A in part *f*.) The sample mean values $\bar{Q}$, $\bar{P}$, and $\bar{A}$ are, respectively, 5,335,000, 11.562, and 60,532. The estimated price elasticity of demand for rutabagas is computed as follows:

$$\hat{E} = \hat{b}\frac{\overline{P}}{\overline{Q}} = -105420\frac{11.562}{5335000} = -0.2285$$

So, rutabaga demand is estimated to be inelastic. The price of rutabagas must fall by approximately 21.88 percent in order for sales of rutabagas to increase by 5 percent:

$$-0.2285 = \frac{+5\%}{\%\Delta P} \quad \Rightarrow \quad \%\Delta P = -21.88\%$$

f. The estimated advertising elasticity of demand for rutabagas is computed as follows:

$$\hat{E}_A = \hat{c}\frac{\overline{A}}{\overline{Q}} = 85.5046\frac{60532}{5335000} = 0.970$$

Rutabaga advertising must increase by approximately 5.15 percent in order for sales of rutabagas to increase by 5 percent:

$$0.970 = \frac{+5\%}{\%\Delta A} \quad \Rightarrow \quad \%\Delta A = 5.15\%$$

g. Since rutabaga prices are determined by market forces of demand and supply, the supply for rutabagas should be estimated using 2SLS.

h. Your estimated supply equation is $\hat{Q}_s = -2,562,672 + 87,214.0P + 60,605.7W$, which comes from the following 2SLS regression printout:

Two-Stage Least-Squares Estimation				
DEP. VARIABLE: Q				
OBS: 21				
VARIABLE	PARAMETER ESTIMATE	STD. ERROR	T-RATIO	P-VALUE
INTERCEPT	-2562672	1413288	-1.81	0.0865
P	87214.0	12119.5	7.20	0.0000
W	60605.7	11770.9	5.15	0.0001

All parameter estimates are statistically significant at the 10 percent level of significance, but only the parameter estimates $\hat{e}$ and $\hat{f}$ are statistically significant at the 5 percent level of significance.

i. The demand and supply functions for rutabagas in 2006 are forecasted to be:

D: $\quad \hat{Q}_{d,2006} = 7,791,014 - 105,420P = (1,378,514 + 85.5 \times 75,000) - 105,420P$

S: $\quad \hat{Q}_{s,2006} = 4,619,103 + 87,214P = (-2,562,672 + 60,605.7 \times 118.5) + 87,214P$

Setting the two forecasted equations for 2006 equal to each other, the forecasted price of rutabagas is found to be 16.466 cents per pound. Then substituting this forecasted price into either the forecasted demand or supply equation gives the forecasted quantity in 2006 as 6,055,169 pounds.

MULTIPLE CHOICE / TRUE-FALSE

1. b   Only answer *b* is *not* a major problem in forecasting. It is usually possible to obtain predicted values for exogenous variables.

2. a   As supply shifts along a stable demand, the movement of supply traces out the demand curve.

3. d   Demand and supply are both identified. Supply contains P_L, which is not in demand; so demand is identified. Demand contains M, which is not in supply; so supply is identified.

4.   c   Since sample observations only reveal where demand and supply intersect, it may not be possible to determine the shape of either the demand or supply curve that generated the points in the sample.

5.   d   2SLS only works on identified demand equations and the usual test procedure using t-ratios or p-values is used to test for statistical significance.

6.   d   Both equations b and c include exogenous variables (Z and W, respectively) that are not in the demand equation.

7.   b   Demand is elastic because $\hat{E} = \hat{b} = -1.10$ and $|-1.10| > 1$.

8.   a $\left| t_{\hat{b}} \right| = 1.10/0.44 = 2.5 > 2.021 \ (= t_{\text{critical}})$

9.   c $\hat{E}_M = \hat{c} = 2.4$

10.   d $\hat{E}_{XY} = \hat{d} = -0.20 < 0 \Rightarrow X$ and Y are complements

11.   b $\%\Delta Q / \%\Delta P_y = -0.20 \Rightarrow \%\Delta Q / +25\% = -0.20 \Rightarrow \%\Delta Q = -5\%$

12.   a $\%\Delta Q / \%\Delta M = 2.4 \Rightarrow 30\% / \%\Delta M = 2.4 \Rightarrow \%\Delta M = +12.5\%$

13.   d   Empirical demand equations are generally estimated using regression analysis.

14.   e   none of the choices are correct: $Q = aP^b M^c P_R^{\ d}$.

15.   b   For linear specifications, elasticities vary. The income elasticity is $c(M/Q)$, where c is constant but M/Q varies.

16.   d   Both are true by the definition of a representative sample.

17.   c   When managers set the price of the firm's product, price is not correlated with the random error term in the firm's demand equation, and OLS is appropriate. If price is determined by the simultaneous interaction of both demand and supply equations, then price will be correlated with the random error term, which creates simultaneous equations bias. This bias can be eliminated by using 2SLS.

18.   e   Variables whose values are determined by a system of equations are called "endogenous" to that system. Market-determined prices are just such variables.

19.   d   Manager-determined prices are determined not by a system of demand and supply equations, but by the manager. Thus, such prices are exogenous variables in a demand (or supply) equation.

20.   d   When a variable is endogenous, its value is determined by all of the exogenous variables in all of the equations, which creates the simultaneity problem. The associated simultaneous equations bias is managed by estimating the equations of the system using the method of two-stage least-squares.

21.   a   The p-value for the estimated trend parameter $\hat{b}$ is less than 0.02, so it is significant at the 2 percent level.

22.   d $\hat{b}$ is the estimated quarterly trend in price (= \$0.80), so the annual rate of increase in price is four times $\hat{b}$, \$3.20.

23.   d   The estimated intercept in quarter $1 = \hat{a} + \hat{c} = 24 + (-8) = 16$.

24.   e   The estimated intercept in quarter $4 = \hat{a} = 24$. Remember, the base quarter is the fourth quarter in this problem.

25.   d   Since all three dummies are negative, the base quarter, which is the fourth quarter, is estimated to have the largest intercept.

26.   a   Since the first quarter dummy is the most negative of the three negative dummies, the first quarter has the smallest intercept value.

27.   e   This pattern follows directly from the pattern of the dummy variables. See answers 7 and 8.

28. b   In the first quarter of 2006, $t = 37$, and $\hat{P}_{37} = 24.0 + 0.8 \times 37 - 8.0 \times 1 = 45.60$.

29. a   In the second quarter of 2006, $t = 38$, and $\hat{P}_{38} = 24.0 + 0.8 \times 38 - 6.0 \times 1 = 48.40$.

30. e   In the third quarter of 2006, $t = 39$, and $\hat{P}_{39} = 24.0 + 0.8 \times 39 - 4.0 \times 1 = 51.20$.

31. d   In the fourth quarter of 2006, $t = 40$, and $\hat{P}_{40} = 24.0 + 0.8 \times 40 = 56$.

32. b $16,000 - 20,000P + 4 \times 16,000 = 80,000 + 15,000P - 7,000 \times 10 \Rightarrow \hat{P}_{2006} = \$2$

33. d $\hat{Q}_{2006} = 80,000 - 20,000 \times 2 = 40,000$ units or $\hat{Q}_{2006} = 10,000 + 15,000 \times 2 = 40,000$ units

34. a   Supply when $P_I = 5$ is $Q = 45,000 + 15,000P$. Set quantity demanded equal to quantity supplied and solve for $P = \$1$. Substituting $P = 1$ into either demand or supply gives the forecast $\hat{Q}_{2006} = 45,000 + 15,000(1) = 60,000$.

35. T   Since both equations include an exogenous variable not in the other equation, then each equation is identified because the *other* equation contains an omitted exogenous variable.

36. F   2SLS can be used to estimate demand as long as demand is identified. The identification status of supply is irrelevant, *unless* you wish to estimate supply.

37. T   Time-series models simply fit a curve to the time-ordered series of values on the variable to be forecast.

38. F   Dummy variables can be used to adjust for many types of occurrences that influence sales, not just seasonal effects. For example, if the sales data include some time periods during which a war was being fought, then a dummy variable for war years and peace years could be added to account for the effect of the war on sales.

39. F   By itself, a negative value of $\hat{b}$ is not sufficient evidence of a downward trend in sales. Unless $\hat{b}$ is shown to be statistically significant at an acceptable level of significance, then it is not possible to reject the hypothesis that $b = 0$ (i.e., there is no trend up or down) without taking an unacceptable risk of committing a Type I error (i.e., reject $b = 0$ when, in fact, b really is zero). Remember, just because the estimate of b is not zero does not mean, by itself, that the true value of b is not zero.

You do a t-test or evaluate the p-value for $\hat{b}$.

40. F   Time-series forecasting may be easier to do than econometric forecasting, but for short-run forecasts the time-series method may be more accurate than some of the more complicated techniques.

Homework Exercises

1. The empirical demand for coal world wide (Q_c = tons per day) is specified to be a linear function of the price of coal (P_c = dollars per ton), the average per capital income in the six largest industrial nations (M = dollars per capita), and the price of crude oil (P_o = dollars per barrel):

    World Demand for Coal: $Q_c = a + bP_c + cM + dP_o$

    a. Specify a linear supply equation that will cause the coal demand function to be identified:

    World Supply of Coal: $Q_c =$ _____.

    Because coal prices are market determined, the empirical demand function for coal is estimated using the 2SLS estimation procedure, which produces the following computer printout:

Two-Stage Least-Squares Estimation				
DEPENDENT VARIABLE: QC				
OBSERVATIONS: 64				
VARIABLE	PARAMETER ESTIMATE	STANDARD ERROR	T-RATIO	P-VALUE
INTERCEPT	1150000.0	253800	4.53	0.0001
PC	–15508.0	3953.0	–3.92	0.0024
M	37.20	9.55	3.90	0.0003
PO	56034.0	14524	3.86	0.0003

    b. The sign of $\hat{b}$ _____ (is, is not) as would be predicted theoretically.

    c. At the 1 percent level of significance, the critical value of the t-statistics is

    _____.

    d. Are the parameter estimates $\hat{a}, \hat{b}, \hat{c}$, and $\hat{d}$ statistically significant at the 1 percent level of significance?

    $\hat{a}$: _____ (significant, NOT significant)

    $\hat{b}$: _____ (significant, NOT significant)

    $\hat{c}$: _____ (significant, NOT significant)

    $\hat{d}$: _____ (significant, NOT significant)

    e. If the price of coal is $26.50 per ton, income per capita is $19,245, and the price of a barrel of crude oil is $18.50, calculate quantity demanded of coal worldwide:

    $\hat{Q}_c =$ _____ tons of coal per day.

    Show your work here:

f. For the values given in part *e*, estimate the elasticities of demand for coal:

  (i) Price elasticity $\hat{E}$ = _____.

  (ii) Income elasticity $\hat{E}_M$ = _____.

  (iii) Cross price elasticity $\hat{E}_{co}$ = _____.

  Show your work here:

g. Using the elasticities estimated in part *f*, calculate the impact on coal consumption if

  (i) The formation of a coal cartel increases coal prices by 20 percent.

  $\%\Delta Q_c$ = _____

  (i) A worldwide economic recovery increases average per capita income in the six largest industrialized nations by 6 percent.

  $\%\Delta Q_c$ = _____

  (ii) Hostilities in the Middle East close the Persian Gulf to shipping causing crude oil prices to rise by 16 percent.

  $\%\Delta Q_c$ = _____

  Show your work here:

2. Suppose a savings and loan association wants to forecast the delinquency rate on home mortgages. Using monthly data, the following trend model is estimated

$$DR_t = a + bt$$

where DR_t = the percentage of mortgage payments delinquent in time period *t*, and t = 1,..,48 (January 2001 through December 2004). The following estimation results are obtained:

DEPENDENT VARIABLE:	DRT	R-SQUARE	F-RATIO	P-VALUE ON F	
OBSERVATIONS:	48	0.7982	181.93	0.0001	
VARIABLE		PARAMETER ESTIMATE	STANDARD ERROR	T-RATIO	P-VALUE
INTERCEPT		2.60	0.74	3.51	0.0010
T		0.030	0.010	3.00	0.0043

a. Does this estimate indicate a significant upward trend in the delinquency rate on home mortgages? In the space below, perform the appropriate *t*-test at the 5 percent significance level.

b.	Perform an *F*-test to determine if the model is statistically significant at the 5 percent level of significance.

c.	Calculate the predicted delinquency rates for January 2005 and March 2005.

$DR_{Jan\ 2005}$ = _____ percent

$DR_{Mar\ 2005}$ = _____ percent

Show your work here:

The trend analysis above indicates that the delinquency rate is rapidly becoming a serious problem for this savings and loan. A management consultant suggests that the trend analysis may be overstating the upward trend because it fails to account for the fact that the months of December and January are consistently much worse months than the rest. The consultant suggests estimating the following model:

$$DR_t = a + bt + cD$$

where *D* is equal to one for the months of December and January, and zero otherwise. The estimation results are:

DEPENDENT VARIABLE: DRT	R-SQUARE	F-RATIO	P-VALUE ON F		
OBSERVATIONS: 48	0.9876	1794.0	0.0001		
VARIABLE	PARAMETER ESTIMATE	STANDARD ERROR	T-RATIO	P-VALUE
INTERCEPT	2.200	0.780	2.82	0.0071
T	0.018	0.004	4.50	0.0001
D	0.810	0.210	3.86	0.0004

d.	Does the new model indicate a significant upward trend in the delinquency rate? Perform the appropriate *t*-test.

e.	Perform a *t*-test to determine whether December and January are significantly worse months for mortgage payments.

f.	Predict the delinquency rates for January 2005 and March 2005.

$DR_{Jan\ 2005}$ = _____ percent

$DR_{Mar\ 2005}$ = _____ percent

Show your work here:

g. Compare your forecasts in parts *c* and *f*. Explain why they differ.

3. A coal-market analyst at Meryl-Long, Inc. estimated the market demand and supply functions for coal in 2004 and obtained the following results:

Demand: $Q = 2,500 - 2.6P + 0.005M + 16.2P_R$

Supply: $Q = 200 + 48P - 4P_I$

where Q = quantity of coal (tons per day), P = real price of coal ($/ton), M = income per capita, P_R = real price of oil ($/100-barrel contract), and P_I = coal miners' wage rate ($/hour). The forecasted values for 2003 are $M = \$40,000$, $P_R = \$1,500$, and $P_I = \$24$.

a. For 2005, the forecasted real price of coal is $_____$ per ton.

b. The forecasted quantity of coal production in 2005 is $_____$ tons per day.

c. A rival consulting firm disagrees with the forecast for the price of oil. Its forecast is $2,600 per 100 barrels based on the belief that OPEC is likely to restrict crude oil supply in 2005. If P_R does equal $2,600, while the forecasted values for M and P_I are unchanged, the new price and output forecasts for 2005 are P_{coal} = $\$_____$ per ton and Q_{coal} = $_____$ tons per day.

d. The forecast of the coal miners' wage rate for 2005 depends on the new union contract that will be negotiated in 2005. If the UMW (United Mine Workers) union manages to win additional concessions that increase the wage rate (P_I) to $30, while the forecasted values of M and P_R are unchanged ($M = \$40,000$, $P_R = \$975$), the new price and output forecasts for 2005 are P_{coal} = $\$_____$ per ton and Q_{coal} = $_____$ tons per day. *Show your work below.*

COMPUTER HOMEWORK EXERCISES

Use a computer regression package, such as the Student Edition of Statistix 8, to work these two computer exercises.

1. Ozark Bottled Water Products, Inc. hired a marketing consulting firm to perform a test marketing of its new brand of spring water called Liquid Ozarka. The marketing experts selected 15 small and medium-sized towns in Arkansas and Missouri for a one-month-long sales test. For one month, Liquid Ozarka was sold at a variety of prices ranging from $3 per gallon to $4 per gallon. Specifically, in three of the markets, price was set by the marketing experts at $3 per gallon. In three more markets, price was set at $3.25 per gallon, and so on. The prices charged in each market (P) are shown in the table below. For each of the 15 market areas, the marketing consultants collected data on average household income (M), the population of the marketing area (N), and the price of a rival brand of bottled water (P_R). At the end of the month, total sales of Liquid Ozarka (Q) were tabulated to provide the following data from which the consultants estimated an empirical demand function for the new product.

Market	P	M	PR	N	Q
1	$3.00	$45,586	$2.75	274,000	7,952
2	3.00	37,521	3.50	13,450	8,222
3	3.00	41,333	2.64	54,150	7,166
4	3.25	47,352	2.35	6,800	6,686
5	3.25	51,450	2.75	11,245	7,715
6	3.25	27,655	3.15	54,500	6,643
7	3.50	30,265	2.55	26,600	5,155
8	3.50	39,542	3.00	158,000	7,127
9	3.50	41,596	2.75	22,500	5,834
10	3.75	42,657	2.45	46,150	5,093
11	3.75	36,421	2.89	8,200	5,828
12	3.75	47,624	2.49	38,500	6,590
13	4.00	50,110	3.15	105,000	6,228
14	4.00	57,421	2.80	92,000	7,218
15	4.00	38,450	2.90	38,720	5,846

Using the marketing data from the 15 test markets shown above, estimate the parameters of the linear empirical demand function:
$$Q = a + bP + cM + dPR + eN$$
If any of the parameter estimates are *not* significant at the 2 percent level of significance, drop the associated explanatory variable from the model and estimate the demand function again.

a. Your estimated linear demand function for Liquid Ozarka is

$\hat{Q} =$ _____.

b. What percentage of the variation in sales of Liquid Ozarka is explained by your estimated demand function?

The marketing consultants describe a "typical" market as one in which the price of Liquid Ozarka is $3.50 per gallon, average household income is $45,000, the price of rival bottled water is $3 per gallon, and the population is 75,000. Answer the following questions for this "typical" market scenario.

c. What is the estimated elasticity of demand for Liquid Ozarka? Is demand elastic or inelastic? What would be the percentage change in price required to increase sales of Liquid Ozarka by 10 percent?

d. What is the estimated income elasticity of demand? Is Liquid Ozarka a normal or inferior good? A 6 percent increase in average household income would be predicted to cause what percentage change in sales of Liquid Ozarka?

e. What is the estimated cross-price elasticity of demand for Liquid Ozarka with respect to changes in price of its rival brand of bottled water? Does the estimated cross-price elasticity have the expected algebraic sign? Why or why not? If the price of the rival brand of water rises by 8 percent, what is the estimated percentage change in sales of Liquid Ozarka?

Using the marketing data from the preceding 15 test markets, estimate the parameters for the log-linear empirical demand function:

$$Q = aP^b M^c P_R^d N^e$$

If any of the parameter estimates are *not* significant at the 2 percent level of significance, drop the associated explanatory variable from the model and estimate the demand function again.

f. Your estimated log-linear demand function for Liquid Ozarka is
    $\hat{Q} =$ _____.

g. Does a log-linear specification work better than a linear specification of demand for Liquid Ozarka? Explain by comparing F-ratios, R^2s, and t-ratios (or p-values).

h. Using the estimated log-linear demand function, compute the price, income, and cross-price elasticities of demand. How do they compare to the estimated elasticities for the linear demand specification?

2. For 2001–2003, Gallaway, Inc. has collected the following data on monthly sales of its Titan II driving club, where Q = the number of units sold per month.

Year	Month	Q	Year	Month	Q	Year	Month	Q
2001	January	6,942	2002	January	8,007	2003	January	7,925
	February	7,348		February	7,698		February	7,326
	March	7,328		March	7,417		March	8,037
	April	8,350		April	8,897		April	9,087
	May	8,619		May	8,607		May	9,303
	June	9,282		June	9,314		June	9,139
	July	8,183		July	8,686		July	8,105
	August	8,317		August	8,539		August	8,321
	September	8,552		September	8,967		September	8,960
	October	7,993		October	8,507		October	7,580
	November	8,198		November	8,359		November	8,562
	December	8,082		December	8,157		December	8,072

a. Management at Gallaway is concerned about sales. They would like to know if there is an upward trend is sales of the Titan II. Use the data above to estimate the monthly trend in sales using a linear trend model of the form: $Q_t = a + bt$. Does your statistical analysis indicate a trend? If so, is it an upward or downward trend and how great is it? Is it a statistically significant trend (use the 5 percent level of significance)?

b. Now adjust your statistical model to account for seasonal variation in club sales. Estimate the following model of sales:

$$Q_t = a + bt + c_1 D1_t + c_2 D2_t + c_3 D3_t$$

where $D1_t = 1$ for the months of January–March or 0 otherwise, $D2_t = 1$ for the months of April–June or 0 otherwise, and $D3_t = 1$ for the months of July–September or 0 otherwise. Do the data indicate a statistically significant seasonal pattern (use the 5 percent level of significance)? If so, what is the seasonal pattern of sales of Titan II clubs?

c. Comparing your estimates of the trend in sales in parts a and b, which estimate is likely to be more accurate? Why?

d. Using the estimated forecast equation from part b, forecast sales of Titan II clubs for January 2004, January 2005, July 2004, and July 2005.

Production and Cost in the Short Run

Learning Objectives

After reading Chapter 8 and working the problems for Chapter 8 in the textbook and in this Workbook, you should be able to:

➤ Understand the information given by a production function.

➤ Compare and contrast technical efficiency and economic efficiency.

➤ Explain the difference between long-run and short-run production time periods.

➤ Compute average product (*AP*) and marginal product (*MP*) and explain the relation among total, average, and marginal products.

➤ Define and explain the law of diminishing marginal product.

➤ Explain the difference between fixed costs and variable costs.

➤ Define and draw graphs of total fixed cost (*TFC*), total variable cost (*TVC*), total cost (*TC*), and short-run marginal cost (*SMC*).

➤ Define and draw graphs of average fixed cost (*AFC*), average variable cost (*AVC*), and average total cost (*ATC*).

➤ Relate short-run costs to the production function using the relations between (i) average variable cost and average product, and (ii) short-run marginal cost and marginal product.

Essential Concepts

1. A *production function* shows the maximum amount of output that can be produced from any specified set of inputs, given the existing technology.

2. *Technical efficiency* is achieved when the maximum possible amount of output is being produced with a given combination of inputs.

3. *Economic efficiency* is achieved when the firm is producing a given amount of output at the lowest possible total cost.

4. Inputs are classified as either *variable* or *fixed* according to whether the level of usage of the input can be readily changed or is extremely difficult (or expensive) to change. In the *short run*, at least one input is a fixed input and all changes in the level of output are accomplished by changing the usage of the variable inputs. In the *long run*, all inputs are variable, and output can be changed by varying the usage of all inputs.

5. In the short run, capital is fixed so that the short-run production function may be written as

$$Q = f(L, \bar{K})$$

which indicates that only changes in the variable input L can change the level of output in the short run.

6. Average product of labor ($AP = Q/L$) and marginal product of labor ($MP = \Delta Q/\Delta L$) are related in the following way:

> When AP is rising (falling), MP is greater (less) than AP. When AP reaches its maximum value, $AP = MP$.

7. The *law of diminishing marginal product* states that as the usage of a variable input increases, a point is reached beyond which its marginal product decreases.

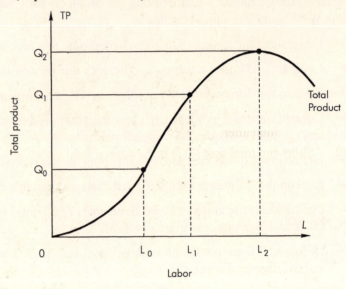

Panel A

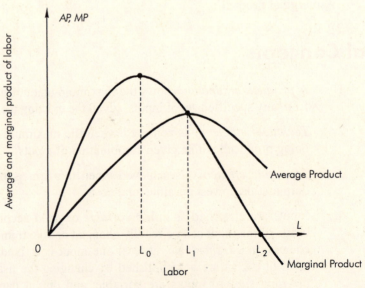

Panel B

8. Panel *A* in the preceding figure shows the typical total product curve (*TP*) when production occurs with only one variable input. The total product curve reflects the following relations:

    a. No output can be produced with zero workers.

    b. Output increases at an increasing rate until L_0 workers are employed producing Q_0 units of output. Over this range marginal product is increasing.

    c. Total product then increases but at a decreasing rate when the firm hires between L_0 and L_2 workers. Over this range *MP* is decreasing.

    d. Average product reaches its maximum value at L_1, where *AP* equals *MP*.

    e. Finally a point will be reached beyond which output will decline, indicating a negative marginal product. In Panel *A*, this occurs for employment levels greater than L_2. The maximum possible total product is thus Q_2.

9. Panel *B* in the figure shows the *AP* and *MP* curves that correspond to *TP* in Panel *A*. Notice that

    a. both curves first rise, reach a maximum, then decline.

    b. marginal product attains a maximum (at L_0) at a lower input level than the level at which average product attains its maximum (at L_1).

    c. while *AP* is always positive, *MP* is zero at L_2 units of labor and is negative thereafter.

10. Short-run total cost (*TC*) is the sum of total variable cost (*TVC*) and total fixed cost (*TFC*):

$$TC = TVC + TFC$$

11. Average fixed cost (*AFC*) is equal to total fixed cost divided by output:

$$AFC = \frac{TFC}{Q}$$

12. Average variable cost (*AVC*) is equal to total variable cost divided by output:

$$AVC = \frac{TVC}{Q}$$

13. Average total cost is equal to total cost divided by output or the sum of average variable and average fixed cost:

$$ATC = \frac{TC}{Q} = AVC + AFC$$

14. Short-run marginal cost (*SMC*) measures the rate of change in *TC* as output varies:

$$SMC = \frac{\Delta TC}{\Delta Q} = \frac{\Delta TVC}{\Delta Q}$$

15. The following figure shows the typical set of short-run average and marginal cost curves. Note the following relations:

    a. *AFC* decreases continuously as output increases (*AFC* is not shown in the figure above, but it is equal to vertical distance between *ATC* and *AVC*).

b. *AVC* is ∪-shaped and *AVC* equals *SMC* at *AVC*'s minimum.

c. *ATC* is ∪-shaped and *ATC* equals *SMC* at *ATC*'s minimum.

d. *SMC* is ∪-shaped and intersects *AVC* and *ATC* at their minimum points. *SMC* lies below (above) *ATC* and *AVC* when *ATC* and *AVC* are falling (rising).

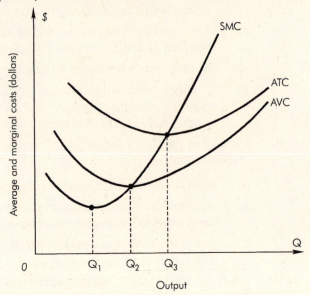

16. In the case of a single variable input, short-run costs are related to the production function by the two relations:

$$AVC = \frac{w}{AP} \quad \text{and} \quad SMC = \frac{w}{MP}$$

where w is the price of the variable input. Since *AP* and *MP* first increase, reach a peak and then decrease, *AVC* and *SMC* first fall, reach a minimum value and then rise.

Matching Definitions

average fixed cost   production
average product of labor   production function
average total cost   short run
average variable cost   short-run marginal cost
economic efficiency   technical efficiency
fixed input   total cost
fixed proportions production total fixed cost
law of diminishing marginal product total variable cost
long run   variable input
marginal product of labor   variable proportions production

1. _____ The creation of goods and services from inputs or resources.

2. _____ A table or mathematical equation showing the maximum amount of output that can be produced from any specified set of inputs, given the existing technology.

3. _____ Production of the maximum level of output that can be obtained from a given combination of inputs.

4. _____ Production of a given amount of output at the lowest possible total cost.

5. _____ An input for which the level of usage cannot readily be changed.

6. _____ An input for which the level of usage may be changed quite readily.

7. _____ That period of time in which the level of usage of one or more inputs is fixed.

8. _____ That period of time in which all inputs are variable, which is sometimes called the *planning horizon.*

9. _____ Production in which a given level of output can be produced with more than one combination of inputs.

10. _____ Production in which one, and only one, ratio or mix of inputs can be used to produce a good.

11. _____ Total product divided by the number of units of labor employed.

12. _____ Additional output attributable to using one more worker holding the use of all other inputs constant.

13. _____ As the level of usage of the variable input increases, other inputs held constant, a point will be reached beyond which the marginal product decreases.

14. _____ Total amount paid for fixed inputs.

15. _____ Total amount paid for variable inputs.

16. _____ The sum of total fixed and total variable costs.

17. _____ Fixed cost per unit of output (i.e., total fixed cost divided by output).

18. _____ Variable cost per unit of output (i.e., total variable cost divided by output).

19. _____ Total cost per unit of output (i.e., total cost divided by output).

20. _____ The change in either total cost or total variable cost per unit change in output.

Study Problems

1. For each of the firm's decisions, determine whether the manager is making a decision in the short run or the long run.

   _____ a. Eckerd's decides to stay open 24 hours a day rather than 16 hours a day.

   _____ b. Harley Davidson builds another production facility.

   _____ c. American Airlines restructures its flight schedules to increase the percentage of seats filled on each of its flights.

   _____ d. Dell Computer adds more workers in its shipping department to speed delivery of new PC orders.

2. Fill in the blanks in the following table:

Usage of Variable Input	Total Product	Marginal Product	Average Product
1........................	_____	_____	4
2........................	_____	8	_____
3........................	18	_____	_____
4........................	_____	_____	5
5........................	_____	−5	_____

The wage rate is $12 per unit of labor. After completing the table, answer the following questions:

a. After _____ units of labor usage, the firm experiences diminishing returns.

b. At _____ units of labor, $SMC = AVC$.

c. The level of output at which $SMC = AVC$ is _____ units of output.

d. Minimum average variable cost = $_____.

e. At the level of labor usage and associated output for which $SMC = AVC$, marginal cost = $_____.

3. Consider a firm using a single variable input and a single fixed input, capital. When the amount of capital is increased:

a. the total product curve will _____.

b. the average product curve will _____.

c. the marginal product curve will _____.

4. Assume labor—the only variable input of a firm—has average and marginal product curves shown in the following figure. The price of labor is $1,000 per unit (i.e., $w = \$1,000$).

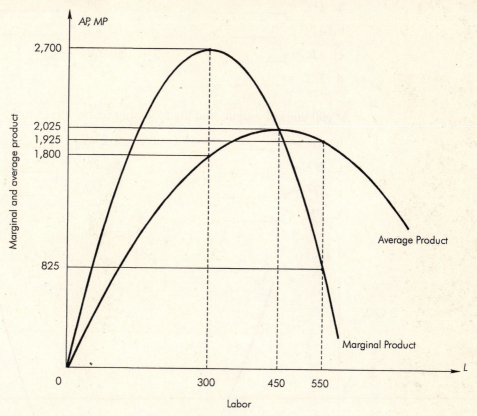

a. At minimum average variable cost, the firm employs _____ units of labor.

b. Minimum average variable cost is reached at _____ units of output.

c. At its minimum value, average variable cost is $_____.

d. Marginal cost reaches its minimum value at _____ units of labor usage, which corresponds to _____ units of output.

e. At its minimum value, marginal cost is $_____.

f. The average variable cost when 550 units of labor are employed is $_____.

g. The marginal cost when 550 units of labor are employed is $_____.

5. Use the figure below to answer these questions:

At 200 units of output, find the following costs:

a. $AFC =$ _____   e. $TVC =$ _____

b. $AVC =$ _____   f. $TC =$ _____

c. $ATC =$ _____   g. $SMC =$ _____

d. $TFC =$ _____

At 600 units of output, find the following costs:

h. $AFC =$ _____   l. $TVC =$ _____

i. $AVC =$ _____   m. $TC =$ _____

j. $ATC =$ _____   n. $SMC =$ _____

k. $TFC =$ _____

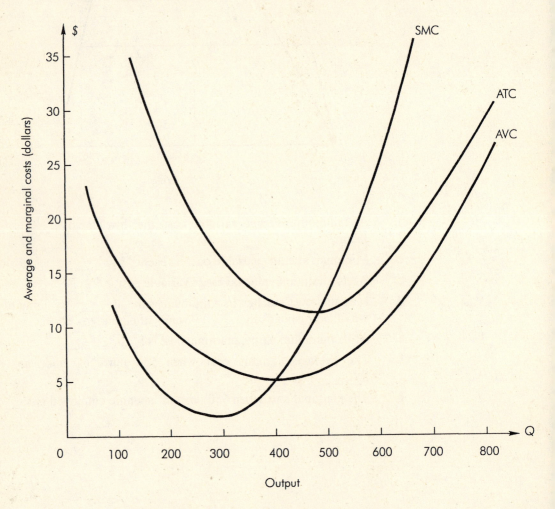

Output

6. Total fixed cost is $150 per week and the price per week of labor is $500 per worker. Fill in the blanks in the table below:

		Product			Total Cost			Average Cost			
Labor	Total	Average	Marginal	Fixed	Variable	Total	Fixed	Variable	Total	Marginal Cost
0	0	XX	XX	___		___	XX	XX	XX	XX
1	2	___	___	___	___	___	___	___	___	___
2	5	___	___	___	___	___	___	___	___	___
3	10	___	___	___	___	___	___	___	___	___
4	16	___	___	___	___	___	___	___	___	___
5	25	___	___	___	___	___	___	___	___	___
6	30	___	___	___	___	___	___	___	___	___
7	34	___	___	___	___	___	___	___	___	___
8	37	___	___	___	___	___	___	___	___	___
9	39	___	___	___	___	___	___	___	___	___
10	40	___	___	___	___	___	___	___	___	___

Multiple Choice / True-False

1. Marginal product equals average product
   a. when marginal product equals zero.
   b. when average product equals zero.
   c. at the inflection point of the total product curve.
   d. at the maximum value of marginal product.
   e. at the maximum value of average product.

2. The economically efficient input combination for producing a given level of output
   a. minimizes the average cost of producing the given level of output.
   b. occurs at the maximum value of the total product curve.
   c. can produce that level of output at the lowest possible total cost.
   d. is determined entirely by the production function.

3. If average product is rising, then marginal product
   a. cannot be falling.
   b. can be either rising or falling, but it must lie above average product.
   c. must lie below average product.
   d. must be rising.

In questions 4–7, suppose that the short-run production function is given by:

Labor	Quantity
0	0
1	3
2	10
3	21
4	24
5	25
6	24
7	14

4. The average product of labor when 3 units of labor are employed is
   a. 3.
   b. 5.
   c. 7.
   d. 11.
   e. −1.

5. The marginal product of the 6th laborer is
   a. 3.
   b. 5.
   c. 7.
   d. 11.
   e. −1.

6. Diminishing marginal returns begin with the
   a. 2nd unit of labor.
   b. 4th unit of labor.
   c. 5th unit of labor.
   d. 6th unit of labor.

7. Marginal product is negative when more than
   a. 3 units of labor are employed.
   b. 4 units of labor are employed.
   c. 5 units of labor are employed.
   d. 6 units of labor are employed.

8. Fixed costs
   a. must be considered in any decision-making process.
   b. do not exist in the long run.
   c. decrease as output rises.
   d. *a* and *b*.
   e. *b* and *c*.

Fill in the missing values and answer questions 9–13.

Q	Total Cost	Fixed Cost	Variable Cost	Average Fixed Cost	Average Variable Cost	Average Total Cost	Marginal Cost
0..........	20	____	____	xx	xx	xx	xx
1..........	____	____	____	____	____	____	20
2..........	____	____	____	____	15	____	____
3..........	____	____	____	____	____	19	____
4..........	____	____	48	____	____	____	____

9. What is total fixed cost?
   a. 10
   b. 15
   c. 20
   d. cannot be determined
   e. none of the above

10. What is total cost when $Q = 1$?
   a. 30
   b. 35
   c. 40
   d. 20
   e. none of the above

11. What is average total cost when $Q = 2$?
   a. 10
   b. 20
   c. 30
   d. 40
   e. none of the above

12. What is marginal cost when $Q = 3$?
   a. 7
   b. 8
   c. 9
   d. 10

13. What is marginal cost when $Q = 4$?
   a. 5
   b. 10
   c. 11
   d. 15
   e. 20

14. When the average product of the variable input is equal to the marginal product,
   a. marginal cost reaches its minimum value.
   b. average variable cost reaches its minimum value.
   c. marginal cost is rising.
   d. both *a* and *c*.
   e. both *b* and *c*.

15. If a firm is producing 5 units of output and the marginal cost for the fifth unit is $7 and the average variable cost for the fifth unit is $3, then the average variable cost for the fourth unit is _____.
   a. 1
   b. 2
   c. 4
   d. 8
   e. none of the above

16. If short-run marginal cost is ∪-shaped, then
   a. total cost increases at an increasing rate, then increases at a decreasing rate.
   b. total variable cost increases at a decreasing rate then increases at an increasing rate.
   c. total variable cost must be *S*-shaped.
   d. all of the above.
   e. both *b* and *c*.

17. Average total cost
   a. increases as output increases.
   b. decreases as output increases.
   c. increases if marginal cost is increasing.
   d. increases if marginal cost is greater than average total cost.
   e. both *c* and *d*.

18. Average fixed cost
   a. increases as output increases.
   b. decreases as output increases.
   c. increases if marginal cost is increasing.
   d. increases if marginal cost is greater than average fixed cost.

19. T   F   A firm that operates in an economically efficient way is also operating in a technically efficient way.

20. T   F   Average fixed cost is not usually graphed with the other average cost curves because average fixed cost can be obtained from average total cost and average variable cost.

21. T   F   If average variable cost is rising, marginal cost must be rising.

22. T   F   Marginal cost measures the change in total variable cost as output changes.

Answers

MATCHING DEFINITIONS

1. production
2. production function
3. technical efficiency
4. economic efficiency
5. fixed input
6. variable input
7. short run
8. long run
9. variable proportions production
10. fixed proportions production
11. average product of labor
12. marginal product of labor
13. law of diminishing marginal product
14. total fixed cost
15. total variable cost
16. total cost
17. average fixed cost
18. average variable cost
19. average total cost
20. short-run marginal cost

STUDY PROBLEMS

1. a. short run; This decision involves increasing the usage of a fixed input, the store.

   b. long run; A new plant allows increased usage of capital inputs that are fixed in the short run.

   c. short run; American Airlines is still using the same number of planes (presumably a fixed input in the short run), but using the planes more intensively.

   d. short run; Dell did not increase the capital resources employed by the shipping department; it is just using more of the variable input labor.

2. The table should look like this:

Usage of Variable Input	Total Product	Marginal Product	Average Product
1......................	4	4	4
2......................	12	8	6
3......................	18	6	6
4......................	20	2	5
5......................	15	–5	3

a. 2; *MP* begins to fall after 2 units of labor are employed.

b. 3; *SMC* will equal *AVC* when $MP = AP$.

c. 18; *TP* is 18 at $L = 3$

d. $2; $AVC = w/AP = 12/6$

e. $2; $SMC = w/MP = 12/6$

3. a. increase (shift upward)

b. increase (shift upward)

c. increase (shift upward)

4. a. 450; *AVC* is minimized when *AP* is maximized.

b. 911,250; Since $AP = Q/L$, $2,025 = Q/450 \Rightarrow Q = 911,250$.

c. $0.49; $AVC = w/AP \Rightarrow \$1,000/2,025$.

d. 300; 540,000; *SMC* is minimized at the level of labor usage where *MP* is maximized. Since $AP = Q/L$ and $AP = 1,800$ at $L = 300$, then $1,800 = Q/300 \Rightarrow Q = 540,000$.

e. $0.37; $SMC = w/MP = \$1,000/2,700$

f. $0.52; $AVC = w/AP = \$1,000/1,925$

g. $1.21; $SMC = w/MP = \$1,000/825$

5. a. $15; the vertical distance between *ATC* and *AVC* at $Q = 200$.

b. $10; read this off the *AVC* curve at $Q = 200$

c. $25; read this off the *ATC* curve at $Q = 200$

d. $3,000; $TFC = AFC \times Q = 15 \times 200$

e. $2,000; $TVC = AVC \times Q = 10 \times 200$

f. $5,000; $TC = ATC \times Q = 25 \times 200$ or $TC = TVC + TFC = 3,000 + 2,000$

g. about $4; read this off the *SMC* curve at $Q = 200$

h. $5; the vertical distance between *ATC* and *AVC* at $Q = 600$

i. $10; read this off the *AVC* curve at $Q = 600$

j. $15; read this off the *ATC* curve at $Q = 600$

k. $3,000; $TFC = AFC \times Q = 5 \times 600$

l. $6,000; $TVC = AVC \times Q = 10 \times 600$

m. $9,000; $TC = ATC \times Q = 15 \times 600$ or $TC = TVC + TFC = 3,000 + 6,000$

n. $25; read this off the *SMC* curve at $Q = 600$

6. Your table should look like this:

Labor	Product Total	Product Average	Product Marginal	Total Cost Fixed	Total Cost Variable	Total Cost Total	Average Cost Fixed	Average Cost Variable	Average Cost Total	Marginal Cost
0	0	0	xx	150	0	150	xx	xx	xx	xx
1	2	2	2	150	500	650	75	250	325	250
2	5	2.5	3	150	1,000	1,150	30	200	230	166.67
3	10	3.3	5	150	1,500	1,650	15	150	165	100
4	16	4	6	150	2,000	2,150	9.37	125	134.37	83.33
5	25	5	9	150	2,500	2,650	6	100	106	55.55
6	30	5	5	150	3,000	3,150	5	100	105	100
7	34	4.85	4	150	3,500	3,650	4.41	102.94	107.35	125
8	37	4.62	3	150	4,000	4,150	4.05	108.11	112.16	166.67
9	39	4.33	2	150	4,500	4,650	3.85	115.38	119.23	250
10	40	4	1	150	5,000	5,150	3.75	125	128.75	500

MULTIPLE CHOICE / TRUE-FALSE

1. e $MP = AP$ at AP's maximum point. Note that answer c is wrong because the inflection point on TP is where MP (not AP) reaches its maximum.

2. c The efficient input combination is the one that minimizes *total*, not average, cost.

3. b MP both rises and falls over the range of labor usage for which AP is rising.

4. c $AP_3 = 21/3 = 7$

5. e $TP_5 = 25$ and $TP_6 = 24 \Rightarrow TP$ falls by one unit. MP for the sixth unit of labor is -1.

6. b MP is smaller for the fourth unit of labor than it is for the third unit of labor.

7. c $MP < 0$ after 5 units of labor are employed.

8. b Fixed costs are the payment to the fixed inputs. Since all inputs are variable in the long run, there are no fixed costs in the long run.

9. c You can see that fixed cost is $20 by noting that when $Q = 0$, $TC = \$20$.

10. c Since SMC for unit 1 is $20, TC for the first unit must be $20 greater than TC when $Q = 0$. Therefore, $TC = 20 + 20 = 40$.

11. e Since $AVC = \$15$, $TVC = \$30$ ($= 2 \times 15$). $TC = TVC + TFC = 30 + 20 = 50$. Therefore, $ATC = TC/Q = 50/2 = \$25$.

12. a $ATC = \$19$ and $TC = \$57$ ($= 3 \times 19$). Since TC is $50 for 2 units, and TC is $57 for 3 units, the marginal cost of the 3rd unit must be $7.

13. c $TC_{Q=4} = TVC + TFC = 48 + 20 = 68$. Since $TC_{Q=3} = \$57$, the marginal cost of the 4th unit must be $11.

14. e When $AP = MP$, AP is at its maximum value. MP is *falling* when $AP = MP$, and thus SMC ($= w/MP$) is rising.

15. b Since $AVC_5 = \$3$, $TVC_5 = \$15$. Given marginal cost of the 5th unit is $7, the total variable cost of 4 units must be $8. Thus $AVC_4 = \$8/4 = \$2$.

16. e   If SMC is $\cup$-shaped, then the slope of TVC first falls, then rises. The only way this can occur is if TVC is S-shaped (i.e., TVC first increases at a decreasing rate, then increases at an increasing rate).

17. d   If marginal exceeds average, then average rises.

18. b   While TFC is constant, AFC declines as Q gets larger.

19. T   All economically efficient firms are technically efficient. The converse is *not* true.

20. T $AFC = ATC - AVC$

21. T   When AVC is rising, SMC exceeds AVC and is rising.

22. T $SMC = \Delta TC/\Delta Q$. Since $\Delta TC = \Delta TVC$ (only TVC varies as Q changes), $SMC = \Delta TVC/\Delta Q$.

Homework Exercises

1. The following figure shows a firm's marginal and average product curves for labor, the only variable input employed by the firm. The wage rate of labor is $200 and the fixed cost is $6,000.

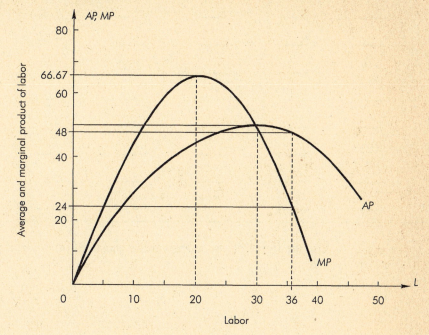

When average variable cost reaches its minimum:

a. Output is _____ units.

b. *AVC* is $_____ and *SMC* is $_____.

c. *ATC* is $_____.

When 36 workers are hired:

d. Output is _____ units.

e. *AVC* is $_____ and *SMC* is $_____ at this output.

f. At the level of output associated with 36 workers, *AVC* is _____ (increasing, decreasing) and *SMC* is _____ (increasing, decreasing).

2. Fill in the blanks in the table below:

Output	TC	TFC	TVC	AFC	AVC	ATC	SMC
0	—	—	—	XX	XX	XX	XX
10	—	—	—	—	—	—	8.0
20	—	—	—	—	4.50	—	—
30	215	—	—	2.00	—	—	—
40	—	—	—	—	—	—	7.2
50	—	—	—	—	6.14	—	8.0
60	452	—	—	—	—	—	—
70	—	—	—	—	—	—	9.0
80	—	—	582	—	—	—	—

3. Use the figure below to answer the questions on the next page.

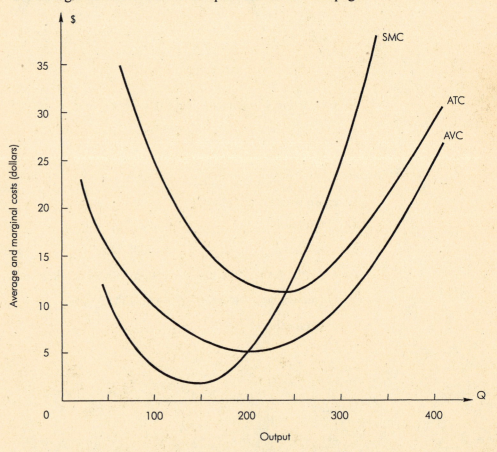

At 100 units of output, find the following costs:

a. $AFC =$ _____   e. $TVC =$ _____

b. $AVC =$ _____   f. $TC \ =$ _____

c. $ATC =$ _____   g. $SMC =$ _____

d. $TFC =$ _____

At 300 units of output, find the following costs:

h. $AFC =$ _____   l. $TVC =$ _____

i. $AVC =$ _____   m. $TC \ =$ _____

j. $ATC =$ _____   n. $SMC =$ _____

k. $TFC =$ _____

Production and Cost in the Long Run

Learning Objectives

After reading Chapter 9 and working the problems for Chapter 9 in the textbook and in this Workbook, you should be able to:

➢ Draw a graph of a typical production isoquant and use the definition of an isoquant to explain why isoquants must be downward sloping.

➢ Discuss the properties of an isoquant.

➢ Construct isocost curves for a given level of expenditure on inputs.

➢ Apply the theory of optimization to find the optimal input combination.

➢ Show graphically that the conditions for minimizing the total cost of producing a given level of output are the same conditions for maximizing the level of output for a given level of total cost.

➢ Construct an expansion path.

➢ Define and illustrate graphically the concept of returns to scale.

➢ Construct a long-run total cost curve from an expansion path.

➢ Explain the concept of economies and diseconomies of scale.

➢ Define economies of scope and explain how to measure economies of scope.

➢ Show the relation between long-run and short-run cost curves.

Essential Concepts

1. In long-run analysis of production, all inputs are variable and isoquants are used to study production decisions. An *isoquant* is a curve showing all possible input combinations capable of producing a given level of output.

2. Isoquants are downward sloping because if greater amounts of labor are used, then less capital is required to produce a given level of output. The *marginal rate of technical substitution* (*MRTS*) is the slope of an isoquant and measures the rate at which the two inputs can be substituted for one another while maintaining a constant level of output

$$MRTS = -\frac{\Delta K}{\Delta L}$$

The minus sign is added in order to make *MRTS* a positive number since $\Delta K/\Delta L$, the slope of the isoquant, is negative.

3. The marginal rate of technical substitution can be expressed as the ratio of two marginal products:

$$MRTS = \frac{MP_L}{MP_K}$$

As labor is substituted for capital, MP_L declines and MP_K rises causing MRTS to diminish.

4. *Isocost curves* show the various combinations of inputs that may be purchased for a given level of expenditure ($\overline{C}$) at given input prices (w and r). The equation of an isocost curve is given by

$$K = \frac{\overline{C}}{r} - \frac{w}{r}L$$

The slope of an isoquant is the negative of the input price ratio ($-w/r$). The K-intercept is $\overline{C}/r$, which represents the amount of capital that may be purchased when all $\overline{C}$ dollars are spent on capital (i.e., zero labor is purchased).

5. A manager can minimize the total cost of producing $\overline{Q}$ units of output by choosing the input combination on the isoquant for $\overline{Q}$ which is just tangent to an isocost curve. Since the optimal input combination occurs at the point of tangency between the isoquant and an isocost curve, the two slopes are equal in equilibrium. Mathematically, the equilibrium condition may be expressed as

$$\frac{MP_L}{MP_K} = \frac{w}{r} \qquad \text{or} \qquad \frac{MP_L}{w} = \frac{MP_K}{r}$$

6. In order to maximize output for a given level of expenditure on inputs, a manager must choose the combination of inputs that equates the marginal rate of technical substitution and the input price ratio, which requires choosing an input combination satisfying exactly the same conditions set forth above for minimizing cost.

7. The *expansion path* is the curve that gives the efficient (least-cost) input combinations for every level of output. The expansion path is derived for a specific set of input prices. Along an expansion path, the input-price ratio is constant and equal to the marginal rate of technical substitution.

8. If all inputs are increased by a factor of c and output goes up by a factor of z, then in general, a producer experiences:

    a. *increasing returns to scale* if $z > c$, because output goes up proportionately *more* than the increase in input usage.

    b. *decreasing returns to scale* if $z < c$, because output goes up proportionately *less* than the increase in input usage.

    c. *constant returns to scale* if $z = c$, because output goes up by the *same* proportion as the increase in input usage.

9. Long-run total cost (LTC) for a given level of output $\overline{Q}$ is given by

$$LTC = wL^* + rK^*$$

where w and r are the prices of labor and capital, respectively, and L^* and K^* is the input combination on the expansion path that minimizes the total cost of producing $\overline{Q}$ units of output.

10. Long-run average cost (LAC) measures the cost per unit of output when the manager can adjust production so that the optimal amount of each input is employed

$$LAC = \frac{LTC}{Q}$$

LAC is ∪-shaped. Falling LAC indicates *economies of scale*, and rising LAC indicates *diseconomies of scale*.

11. Long-run marginal cost (LMC) measures the rate of change in long-run total cost as output changes along the expansion path:

$$LMC = \frac{\Delta LTC}{\Delta Q}$$

LMC is ∪-shaped. LMC lies below (above) LAC when LAC is falling (rising). LMC equals LAC at LAC's minimum value.

12. When constant returns to scale occur over the entire range of output, the firm experiences constant costs in the long run and the LAC curve is flat and equal to LMC at all output levels (see Figure 9.12 on page 370 of the text).

13. *Economies of scope* exist for a multiproduct firm when the joint cost of producing two or more goods is less than the sum of the separate costs of producing the goods. In the case of two goods, X and Y, economies of scope are measured by the fraction

$$SC = \frac{C(X) + C(Y) - C(X,Y)}{C(X,Y)}$$

where SC is greater (less) than zero when (dis)economies of scope exist.

14. The relations between long-run cost and short-run cost can be summarized by the following points:

    a. LMC intersects LAC when the latter is at its minimum point.

    b. At each output where a particular ATC is tangent to LAC, the relevant SMC equals LMC.

    c. For all ATC curves, the point of tangency with LAC is at an output less (greater) than the output of minimum ATC if the tangency is at an output less (greater) than that associated with minimum LAC.

15. Because managers have the greatest flexibility to choose inputs in the long run, costs are lower in the long run than in the short run for all output levels except the output level for which the fixed input is at its optimal level. Thus, the firm's short-run costs can generally be reduced by adjusting the fixed inputs to their optimal long-run levels when the long-run opportunity to adjust fixed inputs arises.

Matching Definitions

constant costs
constant returns to scale
decreasing returns to scale
diseconomies of scale
economies of scale
economies of scope
expansion path

increasing returns to scale
isocost curve
isoquant
long-run average cost
long-run marginal cost
marginal rate of technical substitution
short-run expansion path

1. _____ A curve that displays all the various combinations of inputs that will produce a given amount of output.

2. _____ The rate at which one input is substituted for another along an isoquant.

3. _____ Line that shows all the possible combinations of inputs that can be purchased for a given total cost.

4. _____ A curve showing all of the cost-minimizing levels of input usage for various levels of output.

5. _____ When the usage of all inputs is increased by an equiproportionate amount, output increases by exactly the same proportion.

6. _____ When the usage of all inputs is increased by an equiproportionate amount, output increases by a larger proportionate amount.

7. _____ When the usage of all inputs is increased by an equiproportionate amount, output increases by a smaller proportionate amount.

8. _____ Cost per unit in the long run.

9. _____ The change in long-run total cost per unit change in output.

10. _____ When long-run average cost falls as output increases.

11. _____ When long-run average cost increases with increases in output.

12. _____ Long-run average and marginal costs are equal for all levels of output.

13. _____ The situation in which the joint cost of producing two goods is less than the sum of the separate costs of producing the two goods.

14. _____ Horizontal line showing the cost-minimizing input combinations for various output levels when capital is fixed in the short run.

Study Problems

1. In the following figure, isoquant Q_0 is the isoquant for 1,000 units of output.

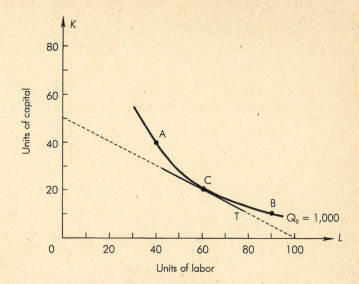

    a. Marginal rate of technical substitution between points A and C is _____.
    b. Marginal rate of technical substitution between points C and B is _____.
    c. Marginal rate of technical substitution at point C is _____.

2. The following graph shows two isocost curves. The price of capital is $100.

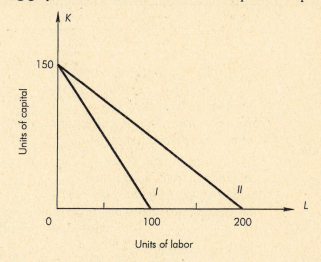

    a. The total cost associated with isocost I is $ 15,000 , and the price of labor is $ 150 .

---

b. The equation for isocost *I* is $K = 150 - 1.5L$. With isocost *I* the firm must give up 1.5 units of capital to purchase one more unit of labor in the market.

c. The total cost associated with isocost *II* is $ 15,000 , and the price of labor is $ 75 .

d. The equation for isocost *II* is $K = 150 - 3/4L$. With isocost *II* the firm must give up .75 units of capital to purchase one more unit of labor in the market.

3. The following figure shows a firm's isoquant for producing 2,000 units of output and four isocost curves. Labor and capital each cost $50 per unit.

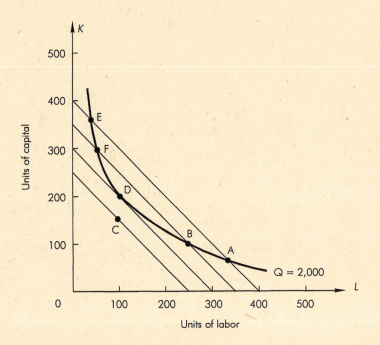

a. At point *A*, the *MRTS* is Less Than (less than, greater than, equal to) the input price ratio, *w/r*. The total cost of producing 2,000 units of output with input combination *A* is $ 20,000 .

b. By moving from *A* to *B*, the firm DECREASES (increases, decreases) labor usage and INCREASES (increases, decreases) capital usage. At point *B* the *MRTS* is Less Than (greater than, less than, equal to) the input price ratio, *w/r*. The movement from *A* to *B* DECREASED (increased, decreased) total cost by $ 2,500 .

$250 * 50 =$
$17,500$

c. At Point *D* the firm MINIMIZES (minimizes, maximizes) the cost of producing 2,000 units of output. The *MRTS* is EQUAL TO (greater than, less than, equal to) the input price ratio, *w/r*.

$300 * 50 = 15000$
$K = 200 * 50 = 10,000$
$L = 100 * 50 = 5,000$

d. The optimal input combination is 100 units of labor and 200 units of capital. At this combination, the total cost of producing 2,000 units is $ 15,000 .

e. At point *E*, the *MP* per dollar spent on CAPITAL is less than the *MP* per dollar spent on LABOR . The total cost of producing 2,000 units of output with input combination *E* is $ 20,000 .

f. The movement from E to F reduces the MP per dollar spent on _____ and increases the MP per dollar spent on _____. This movement _____ (increased, decreased) total cost by $_____.

g. At input combination D, the MP per dollar spent on labor is _____ (greater than, less than, equal to) the MP per dollar spent on capital.

h. Input combination C costs $_____. The firm would not use this combination to produce 2,000 units of output because _____.

4. Your firm produces clay pots entirely by hand even though a pottery machine exists that can make clay pots faster than a human. Workers cost $100 per day and each additional worker can produce 20 more pots per day (i.e., marginal product is constant and equal to 20). Installation of the first pottery machine would increase output by 300 pots per day. Currently your firm produces 1,200 pots per day.

a. Your financial analysis department estimates that the price of a pottery machine is $2,000 per day. Can you reduce the cost of producing 1,200 pots per day by adding a pottery machine to your production process and reducing the amount of labor? Explain why or why not.

b. If a labor union negotiates higher wages so that labor costs rise to $150 per day, does this change your answer to part a? Explain.

c. Suppose your firm wants to expand output to 2,500 pots per day and input prices are $100 and $2,000 per day for labor and capital, respectively. Is it efficient to hire more labor or more capital? Explain using the ratio of marginal products and input prices.

5. The figure below shows a portion of the expansion path for a firm. The price of labor is $75.

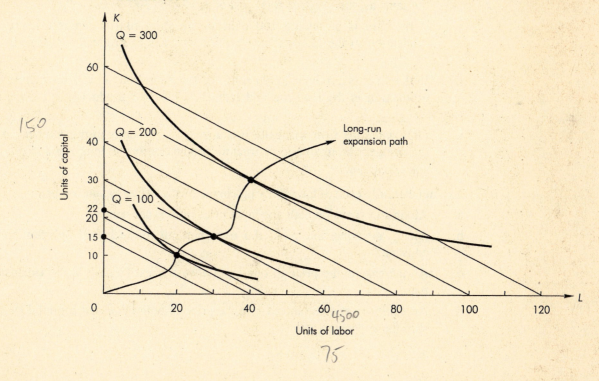

a. The price of capital is $ 150 . Along the expansion path, the marginal rate of technical substitution is equal to $\frac{1}{2}$. w/r

b. To produce 100 units in the long run, a manager would use 20 units of labor and 10 units of capital. The long-run total cost of producing 100 units is $ 3000 .

c. To produce 200 units in the long run, a manager would use 30 units of labor and 15 units of capital. The long-run total cost of producing 200 units is $ 4500 .

d. To produce 300 units in the long run, a manager would use _____ units of labor and _____ units of capital. The long-run total cost of producing 300 units is $_____ .

e. The firm currently operates with 15 units of capital equipment. In the figure above, construct the firm's short-run expansion path and label it "Short-run expansion path."

f. To produce 100 units in the short run, a manager would use _____ units of labor and _____ units of capital. The short-run total cost of producing 100 units is $_____ , which is _____ (more than, less than, the same as) the long-run total cost of producing 100 units.

g. To produce 200 units in the short run, a manager would use _____ units of labor and _____ units of capital. The short-run total cost of producing 200 units is $_____ , which is _____ (more than, less than, the same as) the long-run total cost of producing 200 units.

h. To produce 300 units in the short run, a manager would use _____ units of labor and _____ units of capital. The short-run total cost of producing 300 units is $_____ , which is _____ (more than, less than, the same as) the long-run total cost of producing 300 units.

i. If the firm is producing 100 units in the short run, it can restructure its production in the long-run and reduce its costs of producing 100 units by $_____ .

j. If the firm is producing 300 units in the short run, it can restructure its production in the long-run and reduce its costs of producing 300 units by $_____ .

k. Only when the firm wishes to produce _____ units in the short run will the manager be unable to restructure production in the long run and reduce costs. Explain.

6. Explain carefully each of the following characteristics of an expansion path:

a. Along an expansion path, the input price ratio is constant.

b. Along an expansion path, the marginal rate of technical substitution is constant.

c. An increase in the price of one input always causes a shift in the expansion path.

d. An equiproportionate increase in the price of both labor and capital does not shift the expansion path.

7. You are a management consultant hired by the Rio Loco Vineyards to estimate the costs of raising grapes in an arid region of New Mexico. If labor costs $6,000 per man-year and capital costs $200 per unit annually, you determine that the least-cost input combinations for various levels of grape production are:

Output (bushels/year)	Labor (man-years)	Capital (units/year)
100,000	30	100
200,000	51	270
300,000	56	420
400,000	60	600
500,000	62	640
600,000	84	1,080

a. Complete the table below:

Output	LTC	LAC	LMC
100,000	$_____	$_____	xx
200,000	_____	_____	$_____
300,000	_____	_____	_____
400,000	_____	_____	_____
500,000	_____	_____	_____
600,000	_____	_____	_____

b. Over what range of output do economies of scale exist in the production of grapes?

c. Over what range of output do diseconomies of scale exist in the production of grapes?

Multiple Choice / True-False

For questions 1–5, consider the expansion path illustrated below. The price of capital is $2.

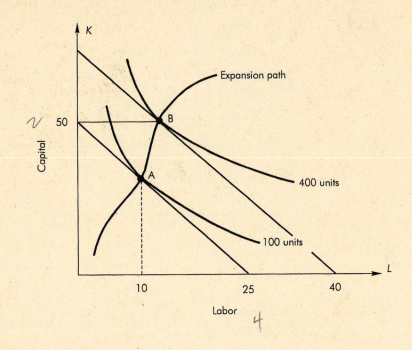

1. What is the price of labor?
   a. $1
   b. $2
   c. $2.50
   d. $3.00
   (e.) $4

2. The efficient amount of capital for producing 100 units of output is
   (a.) 10 units of capital.
   b. 20 units of capital.
   c. 30 units of capital.
   d. 40 units of capital.

3. The marginal rate of technical substitution at point B is _____.
   a. 0.5
   b. 0.25
   c. 1
   (d.) 2 $w/r = 4/2 = 2$
   e. 4

4. The average cost of producing 400 units is
   a. $1.
   b. $0.10.
   c. $4.
   d. $0.40.
   e. $0.50.

5. The efficient amount of labor for producing 400 units of output is
   a. 5.
   b. 10.
   c. 15.
   d. 25.
   e. 50.

6. A ∪-shaped long-run average cost (*LAC*) curve represents
   a. increasing returns and diminishing returns.
   b. fixed costs and variable costs.
   c. economies and diseconomies of scale.
   d. average fixed costs and average variable costs.

7. At any output at which *ATC* is tangent to *LAC*,
   a. $LMC = SMC$.
   b. economies of scale must be present.
   c. long-run total cost (*LTC*) equals short-run total cost (*TC*).
   d. both *a* and *c*.
   e. all of the above.

Questions 8–11 refer to the following:

The price of labor is $20 per unit and the price of capital is $40 per unit.

Optimal input combination

Output	L* 20	K* 40	LTC	LAC	LMC
10	20	8	$ 720	$ 72	xx
20	24	12	960	48	$24
30	32	20	1440	48	48
40	50	24	2,040	51	60

8. When output is 10 units, what is long-run average cost?
   a. $24
   b. $48
   c. $60
   d. $72

9. When output is 20 units, how many units of labor will the firm use?
    a. 22
    b. 24
    c. 30
    d. 50

10. How much does the 30th unit add to long-run total cost?
    a. $24
    b. $48
    c. $60
    d. $72

11. When output is 40 units, how many units of capital will the firm use?
    a. 22
    b. 24
    c. 26
    d. 30

The next three questions refer to the following:

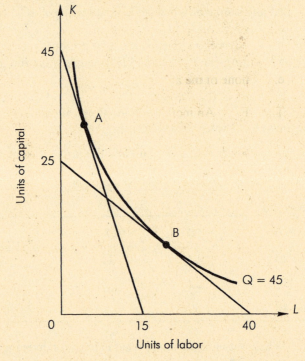

12. What is the marginal rate of technical substitution at point *A?*
    a. 0.3
    b. 1
    c. 1.125
    d. 1.67
    e. none of the above

13. As you move from point *A* to point *B*,
    a.   output is unchanged.
    b.   cost is unchanged.
    c.   the rate at which the firm can substitute labor for capital while holding output constant decreases.
    d.   both *a* and *b*.
    e.   both *a* and *c*.

14. If the firm continues to produce 45 units of output and moves from the combination at *A* to the combination at *B*, it must be true that
    a.   the price of labor decreased relative to the price of capital.
    b.   the price of capital decreased relative to the price of labor.
    c.   the cost of producing 45 units decreased.
    d.   both *b* and *c*.
    e.   none of these are true.

15. A sofa manufacturer currently is using 50 workers and 30 machines to produce 5,000 sofas a day. The wage rate is $200 and the rental rate for a machine is $1,000. At these input levels, another worker adds 200 sofas, while another machine adds 500 sofas. If the firm uses 45 workers and 31 machines instead,
    a.   then its cost will be unchanged, and its output will decrease by 500 units.
    b.   then its cost will be unchanged, and its output will increase by 300 units.
    c.   then its cost will be unchanged, and its output will increase by 500 units.
    d.   then its output will be unchanged, and its cost will decrease by $800.
    e.   none of the above.

16. T   F   An increase in input prices causes a downward shift in each isoquant.

17. T   F   When the production function exhibits constant returns to scale, doubling the usage of all inputs doubles the output.

18. T   F   The expansion path gives the input combinations that minimize the average cost of producing various levels of output.

19. T   F   The efficient input combination is the one that maximizes output and minimizes total cost.

20. T   F   Economies of scale occur when input prices fall as output rises.

Answers

MATCHING DEFINITIONS

1. isoquant
2. marginal rate of technical substitution
3. isocost curve
4. expansion path
5. constant returns to scale
6. increasing returns to scale
7. decreasing returns to scale
8. long-run average cost
9. long-run marginal cost
10. economies of scale
11. diseconomies of scale
12. constant costs
13. economies of scope
14. short-run expansion path

STUDY PROBLEMS

1. a. $1 (= -\frac{20-40}{60-40})$, which is the slope over the interval from A to C.

    b. $0.33 (= -\frac{10-20}{90-60})$, which is the slope over the interval from C to B.

    c. $0.5 (= -\frac{-50}{100})$, which is the slope of the tangent line at point C.

2. a. 15,000; 150. The K-intercept is 150, so the isocost curve represents a cost of $15,000 (= 150×$100). The L-intercept is 100, to w = $150 (= 15,000/100).

    b. $K = 150 - 1.5L$ (or $K = 150 - (150/100)L$ or $15,000 = 150L + 100K$); 1.5

    c. 15,000; $75. The price of labor decreases and causes an outward rotation of the isocost curve.

    d. $K = 150 - 0.75L$ (or $K = 150 - (150/200)L$ or $15,000 = 75L + 100K$); 0.75

3. a. less than; $20,000 (= $50 × 400)

    b. decreases; increases; less than; decreased; $2,500 [= (400–350) × $50]. [Note: For the last part of this answer, you must decide visually that the isocost curve passing through point B intersects the L or K-intercepts at 350. Do not panic, your instructor knows this.]

    c. minimizes; equal

    d. 100; 200; $15,000 (= 300 × $50)

    e. capital; labor; $20,000

    f. labor; capital; decreased; $2,500 (see answer to part b above)

    g. equal to

    h. $12,500 (= 250 × $50); this combination lies below the 2,000 unit isoquant and so 2,000 units cannot be produced with combination C.

4. a. By purchasing one pottery machine, which would increase output by 300 units, 15 laborers could be fired and output would remain exactly equal to 1,200 units per day. This reduces the cost of labor by 15 × $100 = $1,500. The cost of capital increases by $2,000. Clearly, substituting the machine for an equally productive amount of labor (i.e., the 15 workers) increases the total cost of producing 1,200 clay pots per day.

b. Yes, at $150 per worker, the reduction in wage expense is now $15 \times 150 = \$2,250$, which is more than the cost of the machine ($2,000 per day). Thus, the higher wages make buying a machine efficient.

c. $MP_L/w = 20/100 = 0.2$ additional pots per additional dollar spent on labor

$MP_K/r = 300/2,000 = 0.15$ additional pots per extra dollar spent on capital

Since each additional dollar spent on labor increases output by more than an additional dollar spent on capital, it is less costly to expand output by hiring more labor than by buying pottery machines.

5. a. The price of capital is $150. You can discover this by noting in the figure that the slope of the isocost curves is ½. Since the slope of isocost curves equals w/r and you are told that $r = \$150$, you can see that $75/r = ½$ and thus $r = 150$. At every tangency point along the (long-run) expansion path, the slope of the isoquant equals the slope of the isocost line. Since the isocost lines are always parallel, their slopes are constant along the expansion path and equal to $MRTS$, which must be ½ in this case.

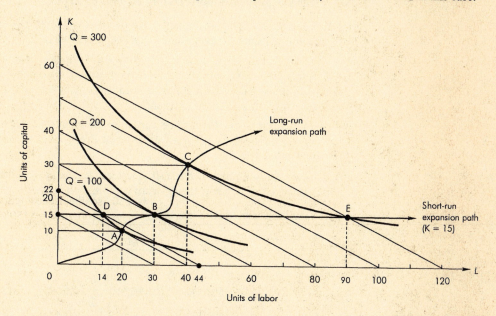

b. 20; 10; $3,000. At point A in the figure above, you can see that the tangency occurs at 20 units of labor and 10 units of capital, which costs $3,000 (= $150 × 20 or $75 × 20 + 150 × 10).

c. 30; 15; $4,500. At point B in the figure above, you can see that the tangency occurs at 30 units of labor and 15 units of capital, which costs $4,500 (= $150 × 30 or $75 × 30 + 150 × 15).

d. 40; 30; $7,500. At point C in the figure above, you can see that the tangency occurs at 40 units of labor and 30 units of capital, which costs $7,500 (= $150 × 50 or $75 × 40 + 150 × 30).

e. The short-run expansion path is a horizontal line at 15 units of capital, which is designated in the figure above as "Short-run expansion path."

f. 14; 15; $3,300; more than. At point D in the figure above, you can see that the 100-unit isoquant is reached with 15 units of capital by employing 14 units of labor at a cost of $3,300 (= $150 × 22 or $75 × 14 + 150 × 15), which is more than the long-run cost of $3,000.

g. 30; 15; $4,500; the same as. At point *B* in the figure above, you can see that the 200-unit isoquant is reached with 15 units of capital by employing 30 units of labor, which costs $4,500 (= $150 × 30 or $75 × 30 + 150 × 15), which is the same as the long-run cost of $4,500.

h. 90; 15; $9,000; more than. At point *E* in the figure, you can see that the 300-unit isoquant is reached with 15 units of capital by employing 90 units of labor at a cost of $9,000 (= $150 × 60 or $75 × 90 + $150 × 15), which is more than the long-run cost of $7,500.

i. $300; This is the difference between the short-run and long-run total costs of producing 100 units (= $3,300 – $3,000).

j. $1,500; This is the difference between the short-run and long-run total costs of producing 300 units (= $9,000 – $7,500).

k. 200; When 200 units are produced in the short-run, the fixed amount of capital (15 units) happens also to be the long-run optimal level of capital, so the costs are equal in the long-run and short-run for 200 units of output.

6. a. An expansion path is derived for a given set of input prices. Thus the input price ratio is constant for every point on an expansion path.

b. The expansion path is a locus of efficient input combinations for each level of output. The efficient input combinations satisfy the condition that *MRTS* = the input price ratio. Since the input price ratio is constant for all *Q* along an expansion path, then *MRTS* must also be constant.

c. An increase in one input price must alter the input price ratio. Thus a different set of input combinations becomes efficient at every level of output, and the expansion path shifts.

d. An equiproportional increase (or decrease) in input prices leaves the input price ratio unchanged. The same capital-labor combination is efficient for every output level.

7. a. Your table should look like this:

Q	LTC	LAC	LMC
100,000	$200,000	$2.00	xx
200,000	360,000	1.80	$1.60
300,000	420,000	1.40	0.60
400,000	480,000	1.20	0.60
500,000	500,000	1.00	0.20
600,000	720,000	1.20	2.20

b. Economies of scale occur over the output range 100,000 to 500,000 bushels/year.

c. Diseconomies of scale set in at outputs greater than 500,000 bushels/year.

MULTIPLE CHOICE / TRUE-FALSE

1. e From the figure, the isocost curves can be seen to have a slope of 2. Since *r* is given to be $2, *w*/2 = 2 ⇒ *w* = $4.

2. c Input combination *A* costs $100 (= $4 × 25 or $2 × 50). Since input combination *A* has 10 units of labor, which cost $40 to buy, $60 remains to be spent on capital. Thus, 30 (= $60/$2) units of capital are used to produce 100 units of output.

3. d At every point on the expansion path, *MRTS* = the slope of the isocost curve. Since the isocost curves have a slope equal to 2, *MRTS* must also equal 2.

4.   d   Total cost of 400 units is $160 (= $4 × 40), so average cost is $160/400 = $0.40.

5.   c $100 is being spent on 50 units of capital, leaving $60 to purchase labor. Since $w =$ $4, 15 units of labor can be purchased (input bundle B).

6.   c   When LAC falls, economies of scale exist. If LAC rises, diseconomies of scale exist.

7.   d   When $ATC = LAC$ at a given Q, LTC must equal TC. It is also true that $LMC = SMC$ at the point of tangency between LAC and ATC.

8.   d $LAC_{10} = \$720/10 = \$72$

9.   b   Since $MC = 24$ for each of the ten extra units (10 units to 20 units), total cost must rise by $240 (= $24 × 10). Thus $TC_{Q\,=\,20}$ must equal $TC_{Q\,=\,20}$ + $240 or $720 + $240 = $960. Once 12 units of capital are purchased by the firm, $480 of the $960 has been spent on capital, leaving $480 to spend on labor. Thus the amount of labor is $480/$20 = 24 units of labor.

10.   b $LMC = \Delta LTC/\Delta Q = (1,440 - 960)/(30 - 20) = \$48$. Each of the units in the interval 20 – 30 cost (on average) an additional $48 to produce. Thus, the 30th unit adds $48 to total cost.

11.   c   50 units of labor and 26 units of capital cost $2,040.

12.   e $MRTS$ at point $A = 45/15 = 3$.

13.   e   Moving from point A to B leaves output unchanged and decreases $MRTS$.

14.   a   To induce managers to move from A to B, labor must become cheaper relative to capital. Note that the slope of the isocost curve (= w/r) is smaller at B than at A.

15.   a   45 workers and 31 machines cost the same as 50 workers and 30 machines. Even though cost is the same, output falls since MP_L/w exceeds MP_K/r.

16.   F   Isoquants do not shift with changes in input prices. Isocost curves do rotate if the relative input price ratio changes, and isocost curves shift parallel if cost changes.

17.   T   With constant returns to scale, $c = z$, and a doubling of inputs leads to an equiproportionate change in output (a doubling in this case).

18.   F   The expansion path is the locus of input combinations that minimize total (not average) cost.

19.   F   This statement is meaningless. The manager can either minimize total cost for a given output or maximize output for a given total cost.

20.   F   Input prices are assumed to be constant along the LAC curve.

Homework Exercises

1. Answer the following questions using the expansion path illustrated below. The price of labor is $4 per unit.

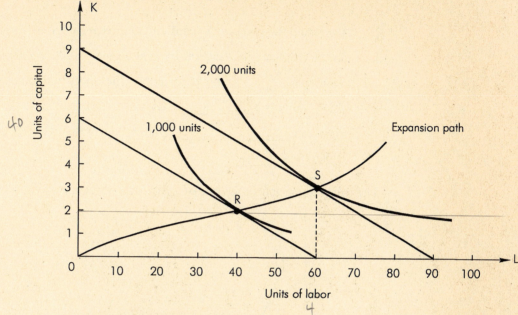

40

a. The price of capital is $ __40__ .

b. In the long run, 1,000 units of output is produced at the lowest possible total cost by employing __40__ units of labor.

c. The marginal rate of technical substitution at point S is __$4/40 = .1$__ .

d. When producing 2,000 units in the long run, the marginal product of the 60th unit of labor (MP_L) is 5. The marginal product of capital (MP_K) must equal __50__ .

e. The equation of the isocost curve passing through point R is
$$K = \underline{6 - .1L}$$

f. In the long run, 2,000 units of output is produced at the lowest possible total cost by employing __3__ units of capital.

g. Is input combination R technically efficient? Explain.

h. Is input combination R economically efficient? Explain.

i. Over the range of output from 1,000 units to 2,000 units, does the firm experience economies or diseconomies of scale? Explain.

j. Construct the short-run expansion path when capital is fixed at 2 units.

k. In the short run with capital fixed at 2 units, 2,000 units can be produced by employing __40__ units of labor. The short-run total cost of producing 2,000 units is $___400___. By restructuring its costs in the long run, the firm can ___Reduce___ (reduce, increase) its total cost of producing 2,000 by $___320 (80)___.

2. The following graph shows one of a firm's isocost curves and isoquants:

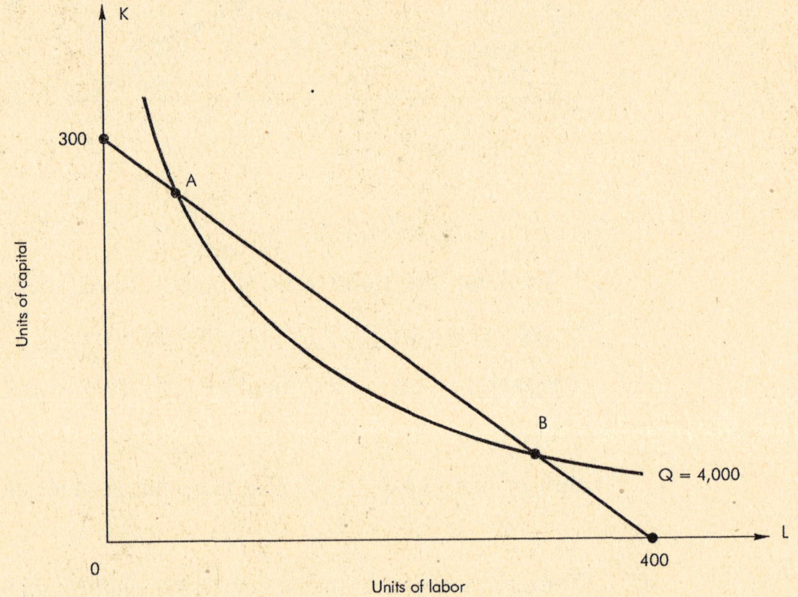

a. Combination A is not an economically efficient method of producing 4,000 units of output because, at A, _____ exceeds _____ or in other words, _____ exceeds _____. The firm should increase _____ and decrease _____.

b. Combination B is not an economically efficient method of producing 4,000 units of output because, at B, _____ exceeds _____, or in other words, _____ exceeds _____. The firm should increase _____ and decrease _____.

c. At the economically efficient method of producing 4,000 units of output the *MRTS* will equal _____.

Production and Cost Estimation

Learning Objectives

After reading Chapter 10 and working the problems for Chapter 10 in the textbook and in this Workbook, you should be able to:

➢ Specify and estimate a short-run production function using a cubic specification of the production function.

➢ Specify and estimate a short-run cost function using a cubic specification.

In order to accomplish these goals, Chapter 10 shows you how to:

➢ Estimate the parameters of a cubic short-run production function by using the technique of regression through the origin.

➢ Find the region of diminishing returns.

➢ Estimate the output level at which AVC reaches its minimum value.

➢ Estimate the parameters of a cubic short-run total variable cost equation along with the associated average variable cost and marginal cost equations.

Essential Concepts

1. The cubic empirical specification for a *short-run* production function is derived from a *long-run* cubic production function. The cubic form of the *long-run* production function is expressed as

$$Q = aK^3L^3 + bK^2L^2$$

2. The properties of a short-run cubic production function $(Q = AL^3 + BL^2)$ are:

a. Holding capital constant at $\overline{K}$ units, the short-run cubic production function is derived as follows:

$$Q = a\overline{K}^3L^3 + b\overline{K}^2L^2$$
$$= AL^3 + BL^2$$

where $A = a\overline{K}^3$ and $B = b\overline{K}^2$

b. The average and marginal products of labor are respectively

$$AP = Q/L = AL^2 + BL \quad \text{and} \quad MP = \Delta Q/\Delta L = 3AL^2 + 2BL$$

c. Marginal product of labor begins to diminish beyond L_m units of labor and average product of labor begins to diminish beyond L_a units of labor, where

$$L_m = -\frac{B}{3A} \quad \text{and} \quad L_a = -\frac{B}{2A}$$

d. In order to have the necessary properties of a production function, the parameters must satisfy the following restrictions:

$$A < 0 \quad \text{and} \quad B > 0$$

3. To estimate a cubic short-run production function using linear regression analysis, you must first transform the cubic equation into linear form:

$$Q = AX + BW$$

where $X = L^3$ and $W = L^2$. In order to correctly estimate the cubic equation, the estimated regression line must pass through the origin; that is, when $L = 0$, $Q = 0$. *Regression through the origin* simply requires the analyst to specify in the computer routine that the origin be suppressed.

4. Short-run cost functions should be estimated using data for which the level of usage of one or more of the inputs is fixed. Usually time-series data for a specific firm are used to estimate short-run cost functions.

5. Collecting data may be complicated by the fact that accounting data are based on expenditures and may not include the firm's opportunity cost of using the various inputs. In particular, capital costs should reflect not only acquisition cost but also the rental income forgone by using (rather than renting) the capital, the depreciation, and any capital gain or loss.

6. The effects of inflation on cost data must be eliminated. To adjust nominal cost figures for inflation, divide each observation by the appropriate price index for that time period.

7. The properties of a short-run cubic cost function ($TVC = aQ + bQ^2 + cQ^3$) are:

a. The average variable cost and marginal cost functions are, respectively,

$$AVC = a + bQ + cQ^2 \quad \text{and} \quad SMC = a + 2bQ + 3cQ^2$$

b. Average variable cost reaches its minimum value at $Q_m = -b/2c$.

c. To conform to the theoretical properties of a cost function, the parameters must satisfy the following restrictions:

$$a > 0, b < 0, \text{ and } c > 0$$

d. The cubic specification produces an S-shaped TVC curve and $\cup$-shaped AVC and SMC curves.

e. Because all three cost curves (TVC, AVC, and SMC) employ the same parameters, it is only necessary to estimate any one of these functions in order to obtain estimates of all three curves.

f. In the short-run cubic specification, input prices are assumed to be constant and are not explicitly included in the cost equation.

Summary of Short-Run Empirical Production and Cost Functions

	Short-run cubic production equations
Total product	$Q = AL^3 + BL^2$
Average product of labor	$AP = AL^2 + BL$
Marginal product of labor	$MP = 3AL^2 + 2BL$
Diminishing marginal returns	beginning at $L_m = -\dfrac{B}{3A}$
Restrictions on parameters	$A < 0$ and $B > 0$

	Short-run cubic cost equations
Total variable cost	$TVC = aQ + bQ^2 + cQ^3$
Average variable cost	$AVC = a + bQ + cQ^2$
Marginal cost	$SMC = a + 2bQ + 3cQ^2$
Average variable cost reaches minimum at	$Q_m = -\dfrac{b}{2c}$
Restrictions on parameters	$a > 0, b < 0, c > 0$

Matching Definitions

empirical production function   regression through the origin
long-run production function   nominal cost data
short-run production function   deflating
cubic production function   user cost of capital
short-run cubic production function

1. _____ The exact mathematical form of the equation to be estimated.

2. _____ Production function in which all inputs are considered variable.

3. _____ Production function in which at least one input is fixed.

4. _____ Production function of the form $Q = aK^3L^3 + bK^2L^2$.

5. _____ Production function of the form $Q = AL^3 + BL^2$.

6. _____ A regression with the intercept parameter suppressed.

7. _____ Data that have not been corrected for the effects of inflation.

8. _____ The process of correcting for inflation by dividing nominal data by a price index.

9. _____ The firm's opportunity cost of using capital.

Study Problems

1. Name the following empirical specifications of production and cost functions:

   a. $TVC = aQ + bQ^2 + cQ^3$ _____

   b. $SMC = a + 2bQ + 3cQ^2$ _____

   c. $Q = aK^3L^3 + bK^2L^2$ _____

   d. $AVC = a + bQ + cQ^2$ _____

   e. $Q = AL^3 + BL^2$ _____

2. What restrictions must be placed on the parameters in the empirical production and cost functions in question 1 above?

3. A firm estimates its long-run production function to be

$$Q = -0.008K^3L^3 + 10K^2L^2$$

Suppose the firm employs 15 units of capital.

   a. The equations for the product curves in the short run are:

   $TP =$ _____

   $AP =$ _____

   $MP =$ _____

   b. At _____ units of labor, marginal product of labor begins to diminish.

   c. At _____ units of labor, average product of labor begins to diminish.

d. Calculate the marginal product and average product of labor when 20 units of labor are employed.

$$MP_{L=20} = \underline{\hspace{2cm}}$$

$$AP_{L=20} = \underline{\hspace{2cm}}$$

4. A firm estimates its cubic production function of the following form

$$Q = AL^3 + BL^2$$

and obtains the following estimation results:

DEPENDENT VARIABLE:	Q	R–SQUARE	F–RATIO	P–VALUE ON F	
OBSERVATIONS:	62	0.7032	142.175	0.0001	
VARIABLE		PARAMETER ESTIMATE	STANDARD ERROR	T–RATIO	P–VALUE
INTERCEPT					
L3		-0.050	0.013	-3.85	0.0003
L2		0.600	0.250	2.40	0.0195

The firm pays $36 per unit for labor services.

a. The estimated total, average, and marginal product functions are:

$$Q = \underline{\hspace{4cm}}$$

$$AP = \underline{\hspace{4cm}}$$

$$MP = \underline{\hspace{4cm}}$$

b. Are the parameters of the correct sign and are they significant? Discuss the *p*-values.

c. Average product reaches its maximum value at _____ units of labor.

d. Average product reaches its maximum value at _____ units of output.

e. At the output level for part *d*, $AVC = \$$ _____ and $SMC = \$$ _____.

f. When labor usage is 7 units, $AVC = \$$ _____ and $SMC = \$$ _____.

5. Consider a firm that estimates the following average variable cost function:

$$AVC = a + bQ + cQ^2$$

The computer printout for the regression analysis is:

DEPENDENT VARIABLE:	AVC	R–SQUARE	F–RATIO	P–VALUE ON F	
OBSERVATIONS:	16	0.9000	58.50	0.0001	
VARIABLE		PARAMETER ESTIMATE	STANDARD ERROR	T–RATIO	P–VALUE
INTERCEPT		75.00	25.00	3.00	0.0102
Q		-2.40	0.40	-6.00	0.0001
Q2		0.06	0.20	3.00	0.0102

a. Determine whether the estimate values of the coefficients indicate a U-shaped AVC curve at the 5 percent level of significance.

b. The marginal cost function associated with this AVC function is
    $SMC =$ _____ .

c. The total variable cost function associated with this function is
    $TVC =$ _____ .

d. AVC reaches its minimum value at $Q_m =$ _____ .

e. Minimum $AVC = \$$ _____ .

Computer Problem

Mercantile Metalworks, Inc. manufactures wire carts for grocery stores. The production manager at Mercantile wishes to estimate an empirical production function for the assembly of carts using the following time-series data for the last 22 days of assembly operations. L is the daily number of assembly workers employed, and Q is the number of carts assembled (completely) for that day. Mercantile pays its assembly workers $160 per day in wages and benefits.

Day	Number of workers L	Number of carts assembled Q	Day	Number of workers L	Number of carts assembled Q
1	15	75	12	40	2,165
2	21	897	13	21	1,534
3	24	1,280	14	27	835
4	32	1,251	15	20	906
5	36	1,315	16	15	102
6	38	2,837	17	36	1,424
7	18	590	18	14	111
8	18	129	19	24	868
9	41	1,572	20	25	916
10	36	2,005	21	32	1,341
11	44	1,024	22	21	806

1. Use a computer regression package, such as the Student Edition of Statistix 8, to estimate the following short-run cubic production function:

$$Q = AL^3 + BL^2$$

Do the parameter estimates have the appropriate algebraic signs? Are they statistically significant at the 1 percent level of statistical significance? How well did the empirical model do in explaining the variation in the number of carts assembled each day?

2. What are the estimated total, average, and marginal product functions from your regression results in Part 1?

3. At what level of labor usage does average product reach its maximum value? In a day, how many carts per worker are assembled when average product is maximized? What is average variable cost when average product is maximized?

4. What is short-run marginal cost when average product is maximized?

5. Beyond what level of *labor employment* does the law of diminishing returns set in? Beyond what level of *output*?

Multiple Choice / True-False

1. Empirical production and cost functions
   a. can be obtained using regression analysis.
   b. require data from actual production operations.
   c. can be used in making profit-maximizing decisions.
   d. are curvilinear functions that can be estimated using regression analysis.
   e. all of the above.

2. Time-series data for a specific firm are often used to estimate short-run cost functions because
   a. over the chosen period of time, a firm will not be able to vary the usage of one or more inputs.
   b. cross-section data would probably include firms with different levels of capital usage.
   c. time-series data are best suited for investment decisions.
   d. both *a* and *b*.
   e. both *b* and *c*.

3. A cubic specification for a short-run cost function is appropriate when the scatter diagram indicates
   a. an *S*-shaped short-run marginal cost curve.
   b. total cost increases at an increasing rate throughout the range of output.
   c. an *S*-shaped short-run total variable cost curve.
   d. an *S*-shaped short-run average total cost curve.
   e. a ∪-shaped short-run total cost curve.

4. The user cost of capital includes
   a. acquisition cost.
   b. depreciation from the use of capital.
   c. capital gains or losses.
   d. revenue foregone by using rather than renting the capital.
   e. all of the above.

5. To adjust cost data for the effects of inflation,
   a. throw out the observations that occur in years with high inflation rates.
   b. deflate cost figures by dividing by an appropriate price index.
   c. inflate cost figures by multiplying by an appropriate price index.
   d. adjust cost data by dividing by the percentage rate of inflation.

6. An estimated short-run cost function
   a. would be used to make price and output decisions.
   b. holds the capital stock constant.
   c. can be estimated using time-series data.
   d. all of the above.

7. For the short-run cost function $AVC = a + bQ + cQ^2$,
   a. the AVC curve is $\cup$-shaped when $a < 0$, $b > 0$, and $c < 0$.
   b. the AVC curve is $\cup$-shaped when $a > 0$, $b < 0$, and $c > 0$.
   c. the corresponding SMC function is $SMC = aQ + 2bQ^2 + 3cQ^3$.
   d. both a and c.
   e. all of the above.

8. A potential problem with cross-section cost data is that
   a. nominal cost data include the effect of inflation.
   b. different firms face different input prices.
   c. at least one input is fixed over time.
   d. both a and b.
   e. none of the above.

The next six questions refer to the following:

A firm estimated its short-run costs using an average variable cost function of the form
$$AVC = a + bQ + cQ^2$$

and obtained the following results. Total fixed cost is $1,000.

DEPENDENT VARIABLE: AVC		R-SQUARE	F-RATIO	P-VALUE ON F	
OBSERVATIONS: 35		0.8713	108.3	0.0001	
VARIABLE		PARAMETER ESTIMATE	STANDARD ERROR	T-RATIO	P-VALUE
INTERCEPT		43.40	13.80	3.14	0.0036
Q		-2.80	0.90	-3.11	0.0039
Q2		0.20	0.05	4.00	0.0004

9. The estimated marginal cost function is:
   a. $SMC = 43.4Q - 1.4Q^2 + 0.07Q^3$
   b. $SMC = 43.4 - 1.4Q + 0.07Q^2$
   c. $SMC = 43.4Q - 5.6Q^2 + 0.6Q^3$
   d. $SMC = 43.4 - 5.6Q + 0.6Q^2$

10. If the firm produces 20 units of output, what is estimated AVC?
    a. $19.40
    b. $67.40
    c. $171.40
    d. $179.40

11. If the firm produces 20 units of output, what is estimated total cost?
     a. $1,348
     b. $1,388
     c. $2,348
     d. $4,428

12. If the firm produces 12 units of output, what is estimated *SMC*?
     a. $38.60
     b. $62.60
     c. $105.80
     d. $197.00

13. At what level of output is *AVC* minimum?
     a. 0.14
     b. 4.67
     c. 7
     d. 28

14. What is the minimum value of *AVC*?
     a. $ 24.50
     b. $ 33.60
     c. $ 72.80
     d. $121.80

15. A cubic specification for a short-run production function is appropriate when the scatter diagram indicates
     a. an *S*-shaped total product curve.
     b. marginal product of labor falls throughout the range of labor usage.
     c. total product is decreasing throughout the range of labor usage.
     d. an *S*-shaped marginal product of labor curve.
     e. a ∪-shaped marginal product of labor curve.

16. T   F   With cross-section data it is not necessary to correct for inflation.

17. T   F   Estimation of a cubic short-run cost function requires that the intercept term be suppressed.

18. T   F   Input prices are commonly omitted in short-run cost estimation because the span of the time-series data set is generally short enough that real input prices do not change much.

19. T   F   Once one of the three cost curves *TVC*, *AVC*, or *SMC* has been estimated, the other two functions cannot be estimated without drawing a new sample of data.

20. T   F   Short-run cost functions are used by firms to make investment decisions while long-run cost functions provide information for output and pricing decisions.

Answers

1. empirical production function
2. long-run production function
3. short-run production function
4. cubic production function
5. short-run cubic production function
6. regression through the origin
7. nominal cost data
8. deflating
9. user cost of capital

STUDY PROBLEMS

1.
   a. short-run cubic cost function
   b. short-run cubic marginal cost function
   c. long-run cubic production function
   d. short-run cubic average variable cost function
   e. short-run cubic production function

2.
   a. $a > 0,\ b < 0,\ c > 0$
   b. same as part a
   c. $A = a\overline{K}^3 < 0$ and $B = b\overline{K}^2 > 0$
   d. same as part a
   e. $A < 0\ \ B > 0$

3.
   a. $TP = -0.008(15)^3 L^3 + 10(15)^2 L^2 = -27L^3 + 2{,}250L^2$

      $AP = -27L^2 + 2{,}250L$

      $MP = 3(-27)L^2 + 2(2{,}250)L = -81L^2 + 4{,}500L$
   b. $L_m = -B/3A = -2{,}250/3(-27) = 27.78$ units of labor
   c. $L_a = -B/2A = -2{,}250/2(-27) = 41.67$ units of labor
   d. $MP_{L=20} = -81(20)^2 + 4{,}500(20) = 57{,}600$

      $AP_{L=20} = -27(20)^2 + 2{,}250(20) = 34{,}200$

4.
   a. $Q = -0.05L^3 + 0.6L^2$

      $AP = -0.05L^2 + 0.6L$

      $MP = 3(-0.05)L^2 + 2(0.6)L = -0.15L^2 + 1.2L$
   b. The signs of both parameters are correct: A is negative, B is positive. The p-values indicate significance at better than the 2 percent level for both parameter estimates.
   c. $L_a = -B/2A = -0.6/-0.1 = 6$

      AP reaches its maximum value when 6 units of labor are employed.
   d. $Q = -0.05(6)^3 + 0.6(6)^2 = 10.8$

      At 10.8 units of output, AP reaches its maximum value.
   e. $AP_{max} = -0.05(6)^2 + 0.6(6) = 1.8$ (or $AP_{max} = Q/L = 10.8/6 = 1.8$)

      So, $AVC = w/AP = 36/1.8 = \$20$

      Since $AP = MP$ when AP is at its maximum value, $AVC = SMC = \$20$ at $L = 6$ and $Q = 10.8$.

      f.   When $L = 7$, $AP = 1.75$ and $MP = 1.05$. Thus, $AVC = 36/1.75 = \$20.57$ and $SMC = 36/1.05 = \$34.29$.

5.   a.   The parameter restrictions are: $a > 0$, $b < 0$, and $c > 0$. In each case, the absolute value of the t-ratio is greater than the critical value of 2.160.

      b. $SMC = 75 - 4.8Q + 0.18Q^2$

      c. $TVC = 75Q - 2.4Q^2 + 0.06Q^3$

      d. $Q_m = -b/2c = 2.4/0.12 = 20$

      f. $AVC_{min} = 75 - 2.4(20) + 0.06(20)^2 = 51$

COMPUTER PROBLEM

1.   Yes, $\hat{A} < 0$ and $\hat{B} > 0$. Both $\hat{A}$ and $\hat{B}$ are statistically significant at better than the 1 percent level. The estimated model explained only about 62 percent of the variation in output. The computer printout looks like this:

DEP. VARIABLE:	Q	R-SQUARE	F-RATIO	P-VALUE ON F	
OBS:	22	0.6198	83.72	0.0000	
VARIABLE		PARAMETER ESTIMATE	STD. ERROR	T-RATIO	P-VALUE
L3		–0.04249	0.01491	–2.85	0.0099
L2		2.77199	0.55584	4.99	0.0001

2. $\hat{Q} = -0.04249L^3 + 2.77199L^2$

     $AP = -0.04249L^2 + 2.77199L = \hat{A}L^2 + \hat{B}L$

     $MP = -0.12747L^2 + 5.54398L = 2\hat{A}L^2 + 3\hat{B}L$

3. $L_a = -B/2A = -(2.77199)/(2 \times -0.04249) = 32.62$ workers per day

     $AP(L_a) = -0.04249(32.62)^2 + 2.77199(32.62) = 45.21$ carts per worker

     $A\hat{V}C = w/AP = \$160/45.21 = \$3.54$ per cart

4.   At maximum AP, $AP = MP$, so $SMC = AVC$, and thus $SMC = \$3.54$. You can verify this result by noticing that MP (at $L = 32.62$) is 45.21. Thus, $SMC = w/MP = \$160/45.21 = \$3.54$, which is exactly the value found in question 3 for AVC.

5. $L_m = 21.75$ workers per day; $\hat{Q}(21.75) = 874$ carts per day

MULTIPLE CHOICE / TRUE-FALSE

1.   e   Empirical production and cost functions are all of these things.

2.   d   To estimate a short-run production function, at least one input must be fixed; that is, usage of one of the inputs must take the same value for each observation in the sample. A time-series on the same firm is usually the best way to accomplish this.

3.   c   An S-shaped total variable cost function requires a cubic specification.

4.   e   The user cost of capital accounts for the cost of acquiring capital, and also any depreciation or capital gains/losses resulting from using and owning capital. The user cost of capital also includes the opportunity cost of using its capital rather than renting it.

5.   b   Nominal dollars are adjusted for the effects of inflation by dividing the nominal dollars by a price index to get real (or constant) dollars.

6.	d	All of these statements are true in general.
7.	b	See Table 10.3 in your textbook.
8.	b	If input prices vary, then they must be included in the model as explanatory variables.
9.	d	$SMC = a + 2bQ + 3cQ^2$, where a = intercept = 43.40, $2b = 2 \times -2.80 = -5.6$, and $3c = 3 \times 0.20 = 0.60$.
10.	b	$AVC_{Q=20} = 43.40 - 2.80 \times 20 + 0.20 \times 20^2 = \$67.40$
11.	c	$TC_{Q=20} = (AVC_{Q=20} \times 20) + TFC = 67.40 \times 20 + 1,000 = \$2,348$
12.	b	$\$62.60 = SMC_{Q=12} = 43.40 - 5.60 \times 12 + 0.60 \times 0.12^2$
13.	c	$AVC_{min} = -b/2c = -(-2.8)/(2 \times 0.2) = 7$
14.	b	$AVC_{Q=7} = \$33.60 = 43.40 - 2.80 \times 7 + 0.20 \times 7^2 = \$67.40$
15.	a	A cubic specification has an S-shape.
16.	T	Correcting for inflation is not necessary because all data are for the same period in time.
17.	F	Regression through the origin is not employed in estimating a cubic short-run *cost* equation but rather in estimating a cubic short-run *production* function.
18.	T	If inflation affects all input prices equiproportionately, real input prices will not vary.
19.	T	Knowing any one equation allows the other two to be derived mathematically.
20.	F	Long-run cost data are used for investment decisions, while short-run cost data are used for output and pricing decisions.

Homework Exercises

1. A firm estimates its cubic production function of the following form:

$$Q = AL^3 + BL^2$$

and obtains the following results:

DEPENDENT VARIABLE: Q		R-SQUARE	F-RATIO	P-VALUE ON F	
OBSERVATIONS: 32		0.7547	92.31	0.0001	
VARIABLE		PARAMETER ESTIMATE	STANDARD ERROR	T-RATIO	P-VALUE
L3		−0.0016	0.0005	−3.20	0.0032
L2		0.4000	0.0950	4.21	0.0002

a. The equations for total product, average product, and marginal product are:

$TP =$ _____

$AP =$ _____

$MP =$ _____

b. The estimated values of A and B are statistically significant at the (exact) levels, _____ and _____, respectively.

c. At _____ units of labor usage, marginal product of labor begins to diminish.

When the wage rate is $300, answer the following questions. (Remember that $AP = Q/L$; $AVC = w/AP$; and $SMC = w/MP$.)

d. Average product of labor reaches its maximum value at _____ units of labor.

e. At the output for part d, average variable cost is $_____ and marginal cost is $_____.

f. When the rate of labor usage is 100 units of labor, output is _____ units. Average variable cost is $_____ and marginal cost is $_____.

2. Suppose Heritage Corporation believes that its total variable costs follow a cubic specification and so it estimates its average variable costs using the following specification:

$$AVC = a + bQ + cQ^2$$

The regression analysis produces the following computer output:

DEPENDENT VARIABLE: AVC	R–SQUARE	F–RATIO	P–VALUE ON F		
OBSERVATIONS: 45	0.6145	33.47	0.0001		
VARIABLE	PARAMETER ESTIMATE	STANDARD ERROR	T–RATIO	P–VALUE	
INTERCEPT	175.0	25.00	7.00	0.0001	
Q	–3.20	0.80	–4.00	0.0003	
Q2	0.08	0.01	8.00	0.0001	

a. Do the estimated coefficients have the required signs to yield a ∪-shaped AVC curve? Discuss the significance using the p-values.

b. Heritage Corporation's marginal cost function is

$SMC = $ _____ .

c. At what level of output does AVC reach a minimum? What is the value of AVC at its minimum?

$Q_{min} = $ _____ $AVC_{min} = $ _____

d. Compute AVC and SMC when Heritage produces 8 units.

$AVC_{Q=8} = $ _____

$SMC_{Q=8} = $ _____

3. **_COMPUTER EXERCISE_**

Use a computer regression package, such as the Student Edition of Statistix 8, to work this computer exercise.

Palm Products Company has collected data on its average variable costs of production for the past 12 months. The costs have been adjusted for inflation by deflating with an appropriate price index. The AVC and associated output data are presented below:

obs	Q	AVC	obs	Q	AVC
1	22	$208	7	45	$172
2	31	202	8	45	158
3	31	206	9	45	173
4	25	214	10	62	170
5	41	174	11	62	152
6	41	203	12	70	175

a. Run the appropriate regression to estimate the parameters for the empirical cost function $AVC = a + bQ + cQ^2$.

b. Using a 10 percent significance level, discuss suitability of the parameter estimates obtained in part _a_. Consider both the algebraic signs and statistical significance of the parameter estimates.

c. Present the estimated average variable cost, total variable cost, and short-run marginal cost functions.

d. At what level of output does AVC reach its minimum value? What is the minimum value of AVC at its minimum?

$$Q_{min} = \text{_____} \qquad AVC_{min} = \text{_____}$$

e. Compute AVC and SMC when Palm Products produces 20 units of output:

$$AVC_{Q=20} = \text{_____}$$

$$SMC_{Q=20} = \text{_____}$$

Is AVC rising or falling when Palm produces 20 units? Explain.

f. At what level of output does SMC equal AVC? How did you get this answer?

Managerial Decisions in Competitive Markets

Learning Objectives

After reading Chapter 11 and working the problems for Chapter 11 in the textbook and in this Workbook, you should be able to:

➤ Discuss three characteristics of perfectly competitive markets.

➤ Apply the basic principles of marginal analysis to determine either (1) the profit-maximizing (or loss-minimizing) level of output, or (2) the profit-maximizing (or loss-minimizing) level of input usage.

➤ Explain why the demand curve facing an *individual* firm in a perfectly competitive industry is perfectly elastic, and why this demand curve is also the marginal revenue curve for a competitive firm.

➤ Explain why a firm should shut down in the short run if market price falls below minimum average variable cost.

➤ Calculate profit margin (or average profit) and explain why profit margin should be ignored when making profit-maximizing decisions.

➤ Explain why fixed costs are irrelevant to a manager's production decision.

➤ Define the concept of long-run competitive equilibrium and explain why a firm in long-run competitive equilibrium produces at the minimum point on long-run average cost.

➤ Give a definition of increasing cost and constant cost industries and draw a long-run industry supply curve for a constant cost industry and for an increasing cost industry.

➤ Explain, using the concept of economic rent, why it is possible for owners of exceptionally productive resources to "get rich" even though economic profit is zero in the long run for competitive markets.

➤ Find the profit-maximizing (or loss-minimizing) level of output for a firm operating in a perfectly competitive market using empirical estimates (or forecasts) of (1) the market price of the commodity, (2) the average variable cost function, and (3) the marginal cost function.

Essential Concepts

1. Perfect competition occurs when a market is described by the following three characteristics:

   i. Firms are price-takers because each firm produces only a very small portion of total market or industry output.

   ii. All firms in the market produce a homogeneous or perfectly standardized product.

   iii. Entry into and exit from the market is unrestricted.

2. The demand curve facing a competitive price-taking firm is horizontal or perfectly elastic at the price determined by the intersection of the market demand and supply curves. Since marginal revenue equals price for a competitive firm, the demand curve is also simultaneously the marginal revenue curve (i.e., $D = MR$). Price-taking firms can sell all they want at the market price. Each additional unit of sales adds to total revenue an amount equal to price.

3. Average profit, which is total profit divided by output (π/Q), is equal to profit margin, which is the difference between price and unit cost ($P - ATC$). The level of output that maximizes total profit occurs at a higher level of output than the output that maximizes profit margin (and average profit). Managers should ignore profit margin (average profit) when making optimal decisions.

4. In the short run, the manager of a firm will choose to produce the output where $P = SMC$, rather than shut down, as long as total revenue is greater than or equal to total variable cost ($TR \geq TVC$) or equivalently, price is equal to or greater than average variable cost ($P \geq AVC$). If price is less than average variable cost ($P < AVC$), the manager will shut down and produce nothing, losing only an amount equal to total fixed costs.

5. Fixed costs are irrelevant in the production decision because the level of fixed cost has no effect on either marginal cost or minimum average variable cost, and thus no effect on the optimal level of output.

6. Summary of the manager's output decision in the short-run:

   i. Average variable cost tells whether to produce; the firm ceases to produce—shuts down—if price falls below minimum AVC.

   ii. Marginal cost tells how much to produce; if $P \geq$ minimum AVC, the firm produces the output at which $P = SMC$.

   iii. Average total cost tells how much profit or loss is made if the firm decides to produce; profit equals the difference between P and ATC multiplied by the quantity produced and sold.

7. The short-run supply curve for an individual price-taking firm is the portion of the firm's marginal cost curve above minimum average variable cost. For market prices less than minimum average variable cost, quantity supplied is zero.

8. The short-run supply curve for a competitive industry can be obtained by horizontally summing the supply curves of all the individual firms in the industry. Short-run supply for a competitive industry is always upward-sloping.

9. In long-run competitive equilibrium, all firms are in profit-maximizing equilibrium ($P = LMC$). Long-run competitive equilibrium occurs because of the entry of new firms into the industry or the exit of existing firms from the industry. The market adjusts so that $P = LMC = LAC$, which is at the minimum point on LAC.

10. The long-run industry supply curve can be either flat (perfectly elastic) or upward sloping depending upon whether the industry is a *constant cost industry* or an *increasing cost industry*, respectively.

    a. For a constant cost industry, as industry output expands, input prices remain constant, and the minimum point on LAC is unchanged. Since long-run supply price equals minimum LAC, the long-run industry supply curve is perfectly elastic (horizontal).

    b. For an increasing cost industry, as industry output expands, input prices are bid up, causing the minimum point on LAC to rise, and long-run supply price to rise. The long-run industry supply curve for an increasing cost industry is upward sloping.

    c. Economic profit is zero for all points on the long-run industry supply curve for both constant and increasing cost industries.

11. *Economic rent* is a payment to the owner of a scarce, superior resource in excess of the resource's opportunity cost. Firms that employ such exceptionally productive resources earn only a normal profit (economic profit is zero) in long-run competitive equilibrium because the potential economic profit from employing a superior resource is paid to the resource as rent.

12. Choosing either output or input usage to maximize profit leads to the same maximum profit level. The profit-maximizing level of *input* usage produces exactly that level of *output* that maximizes profit.

    a. The *marginal revenue product (MRP)* of an additional unit of a variable input is the additional revenue from hiring one more unit of the input. For the variable input labor:

    $$MRP = \frac{\Delta TR}{\Delta L} = P \times MP$$

    When a manager chooses to produce rather than shut down ($TR > TVC$), the optimal level of input usage is found by following this rule: If the marginal revenue product of an additional unit of the input is greater (less) than the price of the input, then that unit should (not) be hired. If the usage of the variable input varies continuously, the manager should employ the amount of the input at which MRP = input price.

    b. *Average revenue product* (ARP) is the average revenue per worker ($ARP = TR/L$). ARP can be calculated as the product of price times the average product of labor:

    $$ARP = \frac{TR}{L} = P \times AP$$

    A manager should shut down operation in the short-run if there is no level of input usage for which ARP is greater than or equal to MRP. When ARP is less than MRP, total revenue is less than total variable cost, and the manager minimizes losses in the short run by shutting down.

13. The following steps that use empirical estimates of price and costs can be employed to find the profit-maximizing rate of production and the level of profit a competitive firm will earn.

Step 1: *Forecast the price of the product.* Use one of the two statistical techniques presented in Chapter 7 of this Workbook (either time-series forecasting or econometric forecasting) to forecast the price of the product.

Step 2: *Estimate average variable cost (AVC) and marginal cost (SMC).* The cubic specification is the appropriate form for estimating a family of short-run cost curves:

$$AVC = a + bQ + cQ^2 \quad \text{and} \quad SMC = a + 2bQ + 3cQ^2$$

Step 3: *Check the shutdown rule.* If $P \geq AVC_{min}$, then the manager should produce. If $P < AVC_{min}$, then the manager should shut down ($Q = 0$). In order to find AVC_{min}, substitute

$$Q_{min} = -\frac{b}{2c}$$

into the equation for AVC:

$$AVC_{min} = a + bQ_{min} + cQ_{min}^2$$

Now compare AVC_{min} to the forecasted price to determine whether or not to produce.

Step 4: *If $P \geq AVC_{min}$, find the output level where $P = SMC$.* The profit-maximizing output level occurs where $P = SMC$. To find the optimal level of output, set forecasted price equal to estimated marginal cost and solve for Q^*:

$$P = a + 2bQ^* + 3cQ^{*2}$$

Step 5: *Compute profit or loss.* Once a manager determines how much to produce, the calculation of total profit is a straightforward matter.

$$\text{Profit} = TR - TC$$
$$= P \times Q^* - AVC \times Q^* - TFC$$
$$= (P - AVC)Q^* - TFC$$

If $P < AVC_{min}$, the firm shuts down, and profit is $-TFC$.

Matching Definitions

average revenue product
constant-cost industry
economic rent
increasing-cost industry
long-run competitive equilibrium
marginal revenue product
perfect competition
perfectly elastic demand
profit margin (or average profit)
quadratic formula
shut down
shutdown price

1. _____ A market structure in which a large number of firms sell a homogenous product or service with no restrictions on entry or exit and each firm is a price-taker.

2. _____ The demand facing a price-taking firm.

3. _____ A firm produces zero output but must still pay its fixed costs.

4. _____ Price minus average total cost.

5. _____ Price below which a firm shuts down in the short run.

6. _____ All firms produce where price equals long-run marginal cost, and economic profits are zero.

7. _____ Industry in which input prices rise as all firms in the industry expand output.

8. _____ Industry in which input prices remain constant as all firms in the industry expand output.

9. _____ Payment in excess of a resource's opportunity cost.

10. _____ The additional revenue earned by hiring one more unit of a variable input.

11. _____ The average revenue per worker.

12. _____ $$X_1, X_2 = \frac{-B \pm \sqrt{B^2 - 4AC}}{2C}$$

Study Problems

1. The manager of a competitive firm will:

   a. Produce rather than shut down if the forecasted price of the product is greater than __AVC__.

   b. Produce and make an economic profit if the forecasted price of the product is greater than __ATC__.

   c. Produce at a loss if the forecasted price is less than __ATC__ but greater than __AVC__.

   d. Shut down if the forecasted price is less than __AVC__.

   e. Minimize loss by producing the level of output where __P__ equals __SMC__ when forecasted price is greater than __AVC__ but less than __ATC__.

   f. Maximize profit by producing the level of output where __P__ equals __SMC__ when forecasted price is greater than __ATC__.

2. Answer the following questions using the cost curves for the price-taking firm shown in the figure below.

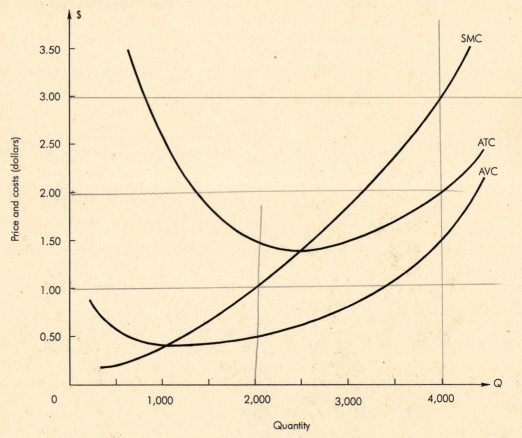

Quantity

   a. If price is $3 per unit of output, draw the marginal revenue curve. The manager should produce __4000__ units.

   b. Since average total cost is $ __4000__ for this output, total cost is $ __4000__ .

c.   The firm makes a profit of $__4000__.

d.   Let price fall to $1, and draw the new marginal revenue curve. The manager should now produce __2000__ units.

e.   At a price of $1, total revenue is now $__2000__ and total cost is $__3000__. The firm makes a loss of $__1000__.

f.   At a price of $1, total variable cost is $__1000__, leaving $__1000__ to apply to fixed cost.

g.   If price falls below $__.50__, the firm will produce zero output.

3.   If a firm is making a loss in the short run, it can do either of two things in the long run:

(i)   _____

(ii) _____

Explain the circumstances under which each of these actions will be taken.

4.   In long-run competitive equilibrium, consumers pay the lowest price for each unit of the good. Explain why.

5.   Consider a competitive, price-taking firm that employs only one variable input, labor, to produce a product that sells for $14 per unit. The wage rate is $24 per unit of labor and total fixed costs are $500. Fill in the blanks in each column of this table as instructed by the questions below:

(1) Units of Labor	(2) Output	(3) Marginal Product	(4) Marginal Revenue Product	(5) Average Product	(6) Average Revenue Product	(7) Marginal Cost	(8) Profit
0	0	___	xx	xx	xx	xx	___
1	8	___	___	___	___	___	___
2	20	___	___	___	___	___	___
3	34	___	___	___	___	___	___
4	45	___	___	___	___	___	___
5	53	___	___	___	___	___	___
6	58	___	___	___	___	___	___
7	61	___	___	___	___	___	___
8	63	___	___	___	___	___	___
9	64	___	___	___	___	___	___
10	62	___	___	___	___	xx	___

a. Fill in the blanks in columns 3 and 5. Marginal product begins to diminish beyond _____ units of labor. Marginal product is negative for the _____th unit of labor. [Note: You will see later in this problem that the profit-maximizing level of labor usage does indeed occur well in the range of diminishing marginal product, but *not* into the range of negative marginal product.]

b. Compute marginal and average revenue products and fill in the blanks in columns 4 and 6. The sixth unit of labor _____ (increases, decreases) _____ (total, marginal) revenue by $_____. Decreasing labor usage from three to two units _____ (increases, decreases) _____ (total, marginal) revenue by $_____.

c. The manager can maximize *total revenue* by hiring _____ units of labor. The maximum possible value of total revenue is $_____.

d. The manager hires _____ units of labor in order to maximize *profit*. At this level of labor usage, *ARP* = _____ which is _____ (greater, less) than *MRP*.

e. Compute marginal cost and fill in the blanks in column 7. At first, marginal cost _____ (rises, falls) as marginal product rises, then marginal cost _____ (rises, falls) as marginal product falls.

f. The profit-maximizing level of output is _____ units because this is the last level of output for which _____ exceeds _____, or equivalently, _____ exceeds _____ .

g. Compute profit and fill in the blanks in column 8. The optimal level of labor employment and the optimal level of output both result in an identical maximum profit level of $_____.

6. A textile firm in a competitive industry employs a particularly efficient manager to run the operations at its production facility. In the textile industry, a plant manager typically makes a salary of $4,500 per month. The textile firm employing the superior manager faces the *LAC* and *LMC* curves shown in the figure below. In long-run competitive equilibrium, the price of the product is $9.

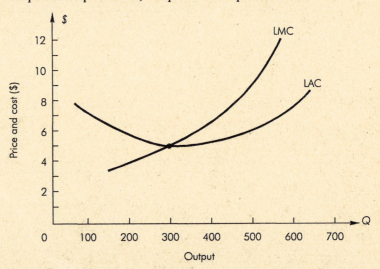

a. A typical textile firm in this competitive industry has a minimum long-run average cost of $_____. The typical textile firm earns economic profit of $_____.

b. The textile firm with the superior plant manager could earn economic profit of $_____ per month, if no rent is paid to the superior manager.

c. The superior plant manager is likely to earn a salary of $_____ per month, $_____ of which is economic rent.

d. If the superior plant manager also owned the textile firm, she would earn $_____ of economic profit. Explain your answer.

7. Consider a price-taking firm in the competitive industry for raw chocolate. The market demand and supply functions for raw chocolate are estimated to be

Chocolate demand: $Q = 10,000 - 10,000P + 2M$
Chocolate supply: $Q = 40,000 + 10,000P - 4,000P_I$

where Q is the number of 10 pound bars per month, P is the price of a 10 pound bar of raw chocolate, income is M, and P_I is the price of cocoa (the primary ingredient input). The manager of ABC Cocoa Products uses time-series data to obtain the following forecasted values of M and P_I for 2005:

$$M = \$25,000 \quad \text{and} \quad P_I = \$10$$

The manager of ABC Cocoa also estimates its average variable cost function to be

$$AVC = 3.0 - 0.0027Q + 0.0000009Q^2$$

Fixed costs at ABC will be $1,600 in 2005.

a. The price of raw chocolate in 2005 is forecasted to be $_____.

b Average variable cost reaches its minimum value at _____ bars of chocolate per month.

c. The minimum value of average variable cost is $_____.

d. Should ABC Cocoa produce or shut down?

e. The marginal cost function for the firm is
$$SMC = \underline{\hspace{6cm}}.$$

f. The optimal level of production for the firm is _____ bars of chocolate per month.

g. The maximum profit (minimum loss) that ABC can expect to earn is $_____.

Next let forecasted price of raw chocolate fall to $1.50.

h. The optimal level of production for ABC is now _____ bars of chocolate per month.

i. The profit (loss) for ABC is forecasted to be $_____.

8. The graphs below show cost, revenue, and profit conditions facing a price-taking firm in a competitive market that faces a market-determined price of $900 per unit. Find the values that belong in blanks $a - k$.

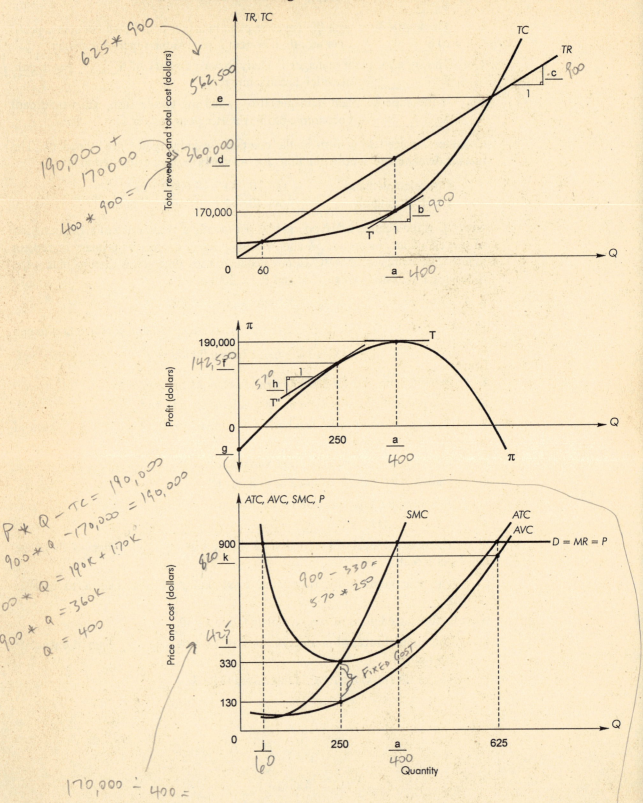

625 * 900

562,500

190,000 +
170000
400 * 900 =
360,000

$-P * Q - TC = 190,000$
$900 * Q - 170,000 = 190,000$
$900 * Q = 190K + 170K$
$900 * Q = 360K$
$Q = 400$

170,000 ÷ 400 =

TR, TC

e — 562,500
d — 360,000
170,000
TC
TR
.c 900
1
b 900
T 1
0   60   a 400   Q

π
190,000 — T
142,5 f
570 h 1
T''
0   250   a 400   π   Q
g

142,570

ATC, AVC, SMC, P
900   D = MR = P
820 k
900 - 330 =
570 * 250
SMC   ATC   AVC
425 i
330   FIXED COST
130
0   j 60   250   a 400   625   Q
Quantity

-130 ÷ 330 = -200 * 250 = -50,000

9. Answer the following questions based on the figure and your answers in Study Problem 8.

    a. What is average fixed cost at 250 units? *200* At 650 units? *80* What is total fixed *50,000* cost at 250 units? At 650 units? Using these values, explain how AFC and TFC are related to increases in Q.

    b. What are the two break-even values of output? *60 + 625* In the top panel, construct a tangent line to TC at each one of the break-even points. At the lower break-even point, is the tangent line steeper or flatter than TR? In the bottom panel, should MR be greater or less than SMC at the lower break-even point? Explain. What happens at the higher output where break-even occurs?

    c. Why is the slope of the profit function zero at the profit-maximizing level of output?

    d. At what level of output is profit margin or average profit maximized? *350* How much more profit can the firm earn by producing the output where $MR = MC$ than by producing where unit costs are minimized? *190K - 142.5K = 47,500*

    e. When the manager is producing 400 units, the firm's marketing director complains that the firm should increase output to 500 units because this will increase revenues by $90,000. If you were the manager of this firm, how would you respond to this advice? *INCREASES COSTS IN EXCESS OF REVENUE*

Multiple Choice / True-False

1. Which of the following statements is *not* a characteristic of a perfectly competitive firm?
    a. Perfectly competitive firms view each other as fierce rivals.
    b. Firms are price-takers.
    c. All firms produce a homogeneous product.
    d. Perfectly competitive markets allow freedom of entry and exit.

2. Since the firm's demand curve is perfectly elastic for a price-taking firm,
    a. $P = MR$.
    b. $P = MRP$.
    c. $P = TR$.
    d. both a and b.
    e. both a and c.

3. In the short run, a firm shuts down when
    a. profit is negative.
    b. $TR < TVC$.
    c. $MRP > ARP$ at the level of labor usage where $MRP = w$.
    d. both b and c.
    e. all of the above.

4. In the short run, a firm continues to produce at a loss when
    a. $TR \geq TFC$.
    b. $P \geq AFC$.
    c. $(TR/Q) \geq (ATC - AFC)$.
    d. both b and c.
    e. both a and c.

5. In a competitive industry the market price of output is $24. A firm is producing that level of output at which average total cost is $30, marginal cost is $25, and average fixed cost is $5. In order to maximize profit (or minimize losses), the firm should
   a. increase output.
   b. decrease output but keep producing.
   c. leave output unchanged.
   d. shut down.

6. In long-run competitive equilibrium,
   a. economic profit is zero.
   b. $P = LMC$.
   c. $P = LAC$.
   d. $P = SMC$.
   e. all of the above.

A firm produces good X and sells the good in a competitive market. The market-determined price of X is $2. Fill in the blanks in the table, and answer questions 7–10.

Total Product	Units of Labor	Marginal Product	Average Product	Marginal Revenue Product	Average Revenue Product
0	0	xx	xx	xx	xx
10	1	⎯⎯	⎯⎯	⎯⎯	⎯⎯
30	2	⎯⎯	⎯⎯	⎯⎯	⎯⎯
48	3	⎯⎯	⎯⎯	⎯⎯	⎯⎯
64	4	⎯⎯	⎯⎯	⎯⎯	⎯⎯
79	5	⎯⎯	⎯⎯	⎯⎯	⎯⎯
93	6	⎯⎯	⎯⎯	⎯⎯	⎯⎯
105	7	⎯⎯	⎯⎯	⎯⎯	⎯⎯
115	8	⎯⎯	⎯⎯	⎯⎯	⎯⎯

7. The marginal revenue product for the third unit of labor is _____.
   a. $18
   b. $48
   c. $16
   d. $9
   e. $36

8. At a wage rate of $22, the firm will hire
   a. 0 units of labor.
   b. 1 unit of labor.
   c. 3 units of labor.
   d. 7 units of labor.
   e. 8 units of labor.

9. At a wage rate of $26, the firm will hire
   a.   0 units of labor.
   b.   1 unit of labor.
   c.   3 units of labor.
   d.   6 units of labor.
   e.   7 units of labor.

10. At a wage rate of $40, the firm will hire
    a.   0 units of labor.
    b.   1 unit of labor.
    c.   3 units of labor.
    d.   7 units of labor.
    e.   8 units of labor.

Use the following figure showing short-run cost curves for a competitive price-taking firm to answer questions 11–15.

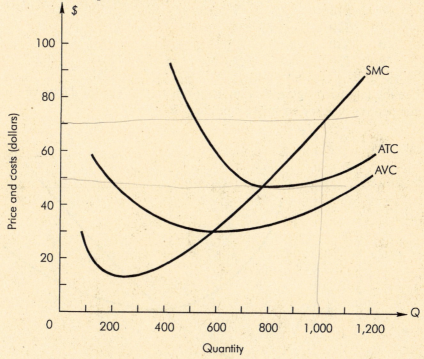

11. If price is $70 how much does the firm produce?
    a.   750 units
    b.   1,000 units
    c.   900 units
    d.   600 units

12. If price is $70 how much profit (loss) does the firm make?
    a.   zero
    b. $16,500
    c. $20,000
    d. $23,000
    e. $15,500

13. Let price be $40. How much does the firm produce?
    a. zero units
    b. 500 units
    c. 600 units
    d. 700 units
    e. 800 units

14. If price is $40, how much profit (loss) does the firm make?
    a. it loses its fixed cost
    b. $5,000
    c. -$7,000
    d. -$4,000
    e. $3,500

15. Below what price will the firm shut down and produce nothing?
    a. $48
    b. $18
    c. $20
    d. $30
    e. $50

Use the following figure showing long-run cost curves for the typical firm in a perfectly competitive industry, to answer questions 16–19.

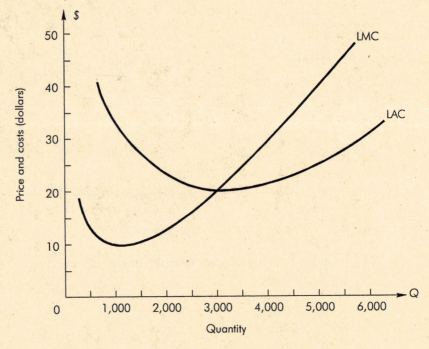

16. If price is $40, the firm will produce _____ units.
    a. 2,000
    b. 3,000
    c. 4,000
    d. 4,500
    e. 5,000

17. If price is $40, how much profit (loss) does the firm make?
   a. $75,000
   b. $60,000
   c. $50,000
   d. $10,000
   e. zero

18. If price is $40 and the firm produces the optimal level of output in this period, what is likely to occur next period?
   a. Each firm will increase output.
   b. Price will fall.
   c. Firms will exit the market.
   d. *b* and *c*.
   e. all of the above.

19. If this industry is in long-run competitive equilibrium the firm will produce _____ units of output and price will be _____.
   a. 1,000; $15
   b. 2,000; $20
   c. 3,000; $20
   d. 4,000; $22
   e. 4,500; $30

For questions 20–28, use the following data for a competitive industry and a price-taking firm that operates in this market. Using time-series data, the market demand and supply functions are estimated to be

Demand: $\hat{Q} = 550 - 10P + 0.01M$

Supply: $\hat{Q} = 400 + 10P - 12.5P_I$

where output is Q, the price of the product is P, income is M, and the price of a key input is P_I. The income forecasted for 2006 is $30,000 and the price of inputs is $52.

Jartech, Inc. is a firm operating in this market. Jartech's average variable cost function is estimated to be

$$A\hat{V}C = 60.0 - 0.08Q + 0.0001Q^2$$

where $A\hat{V}C$ is measured in dollars per unit. Jartech expects to face total fixed costs of $2,500 in 2006.

20. What is the price forecast for 2006?
    a. $15
    b. $20
    c. $35
    d. $40
    e. $55

21. At what output level will Jartech's average variable cost reach its minimum value?
    a. 200 units
    b. 300 units
    c. 400 units
    d. 500 units
    e. 600 units

22. What is the minimum average variable cost?
    a. $0
    b. $55
    c. $45
    d. $44
    e. $20

23. The profit-maximizing (or loss-minimizing) output for Jartech is
    a. 0 units.
    b. 300 units.
    c. 400 units.
    d. 500 units.
    e. 600 units.

24. What is average variable cost at the profit-maximizing level of output?
    a. $0
    b. $20
    c. $44
    d. $45
    e. $50

25. How much profit (loss) does Jartech, Inc. expect to earn?
    a. −$2,500
    b. $2,500
    c. $3,000
    d. −$3,000
    e. $2,000

In questions 26–28, suppose that the 2006 input price forecast is revised to $20 ($P_I =$ $20).

26. What is the revised price forecast for 2006?
    a. $15
    b. $20
    c. $35
    d. $40
    e. $55

27. What is Jartech's profit-maximizing (or loss-minimizing) output?
    a. 0 units
    b. 300 units
    c. 400 units
    d. 500 units
    e. 600 units

28. Under the revised forecast how much profit (loss) does Jartech, Inc. expect to earn?
    a. $0
    b. −$2,500
    c. $2,500
    d. $3,000
    e. −$3,000

29. T   F   A perfectly competitive firm will continue to produce at a loss in the short run as long as total revenue covers the firm's fixed costs.

30. T   F   When we say "fixed costs don't matter," we mean that increasing fixed costs has no effect on profit.

31. T   F   An increase in demand will *not* cause price to rise if the industry is a constant cost industry.

32. T   F   If firms in a competitive industry are making an economic profit, new firms will enter and both price and profit will decrease.

33. T   F   If the owner's superior managerial ability is keeping the firm's costs below those of other firms, the firm will earn economic profit in long-run competitive equilibrium.

34. T   F   If price is greater than marginal cost, the firm should produce less.

Answers

1. perfect competition
2. perfectly elastic demand
3. shut down
4. profit margin (or average profit)
5. shutdown price
6. long-run competitive equilibrium
7. increasing-cost industry
8. constant-cost industry
9. economic rent
10. marginal revenue product
11. average revenue product
12. quadratic formula

STUDY PROBLEMS

1. a. minimum AVC

    b. ATC

    c. ATC; minimum AVC

    d. minimum AVC

    e. P; SMC; minimum AVC; ATC

    f. P; SMC; ATC

2. a. 4,000 units maximizes profit

    b. $2; $8,000

    c. profit = $4,000

    d. 2,000 units to maximize profit

    e. $TR = \$1 \times 2,000 = \$2,000$; $TC = \$1.50 \times 2,000 = \$3,000$; profit = $\$2,000 - \$3,000 = -\$1,000$

    f. $TVC = \$0.50 \times 2,000 = \$1,000$; After paying $1,000 in variable costs, $1,000 in revenue is left to apply toward total fixed costs.

    g. $0.40 (approximately)

3. i. If not already at its optimal level, adjust the usage of the fixed factor to its optimal level for the chosen output.

    ii. Exit the industry.

    Option (i) will be undertaken if adjusting capital usage reduces total cost below revenue.

    Option (ii) will be undertaken if adjusting capital usage cannot eliminate losses in the long run.

4. In the long run, $P = LMC = $ minimum LAC. Not only is price so low that economic profit is zero, but per unit costs are at the lowest possible level, which implies that total costs are minimized for the competitive industry output.

5. Columns 1–8 in your table should look like this:

(1) Units of Labor	(2) Output	(3) Marginal Product	(4) Marginal Revenue Product	(5) Average Product	(6) Average Revenue Product	(7) Marginal Cost	(8) Profit when TFC = $500
0	0	xx	xx	xx	xx	xx	–500
1	8	8	112	8	112	3	–412
2	20	12	168	10	140	2	–268
3	34	14	196	11.33	158.62	1.71	–96
4	45	11	154	11.25	157.5	2.18	34
5	53	8	112	10.6	148.4	3	122
6	58	5	70	9.67	135.38	4.80	168
7	61	3	42	8.71	121.94	8	186
8	63	2	28	7.87	110.18	12	190
9	64	1	14	7.11	99.55	24	180
10	62	–2	–28	6.2	86.8	xx	128

a. 3 units of labor; 10th

b. increases; total; $70; decreases; total; $196

c. 9 units of labor maximizes total revenue (but *not* profit); $896 = TR_{L=9} = ARP \times 9 = 99.55 = P \times Q = 14 \times 64$. As long as *MRP* is positive for an extra unit of labor, hiring that extra unit of labor will increase total revenue.

d. 8 units of labor maximizes profit. This is the last level for which $MRP > w$. $ARP_{L=8} = \$110.18$; greater

e. falls; rises

f. 63; *MR* (or *P*); *SMC; MRP; w*

g. $190

6. a. $9; $0 In long-run competitive equilibrium, price is bid down to the minimum *LAC* of the "typical" firm in the industry. In this problem, the equilibrium price is $9, which means the typical firm has a minimum *LAC* of $9 and earns zero economic profit at a price of $9.

b. $1,500 [= ($9–$6) × 500]. If price is $9, the textile firm in this problem will produce up to the point where its *LMC* equals $9. This occurs at 500 units of output. The average cost to this superior textile producer is $6 per unit (at 500 units of output). So while the typical firm in the industry is earning zero economic profit in long-run equilibrium, this firm with the superior manager is able to earn $1,500 of economic profit per month by producing 500 units at a per unit cost of only $6 ($3 less than the typical firm).

c. $6,000 per month. Since the superior manager generates $1,500 of economic profit, other firms will try to hire this manager. As they compete to hire her, they will be willing to pay up to $1,500 more than the "typical" salary of $4,500. This superior manager, if she negotiates well, should be able to earn $4,500 + $1,500 = $6,000 per month.

d.   As owner of the firm, she would earn zero economic profit (that is, she would pay herself $6,000 per month salary since that is what she could make if she sold her business and went to work for some other firm in the industry). She does, however, earn a salary of $4,500 plus economic rent of $1,500.

7.   a. $Q_d = 60,000 - 10,000P$; $Q_s = 10,000P$
     Solve for $P_{2005} = \$3$

     b. $\hat{Q}_{min} = -b/2c = -(-0.0027)/0.0000018 = 1,500$ units

     c. $A\hat{V}C_{min} = 3 - 0.0027(1,500) + 0.0000009(1,500)^2 = \$0.975$ (97.5 cents)

     d. $P = \$3 > \$0.975 = AVC_{min} \Rightarrow$ produce

     e. $SMC = 3 - 0.0054 - 0.0000027Q^2$

     f.   Set $P = SMC$ and solve for Q^*:

     $$3 = 3 - 0.0054Q + 0.0000027Q^{*2} = 0$$

     $$Q(-0.0054 + 0.0000027Q) = 0$$

     Either $Q = 0$ or $Q = 2,000$. Since the firm should produce and not shut down the optimal output is $Q^* = 2,000$

     g. $TR = P \times Q = \$3 \times 2,000 = \$6,000$

     $$TVC = \$2,400 = AVC \times Q = \left[3 - 0.0027(2,000) + 0.0000009(2,000)^2 \right](2,000) ;$$

     Profit $= \$6,000 - \$2,400 - \$1,600 = \$2,000$

     h.   Set $P = SMC$ again and solve for Q^*:

     $$3 - 0.0054Q^* + 0.0000027Q^{*2} = 1.5$$

     $$Q^* = 1,667 = \frac{-(-0.0054) + \sqrt{(-0.0054)^2 - 4(1.5)(0.0000027)}}{2(0.0000027)}$$

     i. $TR = P \times Q = \$1.50 \times 1,667 = \$2,500$

     $$TVC = \$1,667 = AVC \times Q = \left[3 - 0.0027(1,667) + 0.0000009(1,667)^2 \right](1,667) ;$$

     Profit $= \$2,500 - \$1,667 - \$1,600 = -\$767$

8.   a.   400; $\$900 \times Q - 170,000 = \$190,000 \Rightarrow Q = 400$.

     b. $900; The slope of TC at the profit-maximizing point equals the slope of TR, and the slope of TR is P.

     c. $900; The slope of TR is P (= $900).

     d. $360,000; $TR = P \times Q = \$900 \times 400 = \$360,000$.

     e. $562,500; $TC = ATC \times Q = \$900 \times 625 = \$562,500$.

     f. $142,500; At 250 units, the profit margin (or average profit) is $570 (= $900 − $330) $\Rightarrow$ profit $= \$570 \times 250$.

     g.   −$50,000; At $Q = 0$, profit $= -TFC$. At 250 units, $ATC = \$330$ and $AVC = \$130$, so $TFC = (\$330 - \$130) \times 250$.

     h. $570; The 250th unit adds $900 to total revenue and adds $330 to total cost, and so increases profit by $570 (= $900 − $330). Thus, the slope of the profit function must be $570 at 250 units.

i. $425; $ATC = TC/Q \Rightarrow ATC = \$170,000/400 \Rightarrow ATC = \$425$.

i.   60; Since $P = ATC$ at j, it is a break-even point. In the top panel, the break-even point occurs at 60 units.

k. $820; Since $TFC = \$50,000$ (see part g), it follows that $(\$900 - AVC) \times 625 = \$50,000$. Solving for $AVC \Rightarrow AVC = \$820$.

9.   a.   At 250 units, AFC is $200 (= $330 - $130), and at 650 units, AFC is $80 (=$900 - $820). At 250 units, TFC is $50,000 (= 200×250), and at 650 units, TFC is $50,000 (=$80 \times 625$). As Q increases, AFC declines continuously while TFC is constant.

     b.   Break-even points occur at 60 and 625 units of output. At 60 units, the line tangent to TC is flatter than TR. Thus, in the bottom panel of the figure in Study Problem 8, SMC (which is the value of the slope of the line tangent to TC at 60 units) must be less than MR (which is the slope of TR and equals P). At 650 units, the line tangent to TC is steeper than TR. At 650 units, SMC (which is the value of the slope of the line tangent to TC at 650 units) must be greater than MR.

     c.   At 400 units, profit reaches its maximum value because the slope of TR equals the slope of TC (i.e., $MR = SMC$). Since the 400th unit adds $900 to TR and adds $900 to TC, the change in profit is zero and the tangent line has zero slope at the peak of the profit hill.

     d.   Profit margin (or average profit) is maximized where ATC is minimized, which occurs at 250 units in this problem. By increasing output from 250 to 400 units, the firm can increase its profit by $47,500 (= $190,000 - $142,500).

     e.   Your response: "Yes, increasing production to 500 units will indeed increase revenues by $90,000. Unfortunately, total costs will increase by more than $90,000 because marginal cost exceeds $900 (i.e., MR) for all of these 100 extra units. Thus, increasing output from 400 to 500 units will decrease profit."

MULTIPLE CHOICE / TRUE-FALSE

1.   a   Perfectly competitive firms do not view each other as fierce rivals because each firm is so small relative to the total market that no one firm's increase in sales prevents any other firm from selling as much as it wishes to at the going market price.

2.   a   When demand is horizontal, $P = MR$, and demand is perfectly elastic.

3.   d $TR < TVC \Rightarrow P < AVC \Rightarrow$ shut down and $MRP > ARP \Rightarrow$ shut down

4.   c   Choice c is really $P > AVC$ in disguise since $TR/Q = P$.

5.   d   Since $ATC = 30$ and $AFC = 5$, AVC must be 25. You are told that $SMC = 25$, so the firm must be producing at the minimum point on AVC. Since $P = 24 < AVC_{min}$, the firm should shut down.

6.   e   In long-run competitive equilibrium, $P = LMC = LAC = SMC = ATC$, and profit $= 0$.

7.   e $MRP_{L=3} = MP_{L=3} \times P = 18 \times \$2 = \$36$

8.   d $MRP_{L=7} = \$24 > \$22 > MRP_{L=8} = \$20$

9.   d $MRP_{L=6} = \$28 > \$26 > MRP_{L=7} = \$24$

10. a   At the level of labor usage for which $MRP = \$40$ (i.e., $L = 2$), $MRP_{L=2} = 40 > 30 = ARP_{L=2} \Rightarrow$ shut down

11. b $P = SMC = \$70$ at $Q = 1,000$

12. c $\$20,000 = (P - ATC)Q = (70 - 50)1,000$

13. d $SMC = P = \$40$ at $Q = 700$

14. c $-\$7,000 = (P - ATC)Q = (40 - 50)700$

15.	d	Minimum $AVC = \$30$
16.	e	$P = SMC = \$40$ at $Q = 5{,}000$
17.	a	$\$75{,}000 = (P - LAC)Q = (40 - 25)5{,}000$
18.	b	Price falls because new firms enter and increase supply.
19.	c	Minimum LAC equals $\$20$; 3,000
20.	e	$850 - 10P = -250 + 10P \Rightarrow P = \$55$
21.	c	$\hat{Q}_{min} = -\hat{b}/2\hat{c} = 400 = -(0.08)/0.0002$
22.	d	$A\hat{V}C_{min} = \$44 = 60 - 0.08(400) + 0.0001(400)^2$
23.	d	$SMC = 60 - 0.16Q + 0.0003Q^2 = \$55 \Rightarrow Q^* = 500$
24.	d	$A\hat{V}C_{Q=500} = \$45 = 60 - 0.08(500) + 0.0001(500)^2$
25.	b	Profit $= (\$55 \times 500) - (\$45 \times 500) - \$2{,}500 = \$2{,}500$
26.	c	$850 - 10P = 150 + 10P \Rightarrow P = \$35$
27.	a	$P < A\hat{V}C_{min} = \$45 \Rightarrow$ shut down
28.	b	Profit $= -TFC = -\$2{,}500$
29.	F	It is *variable* costs that must be covered in order to produce.
30.	F	Increasing fixed cost does decrease profit. The level of fixed cost does not affect the production decision. If $P < AVC$, the firm shuts down no matter how high or low fixed costs are. If $P \geq AVC$, the firm produces the level of output where $MR = SMC$, no matter how high or low fixed costs are.
31.	T	A constant-cost industry has a horizontal long-run industry supply curve. In the long-run, an increase in demand will not lead to an increase in price. [Note: In the short-run, the short-run industry supply curve is upward sloping, even for a constant cost industry, and an increase in demand *will* cause price to rise in the short run.]
32.	T	Entry takes place when economic profits are positive and entry increases supply.
33.	F	The owner will earn a normal profit plus rent.
34.	F	Produce more if $P > SMC$

Homework Exercises

1. Consider the cost curves for a price-taking firm in the following figure:

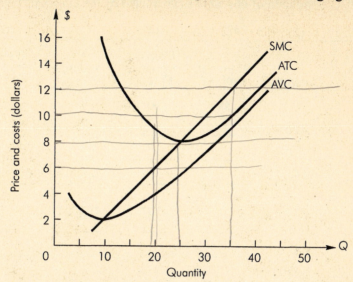

a. When price is $12 per unit of output, the firm maximizes profit by producing ____35____ units.

b. Since average total cost = $____10____ for this output, total cost is $____350____.

c. The firm makes an economic profit (loss) of $____70____.

d. Price falls to $8. The firm now maximizes profit by producing __25__ units.

e. At this output level, total revenue = $____200____ and total cost = $____200____. Therefore the firm earns a profit (loss) of $____0____.

f. Price falls to $6. The firm now maximizes profit by producing ____20____ units.

g. At this output level, average total cost is $____9____ and total cost is $____180____. Total revenue = $____120____ and the firm makes a loss of $____60____.

h. Even though the firm makes a loss, it does not shut down because total variable cost is $____80____, which leaves $____40____ of total revenue to apply toward fixed costs.

i. If price falls below $____2____, the firm shuts down. Explain why.

2. Ajax Corporation is a price-taking firm in a competitive industry that employs only one variable input, labor, to produce a product that sells for $2 per unit. The wage rate is $8 per unit of labor and total fixed costs are $1,000. Fill in the blanks in each column of this table as instructed by the questions below:

(1) Units of Labor	(2) Output	(3) Marginal Product	(4) Marginal Revenue Product	(5) Average Product	(6) Average Revenue Product	(7) Marginal Cost	(8) Profit
0	0	xx	xx	xx	xx	xx	_____
1	400	_____	_____	_____	_____	_____	_____
2	950	_____	_____	_____	_____	_____	_____
3	1,250	_____	_____	_____	_____	_____	_____
4	1,350	_____	_____	_____	_____	_____	_____
5	1,370	_____	_____	_____	_____	_____	_____
6	1,373	_____	_____	_____	_____	_____	_____
7	1,369	_____	_____	_____	_____	_____	_____
8	1,364	_____	_____	_____	_____	_____	_____

a. Fill in the blanks in columns 3 and 5. Marginal product begins to diminish beyond _____ units of labor. Marginal product is negative beyond _____ units of labor.

b. Compute marginal and average revenue products and fill in the blanks in columns 4 and 6. The sixth unit of labor _____ (increases, decreases) total revenue by $_____. Decreasing labor usage from four to three units _____ (increases, decreases) total revenue by $_____.

c. The manager can maximize *total revenue* by hiring _____ units of labor. The maximum possible value of total revenue is $_____.

d. The manager hires _____ units of labor and produces _____ units of output in order to maximize *profit*. At this level of labor usage, $ARP =$ _____ which is _____ (greater, less) than MRP.

e. Compute marginal cost and fill in the blanks in column 7. At first, marginal cost _____ (rises, falls) as marginal product rises, then marginal cost _____ (rises, falls) as marginal product falls.

f. The profit-maximizing level of output is _____ units because this is the last level of output for which _____ exceeds _____, or equivalently, _____ exceeds _____ .

g. Compute profit and fill in the blanks in column 8. The optimal level of labor employment and the optimal level of output both result in an identical maximum profit level of $_____.

h. Now suppose total fixed cost increases to $5,000. Recalculate profit at each level of labor usage (and output) and fill in the blanks in column 9 below. When total fixed cost is $5,000, the optimal level of labor usage is _____ units of labor, and the optimal level of output is _____ units. How high must total fixed costs rise in order for it to be optimal for this firm to shut down? Explain briefly.

(1)	(2)	(9)
Units of Labor	Output	Profit TFC = $5,000
0	0	_____
1	400	_____
2	950	_____
3	1,250	_____
4	1,350	_____
5	1,370	_____
6	1,373	_____
7	1,369	_____
8	1,364	_____

3. Sunnyvale Orchards is one of many small, perfectly competitive firms growing apples for the U.S. market. The forecasted price of apples in 2006 is $23.60 per crate. The management of Sunnyvale Orchards estimates its short-run average variable cost function to be

$$AVC = 20 - 0.04Q + 0.00005Q^2$$

where Q is the number of crates of apples produced each week. Total fixed cost at Sunnyvale Orchards is $1,200 per week.

a. Average variable cost reaches its minimum value at _____ crates of apples per week.

b. The minimum value of average variable cost is $_____ per crate.

c. Sunnyvale faces the marginal cost function $SMC =$ _____

d. Sunnyvale will maximize profit (or minimize loss) by producing _____ crates of apples per week in 2006.

e. Sunnyvale's profit will be $_____ per week. [Note: If a loss occurs, then express profit as a negative value.]

f. If the price of apples falls to $10 per crate, Sunnyvale should produce _____ crates per week, and its profit will be $_____ per week. [Note: If a loss occurs, then express profit as a negative value.]

Managerial Decisions for Firms with Market Power

Learning Objectives

After reading Chapter 12 and working the problems for Chapter 12 in the textbook and in this Workbook, you should be able to:

➤ Define the concept of market power and distinguish between market power and monopoly.

➤ Explain how own-price and cross-price elasticities of demand and the Lerner index can be used to measure the degree of market power possessed by a firm.

➤ Explain why the existence of barriers to entry are necessary for market power in the long run, and list six types of entry barriers.

➤ Find the profit-maximizing output and price for a monopolist in both the short run and long run.

➤ Find the profit-maximizing level of input usage for firms with market power.

➤ Find the profit-maximizing price and output for a monopolistically competitive firm in both the short run and the long run.

➤ Find the profit-maximizing (or loss-minimizing) level of output for a monopoly, or any firm with market power, given estimates or forecasts of (i) the demand function, (ii) the average variable cost function, and (iii) the marginal cost function.

Essential Concepts

1. *Market power* is the ability of a firm to raise price without losing all its sales. Any firm that faces a downward sloping demand curve has market power. Market power gives the firm the ability to raise price above average cost and earn economic profit, if demand and cost conditions so permit.

2. A *monopoly* exists when a single firm produces and sells a particular good or service for which there are no good substitutes, and new firms are prevented from entering the market.

3. The degree to which a firm possesses market power is inversely related to the price elasticity of demand. The less (more) elastic the firm's demand, the greater (less) its degree of market power. The fewer the number of close substitutes consumers can find for a firm's product, the smaller the elasticity of demand (in absolute value), and the greater the firm's market power. When demand is perfectly elastic (demand is horizontal), the firm possesses no market power. The Lerner index

measures the proportionate amount by which price exceeds marginal cost:

$$\text{Lerner index } = \frac{P - MC}{P}$$

Under perfect competition, the index is equal to zero, and the index increases in magnitude as market power increases. The Lerner index can be expressed as $-1/E$, which shows that the index, and market power, vary inversely with the elasticity of demand. The lower (higher) the elasticity of demand (in absolute value), the greater (smaller) the Lerner index and the degree of market power.

4. If consumers view two goods to be substitutes, the cross-price elasticity of demand (E_{XY}) is positive. The higher the (positive) cross-price elasticity, the greater the substitutability between two goods, and the smaller the degree of market power possessed by the two firms.

5. A firm can possess a high degree of market power only when strong barriers to the entry of new firms exist. Six common types of entry barriers are:

   a. *Economies of scale.* When long-run average cost declines over a wide range of output relative to the demand for the product, there may not be room in the market for another large producer to enter the market—at least not without driving price below unit costs making it unprofitable to enter.

   b. *Barriers created by government.* Government barriers to entry, such as licenses and exclusive franchises, have been created in many industries. Patent laws also can, but need not, create strong barriers to entry.

   c. *Input barriers.* When one firm controls a crucial input in the production process, that firm can obviously block entry.

   d. *Brand loyalties.* Over time, firms may develop such strong customer allegiance that new firms cannot find enough buyers at a price that covers cost to make entry worthwhile.

   e. *Consumer lock-in.* For some products or services, consumers may find it costly to switch to another brand, which makes previous consumption decisions costly to change. Potential rivals can be deterred from entering if they believe high switching costs will make it difficult for them to induce many consumers to change brands.

   f. *Network externalities.* Network externalities occur when the value of a product increases as more consumers buy and use the product. Thus, entry of new firms can be deterred if network externalities make it very difficult for new firms to enter markets where firms have established a large base or network of buyers.

6. In the short run

   a. A monopolist will produce a positive output if some price on the demand curve exceeds average variable cost.

   b. A monopolist maximizes profit or minimizes loss by producing the quantity for which $MR = MC$.

   c. If the price exceeds average total cost ($P > ATC$) the firm makes an economic profit.

d.   If price is less than average total cost but greater than average variable cost ($ATC > P > AVC$), the firm suffers an economic loss, but continues to produce in the short run.

e.   If demand falls below average variable cost at every level of output, the firm shuts down and loses only its fixed cost.

7.   In the long run

a.   A manager of a monopoly firm maximizes profit by choosing to produce the level of output where marginal revenue equals long-run marginal cost ($MR = LMC$) as long as $P \geq LAC$.

b.   A monopolist will exit the industry if $P < LAC$.

c.   The manager will adjust plant size to the optimal level. That is, the optimal plant is the one with the short-run average cost curve tangent to the long-run average cost at the profit-maximizing output level.

8.   *Marginal revenue product (MRP)* is the additional revenue attributable to hiring one additional unit of the input: $MRP = \Delta TR / \Delta L$. MRP is also equal to marginal revenue times marginal product: $MRP = MR \times MP$.

9.   When producing with a single variable input, a firm with market power will maximize profit by employing that amount of the input for which marginal revenue product (*MRP*) equals the price of the input when input price is given. The relevant range of the *MRP* curve is the downward sloping, positive portion of *MRP* for which $ARP > MRP$.

10. For a firm with market power, the profit-maximizing condition that the marginal revenue product of the variable input must equal the price of the input ($MRP = w$) is equivalent to the profit-maximizing condition that marginal revenue must equal marginal cost ($MR = MC$). Thus, regardless of whether the manager chooses Q or L to maximize profit, the resulting levels of input usage, output, price and profit are the same in either case.

11. Under *monopolistic competition*, a large number of firms sell a differentiated product. The products, while differentiated, are quite closely related and the products of other firms in the market are close (but not perfect) substitutes for the product sold by the monopolistically competitive firm. The market is monopolistic in that product differentiation creates a degree of market power. It is competitive because of the large number of firms and easy entry.

12. Short-run equilibrium under monopolistic competition is exactly the same as it is for monopoly. Long-run equilibrium in a monopolistically competitive market is attained when the demand curve for each producer is tangent to the long-run average cost curve. Unrestricted entry and exit lead to this equilibrium. At the equilibrium output, price equals long-run average cost, and marginal revenue equals long-run marginal cost.

13. Making profit-maximizing pricing and output decisions for firms with market power can be summarized in the following steps:

Step 1:   *Estimate the demand equation.* Estimate demand for a price-setting firm using the OLS regression procedure, as set forth in Chapter 7. Once the demand equation has been estimated, forecasts for demand-shifting variables (such as $\hat{M}$ and $\hat{P}_R$) are substituted into the estimated demand equation to get

$$Q = a' + bP$$

where $a' = a + c\hat{M} + d\hat{P}_R$

Step 2: *Find the inverse demand equation.* The inverse demand function is derived by solving for P in the estimated demand equation given above

$$P = \frac{-a'}{b} + \frac{1}{b}Q = A + BQ$$

where $a' = a + c\hat{M} + d\hat{P}_R$, $A = -a'/b$, and $B = 1/b$.

Step 3: *Solve for marginal revenue.* When demand is expressed as $P = A + BQ$, marginal revenue is

$$MR = A + 2BQ = \frac{-a'}{b} + \frac{2}{b}Q$$

Step 4: *Estimate average variable cost (AVC) and short-run marginal cost (SMC).* Estimate AVC and SMC functions, as set forth in Chapter 10:

$$AVC = a + bQ + cQ^2$$
$$SMC = a + 2bQ + 3cQ^2$$

Step 5: *Find the output level where MR = SMC.* To find the optimal level of output, the manager sets marginal revenue equal to marginal cost and solves for Q. The larger of the two roots or solutions is the profit-maximizing level of output—unless P (found in Step 6) is less than AVC, and then the optimal level of output is zero.

Step 6: *Find the profit-maximizing price.* Once the optimal quantity, Q^*, has been found, the profit-maximizing price is found by substituting Q^* into the inverse demand equation to obtain the optimal price, P^*:

$$P^* = A + BQ^*$$

As noted above, this price and output will be optimal only if $P \geq AVC$.

Step 7: *Check the shutdown rule.* The manager can calculate the average variable cost at Q^* units by substituting Q^* into the estimated AVC function

$$AVC^* = a + bQ^* + cQ^{*2}$$

If $P^* \geq AVC^*$, then the firm produces Q^* units of output and sells each unit for P^*. If $P^* < AVC^*$, the monopolist shuts down in the short run.

Step 8: *Compute profit or loss.* To compute profit or loss, the manager makes the same calculation regardless of whether the firm operates in a monopoly, oligopoly, or perfectly competitive market

$$\text{Profit} = TR - TC = (P \times Q) - (AVC \times Q) - TFC$$

If $P < AVC$, the firm shuts down, and profit is $-TFC$.

Matching Definitions

consumer lock-in
inverse demand function
Lerner index
marginal revenue product
market definition
market power

monopolistic competition
monopoly
network externalities
strong barrier to entry
switching costs

1. _____ Ability of a firm to raise price without losing all its sales.

2. _____ Firm that produces a good for which there are no close substitutes in a market that other firms are prevented from entering because of entry barriers.

3. _____ Market consisting of a large number of firms selling a differentiated product with low barriers to entry.

4. _____ The identification of the producers and products that compete for consumers in a particular area.

5. _____ A ratio that measures the proportionate amount by which price exceeds marginal cost.

6. _____ Condition that makes it difficult for new firms to enter a market in which economic profits are being earned.

7. _____ Costs consumers incur when they switch to new or different products or services.

8. _____ When high switching costs make previous consumption decisions very costly to change.

9. _____ When a product's value rises as more consumers use it.

10. _____ The additional revenue attributable to hiring an additional unit of a variable input.

11. _____ The demand function with demand price expressed as a function of output.

Study Problems

1. Suppose a monopolist faces the demand and cost curves shown in the figure below.

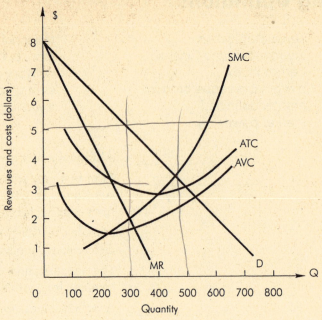

a. The monopolist maximizes profit (minimizes loss) by producing __300__ units of output.

b. The monopolist will sell its output at a price of $__5__ per unit.

c. The monopolist earns a profit (loss) of $__600__.

d. Construct a new demand and marginal revenue curve such that the monopolist earns a loss in the short run but does not shut down.

e. Construct a new demand such that the firm shuts down.

2. a. Explain carefully why firms with market power do not, in general, also maximize total revenue.

b. Under what special condition would firms with market power be able to maximize both profit and total revenue at the same level of output?

3. A monopolist is producing a level of output, 80 units, at which price is $12, marginal revenue is $8, average total cost is $14, average variable cost is $5, and marginal cost is $2.

a. Draw a graph of the demand and cost conditions facing the firm.

b. Is the firm making the profit-maximizing decision? Why or why not? If not, what should the manager do?

4. A manager of a monopolistic competitor faces the following demand and cost schedules:

Quantity	*Price*	*Total Cost*
0	$25	$1,000
100	20	1,800
200	16	2,800
300	10	4,000
400	5	5,400
500	1	7,000

a. The manager should produce __________ units.

b. The manager should charge a price of __________ units.

c. The maximum amount of profit that can be earned is $ __________.

d. If total fixed cost doubles, the firm should produce __________ units. The maximum amount of profit that can be earned is $__________.

5. In the following table columns (1) and (2) show the short-run production function for a monopolist using a single variable input, labor. Columns (2) and (3) show the demand schedule. Total fixed cost is $1,800.

(1) *Labor / week*	(2) *Output / week*	(3) *Price*
0	0	xx
1	50	20
2	110	18
3	150	16
4	180	15
5	200	14
6	210	13

a. Calculate the *MRP* and *ARP* for each level of labor usage.

b. If the weekly wage is $150 how much labor will the firm use and how much will it produce? What is the firm's profit (loss)?

c. If the wage rises to $350 how much labor will the firm use and how much will it produce? What is the firm's profit (loss)?

6. a. Compare short-run profit-maximizing equilibrium for a monopolistic competitor and a monopoly.

b. Compare long-run equilibrium for a monopolistic competitor and a perfect competitor.

7. Explain why, in theory, a monopolist and a monopolistic competitor always sell an output and set a price on the elastic portion of demand.

8. The following figure shows demand, marginal revenue, and long-run costs for a monopolistic competitor.

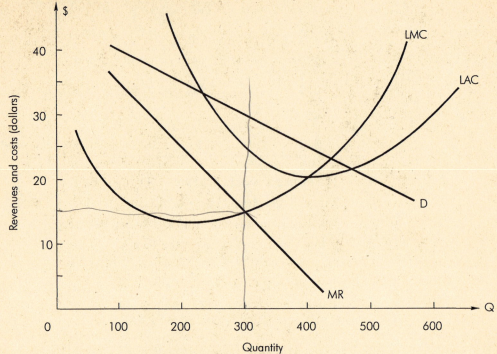

a. With the given demand, what output will the firm produce, what price will it charge, and how much profit (loss) will the firm make?

b. Draw in possible demand and marginal revenue curves when the firm attains long-run equilibrium. What is the firm's economic profit?

c. If these were the cost curves for a perfectly competitive firm in long-run competitive equilibrium, what would output, price, and economic profit be?

9. The demand function for a firm with market power is estimated to be

$$Q = 122,000 - 500P + 4M + 10,000P_R$$

where Q is output, P is price per unit, M is income, and P_R the price of a related good. The manager estimates the values of M and P_R will be \$32,000 and \$4, respectively, in 2005. For 2005, find the following functions:

a. Forecasted demand function

b. Inverse demand function

c. Marginal revenue function

The firm faces an average variable cost function estimated to be

$$AVC = 500 - 0.03Q + 0.000001Q^2$$

where AVC is measured in dollars per unit.

d. The estimated marginal cost function is

$$SMC = \underline{\hspace{6cm}}.$$

e. The profit-maximizing level of output for 2005 is _____ units.

f. The profit-maximizing price for 2005 is $_____.

g. Should the manager produce or shut down?

h. If total fixed cost is expected to be $5 million in 2005, what is the firm's expected profit or loss in 2005?

Multiple Choice / True-False

1. If a firm with market power maximizes profit by producing at the unit elastic point on the demand curve, then

   a. it has no direct competitors.

   b. its marginal cost must be zero at the profit-maximizing level of output.

   c. demand must be perfectly elastic.

   d. it cannot be in long-run equilibrium.

2. Which of the following statements is not always true for a monopolist in short-run equilibrium?

   a. $|E| \geq 1$

   b. $TR > TVC$

   c. $MR = SMC$

   d. $P > MR$

3. If a firm with market power is not making enough profit (in equilibrium),

   a. it will lower price thereby increasing total revenue because demand is elastic.

   b. it will raise price thereby increasing total revenue because demand is inelastic.

   c. it will exit the industry in the long run if economic profit is negative.

   d. it will expand sales until it reaches the unit elastic point on demand.

4. If a monopolist can find buyers for 4 units at a price of $7, and if the marginal revenue due to the 5th unit is $2, the highest price at which the monopolist can find buyers for 5 units must be

   a. $2.

   b. $3.

   c. $4.

   d. $5.

   e. $6.

5. Market power

   a. is the capability to increase price without losing all sales.

   b. exists whenever the firm faces a downward-sloping demand curve.

   c. is greater the less elastic is demand.

   d. is smaller the more positive is the cross-price elasticity of demand.

   e. all of the above.

6. A monopoly is maximizing short-run profit at a point on demand where demand elasticity is –3. What is the Lerner index?
   a. 3
   b. 1/3
   c. 33.3
   d. –3/4

7. Monopolistic competition is similar to monopoly since both market structures have
   a. a small number of firms.
   b. downward-sloping demands for the firms.
   c. economic profit in long-run equilibrium.
   d. easy entry and exit.
   e. all of the above.

8. The *primary* difference between perfect and monopolistic competition is that for monopolistic competition
   a. there is product differentiation.
   b. entry is difficult.
   c. a large number of sellers exists.
   d. consumers have perfect information with respect to prices.

9. In long-run equilibrium under monopolistic competition,
   a. price equals minimum long-run average cost.
   b. price is higher than minimum long-run average cost.
   c. the firms earn less than a normal profit.
   d. firms have the incentive to enter the market.
   e. both *a* and *d*.

Use the following table showing a monopolist's demand schedule and short-run total cost schedule to answer questions 10–13.

Price	Quantity	Total cost
$11	0	$400
10	60	800
9	90	890
8	130	1,050
7	166	1,230
6	196	1,440
5	210	1,800

10. To maximize profit the firm will set a price of $_____ and sell _____ units output.
    a. $10; 60
    b. $9; 90
    c. $8; 130
    d. $7; 166
    e. $6; 196

11. Profit (loss) at the profit-maximizing output is $_____.
    a. $90
    b. $300
    c. −$48
    d. −$10
    e. −$90

12. If the firm reduces price $1 from the profit-maximizing level, marginal revenue is $_____ and marginal cost is $_____.

    a. $0.47; $6
    b. $20; $4
    c. $7; $3
    d. $3.40; $5

13. If the firm reduces price $1 from the profit-maximizing level, profit (loss) will be $_____.
    a. −$48
    b. $62
    c. −$68
    d. −$264
    e. $400

Use the following figure showing cost, demand, and marginal revenue for a monopoly to answer questions 14–16.

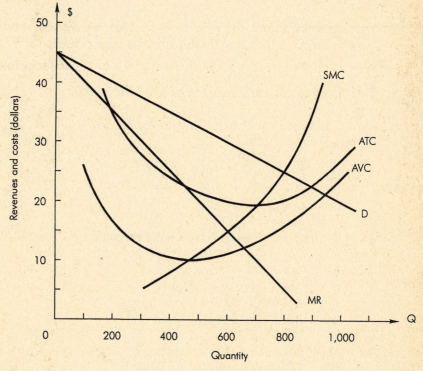

14. What is the profit-maximizing level of output?
    a. 860
    b. 600
    c. 700
    d. 900
    e. 650

15. What is the profit-maximizing price?
    a. $15
    b. $20
    c. $25
    d. $30
    e. $23

16. What is the maximum amount of profit the firm can earn?
    a. $6,000
    b. $10,200
    c. $9,000
    d. $1,200
    e. $8,000

Questions 17–24 involve a profit-maximizing monopolist that produces a product using a single variable input–labor. Using time-series data, the demand function for the monopolist has been estimated as

$$Q = 15,000 - 50P + 0.5M - 300P_R$$

The estimated values for M and P_R in 2005 are $22,000 and $16, respectively. The average variable cost curve for this firm has been estimated as

$$AVC = 200 - 0.12Q + 0.0002Q^2$$

Total fixed costs were forecast to be $100,000 in 2005.

17. The forecasted demand function for 2005 is
    a. $Q = 150,000 - 20P$.
    b. $Q = 20,000 - 0.02P$.
    c. $Q = 80,000 - 0.50P$.
    d. $Q = 21,200 - 50P$.
    e. $Q = 110,000 - 50P$.

18. The forecasted marginal revenue function for 2005 is
    a. $MR = 424 - 0.04Q$.
    b. $MR = 424 - 0.02Q$.
    c. $MR = 110,000 - 0.02Q$.
    d. $MR = 220,000 - 4Q$.
    e. $MR = 16,000 - 2Q$.

19. What is the marginal cost function?
    a. $SMC = 400 - 0.24Q + 0.0001Q^2$
    b. $SMC = 400 - 0.12Q + 0.0004Q^2$
    c. $SMC = 200 - 0.24Q + 0.0006Q^2$
    d. $SMC = 400 - 0.24Q + 0.0004Q^2$

20.	What is the profit-maximizing (or loss-minimizing) level of production?
	a.	0 units
	b.	800 units
	c.	1,000 units
	d.	1,200 units
	e.	1,250 units

21.	What is the value of average variable cost at the optimal level of output?
	a.	$76
	b.	$96
	c.	$112
	d.	$196
	e.	$232

22.	What is the optimal price?
	a.	This is irrelevant as the firm will not produce in the short run.
	b.	$200
	c.	$263
	d.	$408
	e.	$488

23.	The firm's forecasted profit in 2005 is a
	a.	loss of $100,000.
	b.	loss of $48,000.
	c.	profit of $40,800.
	d.	profit of $400,000.
	e.	profit of $565,000.

24.	Now suppose total fixed cost doubles to $200,000 in 2005. The optimal price is now
	a.	$408.
	b.	$488.
	c.	$512.
	d.	$524.
	e.	$600.

25.	T	F	A large negative cross-price elasticity of demand means two goods are easily substitutable, and market power is likely to be weak.

26.	T	F	A monopolist always earns economic profit.

27.	T	F	Like a perfectly competitive firm, a monopolist maximizes profit by producing the level of output for which $P = MC$.

28.	T	F	A high Lerner index indicates a large degree of market power.

29.	T	F	A monopoly should produce and sell on the elastic portion of demand.

30.	T	F	At the output at which $MR = MC$, profit (loss) is the same as at the level of labor usage at which $w = MRP$.

Answers

MATCHING DEFINITIONS

1. market power
2. monopoly
3. monopolistic competition
4. market definition
5. Lerner index
6. strong barrier to entry
7. switching costs
8. consumer lock-in
9. network externalities
10. marginal revenue product
11. inverse demand function

STUDY PROBLEMS

1. a. MR intersects SMC at 300 units

   b. $\$5 = P$ for 300 units.

   c. $ATC_{Q=300} = \$3$, so profit is $(P - ATC)Q = (5 - 3) \times 300 = \$600$.

   d. Demand and marginal revenue should be drawn so that $ATC > P > AVC$.

   e. Draw a demand that lies below AVC at every output level.

2. a. Profit is maximized at the level of output for which $MR = MC$. Total revenue is maximized at the level of output for which $MR = 0$. Since MC is generally positive for all levels of output, the profit-maximizing point where MR equals MC occurs at a lower level of output than that which maximizes total revenue.

   b. If MC is constant and equal to zero, then both total revenue maximization and profit maximization occur at the same output level.

3. a. The following figure illustrates the demand and cost conditions facing the monopolist

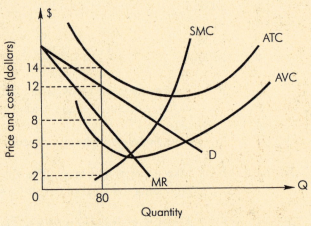

   b. The manager is not minimizing loss. Output should be increased until $MR = SMC$.

4.   a. $Q = 200$ units

        b. $P = \$16$

        c.   Profit = $400

        d.   After doubling TFC to $2,000, the profit-maximizing output is still 200 units. The maximum profit is now –$600.

5.   a.

L	$MRP = MR \times MP$	$ARP = TR/L$
0	xx	xx
1	$1,000	$1,000
2	980	990
3	420	800
4	300	675
5	100	560
6	–70	455

        b. $L = 4$, $Q = 180$. Last unit at which $MRP > w$. $w = \$150 < ARP = \$675$. Profit $= PQ - wL - TFC = \$2,700 - \$600 - \$1,800 = \$300$

        c. $L = 3$, $Q = 150$. Last unit at which $MRP > w$. $w < ARP = 800$. Profit $= \$2,400 - \$1,050 - \$1,800 = -\$450$

6.   a.   In the short run the two are the same; $MR = SMC$ and price given by demand.

        b.   Both firms make zero economic profit, earn a normal profit, and produce an output at which price equals long-run average cost. For a perfect competitor this occurs where price equals minimum LAC equals LMC. For a monopolistic competitor this occurs at a lower output on the downward-sloping portion of LAC and $P > MR = LMC$.

7.   Profit is maximized where $MC = MR$. Since MC is positive (in both the short run and the long run), MR must also be positive, and thus, demand must be elastic.

8.   a. $Q = 300$ (where $LMC = MR$), P is $30 (from demand), and profit is $1,500 [$= (P - LAC)Q = (30 - 25) \times 300$].

        b.   Draw a demand curve that is tangent to LAC on the downward-sloping portion of LAC. The associated MR should equal LMC at tangency quantity. Economic profit is zero since $P = LAC$.

        c. $Q = 400$, $P = \$20$ at minimum LAC. Profit is zero.

9.   a. $Q = 122,000 - 500P + 4(32,000) + 10,000(4) = 290,000 - 500P$

        b.   Solve the demand function for P: $Q - 290,000 = -500P \Rightarrow P = 580 - 0.002Q$

        c. $MR = 580 - 2(0.002)Q = 580 - 0.004Q$

        d. $SMC = 500 - 2(0.03)Q + 3(0.000001)Q^2 = 500 - 0.06Q + 0.000003Q^2$

        e.   Set $MR = SMC$ and solve for Q^*: $580 - 0.004Q = 500 - 0.06Q + 0.000003Q^2$. Solving using the quadratic formula $\Rightarrow Q^* = 20,000$ units

        f. $P^* = 580 - 0.002(20,000) = \$540$

        g. $AVC_{Q = 20,000} = 500 - (0.03 \times 20,000) + 0.000001(20,000)^2 = \$300$. Since $P = \$540 > \$300 = AVC$, the monopolist should produce.

        h.   Profit $= TR - TVC - TFC = (\$540 \times 20,000) - (\$300 \times 20,000) - \$5,000,000 = -\$200,000$

MULTIPLE CHOICE / TRUE-FALSE

1. b   Since profit maximization requires $MR = MC$ and $MR = 0$ when demand is unitary elastic, MC must be zero.

2. b   In short-run equilibrium, a monopolist may have to shut down, and in such a case, $TR < TVC$.

3. c   The monopolist cannot increase profit in the short run because it is already in profit-maximizing equilibrium. In the long run, if profit is negative (i.e., $\pi < 0$), the monopolist will exit the industry.

4. e   Total revenue for 4 units is $28. Marginal revenue for the 5th unit is $2, so total revenue for 5 units is $30. Therefore, the price of 5 units must be $6.

5. e   All choices are correct.

6. b   The Lerner index is equal to $-1/E$.

7. b   Both have market power.

8. a   In perfect competitive products are identical.

9. b $P = LAC$ where LAC slopes downward, rather than at LAC's minimum point.

10. c   This is the last output for which $MR > SMC$.

11. d $TR(= \$8 \times 130) - TC = \$1,040 - \$1,050 = -\$10$.

12. d $MR = (\$1,162 - \$1,040)/36$; $SMC = (\$1,230 - \$1,050)/36$.

13. c $TR - TC = \$1,162 - 1,230 = -\$68$.

14. b $MR = SMC$ at 600.

15. d $P = \$30$ at $Q = 600$.

16. a   Profit $= (P - ATC)Q = (30 - 20) \times 600$.

17. d $Q = 15,000 - 50P + 0.5(22,000) - 300(16) = 21,200 - 50P$

18. a   Inverse demand is $P = 424 - 0.02Q$, so $MR = 424 - 0.04Q$.

19. c   Since $AVC = 200 - 0.12Q + 0.0002Q^2$, $SMC = 200 - 0.24Q + 0.0006Q^2$.

20. b   Setting $MR = SMC$ and solving for $Q \Rightarrow Q^* = 800$ units

21. e $AVC_{Q=800} = 200 - 0.12(800) + 0.0002(800)^2 = \$232$

22. d $P^* = 424 - 0.02(800) = \$408$

23. c   Profit $= TR - TVC - TFC = (\$408 \times 800) - (\$232 \times 800) - 100,000 = \$40,800$.

24. a   Fixed costs don't matter in making optimal decisions, so rising fixed costs have no effect on the profit-maximizing price. P^* remains $408, while profit falls by the amount that total fixed cost rises (i.e., profit falls by $100,000 in this case).

25. F E_{XY} is *positive* for substitutes.

26. F   A monopolist may earn a loss in the short run but never in the long run.

27. F $MR = MC$ for both a perfectly competitive firm and a monopolist. But since $P > MR$ for a monopolist, $P \neq MC$ under monopoly.

28. T   Higher Lerner index indicates a less elastic demand.

29. T   Profit-maximization requires $MR = MC$, and since $MC > 0$, MR must be > 0. And, since demand is elastic when $MR > 0$, profit-maximization occurs in the elastic region of demand.

30. T   The two lead to equivalent outcomes.

Homework Exercises

1. Consider a monopoly that faces the demand and cost curves in the figure below. The firm operates in the short run using a plant designed to produce 850 units optimally.

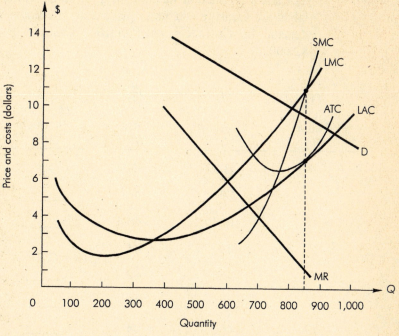

a. In the short run, the manager maximizes profit (or minimizes loss) by producing _____ units.

b. The monopolist charges $_____ per unit for its output.

c. Monopoly profit is $_____.

d. In the long run, the monopolist produces _____ units and sells this output at $_____ per unit. The monopolist earns $_____ profit in the long run.

2. Cascade Enterprises has a patent on a water purifying device that is used mostly by restaurants to soften and purify tap water used in cooking food and cleaning dishes. Cascade Enterprises enjoys a substantial amount of market power in this rather specialized market. In the following table, columns 1 and 2 show a portion of Cascade's production function using a single variable input labor. Quantity and labor are measured in units per month. Columns 2 and 3 show the estimated demand for Cascade's water purifier. Cascade has fixed costs each month of $2,000.

(1) Labor (L)	(2) Quantity (Q)	(3) Price (P)	Marginal Product (MP)	Marginal Revenue (MR)	Marginal Revenue Product (MRP)
4	200	$50	xx	xx	xx
5	280	48	___	___	___
6	340	46	___	___	___
7	390	44	___	___	___
8	430	42	___	___	___
9	450	40	___	___	___
10	460	38	___	___	___

a. Calculate marginal product (MP), marginal revenue (MR), and marginal revenue product (MRP).

b. If Cascade Enterprises must pay a monthly wage rate of $3,000, what is the profit-maximizing levels of labor employment (L^*), output (Q^*), price (P^*), and profit (π^*)?

    i. $L^* =$ _____

    ii. $Q^* =$ _____

    iii. $P^* =$ _____

    iv. $\pi^* =$ _____

c. If the wage rate falls to $1,400 per month, what is the profit-maximizing levels of labor employment (L^*), output (Q^*), price (P^*), and profit (π^*)?

    i. $L^* =$ _____

    ii. $Q^* =$ _____

    iii. $P^* =$ _____

    iv. $\pi^* =$ _____

3. Gemini Robotics, Inc. is a monopoly firm in the market for home robots. The owner-manager of Gemini founded the home robot industry in 2006 on the basis of the following forecasted demand function for home robots in 2006:

$$Q = 9,000 - 0.2P + 0.2M + 56P_B$$

where Q is the number of robots sold, M is the average annual income of potential buyers, and P_B is the price of butlers (in dollars per day). The owner-manager of Gemini expects $M_{2006} = \$50,000/\text{year}$ and $P_B = \$125/\text{day}$.

a. The forecasted demand function in 2006 is

$$Q = \underline{\hspace{4cm}}$$

b. The inverse demand function is

$$P = \underline{\hspace{4cm}}$$

c. The marginal revenue function is

$$MR = \underline{\hspace{4cm}}$$

Suppose Gemini Robotics faces the following estimated average variable cost function:

$$AVC = 40,000 - 200Q + Q^2$$

d. The estimated marginal cost function is

$$SMC = \underline{\hspace{4cm}}$$

e. The optimal level of output for 2006 is \underline{\hspace{2cm}} units.

f. The price of a home robot in 2006 will be \$\underline{\hspace{2cm}}.

g. If Gemini Robotics expects fixed costs in 2006 to be \$15 million, then it can expect to earn a profit (loss) of \$\underline{\hspace{3cm}}.

Strategic Decision Making in Oligopoly Markets

Learning Objectives

After reading Chapter 13 and working the problems for Chapter 13 in the textbook and in this Workbook, you should be able to do the following things

For simultaneous decisions:

➤ Explain why the interdependence of profits for oligopoly firms leads to strategic behavior.

➤ Analyze strategic decisions facing oligopolists making simultaneous decisions by employing the concepts of dominate strategies, dominated strategies, and Nash equilibrium.

➤ Employ best-response curves to find Nash equilibrium decisions in simultaneous decision situations.

For sequential decisions:

➤ Analyze strategic decisions facing oligopolists making sequential decisions by employing the roll-back method of finding best decisions.

➤ Determine whether first or second-mover advantages exist in sequential decisions.

➤ Explain how oligopoly firms may be able to engage in strategic entry deterrence through the use of limit pricing or capacity expansion strategies.

For repeated decisions:

➤ Explain why Nash equilibrium is considered a noncooperative solution for oligopoly decisions and what is meant by the terms "cooperation" and "cheating" in strategic decision making.

➤ Explain why cooperation can sometimes be achieved when decisions are repeated over time.

➤ Explain how to determine whether cooperation (i.e., choosing not to cheat) will increase the present value of a firm.

➤ Discuss four types of facilitating practices that can improve the chances for reaching a cooperative outcome in oligopoly decisions.

➤ Explain why cartel members usually choose to cheat on price-fixing agreements.

➤ Discuss the nature of tacit collusion as a means of achieving cooperative outcomes in oligopoly markets.

Essential Concepts

- Interdependence of firms' profits, which is the distinguishing feature of oligopoly markets, arises when the number of firms in a market is small enough that every firm's price and output decisions affect the demand and marginal revenue conditions of every other firm in the market.

- *Game theory* provides a useful guideline on how to behave in strategic situations involving interdependence. A game is any decision-making situation in which people compete with each other for the purpose of gaining the greatest individual payoff (rather than group payoff) from playing the game.

This chapter is divided into three sections: Section 13.1 examines simultaneous decisions, Section 13.2 examines sequential decisions, and Section 13.3 examines repeated decisions. The *Essential Concepts* for this chapter are presented accordingly.

Simultaneous Decisions:

1. Simultaneous decision games occur when managers must make their individual decisions without knowing the decisions of their rivals.

2. A *dominant strategy* is a strategy or action that always provides the best outcome no matter what decisions rivals make. When a dominant strategy exists, a rational decision maker always chooses to follow its own dominant strategy and predicts that if its rivals have dominant strategies, they will also choose to follow their dominant strategies.

3. A *dominant strategy equilibrium* exists when all decision makers have dominant strategies.

4. A *prisoners' dilemma* arises when all rivals possess dominant strategies, and in dominant strategy equilibrium, they are all worse off than if they had cooperated in making their decisions. In other words, there is a cell in the payoff table that makes every rival better off than in the dominant strategy equilibrium cell.

5. When a firm does not have a dominant strategy, but at least one of its rivals does have a dominant strategy, the firm's manager can predict with confidence that its rivals will follow their dominant strategies. A manager can then choose its own best strategy, knowing the actions that will almost certainly be taken by rivals possessing dominant strategies.

6. *Dominated strategies* are strategies or decisions that are never the best strategy for any of the decisions that rivals might make. Therefore, a dominated strategy would never be chosen and should be ignored or eliminated for decision-making purposes. If, after a first round of eliminating dominated strategies, other strategies become dominated as a result of the first-round elimination, then successive elimination of dominated strategies should continue until no dominated strategies remain in the final payoff table.

7. Strategically astute managers will search first for dominant strategies, and, if no dominant strategies can be discovered, they next look for dominated strategies. When neither form of strategic dominance exists, decision makers must employ a different concept for making simultaneous decisions.

8. In order for all firms in an oligopoly market to be predicting correctly each others' decisions—managers cannot make *best* decisions without making *correct* decisions—all firms must be choosing individually best actions given the predicted actions of their rivals, which they can then believe are correctly predicted. Thus, strategically astute managers look for mutually best decisions.

9. A *Nash equilibrium* is a set of actions or decisions for which all managers are choosing their best actions given the actions they expect their rivals to choose.

10. In Nash equilibrium, no single firm can unilaterally (by itself) make a different decision and do better. This characteristic of Nash equilibrium is called *strategic stability*, and it provides the fundamental reason for believing that strategic decision makers will likely decide on a Nash pair of decisions.

11. When managers face a simultaneous decision-making situation possessing a unique Nash equilibrium set of decisions, rivals can be expected to make the decisions leading to the Nash equilibrium. If there are multiple Nash equilibria, there is generally no way to predict the likely outcome.

12. All dominant strategy equilibria are also Nash equilibria, but Nash equilibria can occur without either dominant or dominated strategies.

13. Economists have developed a tool, called *best-response curves*, to analyze and explain simultaneous decisions when decision choices are continuous rather than discrete. A firm's best-response curve indicates the best decision to make (usually the profit-maximizing one) based on, or accounting for, the decision the firm expects its rival will make. A Nash equilibrium occurs at the price (or output) pair where the firms' best-response curves intersect.

Sequential Decisions:

1. In contrast to simultaneous decisions, the natural process of some decisions requires one firm to make a decision, and then a rival firm, knowing the action taken by the first firm, makes its decision. Such decisions are called *sequential decisions*. Even though they are made at different times, sequential decisions nonetheless involve strategic interdependence. Sequential decisions are linked over time: The best decision a manager can make today depends on how rivals will respond tomorrow.

2. The easiest way to analyze sequential decisions is to use a *game tree*. A game tree is a diagram showing firms' decisions as decision nodes with branches extending from the nodes, one for each action that can be taken at the node. The sequence of decisions usually proceeds from left to right along branches until final payoffs associated with each decision path are reached.

3. When firms make sequential decisions, managers make best decisions for themselves by working backwards through the game tree using the *roll-back method*. The roll-back method (also known as *backward induction*) results in a unique path that is also a Nash decision path: Each firm does the best for itself given the best decisions made by its rivals.

4. If letting your rivals know what you are doing by going first in a sequential decision game increases your payoff (relative to your payoff from going second), then a first-mover advantage exists. Alternatively, if reacting to a decision already made by a rival increases your payoff (relative to your payoff from going first), then a second-mover advantage exists.

---

5. To determine whether the order of decision making can confer an advantage when firms make sequential decisions, the roll-back method can be applied to the game trees for each possible sequence of decisions. If the payoff increases by being the first (second) to move, then a first-mover (second-mover) advantage exists. If the payoffs are identical, then order of play confers no advantage.

6. Managers can make strategic moves to achieve better outcomes for themselves, usually to the detriment of their rivals. Only credible strategic moves matter; rivals ignore any commitments, threats, or promises that will not be carried out should the opportunity to do so arise. There are three types of strategic moves: *commitments*, *threats*, and *promises*.

   a. Managers make commitments by announcing, or demonstrating to rivals in some other way, that they will bind themselves to take a particular action or make a specific decision *no matter what action or decision is taken by its rivals.*

   b. Threats, whether they are made explicitly or tacitly, take the form of a conditional statement, "If you take action *A*, I will take action *B*, which is undesirable or costly to you."

   c. Promises, like threats, are also conditional statements that must be credible to affect strategic decisions. Promises take the form of a conditional statement, "If you take action *A*, I will take action *B* which is desirable or rewarding to you."

Repeated Decisions:

1. Cooperation occurs when oligopoly firms make individual decisions that make every firm better off than they would be in a (noncooperative) Nash equilibrium.

2. Making noncooperative decisions is called "cheating" by game theorists, even though "cheating" does not imply that the firms have made any kind of agreement to cooperate.

3. Cooperation is possible in every prisoners' dilemma decision, but cooperation is not strategically stable when the decision is made only once. In one-time prisoners' dilemmas there can be no future consequences from cheating, so both firms *expect* the other to cheat, which in turn makes cheating the best response for each firm.

4. When decisions are repeated over and over again by the same firms, managers get a chance to punish cheaters. When cheating can be punished by making credible threats of punishment in later rounds of decision making, strategically astute managers can sometimes, but not always, achieve cooperation in prisoners' dilemmas.

5. Cooperation increases a firm's value when the present value of the costs of cheating exceeds the present value of the benefits from cheating. Alternatively, cheating increases a firm's value when the present value of the benefits from cheating outweighs the present value of the costs of cheating. Cooperation is achieved in an oligopoly market when all firms decide not to cheat.

6. A widely studied category of punishment strategies is known in game theory as *trigger strategies*. Managers implement trigger strategies by initially choosing the cooperative action and continuing to choose the cooperative action in successive repetitions of a decision until a rival cheats. The act of cheating then "triggers" a

punishment phase in the next repetition of the game that may last one or more repetitions depending on the nature of the trigger scheme.

7. The two most commonly studied trigger strategies are *tit-for-tat* and *grim strategies*.

   a. In a *tit-for-tat strategy*, cheating triggers punishment in the next decision period, and the punishment continues unless the cheating stops, which triggers a return to cooperation in the following decision period. In other words, if firm *B* cheated in the last decision period, firm A will cheat in this decision period. If firm B cooperated last time, then firm A will cooperate this time.

   b. In a *grim strategy*, cheating triggers punishment in the next decision period, and the punishment continues forever, even if cheaters make cooperative decisions in subsequent periods.

8. Since cooperation usually increases profits, managers frequently adopt legal tactics, known as *facilitating practices*, designed to make cooperation more likely. Four such tactics are price matching, sale-price guarantees, public pricing, and price leadership:

   a. *Price matching*: A firm commits to a price-matching strategy by publicly announcing, usually in an advertisement, that it will match any lower prices offered by its rivals. This largely eliminates the benefit to other firms from cutting their prices, and so price matching discourages noncooperative price-cutting.

   b. *Sale-price guarantees*: Your firm offers a sale-price guarantee by promising customers who buy an item from you today that they are entitled to receive any sale price your firm might offer for some stipulated future period. The primary purpose of this tactic is to make it costly for firms to cut their prices.

   c. *Public pricing*: Publicly available prices, which are timely and authentic, facilitate quick detection of noncooperative price cuts. Early detection of cheating both reduces the present value of benefits from cheating and increases the present value of the costs of cheating, which reduces the likelihood of noncooperative price-cutting.

   d. *Price leadership*: Sometimes one oligopoly firm (the leader) sets its price at a level it believes will maximize total industry profit, and then the rest of the firms (the followers) cooperate by setting the same price. This arrangement, known as price leadership, does not require an explicit agreement among firms and is generally a lawful means of facilitating cooperative pricing.

9. Cartels are the most extreme form of cooperative oligopoly. Essentially a cartel is an explicit collusive agreement among firms to drive up prices by restricting total market output. Cartels are illegal in the United States, Canada, Mexico, Germany, and the European Union.

10. Cartels find it extremely difficult to maintain cooperatively set cartel prices because cartel pricing schemes are usually strategically unstable. The lack of strategic stability of cartels stems from the incentive to cheat by lowering price. The incentive to cut price below the cartel price is great because, when undetected (and unmatched), price cutting occurs along a very elastic single-firm demand curve with the associated lure of much greater revenues for any one firm that cuts price. Of course the lure is great for every firm, and eventually many cartel members begin cutting their prices secretly. This causes price to fall sharply along a much steeper

demand curve that reflects the firm's demand when many cartel members all lower price together.

11. A far less extreme form of cooperation among oligopoly firms is tacit collusion, which occurs when oligopoly firms cooperate without an explicit agreement or any other facilitating practices.

Matching Definitions

best-response curve	payoff table
cartel	price leadership
cheating	price matching
commitments	promises
common knowledge	repeated decisions
cooperation	roll-back method
credible	second-mover advantage
decision nodes	sequential decisions
dominant strategy	simultaneous decision games
dominant strategy equilibrium	strategic behavior
dominated strategies	strategic moves
first-mover advantage	strategic stability
game	successive elimination of dominated
game theory	strategies
game tree	tacit collusion
grim strategy	threats
Nash equilibrium	tit-for-tat strategy
oligopoly	

1. _____ Actions taken by firms to plan for and react to competition from rival firms.

2. _____ A market consisting of a few relatively large firms, each with a substantial share of the market and all recognize their interdependence.

3. _____ An analytical guide or tool for making decisions in situations involving interdependence.

4. _____ Any decision-making situation in which people compete with each other for the purpose of gaining the greatest individual payoff.

5. _____ A situation in which competing firms must make their individual decisions without knowing the decisions of their rivals.

6. _____ A table showing, for every possible combination of decisions players can make, the outcomes or "payoffs" for each of the players in each decision combination.

7. _____ A situation in which all decision makers know the payoff table, and they believe all other decision makers also know the payoff table.

8. _____ A strategy or action that always provides the best outcome no matter what decisions rivals make.

9. _____ Both players have dominant strategies and play them.

10. _____ Strategies that would never be chosen because at least one other strategy provides a higher payoff no matter what rivals choose to do.

11. _____ An iterative decision-making process in which dominated strategies are eliminated to create a reduced payoff table with fewer decisions for managers to consider.

12. _____ A set of actions for which all managers are choosing their best actions given the actions chosen by their rivals.

13. _____ In a Nash equilibrium cell, no decision maker can unilaterally change its decision and improve its individual payoff.

14. _____ A curve indicating the best decision (usually the profit-maximizing one) given the decision the manager believes a rival will make.

15. _____ A decision in which one firm makes its decision first, then a rival firm makes its decision.

16. _____ A diagram showing the structure and payoff of a sequential decision situation.

17. _____ Points in a game tree, represented by boxes, where decisions are made.

18. _____ Method of finding a Nash solution to a sequential decision by looking ahead to future decisions to reason back to the best current decision.

19. _____ A firm can increase its payoff by making its decision first.

20. _____ A firm can increase its payoff by making its decision second.

21. _____ A strategic move that will be carried out because it is in the best interest of the firm making the move to carry it out.

22. _____ Three kinds of actions that can be used to put rivals at a disadvantage: commitments, threats, or promises.

23. _____ Unconditional actions taken for the purpose of increasing payoffs to the committing firms.

24. _____ Conditional strategic moves that take the form, "If you do A, I will do B which is costly to you."

25. _____ Conditional strategic moves that take the form, "If you do A, I will do B which is desirable to you."

26. _____ When firms make decisions that make every firm better off than in a noncooperative Nash equilibrium.

27. _____ When a manager makes a noncooperative decision.

28. _____ Decisions made over and over again by the same firms.

29. _____ Punishment strategies that choose cooperative actions until an episode of cheating triggers a period of punishment.

30. _____ A trigger strategy that punishes after an episode of cheating and returns to cooperation if cheating ends.

31. _____ A trigger strategy that punishes forever after an episode of cheating.

32. _____ A strategic commitment to match any rival's lower price.

33. _____ A firm's promise to give its buyers today any sale price it might offer during a stipulated future period.

34. _____ Informing buyers about prices in a way that makes pricing information public knowledge.

35. _____ A leader firm sets the industry profit-maximizing price and the follower firms cooperate by all setting the same price.

36. _____ A group of firms that agree to limit competitive forces in a market.

37. _____ Cooperation among firms that does not involve an explicit agreement.

Study Problems

1. Two firms, Atlantis and Bacchus, compete primarily by price. Each firm chooses either a high price or a low price simultaneously. The following payoff table shows the profit each firm would earn in each of the four possible decision combinations.

Bacchus
price

		High	Low
Atlantis price	**High**	A $10,000, $10,000	B $5,000, $20,000 _B_
	Low	C $20,000, $5,000 _A_	D $8,000, $8,000 _B_

_A_ (under C-D border)

a. Does Atlantis have a dominant strategy? Why or why not? *Yes, Low*

b. Does Bacchus have a dominant strategy? Why or why not? *Yes, Low*

c. Does Atlantis have a dominated strategy? Explain why or why not.

d. Does Bacchus have a dominated strategy? Explain why or why not.

e. What is the outcome of this simultaneous decision? Why? *Cell D*

f. Is this decision situation a prisoners' dilemma? Explain why or why not. *Yes, Cell A is Better for Both*

g. Is cell C strategically stable? Explain why or why not.

h. Is cell D strategically stable? Explain why or why not.

2. Find the solution to the following advertising decision game between Coke and Pepsi by using the method of successive elimination of dominated strategies.

Pepsi's budget

		Low	Medium	High
Coke's budget	**Low**	A $400, $400	B $320, $720 _P_	C $560, $600 _c_
	Medium	D $500, $300 _c_	E $450, $525 _c_	F $540, $500
	High	G $375, $420	H $300, $378	I $525, $680 _P_

a. Are there any dominant strategies in the original payoff table? *No*

b. In the first round of elimination of dominated strategies, which strategies are eliminated, if any, for Coke? For Pepsi? *Hi - Coke   Low - Pepsi*

c. After the first round of elimination, are there any more dominated strategies to eliminate? If so, identify them.

d. After the first round of elimination, are there any dominant strategies? If so, identify them.

e. The likely outcome of this advertising game is cell *E*.

f. Is the likely outcome a Nash equilibrium? Explain.

g. Is the likely outcome strategically stable? Explain.

3. Find the solution to the following simultaneous pricing decision between Rattler Enterprises and Sidewinder, Inc.

Sidewinder's price

		$100	$200	$300
Rattler's price	$100	A $5,000, $3,600	B ~~R~~ $4,500, $4,200	C ~~S~~ $4,200, $4,500
	$200	D ~~SR~~ $6,000, $7,000	E $4,400, $5,000	F $5,000, $4,600
	$300	G $3,750, $3,200	H ~~S~~ $4,000, $4,200	I ~~R~~ $5,500, $3,600

Annual payoffs in millions of dollars of profit.

a. Rattler's dominant strategy is ___NONE___ ($100, $200, $300, or Rattler has no dominant strategy).

b. Sidewinder's dominant strategy is ___NONE___ ($100, $200, $300, or Sidewinder has no dominant strategy).

c. Rattler's dominated strategy is ___NONE___ ($100, $200, $300, or Rattler has no dominated strategy).

d. Sidewinder's dominated strategy is ___NONE___ ($100, $200, $300, or Sidewinder has no dominated strategy).

e. The likely outcome of this simultaneous pricing decision is for Rattler to set a price of $ _200_ and Sidewinder to set a price of $ _100_ . Explain why you chose this pair of decisions.

4. Managers of two competing automobile lubrication service facilities in a fashionable suburb of Los Angeles must make their pricing decisions simultaneously. Jiff Lube (J) and Oil Can Hank (O) face the following demand and long-run cost conditions, which are common knowledge to the managers

$$Q_J = 50 - 5P_J + 7.5P_O \quad \text{and} \quad LMC_J = LAC_J = \$10$$
$$Q_O = 60 - 6P_O + 6P_J \quad \text{and} \quad LMC_O = LAC_O = \$5$$

The prices, P_J and P_O, are the prices charged by Jiff Lube and Oil Can Hank, respectively, for a full-service lubrication. The quantities, Q_J and Q_O, are the respective quantities of full-service oil changes performed each week. The figure below shows Oil Can Hank's best-response curve, BR_O. Only one point on Jiff Lube's best-response curve, point G, is shown in the figure.

a. Find a second point on Jiff Lube's best-response curve by finding the best response when Jiff Lube believes Oil Can Hank will set a price of $7.50. Plot this price pair on the graph, label it H, draw the best-response curve for Jiff Lube, and label it BR_J.

b. What prices do you expect Jiff Lube and Oil Can Hank to set? Explain why. Label this price pair point N on the graph.

c. How much weekly profit does Jiff Lube make at point N? Oil Can Hank?

d. Explain carefully why the pair of prices at point G in the figure is not likely to be chosen by Jiff Lube and Oil Can Hank.

e. Suppose the managers of the two firms decide to cooperate with each other by agreeing to set prices $P_J =$ $30 and $P_O =$ $30. Label this point C in the figure. How much weekly profit does Jiff Lube make at point C? Oil Can Hank?

f. Why didn't you give point C as your answer to part b?

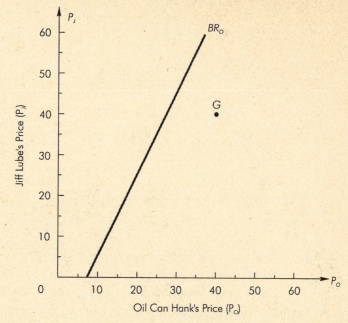

5. Sony and Zenith must each decide which technology to utilize in building their 2005 model high definition television (HDTV) sets: either Alpha technology or Beta technology. Sony has a technological advantage in using Alpha technology and Zenith has a technological advantage in using Beta technology. The payoff table below shows the profit outcomes for both firms in the various possible technology choice outcomes.

Zenith

		Alpha	*Beta*
Sony	**Alpha**	A $16, *$12* 7 5	B $11, *$10*
	Beta	C $9, *$8*	D $13, *$15* 7 5

Payoffs in billions of dollars of profits.

Suppose the technology decision between Alpha and Beta will be made *simultaneously*. Answer the following questions:

a. Sony's dominant strategy is _____NONE_____ (Alpha, Beta, neither: it has no dominant strategy).

b. Zenith's dominant strategy is _____NONE_____ (Alpha, Beta, neither: it has no dominant strategy).

c. This simultaneous decision game has TWO Nash equilibrium cells: __A__ (A, B, C, D) and __D__ (A, B, C, D).

Now suppose that Sony decides to make a strategic commitment to one of the technologies so that it can make the first move in a *sequential* decision game.

d. Complete the following game tree for the sequential game in which Sony moves first, by filling in the blanks using the information in the preceding payoff table.

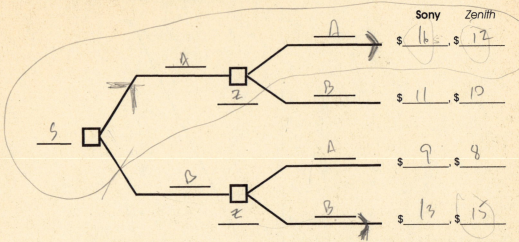

	Sony	Zenith
A	$ 16	$ 12
B	$ 11	$ 10
A	$ 9	$ 8
B	$ 13	$ 15

e. For the sequential game in part *d*, use the roll-back method to find the Nash equilibrium decision path. Circle this decision path on the game tree above. Sony earns a profit of $ 16 and Zenith earns a profit of $ 12 .

Suppose instead that Zenith decides to make a strategic commitment to one of the technologies so that it can make the first move in a sequential decision game.

f. Complete the following game tree for the sequential game in which Zenith moves first, by filling in the blanks using the information in the payoff table.

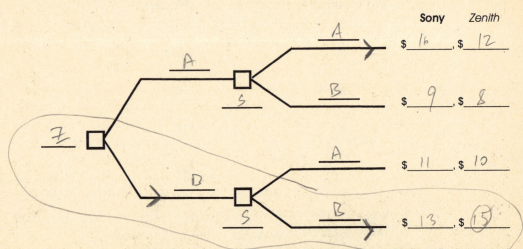

	Sony	Zenith
A	$ 16	$ 12
B	$ 9	$ 8
A	$ 11	$ 10
B	$ 13	$ 15

g. For the sequential game in part *f*, use the roll-back method to find the Nash equilibrium decision path. Circle this decision path on the game tree above. Sony earns a profit of $ 13 and Zenith earns a profit of $ 15 .

h. Does either firm have a first-mover advantage? Explain.

i. Does either firm have a second-mover advantage? Explain.

6. Corsicana is a very small town with two fast-food restaurants, BK and Mac, situated on opposite corners of the only busy intersection in town. BK and Mac compete on the basis of the prices they set for their burger, fry, and soda combination meals. The *Corsicana Gazette*, the local newspaper in which they advertise their prices, is published once a month. On the last day of the month, BK and Mac simultaneously choose their combo meal prices, which will remain in effect for all of the next month.

   The managers at BK and Mac only consider two possible prices: a low price of $3 or a high price of $4. The monthly profits from each of the four possible combinations of decisions are given in the following table:

BK's combo price

		Low ($3)	High ($4)
Mac's combo price	**Low ($3)**	A $3,000, *$5,500*	B $6,500, *$5,000*
	High ($4)	C $2,000, *$9,000*	D $5,000, *$8,000*

Payoffs in dollars of monthly profit.

   a. Is the pricing decision facing Mac and BK a prisoners' dilemma? Why or why not?

   b. What is the cooperative outcome? What is the noncooperative outcome?

   c. Which cell(s) represent cheating in the pricing decision? Explain.

   d. If Mac and BK make their pricing decision just one time, what are their pricing decisions likely to be? Explain.

7. For the monthly pricing decision in Problem 6:

   a. Can Mac make a credible threat to punish BK with a retaliatory price cut?

   b. Can BK make a credible threat of a retaliatory price cut if Mac cheats?

8. Suppose in Problem 6 Mac and BK repeat their simultaneous pricing decisions every month. They had been cooperating, but now Mac's manager is thinking about whether to cheat or to continue cooperating. Mac's manager believes that, in such a small town, it can only get away with cheating for two months before town gossip reaches BK's manager and retaliation begins.

   After BK's manager discovers the cheating, Mac's manager expects to be punished for two months (called the "eye-for-an-eye" strategy in Corsicana). After two months of punishment, Mac's manager expects the two firms will stop feuding and return to cooperation. Mac's manager employs a discount rate of 0.5 percent per month for computing present values.

   a. What is the monthly (undiscounted) gain to Mac from cheating? What is the present value of the benefit from cheating?

   b. What is the monthly (undiscounted) cost of punishment to Mac? What is the present value of the cost of cheating?

   c. Will the manager of Mac choose to cooperate or cheat? Explain.

   d. Suppose Mac's manager begins discounting future benefits and costs at a rate of 60 percent per month. Will Mac now choose to cooperate or cheat?

Multiple Choice / True-False

1. In an oligopoly market,
   a. a firm must lower price in order to sell more output.
   b. each firm faces a demand curve that depends on how the firm's rivals behave.
   c. a few firms account for a large portion of industry sales.
   d. both *a* and *b*.
   e. all of the above.

2. What is a dominant strategy?
   a. A strategy that provides the best possible outcome for both firms.
   b. A strategy that would never be the best choice.
   c. A strategy that leads to the best outcome for a firm no matter what decision rivals make.
   d. both *a* and *c*.

3. Profits are interdependent in oligopoly markets because
   a. products are differentiated.
   b. managers are trying to set prices cooperatively in order to maximize total industry profit.
   c. entry into the market is restricted by some form of entry barrier.
   d. each firm in the market is relatively large.
   e. all of the above.

4. Which of the following is NOT an implication of oligopoly interdependence?
   a. Strategic behavior.
   b. The need to get into the heads of rival managers.
   c. Making decisions that result in the equating of marginal revenue and marginal cost.
   d. Thinking ahead in sequential decisions to anticipate rivals' future actions.

5. At the point of intersection of two best-response curves,
   a. each manager is unable to achieve a higher payoff through any unilateral change of strategy.
   b. each manager is doing his or her part to reach a Nash equilibrium.
   c. total industry profit is maximized.
   d. each firm is making the greatest possible individual profit.
   e. both *a* and *b*.

6. A second-mover advantage
   a. exists when a firm can earn greater profit by reacting to earlier decisions made by rivals.
   b. always arises when there is not a first-mover advantage in a sequential decision.
   c. arises because rivals have imperfect information about payoffs.
   d. none of the above.

7. A credible commitment is
    a. always irreversible.
    b. a way of becoming the first-mover in sequential decision situation.
    c. an unconditional strategic move.
    d. both *a* and *c*.
    e. all of the above.

8. A conditional strategic move, such as a threat or promise, can be credible only if
    a. rivals believe the manager making the move can be *trusted* to follow through on any commitment, threat, or promise that he or she makes.
    b. the strategic move harms rivals.
    c. it can increase each firm's payoff.
    d. it leads to a Nash equilibrium outcome.
    e. none of the above.

9. Which of the following are trigger strategies?
    a. eye-for-an-eye
    b. tit-for-tat
    c. grim
    d. both *b* and *c*.
    e. all of the above.

10. In every prisoners' dilemma situation, cooperation
    a. is possible.
    b. reduces the payoff to at least one of the firms.
    c. reduces the payoff to all players.
    d. is likely.
    e. both *c* and *d*.

11. In a one-time prisoners' dilemma decision,
    a. all firms expect the other firms to cheat.
    b. cheating is usually not a value-maximizing decision.
    c. cheating is less likely when the discount rate is low.
    d. cheating is less likely when the discount rate is high.

12. In a repeated decision for which the present value of the benefits of cheating are less than the present value of the costs of cheating,
    a. deciding not to cheat is a value-maximizing decision.
    b. deciding to cooperate is a value-maximizing decision.
    c. deciding to cheat is a value-maximizing decision.
    d. both *a* and *b*.

13. In the United States, firms that engage in cooperative efforts to coordinate pricing
    a. are always in violation of antitrust laws.
    b. may face federal charges of illegal collusion if they cannot provide evidence that the coordination of prices was in the best interest of consumers.
    c. are simply trying to reach a Nash equilibrium and are not viewed by courts as necessarily breaking any laws.
    d. both *b* and *c*.

14. Punishment for cheating on pricing agreements usually takes the form of
    a.   a retaliatory advertising campaign.   c.   a legal suit.
    b.   a retaliatory price cut.   d.   a monetary fine.

15. Cooperation is achieved in an oligopoly market when
    a.   most of the firms in the market decide not to cheat.
    b.   some of the firms in the market decide not to cheat.
    c.   at least one of the firms in the market decides not to cheat.
    d.   all of the firms in the market decide not to cheat.

16. Price matching
    a.   is a strategic commitment.
    b.   is a flexible pledge to match any lower prices offered by rivals.
    c.   must be irreversible in order to have the desired effect.
    d.   both *a* and *c*.
    e.   both *b* and *c*.

17. Price leadership
    a.   is rather uncommon today.
    b.   is a pricing arrangement in which one firm in an oligopoly agrees to act as a cartel manager and set a price that will maximize the profits of all the firms in the oligopoly market.
    c.   would not be useful to a dominant firm if it could eliminate all its rivals through a price war.
    d.   none of the above.

18. T   F   All dominant strategy equilibria are also Nash equilibria.

19. T   F   In simultaneous decisions, all firms make their decisions at precisely the same time.

20. T   F   In order for a set of predicted decisions to be mutually correct they must also be mutually best decisions.

21. T   F   When there is a first-mover advantage, firms making decisions first always makes more profit than firms making their decisions second.

22. T   F   When oligopoly firms make Nash decisions that are also mutually best decisions for the firms, this indicates the firms are cooperating in their decision making and may be violating antitrust laws.

23. T   F   Cheating can occur even if managers have not made any explicit or implicit arrangements to cooperate.

24. T   F   Cooperation is more likely to occur the more difficult it is to monitor the prices of rivals.

25. T   F   Cartel members have an incentive to cheat by secretly lowering their own prices below the agreed upon cartel price because they individually face highly elastic demand curves.

Answers

MATCHING DEFINITIONS

1. strategic behavior
2. oligopoly
3. game theory
4. game
5. simultaneous decision games
6. payoff table
7. common knowledge
8. dominant strategy
9. dominant strategy equilibrium
10. dominated strategies
11. successive elimination of dominated strategies
12. Nash equilibrium
13. strategic stability
14. best-response curve
15. sequential decisions
16. game tree
17. decision nodes
18. roll-back method
19. first-mover advantage
20. second-mover advantage
21. credible
22. strategic moves
23. commitments
24. threats
25. promises
26. cooperation
27. cheating
28. repeated decisions
29. trigger strategies
30. tit-for-tat strategy
31. grim strategy
32. price matching
33. sale-price guarantee
34. public pricing
35. price leadership
36. cartel
37. tacit collusion

STUDY PROBLEMS

1.   a.   Yes. Atlantis' best price is low no matter what it expects Bacchus to charge. If Bacchus is expected to price high, Atlantis would rather earn $20,000 by pricing low than earn $10,000 by pricing high. Alternatively, if Bacchus is expected to price low, Atlantis would rather earn $8,000 by pricing low than earn $5,000 by pricing high.

       b.   Yes. Bacchus' best price is low no matter what it expects Atlantis to charge. If Atlantis is expected to price high, Bacchus would rather earn $20,000 by pricing low than earn $10,000 by pricing high. Alternatively, if Atlantis is expected to price low, Bacchus would rather earn $8,000 by pricing low than earn $5,000 by pricing high.

c. Yes. Since Atlantis would never find it best to price high no matter what decision Bacchus might make, high is a dominated strategy.

d. Yes. Since Bacchus would never find it best to price high no matter what decision Atlantis might make, high is a dominated strategy.

e. Because both firms have dominant strategies, a dominant strategy equilibrium exists and is likely to occur. It is also true that by eliminating the dominated strategy (high) for both firms leaves **Low**, *Low* as the likely outcome.

f. Yes, this is a prisoners' dilemma because when both firms choose their dominant strategies they each are worse off than if they could cooperate. In this decision situation, they could cooperate by both setting high prices and both firms would earn $2,000 more profit in cell A.

g. No. In cell C, if Bacchus expects Atlantis to price low, then Bacchus can unilaterally increase its profit by choosing to price low and earn $3,000 more in cell D. Strategic stability requires that neither firm can unilaterally change its decision and increase its payoff.

h. Yes. In cell D neither firm can change its own pricing decision by itself and earn greater profit.

2. a. No.

b. In the first round of elimination of dominated strategies, **High** is eliminated for Coke and *Low* is eliminated for Pepsi.

c. Yes. In the second round of elimination of dominated strategies, *High* can be eliminated for Pepsi. Coke has no dominated strategies after the first round.

d. Yes. In the second round, *Medium* is a dominant strategy for Pepsi. Coke has no dominant strategy.

e. E (**Medium**, *Medium*)

f. Yes, cell E is a Nash equilibrium because **Medium**, *Medium* is a mutually best pair of decisions: Coke and Pepsi are both making their best decisions given the anticipated or expected decision of their rival.

g. Yes. In cell E, neither Coke nor Pepsi can, by itself (i.e., unilaterally), make a different decision and reach a higher level of profit.

3. a. Rattler has no dominant strategy.

b. Sidewinder has no dominant strategy.

c. Rattler has no dominated strategy.

d. Sidewinder has no dominated strategy.

e. $200; $100 (cell D). The pair of decisions in cell D is a Nash equilibrium pair of decisions. In cell D, Rattler is doing the best it can for itself given that it expects Sidewinder to set a price of $100. In cell D, Sidewinder is doing the best it can for itself given that it expects Rattler to set its price at $200. Cell D is, of course, strategically stable since neither firm can unilaterally change its decision and make higher profit.

4. a. Substitute $P_O = \$7.50$ into Jiff Lube's demand function to get $Q_J = 106.25 - 5P_J (= 50 - 5P_J + 7.5 \cdot 7.50)$. Next take the inverse of this demand to get Jiff Lube's inverse demand function: $P_J = 21.25 - 0.2Q_J$. Now you can get Jiff Lube's marginal revenue function: $MR_J = 21.25 - 0.4Q_J$. Now set $MR_J = LMC_J$ and solve for Jiff Lube's profit-maximizing output when Oil Can Hank charges $7.50: $MR_J = LMC_J \Rightarrow 21.25 - 0.4Q_J = 10 \Rightarrow Q_J^* = 28.125$. Substitute Q_J^* into Jiff Lube's inverse demand function to find Jiff Lube's best-response to Oil Can Hank's price of $7.50: $P_J^* = \$15.62 = 21.25 - 0.2(28.125)$. So, point H is $P_J = \$15.62$ and P_O $7.50. Point H and the graph of BR_J are shown in the following figure.

b. In a simultaneous decision, managers can be expected to set the Nash prices, which are mutually best prices. Nash prices are found at the intersection of the two best-response curves. Point N, the point of intersection, occurs at $P_J = \$25$ and $P_O = \$20$.

c. Jiff Lube's profit (π_J) at point N is.

$$\pi_J = (25-10)(50-5\cdot25+7.5\cdot20) = \$15\cdot75 = \$1,125/\text{week}.$$

Oil Can Hank's profit (π_O) at point N is:

$$\pi_O = (20-5)(60-6\cdot20+6\cdot25) = \$15\cdot90 = \$1,350/\text{week}. .$$

d. Jiff Lube's manager does not believe Oil Can Hank will set its price at \$40 when Jiff Lube's sets its price at \$40. Both managers know that Oil Can Hank's best response to Jiff Lube's price of \$40 is for Oil Can Hank to lower price to \$27.50 (read this number off the graph).

e. Jiff Lube's profit at point C is:

$$\pi_J = (30-10)(50-5\cdot30+7.5\cdot30) = \$20\cdot125 = \$2,500/\text{week}$$

Oil Can Hank's profit at point C is:

$$\pi_O = (30-5)(60-6\cdot30+6\cdot30) = \$25\cdot60 = \$1,500/\text{week}$$

Both firms make greater profit at point C than at point N.

f. Since the firms are making simultaneous decisions and cannot cooperate, point C will not be chosen, and point N is the expected outcome.

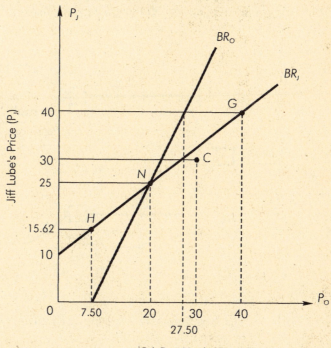

Oil Can Hank's Price (P_O)

5. a. It has no dominant strategy
   b. It has no dominant strategy
   c. cells A and D are Nash equilibrium cells
   d and e. $16 billion; $12 billion. See the figure below:

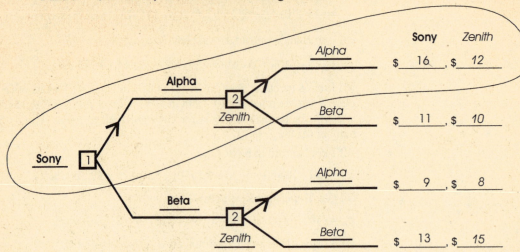

f and g. $13 billion; $15 billion. See the figure below:

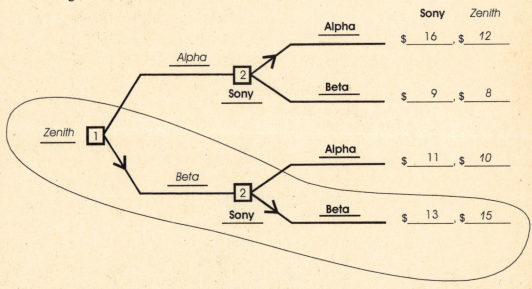

   h. Yes, both firms have a first-mover advantage because each firm makes more profit by going first.
   i. No. Neither firm makes more profit by going second.

6. a. Yes. Both firms have dominant strategies, and the dominant strategy equilibrium makes both BK and Mac worse off than if they cooperated to reach cell D.
   b. cooperate = High, *High* in cell D

      noncooperative = Low, *Low* in cell A
   c. In game theory, cheating means making a decision other than the cooperative decision. So, BK cheats in cell C, and Mac cheats in cell B.

d. When the decision is made just once, both managers know that no punishment for cheating is possible. So, neither manager believes the other will cooperate since unilateral cheating against a cooperating rival will increase the profit of the cheater. Consequently, the dominant strategy equilibrium, which is also the Nash equilibrium, is likely to occur.

7. a. Yes. In cell C in which BK is cheating on Mac by pricing low while Mac prices high, Mac can increase its profit by $1,000 (= $3,000 −$2,000) by carrying out its threat to lower price (i.e., by moving from cell C to cell A).

   b. Yes. In cell B in which Mac is cheating on BK by pricing low while BK prices high, BK can increase its profit by $500 (= $5,500 −$5,000) by carrying out its threat to lower price (i.e., by moving from cell B to cell D).

8. a. $1,500 per month; $2,977.65 $= \dfrac{\$1,500}{(1.005)^1} + \dfrac{\$1,500}{(1.005)^2}$

   b. $2,000 per month; $3,930.79 $= \dfrac{\$2,000}{(1.005)^3} + \dfrac{\$2,000}{(1.005)^4}$

   c. Since $PV_{Costs \; of \; cheating} > PV_{Benefits \; of \; cheating}$, Mac will choose not to cheat and will cooperate.

   d. At a whopping 60 percent per month discount rate, Mac will choose to cheat since

$$PV_{Benefits \; of \; cheating} > PV_{Costs \; of \; cheating}$$
$$\$1,523.44 > \$793.46$$

MULTIPLE CHOICE / TRUE-FALSE

1. e Because the firms in an oligopoly market are large relative to total market output, they will have some degree of market power and their individual decisions will affect every other rivals' demand.

2. c Be careful here. A firm has a dominant strategy if one strategy choice is the best strategy for each and every decision rivals might make. In a prisoners' dilemma, however, both players have a dominant strategy but there exists a set of decisions that provides a higher payoff for both players than they receive in the dominant strategy equilibrium.

3. d When firms have relatively large shares of total market sales their individual pricing, output, and advertising decisions will have an impact on the entire market, which makes the profits of the oligopoly firms interdependent.

4. c In every kind of market structure, managers maximize profit by making decisions that equate marginal revenue and marginal cost, regardless of whether there is interdependence of profits.

5. e The intersection of the best-response curves yields a strategically stable (Nash) equilibrium, but this does not imply that the firms are maximizing either their own individual profit (there is usually a better point for each firm) or their joint profits.

6. a Going second in a sequential decision situation can be advantageous if the second-mover can increase its payoff by knowing its rival's action before it makes its best decision.

7. e A credible commitment is an unconditional strategic move that must be irreversible in order to seize the first move in a strategic decision situation.

8. e To be credible, the threatened or promised action must be the best action to take when the time comes to make good on the threat or promise.

9. d Tit-for-tat and grim strategies are the two most widely known trigger strategies.

10.	a	This is one of the characteristics of a prisoners' dilemma situation.
11.	a	Regardless of the discount rate, in a one-time prisoners' dilemma rivals expect each other to cheat since there can be no punishment for cheating in a one-time game.
12.	d	If $PV_{Benefits\ of\ cheating} < PV_{Costs\ of\ cheating}$, then cheating would decrease the present value of a firm. Consequently, deciding not to cheat and to cooperate instead is consistent with maximizing the value of the firm.
13.	a	Any form of coordinating prices is illegal per se in the United States.
14.	b	Because cooperation in setting prices is illegal, managers cannot challenge noncooperative behavior in court or impose fines.
15.	d	In an oligopoly market, all the firms need to decide not to cheat in order for cooperation to occur.
16.	d	Price matching is a strategic commitment–and so must be irreversible in order to be credible–to match any lower prices offered by rivals.
17.	d	None of these statements characterize price leadership.
18.	T	In dominant strategy equilibrium, both firms are doing the best they can *no matter what* their rivals choose so they must also be doing the best they can *given* what their rivals choose.
19.	F	To be a simultaneous decision, the firms cannot know at the time they make their decisions what decisions their rivals have made, are making, or will make.
20.	T	In order for all managers to believe they are correctly predicting their rivals' decisions, they must predict that all rivals are making the best decisions for themselves given the decisions they all expect their rivals to make.
21.	F	If a firm experiences a first-mover advantage, then it earns a greater payoff *for itself* by going first than by going second. This does *not* mean that it earns a higher payoff *than its rivals* by going first.
22.	F	Nash decision making is not a sign of cooperation. The firms are only doing best for themselves given what they expect their rivals will do. It is frequently the case that if rivals could indeed collude or cooperate, they could all do better individually at decision sets other than the Nash point.
23.	T	Cheating does not imply that rivals have explicitly or tacitly agreed to cooperate.
24.	F	Cheating is more likely to occur the more difficult it is to monitor rivals' prices.
25.	T	Any *one* member of the cartel believes it can cut price and gain a great deal of sales because demand is quite elastic when only *one* cartel member cuts price.

Homework Exercises

1. The *Tampa Tribune* and the *St. Petersburg Times* compete for readers in the Tampa Bay market for newspapers. Recently, both newspapers considered changing the prices they charge for their Sunday editions. Suppose they considered the following payoff table for making a *simultaneous* decision to charge either a low price of $0.50 or a high price of $1.00:

St. Petersburg Times

		Low Price $0.50	High Price $1.00
Tampa Tribune	Low price $0.50	A $45,000, $30,000 TT SP	B $35,000, $20,000
	High price $1.00	C $40,000, $45,000 SP	D $50,000, $40,000 TT

Payoffs in dollars of profit per Sunday edition.

a. *St. Petersburg Times*' dominant strategy is __Low__ (low price, high price, it has no dominant strategy).

b. *Tampa Tribune's* dominant strategy is __None__ (low price, high price, it has no dominant strategy).

c. *St. Petersburg Times*' dominated strategy is __High__ (low price, high price, it has no dominated strategy).

d. *Tampa Tribune's* dominated strategy is __None__ (low price, high price, it has no dominated strategy).

e. Cell __A__ is a Nash equilibrium.

f. The Nash equilibrium cell in part *e* __is not__ (is, is not) a dominant strategy equilibrium.

g. Cell D __is not__ (is, is not) strategically stable. Explain briefly in the space provided below:

2. Now suppose the newspaper pricing decision in Homework Exercise 1 is made sequentially. Using the payoff table in the previous exercise, complete the two sequential game trees on the next page. In the first game tree (the top one), let the *St. Petersburg Times* make the first pricing decision. In the second game tree (the bottom one), let the *Tampa Tribune* go first. After you complete the two game trees, solve both sequential decision games using the roll-back method. Circle the solution path on each game tree. Then, after solving both sequential decision games, answer the following questions:

a. The *St. Petersburg Times* experiences a ___1st___ (first-mover advantage, second-mover advantage, neither a first- nor a second-mover advantage). Explain your answer.

b. The *Tampa Tribune* experiences a ___2ND___ (first-mover advantage, second-mover advantage, neither a first- nor a second-mover advantage). Explain your answer.

c. Can you predict which newspaper is likely to go first in this sequential decision? Explain. [Hint: Remember that the payoff table is common knowledge to both managers.]

Tampa Tribune goes first

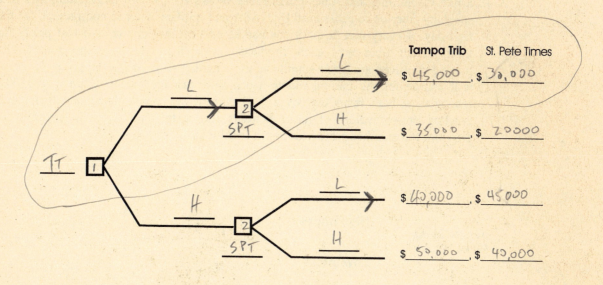

	Tampa Trib	St. Pete Times
L	$ 45,000	$ 30,000
H	$ 35000	$ 20000
L	$ 40,000	$ 45000
H	$ 50,000	$ 40,000

St. Petersburg Times goes first

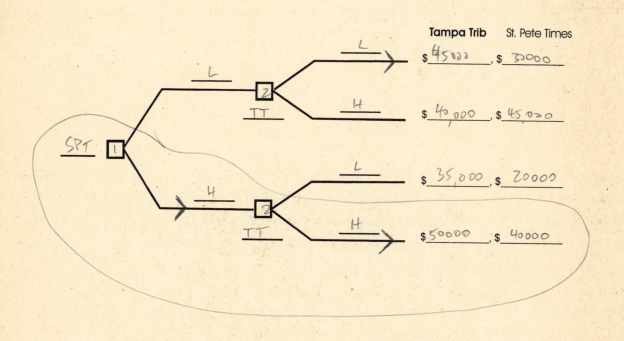

	Tampa Trib	St. Pete Times
L	$ 45000	$ 30000
H	$ 40,000	$ 45,000
L	$ 35,000	$ 20000
H	$ 50000	$ 40000

3. Smith Cable, Inc. and Jones Glass Fibre Works are the two largest suppliers of a specialty fiber-optic cable used by NASA and military defense contractors. On the first day of every month, both companies post on the Internet a list of prices for their various fiber-optic cable products—either high prices or low prices. The pricing decisions are made simultaneously (neither firm knows the prices the other will charge for the current month when their pricing decisions are made). The managers at both firms employ a 1.75 percent per month discount rate for calculating present values of future benefits and costs. The following payoff table provides the monthly profits for Smith and Jones:

Smith Cable, Inc.

		High prices	Low prices
Jones Glass Fibre Works	High prices	A $7, $4	B $2, $5.5
	Low prices	C $8, $1	D $4, $2

Payoffs in dollars of monthly profit

The managers of both firms believe that they can get away with cheating for one month but believe they will then be punished for two months when they get caught.

a. Smith Cable will choose to _____ (cheat, cooperate) because the present value of the benefits of cheating equals $_____ million while the present value of the costs of cheating equals $_____ million.

Show your computations here:

b. Jones Fibre will choose to _____ (cheat, cooperate) because the present value of the benefits of cheating equals $_____ million while the present value of the costs of cheating equals $_____ million.

Show your computations here:

Advanced Techniques for Profit Maximization

Learning Objectives

After reading Chapter 14 and working the problems for Chapter 14 in the textbook and in this Workbook, you will learn how to handle a number of managerial decision situations that are more complicated than the problem of maximizing profit when a firm produces one product in one plant and sells the product in one market where structural entry barriers protect any profit the firm might earn by pricing where $MR = MC$ on the demand curve. In this chapter you will learn:

➤   How to choose individual production levels at multiple plants owned by a firm in order to minimize the total cost of producing a given amount of total output for a firm.

➤   Why a popular pricing technique, cost-plus pricing, usually fails to result in the profit-maximizing price and how to apply the technique when costs are constant and demand is linear to achieve profit-maximization.

➤   How to set different prices for a good that can be sold in different markets to buyers with differing elasticities of demand in order to increase total revenue (and profit).

➤   How to make profit-maximizing decisions when producing multiple products that are related either in consumption or in production.

➤   Why it is difficult, but not impossible, to create strategic barriers to entry by either limit pricing or capacity expansion.

Essential Concepts

MULTIPLE PLANTS

1.   If a firm produces in two plants, A and B, it should allocate production between the two plants so that $MC_A = MC_B$. The optimal total output for the firm is that output for which $MR = MC_T$. Hence, for profit maximization, the firm should produce the level of total output and allocate this total output between the two plants so that

$$MR = MC_T = MC_A = MC_B$$

COST-PLUS PRICING

2.   Cost-plus pricing is a common technique for pricing when firms cannot or do not wish to estimate demand an cost conditions and apply the MR = MC rule to find the profit-maximizing price and output on the firm's demand curve.

3.   The price charged represents a markup (margin) over average cost:

$$P = (1+m)ATC$$

where m is the markup on unit cost (expressed as a fraction, rather than a percentage).

4. Cost-plus pricing does not generally produce the profit-maximizing price because (1) it fails to incorporate information about demand and marginal revenue, and (2) it utilizes average, not marginal, cost to compute price.

5. When costs are constant, yields the profit-maximizing price when the optimal markup, m^*, is applied to average variable costs as follows:

$$P = (1+m^*)AVC$$

and the optimal markup is chosen according to the following relation with price elasticity of demand:

$$m^* = -\frac{1}{1+E^*}$$

where E^* is the price elasticity at the profit-maximizing point of the firm's demand.

6. When demand is linear and costs are constant ($SMC = AVC$), the profit-maximizing value for E^* is

$$E^* = 1 + \frac{A}{0.5(AVC - A)}$$

where A is the price-intercept of the linear demand curve and AVC is the constant average variable cost (fixed costs, as always, must be ignored).

MULTIPLE MARKETS

7. If a firm sells in two distinct markets, 1 and 2, it should allocate output (sales) between the two markets such that $MR_1 = MR_2$. The optimal level of total output for the firm is that at which $MR_T = MC$. Hence, for profit maximization, the firm should produce the level of output and allocate the sales of this output between the two markets so that

$$MR_T = MC = MR_1 = MR_2$$

MULTIPLE PRODUCTS

Related in Consumption

8. Defining the two products to be X and Y, the firm will produce and sell those levels of output for which

$$MR_X = MC_X \quad \text{and} \quad MR_Y = MC_Y$$

Since the products are related in consumption, MR_X is a function not only of Q_X but also of Q_Y, as is MR_Y. Therefore, the marginal conditions for the two products must be satisfied simultaneously.

Related in Production as Substitutes

9. If a firm produces two products, X and Y, that compete for the firm's limited production facilities, the firm should allocate the production facility so that the marginal revenue product of the production facility is equal for the two products, $MRP_X = MRP_Y$. If in the long run the firm can vary its usage of (or size of) the production facility, the optimal level of usage of the facility is that at which $MRP_T = MC$. Hence, for profit maximization the firm should select the level of

usage of its production facility and allocate this level of usage between the production of the two products so that

$$MRP_T = MC = MRP_X = MRP_Y$$

Related in Production as Complements

10. To maximize profit, the manager produces the level of joint product where the joint marginal revenue equals marginal cost: $MR_J = MC$. If the profit-maximizing level of joint production exceeds the output where the MR_J kinks, then, for the good with negative marginal revenue, the units beyond the point of zero marginal revenue are disposed of rather than sold in the market. The profit-maximizing prices are found using the demand functions for the two goods.

STRATEGIC ENTRY DETERRENCE

11. Strategic entry deterrence occurs when an established firm (or firms) makes strategic moves designed to discourage or even prevent the entry of a new firm or firms into a market. Two types of strategic moves designed to manipulate the beliefs of potential entrants about the profitability of entering are limit pricing and capacity expansion.

Limit pricing

12. Under certain circumstances, an oligopolist, or possibly a monopolist, may be able to make a credible commitment to charge forever a price lower than the profit-maximizing price in order to discourage new firms from entering the market.

Capacity Expansion

13. Sometimes an established firm can make its threat of a price cut in the event of entry credible by irreversibly increasing its plant capacity. When increasing production capacity results in lower marginal costs of production for an established firm, the established firm's best response to entry of a new firm may then be to increase its own level of production, which requires the established firm to cut its price in order to sell the extra output.

Matching Definitions

capacity expansion as a barrier to entry
complements in consumption
complements in production
cost-plus pricing
limit pricing
price discrimination
strategic entry deterrence
substitutes in consumption
substitutes in production
total marginal cost curve

1. _____ Horizontal summation of all plants' marginal cost curves, which gives the addition to total cost attributable to increasing total output by one unit.

2. _____ A method of determining price by setting price equal to average total cost plus a portion (m) of average cost as a markup.

3. _____ Firms charge different groups of customers different prices for the same good or service.

4. _____ Products that are used together and purchased together.

5. _____ Products are substitutes and buyers purchase only one of the firm's products.

6. _____ Goods, produced by the same firm, that compete for limited production facilities.

7. _____ Two or more goods that are produced using a common input.

8. _____ Strategic moves taken by established firms to prevent entry of new firms.

9. _____ Strategy in which an established firm irreversibly expands capacity to make credible its threat to decrease price if entry occurs.

Study Problems

1. Atlas Manufacturing, a firm with market power, produces in two plants, A and B. The estimated marginal cost functions of the two plants are

$$MC_A = 10 + 0.05Q_A$$
$$MC_B = 20 + 0.01Q_B$$

a. The inverse marginal cost functions are

$Q_A =$ _____

$Q_B =$ _____

b. Set $MC_A = MC_T$ and $MC_B = MC_T$ in the inverse marginal cost functions in part *a*. Solve for the total output, $Q_T = Q_A + Q_B$ as a function of MC_T:

$Q_T =$ _____

c. Take the inverse of the Q_T function in part *b* to find the total marginal cost function:

$MC_T =$ _____

d. Beyond _____ units of total production, the firm uses *both* plants for production.

e. If the manager of the firm wants to produce 350 units at the least possible total cost, the optimal production levels in the two plants are

$Q_A =$ _____

$Q_B =$ _____

f. Construct MC_A, MC_B, and MC_T on the axes provided below. Check your answers to parts *d* and *e*.

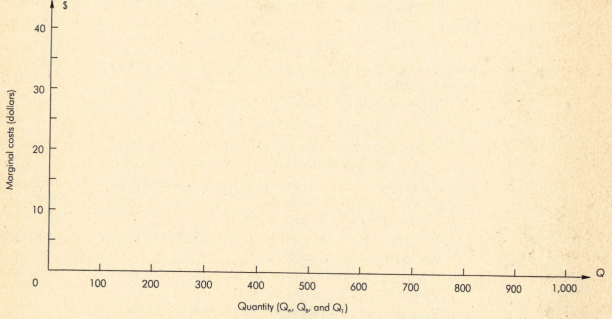

Quantity (Q_A, Q_B, and Q_T)

g. If the manager of Atlas decides to produce 100 units, _____ units should be produced in plant A and _____ units in plant B.

The estimated (inverse) demand function for Atlas Manufacturing is
$$P = 40 - 0.009375Q$$

h. The marginal revenue function is $MR = $ _____.

i. The optimal level of total output is _____ units.

j. Atlas Manufacturing will divide the total output between plants A and B as

$Q_A = $ _____ units

$Q_B = $ _____ units.

k. Atlas Manufacturing will charge $ _____ for its product.

l. Construct the demand and marginal revenue lines on the axes above. Check your answers to parts $i, j,$ and k.

2. Bruce Slover is the senior production and pricing manager at DrillQuick, a Houston-based company that manufactures a patented drill bit called the "Blaster," which is used in the petroleum industry. His company has historically used a 25 percent markup on the average total costs of producing Blasters. The average variable cost of production is constant and equal to $7,500 per bit. Total fixed cost is $50,000 per quarter-year of production. DrillQuick currently produces 250 bits per quarter.

a. The average variable cost of producing a Blaster bit is $ _____, which also equals the _____ (average total, short-run marginal, average fixed) cost of production. Average fixed cost of production is $ _____. Average total cost of producing a Blaster bit is $ _____.

b. Using a 25 percent markup on average total cost, Slover calculates the cost-plus price for a Blaster bit to be $ _____ per bit. DrillQuick earns quarterly profit of $ _____ by selling 250 bits per quarter.

Slover wants to determine whether cost-plus pricing is yielding the maximum possible profit for DrillQuick. After undertaking a statistical estimation of demand for Blaster drill bits, he estimates DrillQuick faces the following linear demand for its bits:

$$Q = 640 - 0.04P$$

where Q is the number of Blaster bits demanded each quarter and P is the price charged for Blaster bits.

c. The inverse demand for Blaster bits is $P = $ _____.

d. The marginal revenue for Blaster bits is $MR = $ _____.

e. Setting $MR = SMC$, Slover discovers that DrillQuik should be producing _____ bits per quarter in order to maximize its profit.

f. Based on the estimated demand, Slover discovers that the profit-maximizing price is $ _____, which is _____ (higher than, lower than, equal to) the cost-plus price in part b.

g. Using the $MR = SMC$ approach to set price, Slover calculates that DrillQuik can earn economic profit of $ _____ each quarter, which is _____ (more than, less than, the same as) the profit earned using cost-plus pricing.

h. Explain why you would expect the outcome for profits in part g.

i. If the president of DrillQuick insists that Slover continue using markup pricing, then Slover should suggest to his boss that DrillQuick use the following formula $P = (1 + m^*) \times$ _____ (ATC, AVC, SMC), where m^* equals _____. Verify that this formula gives the price found in part d.

3. Belmont Industries sells its product in two distinct markets. The demand functions for these two markets are estimated to be

$$Market\ 1: \quad Q_1 = 25,000 - 5,000P_1$$
$$Market\ 2: \quad Q_2 = 40,000 - 5,000P_2$$

Belmont Industries' marginal cost function is $MC = 1.25 + 0.0001Q$.

a. Find Belmont Industries' inverse demand functions.

$$Market\ 1: \quad P_1 = \underline{\hspace{3cm}}$$
$$Market\ 2: \quad P_2 = \underline{\hspace{3cm}}$$

b. Find Belmont's marginal revenue and inverse marginal revenue functions.

Market 1: $MR_1 =$ _____ $Q_1 =$ _____

Market 2: $MR_2 =$ _____ $Q_2 =$ _____

c. Belmont's total marginal revenue function is $MR_T =$ _____ .

d. On the axes below, construct lines for MR_1, MR_2, and MR_T.

Quantity (Q_1, Q_2, and Q_T)

e. Belmont Industries' profit is maximized by producing and selling a total of _____ units.

f. The manager of Belmont Industries maximizes profit by selling _____ units in market 1 and selling _____ units in market 2.

g. In order to maximize profit, the manager must set prices in the two markets as

$$P_1^* = \$\underline{\hspace{2cm}}$$
$$P_2^* = \$\underline{\hspace{2cm}}$$

h. Measured at the prices in part g, the point elasticities of demand are

$$E_1 = \underline{\hspace{2cm}}$$
$$E_2 = \underline{\hspace{2cm}}$$

The higher price is charged in the _____ (less, more) elastic market.

i. In the preceding figure in which you have constructed marginal revenue and demand curves, now construct the marginal cost curve and verify that you have correctly calculated the profit-maximizing prices and outputs.

4. Consider a firm with market power that sells a "regular" and "deluxe" version of a product. The manager estimates the demand functions for the two products are

$$Q_R = 800 - 60P_R + 40P_D$$
$$Q_D = 1,000 - 40P_D + 20P_R$$

By solving the demand functions simultaneously, the manager obtains the following estimated inverse demand functions:

$$P_R = 45 - 0.025Q_R - 0.025Q_D$$
$$P_D = 47.5 - 0.0375Q_D - 0.0125Q_R$$

The marginal cost functions are estimated to be

$$MC_R = 0.5 + 0.01Q_R$$
$$MC_D = 0.6 + 0.01Q_D$$

a. Verify that the manager correctly performed the derivation of the inverse demand functions from the demand functions.

b. The marginal revenue functions are:

$$MR_R = \underline{\hspace{4cm}}$$
$$MR_D = \underline{\hspace{4cm}}$$

c. The profit-maximizing levels of output and prices are:

$Q_R = \underline{\hspace{2cm}}$ units $P_R = \$\underline{\hspace{2cm}}$

$Q_D = \underline{\hspace{2cm}}$ units $P_D = \$\underline{\hspace{2cm}}$

5. Simpson Corporation produces two products (X and Y) that are substitutes in production. The demand functions for the two products are forecasted to be

$$Q_X = 120 - 6P_X$$
$$Q_Y = 48 - 4P_Y$$

The manufacturing process uses a common production facility, and the outputs of the two products are determined by the amounts of time the facility is employed to produce them:

$$Q_X = 1.0H_X$$
$$Q_Y = 2.0H_Y$$

where H_X and H_Y are the number of hours per week the production facility is used to produce good X and good Y, respectively. The marginal cost for using the production facility is estimated to be

$$MC = 9 + 0.1H_T$$

where H_T is the total number of hours per week that the plant operates ($H_T = H_X + H_Y$).

a. The marginal revenue products of the production facility in X and Y are

$$MRP_{H_X} = \underline{\hspace{5cm}}$$

$$MRP_{H_Y} = \underline{\hspace{5cm}}$$

b. The marginal revenue product of total hours of plant operation, MRP_T, is

$$MRP_T = \underline{\hspace{6cm}}.$$

c. The profit-maximizing level of usage of the production facility is _____ hours per week. The optimal allocation of the production facility between the production of X and Y is

$$H_X = \underline{\hspace{2cm}}$$

$$H_Y = \underline{\hspace{2cm}}$$

d. The profit-maximizing outputs and prices are

$$Q_X^* = \underline{\hspace{2cm}} \quad \text{and} \quad P_X^* = \underline{\hspace{2cm}}$$

$$Q_Y^* = \underline{\hspace{2cm}} \quad \text{and} \quad P_Y^* = \underline{\hspace{2cm}}$$

6. Waring Chemical Supply produces styrene and ulene, which are complements in production. The production process yields equal amounts of both products. The owner and manager of Waring Chemical Supply must decide how much styrene and ulene to produce and sell and what prices to charge. The owner wants to make the pricing and production decisions in a way that maximizes the profit of the firm.

The forecasted monthly demand for styrene and ulene are

$$Q_S = 10,000 - 50P_S \quad \text{and} \quad Q_U = 12,000 - 40P_U$$

where quantities are measured in gallons demanded per month and prices are expressed in dollars per gallon. The owner of Waring Chemical estimates that marginal cost of producing the joint products is

$$MC = 200 - 0.06Q_J$$

where Q_J is the number of gallons of joint product ($Q_J = Q_S = Q_U$).

a. Derive the marginal revenue functions for styrene and ulene

$$MR_S = \underline{\hspace{5cm}}$$

$$MR_U = \underline{\hspace{5cm}}$$

Construct these two marginal revenue functions on the axes provided on the following page.

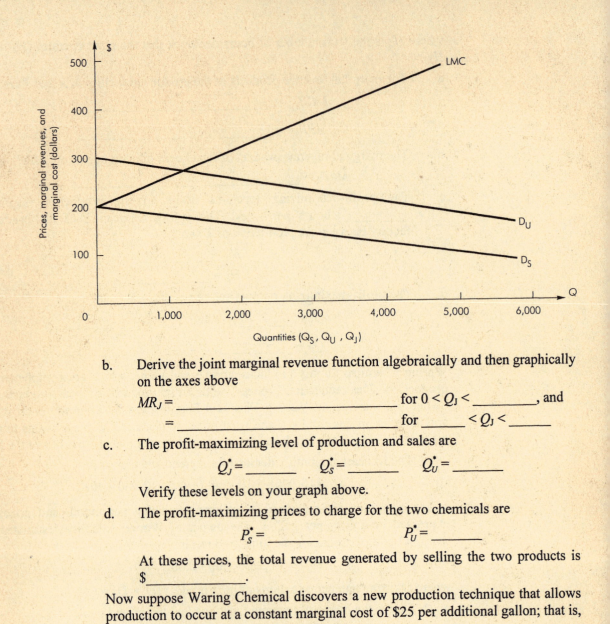

b. Derive the joint marginal revenue function algebraically and then graphically
    on the axes above

    $MR_J =$ _____ for $0 < Q_J <$ _____, and

    $\quad\; =$ _____ for _____ $< Q_J <$ _____

c. The profit-maximizing level of production and sales are

    $Q_J^* =$ _____ $Q_S^* =$ _____ $Q_U^* =$ _____

    Verify these levels on your graph above.

d. The profit-maximizing prices to charge for the two chemicals are

    $P_S^* =$ _____ $P_U^* =$ _____

    At these prices, the total revenue generated by selling the two products is
    $ _____ .

Now suppose Waring Chemical discovers a new production technique that allows
production to occur at a constant marginal cost of $25 per additional gallon; that is,
the new marginal cost function is $MC = 25$.

e. The profit-maximizing level of production of the joint product is _____
    gallons per week. The amount sold each week is _____ gallons of styrene
    and _____ gallons of ulene. In order to maximize profit, the manager
    must dispose of _____ units of _____ each week rather than sell
    those units.

f. The profit-maximizing prices to charge for the two chemicals are

    $P_S^* =$ _____ $P_U^* =$ _____

    At these prices, the total revenue generated by selling the two products is
    $ _____ .

7. Burger Doodle, the only seller of gourmet hamburgers in a trendy shopping mall in Kansas City, charges $10 per burger (the profit-maximizing price for a monopolist) and makes $180,000 of profit per year. Designer Burger wants to open a competing burger restaurant in the mall. The owner-manager of Burger Doodle knows that if he lowers his burger price to $6 and Designer Burger chooses to enter the market, Burger Doodle can make $100,000 of annual profit while Designer Burger (facing higher costs) would suffer a loss of $50,000 per year. If Burger Doodle charges $6 and Designer Burger decides not to enter, then Burger Doodle makes $150,000. The owner-manager also knows that if he keeps his price at the monopoly price of $10 and Designer Burger decides to enter, Burger Doodle will make $120,000 of profit annually while Designer Burger will make $100,000 annually. Burger Doodle must make its pricing decision first, and then Designer Burger will decide whether to enter the market or stay out.

    a. The diagram below shows the game tree facing the owner-manager of Burger Doodle should he wish to try to deter Designer Burger from entering his market by lowering his price to $6, the prospective limit price. Fill in the blanks to complete the following game tree (payoffs are annual profits).

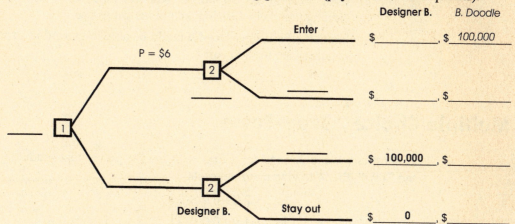

    b. What condition must be met in order for Burger Doodle to be able to successfully implement a limit pricing strategy to deter Burger Designer from entering?

    c. Assuming the condition set forth in part b is met, show that setting the limit price of $6 per burger will indeed deter entry of Designer Burger by using the roll-back method to find the likely outcome. Circle this decision path in the game tree above.

    d. Suppose the necessary condition for successful limit pricing (discussed in part b) cannot be achieved. The following diagram shows the game tree for the limit pricing decision when Burger Doodle can react to entry by Designer Burger by changing its initial price to the Nash price for two firms ($P_N =$ $7.50). Fill in the missing blanks to complete the game tree.

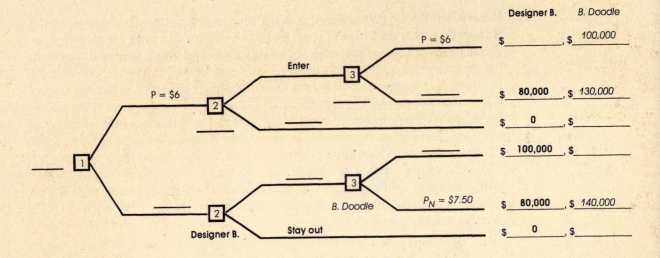

Designer B.   B. Doodle

P = $6 $_____ , $ _100,000_

Enter

P = $6 $_80,000_ , $ _130,000_

$___0___ , $_____

$_100,000_ , $_____

B. Doodle $P_N = \$7.50$ $_80,000_ , $ _140,000_

Stay out $___0___ , $_____

Designer B.

e.   Using the roll-back method in the above game tree, show that setting the limit price of $6 per burger will *not* deter entry of Designer Burger by circling the likely decision path in the game tree.

f.   Explain how Burger Doodle might be able to expand its capacity to meet the condition set forth in part *b*.

Multiple Choice / True-False

In questions 1 and 2, consider a firm with market power that produces in two plants (1 and 2) with the following marginal costs:

$$MC_1 = 2.0 + 0.001Q_1$$
$$MC_2 = 1.0 + 0.001Q_2$$
$$MC_T = 1.5 + 0.0005Q \quad \text{(for } Q_T > 1,000\text{)}$$

where cost is measured in dollars. The firm's demand function is estimated to be

$$Q = 22,000 - 4,000P$$

1.   The manager maximizes profit by producing and selling
   a.   2,000 units at a price of $3.50 per unit.
   b.   2,500 units at a price of $3.75 per unit.
   c.   5,500 units at a price of $4.25 per unit.
   d.   3,000 units at a price of $4.00 per unit.
   e.   4,000 units at a price of $4.50 per unit.

2.   To minimize the total cost of producing the profit-maximizing level of output, the manager allocates output between the two plants so that
   a. $Q_1 = 1,000$ and $Q_2 = 2,000$.
   b. $Q_1 = 1,500$ and $Q_2 = 2,500$.
   c. $Q_1 = 2,000$ and $Q_2 = 3,000$.
   d. $Q_1 = 2,250$ and $Q_2 = 3,500$.

3. Which of the following are practical problems that arise with the implementation of cost-plus pricing?
    a. For short-run pricing applications, the fraction of fixed costs to include in the computation is completely arbitrary.
    b. Determining the value of average total cost to multiply by $1 + m$ is difficult when unit costs vary with the level of output level.
    c. Choosing the markup (m) to employ is largely a guessing game.
    d. all of the above.
    e. both b and c.

4. If a firm's long-run costs are constant and its optimal elastiticity is known to be −3.0, then the markup on LAC that will maximize profit is
    a. 5 percent.   d. 100 percent.
    b. 20 percent.   e. 200 percent.
    c. 50 percent.

5. There are two *theoretical* reasons why the cost-plus pricing method of setting price is not likely (except by luck) to result in profit-maximization. Find these two theoretical problems with cost-plus pricing in the choices below.
    a. The cost-plus pricing formula uses average instead of marginal cost.
    b. The cost-plus pricing formula fails to include any information about demand or marginal revenue.
    c. The cost-plus pricing formula is a linear function of average cost, and thus can only be applied in linear demand situations.
    d. both a and b.
    e. both b and c.

In questions 6–8, a firm with market power can divide its sales into two submarkets, the demands and marginal revenues of which are shown in the figure below.

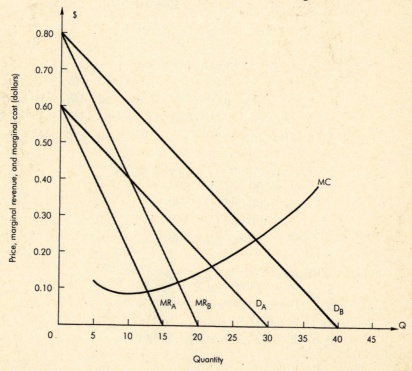

6. The total output of the monopolist is
   a. 5 units.
   b. 10 units.
   c. 15 units.
   d. 20 units.
   e. 25 units.

7. In order to maximize profit, how must the total output be distributed between markets?
   a. $Q_A = 5$ and $Q_B = 10$
   b. $Q_A = 10$ and $Q_B = 15$
   c. $Q_A = 15$ and $Q_B = 25$
   d. $Q_A = 15$ and $Q_B = 10$

8. What prices should be charged in each of the markets?
   a. $P_A = \$0.30$ and $P_B = \$0.20$
   b. $P_A = \$0.20$ and $P_B = \$0.40$
   c. $P_A = \$0.40$ and $P_B = \$0.50$
   d. $P_A = \$0.25$ and $P_B = \$0.35$

In questions 9–11 use the following:

A firm produces two products, X and Y, which are related in consumption. After estimating the demand functions and solving them simultaneously, the manager determines the inverse demand functions to be

$$P_X = 36 - 0.0025Q_X - 0.01Q_Y$$
$$P_Y = 45 - 0.0125Q_Y - 0.03Q_X$$

The marginal cost functions are estimated to be

$$MC_X = 22 + 0.015Q_X$$
$$MC_Y = 12 + 0.005Q_Y$$

9. The marginal revenue functions are
   a. $MR_X = 36 - 0.005Q_X - 0.01Q_Y$ and $MR_Y = 45 - 0.025Q_Y - 0.03Q_X$
   b. $MR_X = 72 - 0.005Q_X - 0.02Q_Y$ and $MR_Y = 90 - 0.025Q_Y - 0.06Q_X$
   c. $MR_X = 36 - 0.005Q_X - 0.02Q_Y$ and $MR_Y = 45 - 0.025Q_Y - 0.06Q_X$
   d. $MR_X = 36 - 0.005Q_X - 0.03Q_Y$ and $MR_Y = 45 - 0.025Q_Y - 0.09Q_X$

10. What are the optimal levels of X and Y?
    a. $Q_X = 300$ and $Q_Y = 800$
    b. $Q_X = 600$ and $Q_Y = 400$
    c. $Q_X = 300$ and $Q_Y = 300$
    d. $Q_X = 200$ and $Q_Y = 600$

11. What are the optimal prices for X and Y?
    a. $P_X = \$25.00$ and $P_Y = \$25.50$
    b. $P_X = \$30.00$ and $P_Y = \$32.50$
    c. $P_X = \$21.50$ and $P_Y = \$20.00$
    d. $P_X = \$27.25$ and $P_Y = \$26.00$

For questions 12–14, use the figure below that shows the *MRP* curves for products A and B, which are substitutes in production. The marginal cost of using the production facility is estimated to be constant and equal to $2,000:

$$MC = 2,000$$

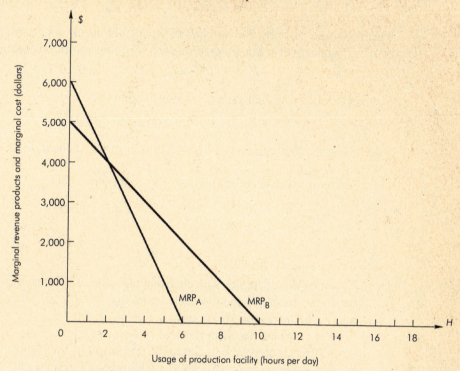

Usage of production facility (hours per day)

12. What is the optimal number of hours per day that the production facility should be used?
    a. 6 hours per day
    b. 8 hours per day
    c. 10 hours per day
    d. 12 hours per day
    e. 14 hours per day

13. How should the total number of hours be allocated to production of A and B?
    a. $H_A = 2$ hours and $H_B = 4$ hours
    b. $H_A = 4$ hours and $H_B = 4$ hours
    c. $H_A = 5$ hours and $H_B = 5$ hours
    d. $H_A = 4$ hours and $H_B = 6$ hours

14. Suppose the marginal cost of using the production facility is $MC = 1,000$. How should the total number of hours be allocated to production of A and B?
    a. $H_A = 5$ hours and $H_B = 8$ hours
    b. $H_A = 4$ hours and $H_B = 4$ hours
    c. $H_A = 2.5$ hours and $H_B = 3.5$ hours
    d. $H_A = 4$ hours and $H_B = 6$ hours

In questions 15–18, consider Jupiter Bicycle Company, a firm that manufactures two types of bicycles, road bikes and dirt bikes. The two bicycles are substitutes in production and must share Jupiter's production facility. The two bicycles have the following "production functions":

$$Q_R = 2.0H_R \quad \text{and} \quad Q_D = 4.0H_D$$

where H_R and H_D are the number of hours per week spent producing road and dirt bicycles, respectively. The inverse demand functions are forecasted to be

$$P_R = 900 - 25Q_R \quad \text{and} \quad P_D = 500 - 3.125Q_D$$

The marginal cost of the firm's plant is estimated to be

$$MC = 300 + 50H_T$$

where H_T is the total number of hours Jupiter operates its bicycle factory.

15. Jupiter maximizes profit by operating its bicycle plant _____ hours per week.
    a. 6
    b. 8
    c. 12
    d. 14

16. The manager of Jupiter Bicycle Company should allocate the total number of hours between road bikes and dirt bikes as follows:
    a. 4 hours on road bicycles and 4 hours on dirt bicycles
    b. 4 hours on road bicycles and 10 hours on dirt bicycles
    c. 6 hours on road bicycles and 6 hours on dirt bicycles
    d. 6 hours on road bicycles and 8 hours on dirt bicycles

17. Jupiter's weekly output of the two bicycles should be
    a. 8 road bicycles per week and 40 dirt bicycles per week.
    b. 12 road bicycles per week and 24 dirt bicycles per week.
    c. 8 road bicycles per week and 16 dirt bicycles per week.
    d. 10 road bicycles per week and 20 dirt bicycles per week.

18. Jupiter should charge the following prices for the two bicycles:
    a. $P_R = \$100$ and $P_D = \$95$
    b. $P_R = \$200$ and $P_D = \$175$
    c. $P_R = \$700$ and $P_D = \$375$
    d. $P_R = \$350$ and $P_D = \$125$

19. Limit pricing can be difficult to practice successfully because
    a. incumbents usually do better after a new firm enters by raising their prices.
    b. incumbents usually do better after a new firm enters by lowering their prices.
    c. new entrants frequently wish to engage in a price war to gain market share.
    d. highly differentiated products make it difficult to raise price profitably.
    e. knowledge is seldom common.

20. Increasing plant capacity can serve as a barrier to entry if
    a. an increase in plant capacity lowers the marginal costs of production for an established firm.
    b. the increase in plant capacity is reversible.
    c. the increase in plant capacity is irreversible.
    d. both *a* and *b*.
    e. both *a* and *c*.

Answers

MATCHING DEFINITIONS

1. total marginal cost curve
2. cost-plus pricing
3. price discrimination
4. complements in consumption
5. substitutes in consumption
6. substitutes in production
7. complements in production
8. strategic entry deterrence
9. limit pricing
10. capacity expansion as a barrier to entry

STUDY PROBLEMS

1. a. Take the inverses of the *MC* functions. [See Exercises 2*a* and 2*b* in the *Review of Fundamental Mathematics* at the beginning of this Workbook.]

$$Q_A = -200 + 20MC_A$$
$$Q_B = -2,000 + 100MC_B$$

   b. After setting $MC_A = MC_B = MC_T$, which forces the manager to minimize total cost:

$$Q_T = Q_A + Q_B = (-200 + 20MC_T) + (-2,000 + 100MC_T) = -2,200 + 120MC_T$$

   c. Taking the inverse of $Q_T = -2,200 + 120MC_T$:

$$MC_T = 18.33 + 0.00833Q_T$$

   d. To find the kink point of MC_T, set *MC* in the low-cost plant equal to the minimum value of the marginal cost in the high-cost plant and solve for Q_{kink} (see page 579 of your textbook). In this problem, plant A is the low-cost plant and plant B is the high-cost plant (see footnote 2 on page 580 of your textbook):

$$10 + 0.05Q = 20$$
$$Q_{kink} = 10/0.05 = 200 \text{ units}$$

   e. Since $Q_T = 350$, substitute 350 into the MC_T function to find $MC_T = \$21.25$ ($= 18.33 + 0.00833 \times 350$). Then find Q_A^* and Q_B^* by substituting $21.25 into the two inverse marginal cost functions

$$Q_A^* = 225(= -200 + 20 \times 21.25)$$
$$Q_B^* = 125(= -2,000 + 100 \times 21.25)$$

   f. See MC_A, MC_B, and MC_T in the following figure. Note that at $MC_T = \$21.25$, $MC_A = MC_B$ and $Q_A = 125$, $Q_B = 225$, and $Q_T = 350$.

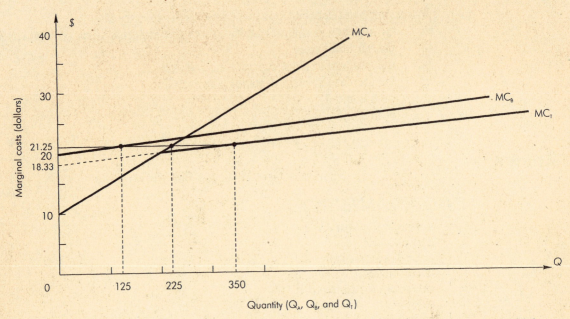

g. 100; 0 Since $Q_T < Q_{kink}$, all output is produced in the low-cost plant A and high-cost plant B is shut down.

h. $MR = 40 - 0.01875Q$

i. Set $MR = MC_T$ and solve for Q_T:

$$40 - 0.01875Q_T = 18.33 + 0.0083Q_T \Rightarrow Q_T^* = 800$$

j. $MC_T(800) = \$25$; $Q_A^* = 300 \ (= -200 + 20 \times 25)$; $Q_B^* = 500 \ (= -2,000 + 100 \times 25)$

k. $P^* = \$32.50 \ (= 40 - 0.009375 \times 800)$

l. See the figure below.

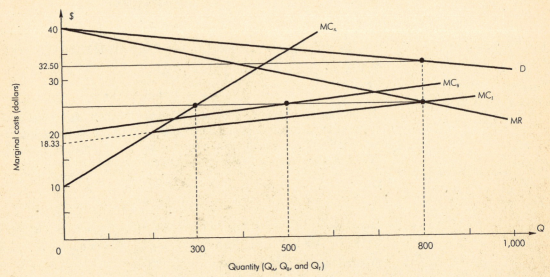

2. a. \$7,500 (this value is given in the problem); SMC (Recall that when short-run costs are constant, $SMC = AVC$ and when long-run costs are constant, $LMC = LAC$); \$200 $(= TFC/Q = \$51,000/255)$; $ATC = \$7,700 \ (= AVC + AFC)$

b. \$9,625 $(= 1.25 \times ATC = 1.25 \times \$7,700)$; \$490,875 $[=(P - ATC)Q = (\$9,625 - \$7,700) \times 255]$

c. $P = 16,000 - 25Q$

d. $MR = 16,000 - 50Q$

e. $Q^* = 170$ bits per quarter $(MR = SMC \Rightarrow 16,000 - 50Q = 7500 \Rightarrow Q^* = 170)$

f. $P^* = \$11,750\ (= 16,000 - 25 \times 170)$; higher than

g. $\$671,500\ [= (P^* - AVC)Q^* - TFC = (11,750 - 7,500) \times 170 - 51,000]$

h.   Since cost-plus pricing does NOT generally result in profit-maximization, the profit using the $MR = MC$ approach will be higher because it gives the best possible profit outcome.

i. AVC (because fixed costs must be ignored); $m^* = 0.5667$

To get m^*, you must first compute E^*, then apply the formula $m^* = -\dfrac{1}{1 + E^*}$:

$$E^* = 1 + \frac{A}{0.5(AVC - A)} = 1 + \frac{16,000}{0.5(7,500 - 16,000)} = 1 + \frac{16,000}{-4,250}$$

$$= 1 + (-3.7647) = -2.7647$$

$$m^* = -\frac{1}{1 + E^*} = -\frac{1}{1 + (-2.7647)} = 0.5667$$

To verify this procedure gives the profit-maximizing price:
$$P^* = (1 + m^*)AVC = (1.5667) \times 7,500 = \$11,750\checkmark$$

3. a. $P_1 = 5 - 0.0002Q_1$ and $P_2 = 8 - 0.0002Q_2$

    b. $MR_1 = 5 - 0.0004Q_1 \Rightarrow Q_1 = 12,500 - 2,500MR_1$

          $MR_2 = 8 - 0.0004Q_2 \Rightarrow Q_2 = 20,000 - 2,500MR_2$

    c.   Set $MR_1 = MR_2 = MR_T$ and sum:

          $$Q_1 + Q_2 = Q_T = (12,500 - 2,500MR_1) + (20,000 - 2,500MR_2)$$

          $$Q_T = 32,500 - 5,000MR_T \Rightarrow MR_T = 6.5 - 0.0002Q_T \text{ (for } Q_T > 7,500)$$

          [Note: To find the kink, set $MR_2 = 5$ and solve for Q_{kink}.]

    d.   See the figure below.

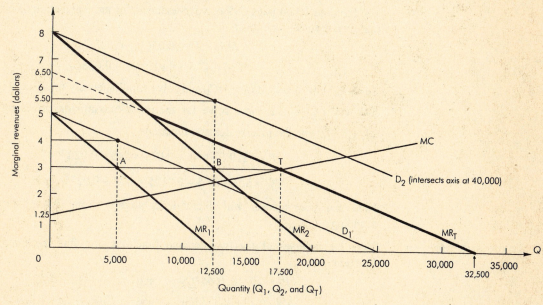

e. $MR_T = MC_T \Rightarrow Q_T = 17{,}500$ units

f. MR_T (17,500) = \$3. Substitute \$3 into both inverse marginal revenue functions:

$$Q_1 = 5{,}000 \; (= 12{,}500 - 2{,}500 \times 3)$$
$$Q_2 = 12{,}500 \; (= 20{,}000 - 2{,}500 \times 3)$$

g. $P_1 = 5 - 0.0002(5{,}000) = \$4$

       $P_2 = 8 - 0.0002(12{,}500) = \$5.50$

h. $E_1 = -4$ [= 4/(4−5)]; $E_2 = -2.2$ [= 5.50/(5.50−8)]; Market 2 has the less elastic demand since $|E_2| < |E_1|$. Remember, the higher price is charged in the market with the less elastic demand.

i.   See the previous figure.

4.   a.   Follow the substitution procedure described in footnote 9 on page 599 of your textbook:

First, using the equation for Q_R, solve for P_R:

$$P_R = 13.33 - 0.0167Q_R + 0.67P_D$$

Next, using the equation for Q_D, solve for P_D:

$$P_D = 25 - 0.025Q_D + 0.5P_R$$

[Note: You could alternatively have solved for P_D in the equation for Q_R and for P_R in the equation for Q_D.]

Now, cross-substitute the solution for P_R into the equation for P_D and the solution for P_D into the equation for P_R:

$$P_D = 25 - 0.025Q_D + 0.5[13.33 - 0.0167Q_R + 0.67P_D]$$
$$P_R = 13.33 - 0.0167Q_R + 0.67[25 - 0.025Q_D + 0.5P_R]$$

Now P_D is expressed as a function of Q_D and Q_R, as is P_R:

$$P_R = 45 - 0.025Q_R - 0.025Q_D$$
$$P_D = 47.5 - 0.0375Q_D - 0.0125Q_R$$

This verifies that the inverse demand functions can indeed be derived from the estimated demand functions.

b.   See footnote 10 on page 599 of your textbook for an explanation of how to get the marginal revenue functions:

$$MR_R = 45 - 0.05Q_R - 0.025Q_D$$
$$MR_D = 47.5 - 0.0125Q_R - 0.075Q_D$$

c.   Set $MR_R = MC_R$ and $MR_D = MC_D$ and solve simultaneously for Q_R and $Q_D \Rightarrow Q_R^* = 545$ and $Q_D^* = 472$. Now solve for the profit-maximizing prices by substituting Q_R^* and Q_D^* into the inverse demand functions

$$P_R^* = \$19.57 = 45 - 0.025 \times 545 - 0.025 \times 472$$

$$P_D^* = \$23 = 47.5 - 0.0125 \times 472 - 0.0375 \times 545$$

Note that your answer will likely differ slightly from this answer because of rounding.

5.   a.   Take the inverses of the two demand functions and find the marginal revenue functions

$$P_X = 20 - 0.16667Q_X \qquad \text{and} \qquad P_Y = 12 - 0.25Q_Y$$
$$MR_X = 20 - 0.3333Q_X \qquad \text{and} \qquad MR_Y = 12 - 0.5Q_Y$$

Express marginal revenues as functions of facility hours, H_X and H_Y, by substituting the production relations, $Q_X = 1.0H_X$ and $Q_Y = 2.0H_Y$:

$$MR_X = 20 - 0.3333H_X \quad \text{and} \quad MR_Y = 12 - 0.5(2H_Y) = 12 - H_Y$$

Now derive the *MRP* functions

$$MRP_{Hx} = MR_X \times MP_{Hx} = (20 - 0.3333H_X) \times 1 = 20 - 0.3333H_X$$

$$MRP_{Hy} = MR_Y \times MP_{Hy} = (12 - H_Y) \times 2 = 24 - 2H_Y$$

b. Take inverses of the *MRP* functions

$$H_X = 60 - 3MRP_{Hx}$$

$$H_Y = 12 - 0.5MRP_{Hy}$$

Sum $H_X + H_Y$ to get H_T (Remember, optimal plant usage requires $MRP_{Hx} = MRP_{Hy} = MRP_T$.):

$$H_T = (60 - 3MRP_T) + (12 - 0.5MRP_T) = 72 - 3.5MRP_T$$

Finally, take the inverse to get MRP_T as a function of H_T

$$MRP_T = 20.57143 - 0.28714H_T$$

c. To find the optimal, or profit-maximizing, level of usage of the production facility, set $MRP_T = MC$ and solve for H_T^*

$$MRP_T = 20.57143 - 0.28714H_T = 9 + 0.1H_T \Rightarrow H_T^* = 30 \text{ hours per week.}$$

MRP_T at the optimal level of hours is found by substituting H_T^* into MRP_T:

$$MRP_T^* = 12 \ (= 20.571 - 0.2875 \times 30)$$

Because optimal allocation of plant time between the two goods X and Y requires satisfying the equimarginal principle, $MRP_{Hx} = MRP_{Hy} = MRP_T$, H_X^* and H_Y^* are found by evaluating the inverse *MRP* functions at MPR_T^*

$$H_X^* = 60 - 3 \times 12 = 24$$

$$H_Y^* = 12 - 0.5 \times 12 = 6$$

d. The profit-maximizing outputs and prices are found as follows:

$$Q_X^* = 1.0H_X^* = 24 \text{ units per week} \quad \text{and} \quad P_X^* = 20 - 0.16667 \times 24 - \$16$$

$$Q_Y^* = 2.0H_Y^* = 12 \text{ units per week} \quad \text{and} \quad P_Y^* = 12 - 0.25 \times 12 = \$9$$

6. a. First find the inverse demand functions:

$$P_S = 200 - 0.02Q_S \quad \text{and} \quad P_U = 300 - 0.025Q_U$$

Then, the marginal revenue functions are easily written as

$$MR_S = 200 - 0.04Q_S \quad \text{and} \quad MR_U = 300 - 0.05Q_U$$

See the figure on page 320 for the graphs of these two *MR* functions.

b. The joint marginal revenue function is derived by summing $MR_S + MR_U = MR_J$ at all output levels ($Q_S = Q_U = Q_J$) for which both MR_S and MR_U are positive. When one of the *MR*s becomes zero, it is no longer vertically summed. In this problem, MR_S becomes negative beyond 5,000 gallons. Thus, the joint marginal revenue function is the (vertical) sum of both *MR*s only over the range of output 0 to 5,000. MR_U becomes negative beyond 6,000 gallons, so for the range $5,000 < Q_J < 6,000$, $MR_J = MR_U$. The algebraic summing is done as follows:

For $0 < Q_J < 5,000$:

$$MR_J = MR_S + MR_U = 200 - 0.04Q_J + 300 - 0.05Q_J$$

$$= 500 - 0.09Q_J$$

For $5,000 < Q_J < 6,000$:

$$MR_J = MR_U$$

$$= 300 - 0.05Q_J$$

c. To find the profit-maximizing levels of production and sales, MR_J is set equal to MC, and the solution is Q_J^* which, by the joint nature of production, is also Q_S^* and Q_U^*:

$$MR_J = MC \Rightarrow 500 - 0.09Q_J = 200 + 0.06Q_J \Rightarrow Q_J^* = 2{,}000 \text{ gallons per month}$$

Since each gallon of the joint product yields one gallon of styrene and one gallon of ulene, $Q_S^* = 2{,}000 = Q_U^*$. At $Q_J = 2{,}000$, both MRs are positive, so all 2,000 units of each product will be sold.

d. The profit-maximizing prices are

$$P_S^* = 200 - 0.02 \times 2{,}000 = \$160$$

$$P_U^* = 300 - 0.05 \times 2{,}000 = \$250$$

The associated total revenues are

$$TR_S^* = \$160 \times 2{,}000 = \$320{,}000$$

$$TR_U^* = \$250 \times 2{,}000 = \$400{,}000$$

$$TR_{total} = TR_S^* + TR_U^* = \$720{,}000$$

e. When $MC = 25$; $MR_J = MC$ at more than 5,000 gallons of chemical. Thus, $MR_J = 300 - 0.05Q_J$. Setting $MR_J = MC$ and solving for Q_J shows that $Q_J^* = 5{,}500$. Thus, Waring Chemical *produces* 5,500 gallons of both styrene and ulene, but *sells* all of the ulene while *selling* only 5,000 gallons of styrene (i.e., disposes of 500 gallons of styrene).

f. The profit-maximizing prices are

$$P_S^* = 200 - 0.02 \times 5{,}000 = \$100$$

$$P_U^* = 300 - 0.05 \times 2{,}000 = \$162.50$$

The associated total revenues are

$$TR_S^* = \$100 \times 5{,}000 = \$500{,}000$$

$$TR_U^* = \$162.50 \times 5{,}500 = \$893{,}750$$

$$TR_{total} = TR_S^* + TR_U^* = \$1{,}393{,}750$$

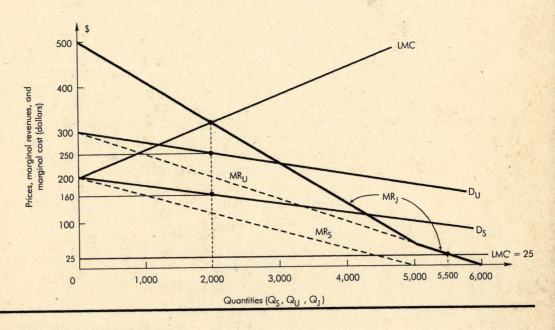

7.   a.   See the blanks in the game tree below

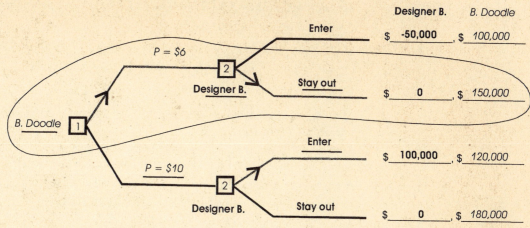

b.   Burger Doodle must be able make an irreversible commitment to price at $6 per burger. Otherwise, Designer Burger will believe it can enter, and then Burger Doodle will see that pricing at $10 gives it $120,000 of profit, which is more than the $100,000 of profit it makes by sticking to the limit price of $6 (after Designer Burger enters).

c.   If Burger Doodle can make an irreversible decision to price at $6, the decision path is shown in the game tree above. Limit pricing succeeds in deterring entry.

d.   See the blanks in the game tree below

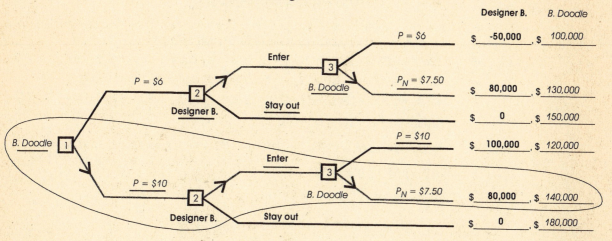

e.   The circled path in the game tree above shows that entry cannot be deterred. Whether Burger Doodle prices at $6 or $10 initially (at decision node 1), it will change its price to the Nash price of $7.50 after Designer Burger chooses to enter (which it will do).

f.   If Burger Doodle, by expanding its capacity, is able to lower sufficiently its marginal costs of production, it can then make its threat (or its commitment) to maintain its price at $6. Once Designer Burger believes Burger Doodle will stick to its $6 price, Designer Burger will choose not to enter.

1. e   Set $MR = MC_T$: $MR = 5.5 - 0.0005Q_T = 1.5 + 0.0005Q_T$. Solve for $Q^* = 4,000$ units

            $P = 5.5 - 0.00025 \times 4,000 = \$4.50$

2. b $MC_T = 0.0005(4,000) + 1.5 = 3.5$. Set $MC_1 = MC_2 = 3.5$ in the inverse MC functions:

$$Q_1^* = 1,000 \times 3.5 - 2,000 = 1,500 \text{ units}$$

$$Q_2^* = 1,000 \times 3.5 - 1,000 = 2,500 \text{ units}$$

3. e MR_T (the horizontal sum of MR_A and MR_B which you must construct on the graph) intersects MC at 25 units.

4. e   Both b and c are practical problems with cost-plus pricing. Choice a cannot be correct because fixed costs do not matter in making optimal pricing decisions.

5. c   If $E^* = -3$, then $m^* = -1/(1 + E^*) = 1/2$. Thus, 50 percent is the optimal markup.

6. d   Both a and b are theoretical problems with cost-plus pricing.

7. b $MR_T = 0.20 = MR_A = MR_B$ when $Q_A = 10$ and $Q_B = 15$

8. c   Reading off D_A and D_B: $P_A = \$0.40$ and $P_B = \$0.50$

9. a   See footnote 10, page 599 of your textbook.

10. a $MR_X = 36 - 0.005Q_X - 0.01Q_Y = 22 + 0.015Q_X = MC_X$

            $MR_Y = 45 - 0.025Q_Y - 0.03Q_X = 12 + 0.005Q_Y = MC_Y$

            Solving for optimal outputs: $Q_X^* = 300$ units and $Q_Y^* = 800$ units

11. d $P_X^* = 36 - 0.0025(300) - 0.01(800) = \$27.25$

            $P_Y^* = 45 - 0.0125(800) - 0.03(300) = \$26.00$

12. c $MRP_T = 2,000$ at 10 hours per day (You must construct total marginal revenue product by horizontal summations of MRP_A and MRP_B.)

13. d $MRP_A = MRP_B = 2,000$ at $H_A = 4$ hours per day and $H_B = 6$ hours per day.

14. a $MRP_A = MRP_B = 1,000$ at $H_A = 5$ hours per day and $H_B = 8$ hours per day.

15. d $MRP_R = 1,800 - 200H_R$ and $MRP_D = 2,000 - 100H_D$. $MRP_T = 1,933.33 - 66.67H_T$

            Setting $MRP_T = MC \Rightarrow H_T^* = 14$.

16. b   At $H_T^* = 14$, $MRP_T^* = 1,000$. Set $MRP_R = MRP_D = 1,000$ and solve for H_R^* and H_D^*

            $H_R^* = 9\,M - 0.005 \times 1,000 = 4$

            $H_D^* = 20 - 0.1 \times 1,000 = 10$

17. a $Q_R^* = 2H_R^* = 2 \times 4 = 8$ road bikes per week

            $Q_D^* = 4H_D^* = 4 \times 10 = 40$ dirt bikes per week

18. c $P_R^* = 900 - 25 \times 8 = \$700$

            $P_D^* = 500 - 3.125 \times 40 = \$375$

19. a   New entrants know that, in most cases, incumbent firms will not want to keep prices low if the entrant does indeed carry out its plans to enter the market. Consequently, the threat by incumbents to keep prices low to punish entry is not a credible threat in most cases.

20. e   Increased plant capacity can served as an entry barrier only if it is an irreversible commitment that lowers marginal costs, which thereby makes higher output and lower prices a credible threat.

Homework Exercises

1. Consider a firm with market power that produces its product in two plants, A and B. The marginal cost curves, as well as the demand and marginal revenue curves, are shown in the figure below.

   a. Construct the total marginal cost function in the figure. Label this curve MC_T.
   b. The profit-maximizing level of total output is _____ units. At this level of production, marginal cost = $_____ and marginal revenue = $_____.
   c. The manager minimizes the total cost of producing the total output in part b by producing _____ units in plant A and producing _____ units in plant B.
   d. The profit-maximizing price of the output is $_____ per unit.

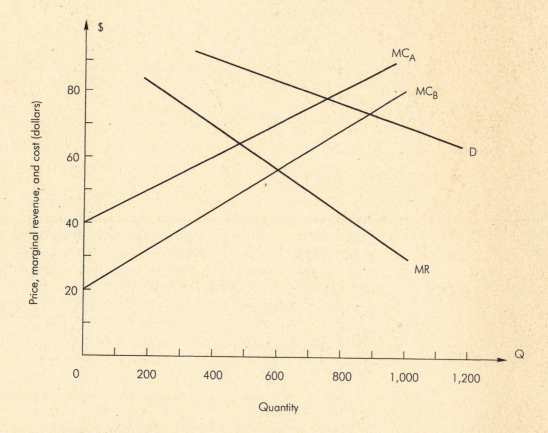

2. Dr. Rogers takes a managerial economics course at Feenix College of International Business Strategy and learns that cost-plus pricing is the best way to ensure that she earns a "desirable" or "reasonable" level of profit. She decides that her skills as a pediatric physician should earn 75% as much as the costs of providing health care services, so she chooses a markup of 75% on her average total costs.

   Dr. Rogers, a respected pediatric physician, has a reputation for being one of the best "baby and kid doctors" in the area. Dr. Rogers enjoys a rather substantial degree of market power in this market. A marketing research firm has estimated the demand for her work as a linear function of the price she decides to charge:

$$Q = 600 - 0.2P$$

where Q is the number of pediatric examinations performed each month, and P is the average price of a pediatric exam. Her accountant tells her that her average variable costs are constant and equal to $225 per exam. Her total fixed cost each month is $36,000 per month.

a. Derive the inverse demand for Dr. Rogers's pediatric exams.

$$P = \underline{\hspace{6cm}}$$

b. Derive the marginal revenue for Dr. Rogers's pediatric exams.

$$MR = \underline{\hspace{6cm}}$$

Currently Dr. Rogers has a full schedule of patients and enjoys a waiting list each month of about 25 patients who cannot get in to see her. She plans her work schedule to work 20 days per month and to see 20 patients per work day, which allows her to see 400 patients per month. Currently, she charges a price (on average) of $350 per patient.

c. Explain why Dr. Rogers currently experiences a waiting list of 25 patients each month.

d. Currently, Dr. Rogers's costs to service 400 patients per month are

$$AVC = \$\underline{\hspace{2cm}}, \quad AFC = \$\underline{\hspace{2cm}}, \quad \text{and } ATC = \$\underline{\hspace{2cm}}$$

The doctor's monthly profit is $\underline{\hspace{4cm}}$.

e. As previously mentioned, Dr. Rogers decides to begin setting her price using a 75 percent markup on her current average total costs (use ATC from part d):

$$m = \underline{\hspace{2cm}} \quad \text{and } P = \$\underline{\hspace{2cm}}$$

f. The doctor computes her expected profit from her decision to begin implementing cost-plus pricing by using the cost-plus price (computed in part e above), and she (incorrectly) believes she will continue to see 400 patients each month after implementing the cost-plus price in part e. By treating 400 patients, she predicts her profit will be $\underline{\hspace{4cm}}$ per month. Her actual profit when she implements the price in part e will be $\underline{\hspace{4cm}}$, which is less than the amount she expects. Explain why.

g. Dr. Rogers, while happy that cost-plus pricing has improved her profits, is troubled by her profit shortfall. She picks up a copy of Thomas and Maurice's *Managerial Economics* text, and, after reading Chapter 12, she applies the $MR = MC$ rule to find her profit-maximizing price, number of patients, and profit:

$$P^* = \$\underline{\hspace{2cm}}, \quad Q^* = \underline{\hspace{2cm}}, \quad \text{and maximum profit} = \$\underline{\hspace{3cm}}$$

h. Explain why her implementation of cost-plus pricing in part e failed to maximize her profit.

i. Is there any way for Dr. Rogers to employ cost-plus pricing to find P^* in part g? If so, carry out the computations to show that P^* can be obtained in this case using cost-plus pricing.

3.   Good-Looking Pants, Inc. sells designer jeans in the United States and Europe. For 2005, Good-Looking has estimated its demand functions in both markets to be

$$United States: \quad Q_{US} = 80,000 - 1,000P_{US}$$
$$Europe: \quad Q_E = 40,000 - 666.67P_E$$

The estimated marginal cost of producing jeans in 2005 is

$$MC = 12.5 + 0.0005Q$$

a.   The inverse demand functions and marginal revenue functions are

$P_{US} = $ _____ $P_E = $ _____

$MR_{US} = $ _____ MR_E _____

b.   The total marginal revenue function for Good-Looking Pants is

$MR_T = $ _____

c.   The manager of Good-Looking Pants will maximize the firm's profit by pro-ducing _____ pairs of designer jeans in 2005.

d.   Profit is maximized by splitting the total output of jeans between U.S. buyers and European buyers in the following way:

$Q_{US} = $ _____ pairs of jeans

$Q_E = $ _____ pairs of jeans

e.   The profit-maximizing price of a pair of Good-Looking jeans is $_____ in the United States and $_____ in Europe.

f.   The _____ (higher, lower) price must be charged to the buyer in the more elastic market. Compute the point elasticities of demand in both markets at the prices set in part *d* in order to verify your answer.

$E_{US} = $ _____

$E_E = $ _____

Decisions Under Risk and Uncertainty

Learning Objectives

After reading Chapter 15 and working the problems for Chapter 15 in the textbook and in this Workbook, you should be able to:

➤ Distinguish between decision making under uncertainty and under risk.

➤ Compute the expected value, variance, standard deviation, and coefficient of variation of a probability distribution.

➤ Apply the expected value rule, the mean-variance rules, and the coefficient of variation rule to make decisions under risk.

➤ Define three risk preference categories: risk averse, risk neutral, and risk loving, and relate these attitudes toward risk to the shape of the utility of profit curve.

➤ Find the optimal level of a risky activity (when the variances of marginal benefit and marginal cost are constant) by setting $E(MB) = E(MC)$.

➤ Apply (1) the maximax rule, (2) the maximin rule, (3) the minimax regret rule, and (4) the equal probability rule to make decisions under uncertainty.

Essential Concepts

1. Conditions of *risk* occur when a manager must make a decision for which the outcome is not known with certainty. Under conditions of risk, the manager can make a list of all possible outcomes and assign probabilities to the various outcomes. *Uncertainty* exists when a decision maker cannot list all possible outcomes and/or cannot assign probabilities to the various outcomes.

2. In order to measure the risk associated with a decision, the manager can examine several characteristics of the probability distribution of outcomes for the decision. A *probability distribution* is a table or graph showing all possible outcomes or payoffs for a decision and the probability that each outcome will occur.

3. In order to measure the risk associated with a decision, several statistical characteristics of the probability distribution can be employed:

   a. The *expected value (or mean)* of a probability distribution is

$$E(X) = \text{Expected value of } X = \sum_{i=1}^{n} p_i X_i$$

   where X_i is the ith outcome of a decision, p_i is the probability of the ith

outcome, and n is the total number of possible outcomes in the probability distribution. The expected value of a distribution does *not* give the actual value of the random outcome, but rather indicates the "average" value of the outcomes if the risky decision were to be repeated a large number of times.

b. The *variance* (a measure of *absolute* risk) of a probability distribution measures the dispersion of the outcomes about the mean or expected outcome. The variance is calculated as

$$Variance(X) = \sigma_x^2 = \sum_{i=1}^{n} p_i (X_i - E(X))^2$$

The higher (lower) the variance, the greater (lower) the risk associated with a probability distribution.

c. The *standard deviation* is the square root of the variance:

$$\sigma_x = \sqrt{Variance(X)}$$

The higher (lower) the standard deviation, the greater (lower) the risk.

d. When the expected values of outcomes differ substantially, managers should measure the riskiness of a decision relative to its expected value using the coefficient of variation (a measure of *relative* risk):

$$\upsilon = \frac{Standard\ deviation}{Expected\ value} = \frac{\sigma}{E(X)}$$

4. While no single decision rule guarantees that profits will actually be maximized, there are a number of decision rules that managers can use to help them make decisions under risk. Decision rules do not eliminate the risk surrounding a decision, they just provide a method of systematically including risk in the process of decision making. The three rules presented in this chapter are (1) the expected value rule, (2) the mean-variance rules, and (3) the coefficient of variation rule. These three rules are summarized below:

Summary of Decision Rules Under Conditions of Risk

Expected value rule	Choose the decision with the highest expected value.
Mean-variance rules	Given two risky decisions A and B: If decision A has a higher expected outcome and a lower variance than decision B, decision A should be made. If both decisions A and B have identical variances (or standard deviations), the decision with the higher expected value should be made. If both decisions A and B have identical expected values, the decision with the lower variance (standard deviation) should be made.
Coefficient of variation rule	Choose the decision with the smallest coefficient of variation.

5. Which rule is best?

    When a decision is to be made repeatedly, with identical probabilities each time, the expected value rule provides managers with the most reliable rule for maximizing (expected) profit. The average return of a given risky course of action repeated many times will approach the expected value of that action.

    When a manager makes a one-time decision under risk, there will not be any follow-up repetitions of the decision to "average out" a bad outcome (or a good outcome). Unfortunately, there is no best rule to follow when decisions are not repetitive.

    The rules for risky decision making should be used by managers to help analyze and guide the decision-making process. Ultimately, making decisions under risk (or uncertainty) is as much an art as it is a science.

6. The actual decisions made by a manager depend upon the manager's willingness to accept risk. To allow for different attitudes toward risk-taking in decision making, modern decision theory treats managers as deriving utility or satisfaction from the profits earned by their firms. Just as consumers derived utility from consumption of goods in Chapter 6, in *expected utility theory*, managers are assumed to derive utility from earning profits.

7. Expected utility theory postulates that managers make risky decisions in a way that maximizes the expected utility of the profit outcomes, where the expected utility of a risky decision is the sum of the probability-weighted utilities of each possible profit outcome:

$$E[U(\pi)] = p_1 U(\pi_1) + p_2 U(\pi_2) + ... + p_n U(\pi_n)$$

$U(\pi)$ is the manager's utility function for profit that measures the utility associated with a particular level of profit. The utility function for profit gives an index value to measure the level of utility experienced when a given amount of profit is earned. The relation between an index of utility and the level of profit earned is assumed to be an upward-sloping curve.

8. A manager's attitude toward risk is determined by the manager's *marginal utility of profit*:

$$MU_{\text{profit}} = \Delta U(\pi) / \Delta \pi$$

Marginal utility, then, measures the slope of the upward-sloping $U(\pi)$ curve. It is the slope of the utility curve, or marginal utility, that determines a managers attitude toward risk:

a. People are said to be *risk averse* if, facing two risky decisions with equal expected profits, they choose the less risky decision.

b. Someone who chooses the more risky of two decision when the expected profits are the same is said to be *risk loving*.

c. A *risk neutral* person is indifferent between risky decisions that all have the same expected profit.

9. A manager's attitude toward risky decisions can be related to his or her marginal utility of profit. Someone who experiences diminishing (increasing) marginal utility for profit will be a risk averse (risk loving) decision maker. Someone whose marginal utility of profit is constant is risk neutral.

10. If a manager maximizes expected utility for profit, the decisions can differ from decisions reached using the three decision rules discussed for making risky decisions. In the case of a risk-neutral manager, however, the decisions are the same under maximization of expected profit and maximization of expected utility of profit.

11. In the case of uncertainty, decision science can provide very little guidance to managers beyond offering them some simple decision rules to aid them in their analysis of uncertain situations. Four basic rules for decision making under uncertainty are summarized in the following table.

Summary of Decision Rules Under Conditions of Uncertainty

Maximax rule	Identify the best outcome for each possible decision and choose the decision with the maximum payoff.
Maximin rule	Identify the worst outcome for each decision and choose the decision associated with the maximum worst payoff.
Minimax regret rule	Determine the worst potential regret associated with each decision, where the potential regret associated with any particular decision and state of nature is the improvement in payoff the manager could have experienced had the decision been the best one when that state of nature actually occurred. The manager chooses the decision with the minimum worst potential regret.
Equal probability rule	Assume each state of nature is equally likely to occur and compute the average payoff for each equally likely possible state of nature. Choose the decision with the highest average payoff.

Matching Definitions

certainty equivalent
coefficient of variation
coefficient of variation rule
equal probability rule
expected utility
expected utility theory
expected value
expected value rule
marginal utility of profit
maximax rule
maximin rule
mean of the distribution

mean-variance analysis
minimax regret rule
payoff matrix
potential regret
probability distribution
risk
risk averse
risk loving
risk neutral
standard deviation
uncertainty
variance

1. _____ A decision-making situation in which a manager can list all possible outcomes and assign probabilities to the occurrence of each one.

2. _____ A situation in which the manager cannot list all possible outcomes and/or cannot assign probabilities to the outcomes.

3. _____ A table or graph showing all possible outcomes for a decision and the probabilities that each outcome will occur.

4. _____ The weighted average of the outcomes, with the probabilities of each outcome serving as the respective weights.

5. _____ Expected value of a distribution.

6. _____ A measure of the dispersion of a distribution around its mean.

7. _____ Square root of the variance.

8. _____ Standard deviation divided by the expected value of the probability distribution.

9. _____ Choosing the decision with the highest expected value.

10. _____ Method of decision making that uses both the mean and the variance to make decisions.

11. _____ A decision-making method that chooses the decision with the lowest coefficient of variation.

12. _____ A decision-making theory that accounts for the decision-maker's attitude toward risk.

13. _____ The sum of the probability-weighted utilities of each possible profit outcome.

14. _____ The amount by which total utility increases for each additional dollar of profit that the firm makes.

15. _____ A decision maker who chooses the less risky project when two projects have an equal expected profit.

16. _____ A decision maker who chooses the project with the higher risk when two projects have an equal expected profit.

17. _____ The decision maker who ignores risk and focuses only on the expected value of decisions.

18. _____ The dollar amount to be received with certainty that a manager would be just willing to trade for the opportunity to engage in a risky decision.

19. _____ A decision-making guide in which the manager identifies for each possible decision the best outcome that could occur and then chooses the decision that would give the maximum payoff of all the best outcomes.

20. _____ A table with rows corresponding to the various decisions and columns corresponding to the various states of nature.

21. _____ A decision-making guide in which the manager identifies the worst outcome for each decision and makes the decision associated with the maximum worst payoff.

22. _____ For a given decision and state of nature, the improvement in payoff the manager could have experienced had the decision been the best one when that state of nature actually occurred.

23. _____ A decision-making guide that requires managers make to the decision with the minimum worst potential regret.

24. _____ A decision-making guide that assumes each state of nature has an equal probability of occurring; the manager then calculates the average payoff for each decision and chooses the decision with the highest average payoff.

Study Problems

1. Consider the following two probability distributions for sales:

| | Probability | |
Sales	Distribution A (percent)	Distribution B (percent)
100	20	5
200	40	20
300	20	50
400	15	20
500	5	5

a. Calculate the expected sales for both of these probability distributions.

$E(Sales_A) = $ _____

$E(Sales_B) = $ _____

b. Calculate the variance and standard deviation for both of the probability distributions.

$\sigma_A^2 = $ _____ and $\sigma_A = $ _____

$\sigma_B^2 = $ _____ and $\sigma_B = $ _____

Distribution _____ is more risky than distribution _____.

c. Calculate the coefficient of variation for both distributions

$\upsilon_A = $ _____

$\upsilon_B = $ _____

Distribution _____ has greater risk relative to its mean than distribution _____.

2. Texas Petroleum Company is a producer of crude oil that is considering two drilling projects with the following profit outcomes and associated probabilities:

Drilling Project A		Drilling Project B	
Profit	Probability (percent)	Profit	Probability (percent)
−$300,000	10	−$600,000	15
100,000	60	100,000	25
500,000	20	300,000	40
600,000	10	1,000,000	20

a.   Compute the expected profit for both drilling projects.

$E(Profit_A) = $ _____ and $E(Profit_B) = $ _____

b.   Based on the expected value rule, Texas Petroleum should choose drilling project _____ .

c.   Compute the standard deviations of both projects:

$\sigma_A = $ _____ and $\sigma_B = $ _____

d.   Which drilling project has the greater (absolute) risk?

e.   Use mean-variance rules, if possible, to decide which drilling project to undertake. Explain.

f.   Compute the coefficient of variation for both projects:

$\upsilon_A = $ _____ and $\upsilon_B = $ _____

Using the coefficient of variation rule, Texas Petroleum should choose project _____ .

3.   A manager's utility function for profit is $U(\pi) = 35\pi$, where π is the dollar amount of profit. The manager is considering a risky decision with the four possible profit outcomes shown below. The manager makes the following subjective assessments about the probability of each profit outcome:

Probability	Profit Outcome
0.05	-$15,000
0.40	-$1,000
0.50	$5,000
0.05	$10,000

a.   The expected profit is _____ .

b.   The expected utility of profit is _____ .

c.   The marginal utility of an extra dollar of profit is _____ .

d.   The manager is risk _____ because the marginal utility of profit is _____ .

4.   Suppose the manager of a firm has a utility function for profit $U(\pi) = 12\ln(\pi)$, where π is the dollar amount of profit. The manager is considering a risky project with the following profit payoffs and probabilities:

Probability	Profit Outcome	Marginal Utility of Profit
0.10	$1,000	xx
0.20	$2,000	_____
0.30	$3,000	_____
0.40	$4,000	_____

a. The expected profit is _____.

b. The expected utility of profit is _____.

c. Fill in the blanks in the following table showing the marginal utility of an additional $1,000 of profit.

d. The manager is risk _____ because the marginal utility of profit is _____.

5. A firm is making production plans for next quarter, but the manager does not know what the price of the product will be next month. She believes there is a 30 percent chance that price will be $500 and a 70 percent chance that price will be $750. The four possible profit outcomes are

	Profit (loss) when price is	
	$500	$750
Option A: produce 1,000 units	−$12,000	$80,000
Option B: produce 2,000 units	−$20,000	$150,000

a. Option _____ maximizes expected profit.

b. Option _____ is the riskier of the two options.

c. The manager _____ (can, cannot) apply mean-variance rules in this decision. If the manager can use mean-variance rules, the manager would choose Option _____.

d. Using the coefficient of variation rule, the manager chooses Option _____.

6. Suppose the manager in Problem 5 has absolutely no idea about the probabilities of the two prices occurring. Which option would the manager choose under each of the following rules?

a. Maximax rule _____

b. Maximin rule _____

c. Minimax regret rule _____

d. Equal probability rule _____

Multiple Choice / True-False

Answer questions 1–3 using the following probability distribution for profit:

Profit	Probability
$30	0.10
$40	0.30
$50	0.50
$60	0.10

1. The expected profit for the profit distribution above is _____.
   a. $0.10(30) + 0.3(40) + 0.5(50) + 0.10(60)$
   b. $0.10^2(30) + 0.3^2(40) + 0.5^2(50) + 0.10^2(60)$
   c. $0.10(30 - 46)^2 + 0.30(40 - 46)^2 + 0.50(50 - 46)^2 + 0.10(60 - 46)^2$
   d. $(30 + 40 + 50 + 60)/2$
   e. both b and d.

2. The variance for the profit distribution above is _____.
   a. 64
   b. 46
   c. 54
   d. 8

3. The coefficient of variation for the distribution above is _____.
   a. 0.17
   b. 5.75
   c. 0.50
   d. 1.39

Answer questions 4–10 using the following table that shows the various profit outcomes for different projects when the price of the product is $10 or $20.

	Profit	
Project	P = $10	P = $20
A	$40	$120
B	$55	$70
C	–$10	$200

4. Using the maximax rule, a manager would choose _____.
   a. Project A
   b. Project B
   c. Project C
   d. Either Project A or Project C

5. Following the maximin rule, a manager would choose _____.
   a. Project A
   b. Project B
   c. Project C

6. Which project has the minimum worst potential regret?
   a. Project A
   b. Project B
   c. Project C

7. Under the equal probability rule, which project should be chosen?
   a. Project A
   b. Project B
   c. Project C
   d. Either Project A or C

Now suppose the manager in questions 4–7 above is able to determine that product price is likely to follow the probability distribution below:

Price	Profitability
$10	60%
$20	40%

8. Which project should be chosen under the expected value rule?
   a. Project A
   b. Project B
   c. Project C

9. Using mean-variance rules, which project would the manager choose?
   a. Project A
   b. Project B
   c. Project C
   d. Cannot apply mean-variance rules for these projects

10. Which project should be chosen under the coefficient of variation rule?
   a. Project A
   b. Project B
   c. Project C

11. Risk exists when
    a. all possible outcomes are known but probabilities can't be assigned to the outcomes.
    b. all possible outcomes are known and probabilities can be assigned to each.
    c. all possible outcomes are known but only objective probabilities can be assigned to each.
    d. future events can influence the payoffs but the decision maker has some control over their probabilities.
    e. both c and d.

12. Using the minimax regret rule the manager makes the decision
    a. with the smallest worst-potential regret.
    b. with the largest worst-potential regret.
    c. knowing he will not regret it.
    d. that has the highest expected value relative to the other decisions.

13. In the maximin strategy, a manager choosing between two options will choose the option that
    a. has the highest expected profit.
    b. provides the best of the worst possible outcomes.
    c. minimizes the maximum loss.
    d. both a and b.
    e. both b and c.

14. In making decisions under risk
    a. maximizing expected value is always the best rule.
    b. mean variance analysis is always the best rule.
    c. the coefficient of variation rule is always best.
    d. maximizing expected value is most reliable for making repeated decisions with identical probabilities.
    e. none of the above.

15. A probability distribution
    a. is a way of dealing with uncertainty.
    b. lists all possible outcomes and the corresponding probabilities of occurrence.
    c. shows only the most likely outcome in an uncertain situation.
    d. both a and b.
    e. both a and c.

16. The variance of a probability distribution is used to measure risk because a higher variance is associated with
    a. a wider spread of values around the mean.
    b. a more compact distribution.
    c. a lower expected value.
    d. both a and b.
    e. all of the above.

The next three questions refer to the following probability distribution for profit:

Profit	Probability
$30	0.05
40	0.25
50	0.60
60	0.10

17. What is the expected profit for this distribution?
   a. $11,875
   b. $46
   c. $47.50
   d. $48.75
   e.   none of the above.

18. What is the variance of this distribution?
   a.   48.75
   b.   2,376
   c.   525
   d.   70
   e.   11.875

19. What is the coefficient of variation for this distribution?
   a.   1.67
   b.   0.675
   c.   18.6
   d.   0.147
   e.   1.03

20. T   F   Given two projects, A and B, if $E(\pi_A) > E(\pi_B)$ and $\sigma_A^2 > \sigma_B^2$, then the manager should select project A using mean-variance analysis.

21. T   F   Given two projects, A and B, if $E(\pi_A) = E(\pi_B)$ and, $\sigma_A^2 < \sigma_B^2$, then the manager should select project A using mean-variance analysis.

22. T   F   Employing the expected value rule guarantees that a manager will always earn the greatest return possible, a return equal to the expected value.

23. T   F   Suppose a person has two alternatives: (A) receive $1,000 with certainty, or (B) flip a coin and receive $2,000 if a head comes up or nothing ($0) if a tail comes up. A risk-averse person will take the $1,000 with certainty (alternative A).

24. T   F   When net benefit has the same variance at all relevant levels of activity, a risk-loving manager will undertake more of the risky activity than will a risk-averse manager.

Answers

MATCHING DEFINITIONS

1. risk
2. uncertainty
3. probability distribution
4. expected value
5. mean of the distribution
6. variance
7. standard deviation
8. coefficient of variation
9. expected value rule
10. mean-variance analysis
11. coefficient of variation rule
12. expected utility theory
13. expected utility
14. marginal utility of profit
15. risk averse
16. risk loving
17. risk neutral
18. certainty equivalent
19. maximax rule
20. payoff matrix
21. maximin rule
22. potential regret
23. minimax regret rule
24. equal probability rule

STUDY PROBLEMS

1. a. $E(\text{Sales}_A) = (0.20 \times 100) + (0.40 \times 200) + (0.20 \times 300) + (0.15 \times 400) + (0.05 \times 500) = 245$

   $E(\text{Sales}_B) = (0.05 \times 100) + (0.20 \times 200) + (0.50 \times 300) + (0.20 \times 400) + (0.05 \times 500) = 300$

   b. $\sigma_A^2 = (100 - 245)^2(0.2) + (200 - 245)^2(0.4) + (300 - 245)^2(0.2) + (400 - 245)^2(0.15) + (500 - 245)^2(0.05) = 12,475$

   $\sigma_A = (12,475)^{.5} = 111.69$

   $\sigma_B^2 = (100 - 300)^2(0.05) + (200 - 300)^2(0.2) + (300 - 300)^2(0.5) + (400 - 300)^2(0.20) + (500 - 300)^2(0.05) = 8,000$

   $\sigma_B = (8,000)^{.5} = 89.44$

   Distribution A is more risky than distribution B because $\sigma_A^2 < \sigma_B^2$.

   c. $\upsilon_A = $ standard deviation / expected value $= 111.69/245 = 0.456$

   $\upsilon_B = $ standard deviation / expected value $= 89.44/300 = 0.298$

   Distribution A has greater relative risk than distribution B because $\upsilon_A > \upsilon_B$.

2. a. $E(\text{Profit}_A) = (-300,000 \times 0.10) + (100,000 \times 0.60) + (500,000 \times 0.20) + (600,000 \times 0.10) = \$190,000$

   $E(\text{Profit}_B) = (-600,000 \times 0.15) + (100,000 \times 0.25) + (300,000 \times 0.40) + (1,000,000 \times 0.20) = \$255,000$

   b. Project B (It has the larger expected profit.)

c. $\text{Variance}_A = (-300{,}000 - 190{,}000)^2(0.10) + (100{,}000 - 190{,}000)^2(0.60) + (500{,}000$
$- 190{,}000)^2(0.20) + (600{,}000 - 190{,}000)^2(0.10)$
$= 64{,}900{,}000{,}000$

$\sigma_A = (64{,}900{,}000{,}000)^{0.5} = 254{,}755$

$\text{Variance}_B = (-600{,}000 - 255{,}000)^2(0.15) + (100{,}000 - 255{,}000)^2(0.25) + (300{,}000$
$- 255{,}000)^2(0.40) + (1{,}000{,}000 - 255{,}000)^2(0.20)$
$= 27{,}475{,}000{,}000$

$\sigma_B = (227{,}475{,}000{,}000)^{0.5} = 476{,}943$

d. Project B has higher (absolute) risk than Project A since $\sigma_B > \sigma_A$.

e. The expected profit in project B exceeds the expected profit in project A, but project B has a higher variance than A. The manager at Texas Petroleum must make a tradeoff between risk and return in order to decide which of the two projects to choose. Mean-variance rules cannot be employed to make decision when a tradeoff between risk and return is involved.

f. $\upsilon_A = 254{,}755/190{,}000 = 1.34$ and $\upsilon_B = 476{,}943/255{,}000 = 1.87$

Project B has higher relative risk. Under the coefficient of variation rule, Project A is chosen.

3. a. $E(\pi) = 0.05(-\$15{,}000) + 0.40(-\$1{,}000) + 0.50(\$5{,}000) + 0.05(\$10{,}000)$
$= \$1{,}850$

b. $E[U(\pi)] = 0.05 \times U(-\$15{,}000) + 0.40 \times U(-\$1{,}000) + 0.50 \times U(\$5{,}000) +$
$0.05 \times U(\$10{,}000)$
$= 0.05(-525{,}000) + 0.40(-35{,}000) + 0.50(175{,}000) + 0.05(350{,}000)$
$= 64{,}750$

c. 35

d. neutral; constant

4. a. $E(\pi) = 0.10(\$1{,}000) + 0.20(\$2{,}000) + 0.30(\$3{,}000) + 0.4(\$4{,}000)$
$= \$3{,}000$

c. $E[U(\pi)] = 0.10 \times U(\$1{,}000) + 0.20 \times U(\$2{,}000) + 0.30 \times U(\$3{,}000) +$
$0.40 \times U(\$40{,}000)$
$= 0.10(82.89) + 0.20(91.21) + 0.30(96.08) + 0.40(99.53)$
$= 95.17$

c. 8.32; 4.87; 3.45 (in the three blanks)

d. averse; decreasing

5. a. B

b. B

c. cannot; blank

d. B

6. a. B

b. A

c. B

d. B

1. a   This follows directly from the definition of expected value. E(Profit) = $46.

2. a $Var(\pi) = (30 - 46)2(0.10) + (40 - 46)2(0.30) + (50 - 46)2(0.50) + (60 - 46)2(0.10) = 64$

3. a   The coefficient of variation $= \sigma/E(\pi) = 8/46 = 0.17$

4. c   Project C has the greatest best-outcome.

5. b   Project B has the maximum worst possible outcome (= $55).

6. c   The worst regrets are 80, 130, and 65 for Projects A, B, and C, respectively. Project C has the smallest potential regret.

7. c   The average profit for Project C is 190/2 = $85, which is higher than for Projects A or B.

8. c $E(\pi_A) = \$72$, $E(\pi_B) = \$61$, and $E(\pi_C) = \$74$. Project C has the highest $E(\pi)$.

9. d   Project C has the highest $E(\pi)$ and the highest σ^2. Since a tradeoff between expected return and risk is involved, mean-variance analysis cannot be applied.

10. b   Project B has the lowest coefficient of variation: $\upsilon_A = 0.54$, $\upsilon_B = 0.12$, $\upsilon_C = 1.39$.

11. b   This is the definition.

12. a   This is the definition.

13. e   Both statements are correct.

14. d   Unless a decision is made repeatedly with identical probabilities, there is no clearly best rule to follow.

15. b   This is the definition of a probability distribution.

16. a   The higher the variance, the greater the dispersion of outcomes and the greater is the risk.

17. c $\$47.50 = 0.05(30) + 0.25(40) + 0.60(50) + 0.10(60)$

18. a $48.75 = 0.05(30-47.50)^2 + 0.25(40-47.50)^2 + 0.60(50-47.50)^2 + 0.10(60-47.50)^2$

19. d $0.147 = (48.74)^{0.5}/47.50$

20. F   Even though the expected value of Project A is higher than B's expected value, Project A has a higher variance (is riskier) than B. Projects A and B cannot be ranked using mean-variance analysis in this case.

21. T   Project A should be chosen since it has a lower risk and an equal expected return.

22. F   The expected value rule only guarantees the greatest return *on average*, if the decision is made a very large number of times. When the decision is made repeatedly, the expected value rule provides the most reliable rule for maximizing profit.

23. T   Although the expected value of alternative B is $1,000, a risk-averse decision maker takes the $1,000 with certainty (alternative A).

24. F   When risk is the same at all levels of activity (i.e., constant variance of net benefit), the optimal level of a risky activity is the same for both risk averse and risk loving managers. It is also the same for risk-neutral managers.

Homework Exercises

Star Products, Inc. faces uncertain demand conditions in 2006. Management at Star Products is considering three different levels of output for 2006: 1, 1.5, or 2 million units. Management has determined that the following profit levels will occur under weak and strong demand conditions:

Output Level	Profit (in $millions) if Demand is	
	Weak	Strong
1 million units	60	175
1.5 million units	50	200
2.0 million units	−50	400

1. Using each of the four rules for decision making under uncertainty, determine the output level of 2006.

    Maximax rule   _____ units of output

    Maximin rule   _____ units of output

    Minimax regret rule   _____ units of output

    Equal probability rule   _____ units of output

2. Now suppose that management believes the probability of weak demand in 2006 is 25% and the probability of strong demand is 75%. Compute the expected profit, variance, standard deviation, and coefficient of variation for each level of output:

Output	$E(\pi)$	σ^2	σ	υ
1 million units	_____	_____	_____	_____
1.5 million units	_____	_____	_____	_____
2.0 million units	_____	_____	_____	_____

3. Based on the expected value rule, Star Products should produce _____ units in 2006.

4. Using mean-variance analysis, which level of output should be chosen? Explain your answer.

5. Using the coefficient of variation rule, Star Products should produce _____ units in 2006. Explain briefly.

6. Suppose the manager's utility function for profit is $U(\pi) = 100\pi$. Calculate the expected utility of profit for each of the three output decisions:

Output	$E[U(\pi)]$
1 *million units*	_____
1.5 *million units*	_____
2.0 *million units*	_____

To maximize the expected utility of profit, the manger should choose to produce _____ units in 2006. Explain why this decision is the same as the decision in question 3 above.